ARD AND QUINNEY'S CRIMINAL
AVIOR SYSTEMS

ant classic, familiar to virtually all criminologists, *Clinard and Quinney's Criminal Behavior Revised Edition* begins with a discussion of the construction of types of crime and then and utilizes a useful typology of criminal behavior systems. It classifies crime into seven among them: violent personal crime, occasional property crime, public order crime, nal crime, corporate crime, organized crime, and political crime. They examine the areer of the offender in each category, public and legal attitudes toward these individu- t systems they may have, attitudes of the offenders, and other features. The discussion tegory of crime is thorough and enlightening and takes the reader far in understanding problem of crime and establishing intelligent definitions to study it.

w edition looks at the criminal landscape of the twenty-first century, capturing both ous advancements in theory and research in the field of criminology, as well as many anges that have taken place in law, mass media, the economy, culture, and the politi- that directly affect the book's coverage of various types of crimes. A global perspective he book's relevance to include a variety of different societies. Crimes newly examined tion include identity theft, domestic violence, arson, hate crimes, cybercrime, campus ult, police brutality, Ponzi schemes, human trafficking, and terrorism. Finally, alterna- nventional criminal justice are considered, including such approaches as peacemaking, justice, private justice, problem solving, harm reduction, naming and shaming, and d external controls.

predecessors, *Clinard and Quinney's Criminal Behavior Systems: A Revised Edition* will l to criminologists formulating their own theories and research on criminal behavior as students in criminology and sociology courses on how to view and study crime.

Treviño is Professor of Sociology at Wheaton College. He is the author and editor of sev-
inc‾ of G. Wright Mills (2012); *Classic Writings in Law and Society,*
tion he Legal System (2008); *George*
s: F : *A Multidisciplinary Approach*
th   Goffman's Legacy (2003); *Talcott*
lay 1); and *The Sociology of Law:*
d Co   rom Boston College, his M.A.

from Northern Arizona University, and his B.A. from the University of North Texas. He
as President of the Justice Studies Association (2000–2002), President of the Society for
of Social Problems (2010–2011), and was a Fulbright Scholar to the Republic of Mold

Richard Quinney is a renowned American sociologist, writer, and photographer
his philosophical and critical approach to crime and social justice. After earning hi
Sociology from the University of Wisconsin, he taught at several universities on the
and in the Midwest. He is author of several books, including *Criminal Behavior Sy*
published in 1967), *The Problem of Crime* (1970), *The Social Reality of Crime* (1974),
Legal Order (1974), *Criminology* (1975), *Class, State, and Crime* (1977), *Providence* (19
Existence (1982), *Criminology as Peacemaking* (1991), *Erich Fromm and Critical Criminol*
Bearing Witness to Crime and Social Justice (2000), and *Storytelling Sociology* (2004). He w
the prestigious Edwin Sutherland Award in 1984 by the American Society of Crimi
his contributions to criminological theory. He is currently Professor Emeritus of Sc
Northern Illinois University.

The late **Marshall B. Clinard** was Quinney's coauthor on the first, second, and third
Criminal Behavior Systems. The late John Wildeman joined them on the third edition.

NARD AND QUINNEY'S
IMINAL BEHAVIOR
STEMS

vised Edition

:h Edition

ier Treviño

:ledge
Francis Group
ID LONDON

Fourth edition published 2019
by Routledge
52 Vanderbilt Avenue, New York, NY 10017

and by Routledge
2 Park Square, Milton Park, Abingdon, Oxon, OX14 4RN

Routledge is an imprint of the Taylor & Francis Group, an informa business

© 2019 Taylor & Francis

First edition published by Holt, Rinehart and Winston, Inc. 1967
Third edition published by Anderson Publishing Co. 1994

Library of Congress Cataloging-in-Publication Data
A catalog record has been requested for this book

ISBN: 978-0-367-02664-6 (hbk)
ISBN: 978-0-367-02665-3 (pbk)
ISBN: 978-0-429-39846-9 (ebk)

Typeset in Bembo
by Swales & Willis Ltd, Exeter, Devon, UK

CONTENTS

FOREWORD

Richard Quinney

A long time ago—when the world was new—I asked Marshall Clinard what he thought about creating a typology of criminal behavior. As a graduate student in sociology at the University of Wisconsin at the end of the 1950s, I had read his *Sociology of Deviant Behavior* and been impressed by his delineation of types of delinquent and criminal behavior based on a continuum of the careers of offenders. This was a time when several sociologists were constructing typologies of various kinds. I had studied with Howard P. Becker and was working on a dissertation under his direction when he died unexpectedly in the summer of 1960, as I was about to leave for my first teaching job, at St. Lawrence University. Marshall was returning from research in India, and before I left I asked him to be the advisor for my dissertation. He agreed. Thus my turn from social theory, with emphasis on the sociology of knowledge and religion, to criminology.

Obviously, there was something about the construction of typologies that appealed to my intellectual interests. While studying with Becker, I had been inspired by his constructed types of sacred and secular. He had elaborated the constructive process in articles and books, especially in *Social Thought from Lore to Science*. Eventually, the many efforts in typology construction would be presented and analyzed in John McKinney's *Constructive Typology and Social Theory* (1966). By then, I had completed my dissertation and moved to teaching jobs, first at the University of Kentucky and then at New York University. During those years, Marshall and I had been writing what would be the first edition of our *Criminal Behavior Systems: A Typology* (1967).

Marshall and I kept in contact and were colleagues and friends for 50 years, until his death in 2010 at the age of 98. There would be a second and a third edition of *Criminal Behavior Systems*. You could say that it was this book that was the thread that held us together. But certainly there was more: frequent visits over these years, travel together to India and Kathmandu, letter exchanges now comprising a thick file in a drawer beside my desk, reading and commenting on books that we wrote individually, and advice and encouragement to each other along the way. This revision of our book brings us together one more time—good fortune in the guise of an academic life.

A couple of years ago, Javier Treviño surprised me when he suggested that it was time for a new edition of what he called "a classic." I made a few suggestions, mainly about the dimensions of the typology and the naming of the constructed types. I continue to recognize that what we call "crime" is so diverse that any explanation needs to be restricted to specifically designated behaviors, and not only to the behaviors of those defined as "criminal" but to the process of defining behavior as criminal and to the reactions (including legal reactions) of the public. Moreover, the underlying social, political, and economic context must be central to understanding, to explaining, what is defined as a crime. My years of work as a critical criminologist are crucial to my thoughts about the construction of a typology of crime. This revision by Javier incorporates the many developments in criminology since the earlier editions of the book. We, you, and I, give our thanks to Javier for his careful and extensive work on this new edition.

PREFACE

Clinard and Quinney's Criminal Behavior Systems is a revised and updated version of previous editions of the book *Criminal Behavior Systems: A Typology*. The project's conceptual and editorial lineage began years ago when Marshall B. Clinard, while an undergraduate student at Stanford University, took a criminology course in which Edwin H. Sutherland's *Criminology* (1924) was used as the textbook.[1] In it, Sutherland stated, "A great deal of effort has been devoted to the attempt to *classify* crimes. Most of the results must be regarded as useless."[2] The book left such an indelible mark on Clinard's thinking that he opted to undertake work toward the Ph.D. degree at the University of Chicago where Sutherland was teaching at the time. Shortly after arriving in Chicago, in 1935, Sutherland hired Clinard as his research assistant. "In Sutherland's role as my mentor," wrote Clinard almost three-quarters of a century later,

> He exercised a decisive influence on my career. While working as his research assistant, he had me read each day a variety of newspapers to look for and cut out articles on corporate crime. He then had me *classify* [italics added] the offenses described in newspaper articles based on several factors, including the nature of the particular violation committed.[3]

In the fourth edition of Sutherland's book, retitled *Principles of Criminology*, published in 1939, he introduced the concept of "behavior systems" in crime. As he explained,

> It is understood that certain crimes cluster in systems, are organized, are combined with other behavior in such manner as to form systems, and that certain other crimes stand somewhat isolated and outside of systems.[4]

The first attempt to implement Sutherland's concept of behavior systems and devise crime typologies was conducted by Clinard and Richard Quinney, his former student at the University of Wisconsin. In *Criminal Behavior Systems: A Typology* (1967), they explained that because crime covers a wide and diverse range of phenomena, "we feel that continued progress in criminology will largely depend on the study of *types* of crime."[5] The typological structure in that book was inspired by Clinard's "Selected Types of Delinquent and Criminal Behavior," which first appeared in his *Sociology of Deviant Behavior* (1957), a text that has become a standard in sociology and criminology.[6]

In order to present the forms of criminal behavior systematically, Clinard and Quinney formulated a typology based on eight types of crime: (1) violent personal crime, (2) occasional property crime, (3) occupational crime, (4) political crime, (5) public order crime, (6) conventional crime, (7) organized crime, and (8) professional crime. The typology encompassed four sociological dimensions: "the criminal career of the offender," "group support of the criminal behavior," "correspondence between criminal behavior and legitimate behavior," and "societal reaction." Their typology formed the framework for selecting, for the book, research articles on the eight types of crime. The articles consisted of previously published research studies as well as original ones prepared especially for the volume.

The second edition of *Criminal Behavior Systems: A Typology* (1973) was revised in several ways.[7] First, it dropped the readings format in favor of a greater discussion of each type of crime as well as of greater integration of research that had, up to that point, been conducted on each type. Second, in considering Quinney's notion that crime is a category of human behavior that is created and imposed by authorized political agents through the formulation of criminal definitions,[8] Clinard and Quinney felt that in their original conceptualization of the dimensions they "had not properly considered how certain offenses relating to each type had become defined as crimes nor the differences in the legal processing of each type." Thus, they developed more fully the dimension of "societal reaction" by dividing it into two: "legal aspects of selected offenses" and "societal reaction and legal processing." Third, they added a new type, *corporate* criminal behavior, to the original eight types of crime. Their rationale for doing so was that "this new type distinguishes between the complex criminal behavior of large corporations and other kinds of occupational criminal behavior." Building on earlier work by Quinney,[9] Clinard and Quinney added conceptual clarity to Sutherland's amorphous concept of "white-collar crime" by delineating its two principal forms: occupational crime, which involves the violation of criminal law committed by individuals in the course of their legitimate occupations, and corporate crime, which involves crimes by the corporation and crimes by corporate officials.[10]

For the third edition of *Criminal Behavior Systems: A Typology* (1994) John Wildeman, who had been a student of Quinney's at New York University, was recruited as coauthor.[11] A typological revision consisted of clarifying further and clearly distinguishing the categories of occupational crime and corporate crime. The category of political crime was greatly expanded and included discussion of nonviolent responses to offenders on the part of the state, based on Quinney's pioneering work on peacemaking criminology.[12]

The present edition has been retitled *Clinard and Quinney's Criminal Behavior Systems: A Revised Edition* as testimony to the fact that it was the conceptualization of criminal behavior systems that made the book a classic in criminology. This volume, authored by A. Javier Treviño, Quinney's former student at Boston College, continues the legacy of the previous editions by maintaining focus on criminal behavior systems and discussion of recent research studies that relate to the systems. Quinney revised the list of types in the typology and renamed the theoretical dimensions on which the typologies are based. These are now labeled "definition of behavior as criminal," "sociology of criminal behavior," and "social reaction to criminal behavior." Treviño updated the language and research to make it more relevant, informative, and appealing to current readers. Greater focus is given to alternative responses to mainstream criminal justice approaches. These responses are in the tradition of peacemaking, restorative justice, and transformative justice.

It is our hope that our typology of criminal behavior systems continues to be of use to a new generation of students in the field of criminology and to criminologists formulating their own theories and research on criminal behavior. Our work is indebted to those criminologists who have devoted their attention to the study of the various types of criminal behavior.

Notes

1 Edwin H. Sutherland, *Criminology* (Philadelphia: J.B. Lippincott, 1924).
2 Ibid., 22.
3 Marshall B. Clinard, "How I Became a Criminologist," in *Studies in Symbolic Interaction*, ed. by Norman K. Denzin (Bingley, UK: Emerald, 2008), 31:133–142, 136.
4 Edwin H. Sutherland, *Principles of Criminology*, 4th edition (Philadelphia: J.P. Lippincott, 1939), 230.
5 Marshall B. Clinard and Richard Quinney, *Criminal Behavior Systems: A Typology* (New York: Holt, Rinehart and Winston, 1967), v.
6 Marshall B. Clinard, *Sociology of Deviant Behavior* (New York: Rinehart, 1957). That classificatory scheme consisted of several categories of offenders based on a continuum ranging from "non-career" types to "criminal-offender" types.
7 Marshall B. Clinard and Richard Quinney, *Criminal Behavior Systems: A Typology*, 2nd edition (New York: Holt, Rinehart and Winston, 1973).
8 Richard Quinney, *The Social Reality of Crime* (New York: Little, Brown, 1970).
9 Richard Quinney, "The Study of White Collar Crime: Toward a Reorientation in Theory and Research," *Journal of Criminal Law, Criminology and Police Science* 55, no. 2 (1964): 208–214.
10 Clinard, along with Peter C. Yeager, later clarified that corporate crime included crimes committed by corporate officials with the aim of benefitting the corporation. See Marshall B. Clinard and Peter C. Yeager, *Corporate Crime* (New York: Free Press, 1980).
11 Marshall B. Clinard, Richard Quinney, and John Wildeman, *Criminal Behavior Systems: A Typology*, 3rd edition (Cincinnati: Anderson Publishing, 1994).
12 Harold E. Pepinsky and Richard Quinney, eds., *Criminology as Peacemaking* (Bloomington: Indiana University Press, 1991).

1
A TYPOLOGY OF CRIMINAL BEHAVIOR SYSTEMS

We all try to give meaning to our existence. Our common goal is to make the world understandable and familiar, thus rendering it amenable to order, prediction, and control. A principal way we achieve understanding is by generalizing beyond the singular, the unique, and the particular. Whether we are participants or observers of the social scene, we understand largely by searching for recurrent and uniform patterns. Thus, it is through abstraction that we are able to comprehend the world of concrete experience.

All phenomena are unique in time and space. Nothing ever recurs exactly as before. But in order to reduce the complexity of our experiences, we tend to compartmentalize the infinite variety of life. We construct images or concepts in our attempt to "know" the world around us. These constructs are a reduction of our intricate and manifold experiences, a reduction that treats occurrences *as if* they were similar, recurrent, and general. Events are placed into categories. Phenomena thus become comparable, and comparison is the beginning of scientific and philosophical reflection.

Thus, as with all human endeavors, the systematic study of behavior is based on an ordering of the diversified world of discrete phenomena. This is accomplished in the sciences by the development of classifications, where concrete occurrences are ordered and compared by categorizing single observations into typologies. As abstractions, these constructed types deviate from the concrete in that they combine and accentuate attributes relevant to a particular analysis. A constructed type consists of characteristics with empirical referents that serve as a basis for comparison of empirical cases.[1]

Typologies have been used for centuries in the study of physical and human phenomena. For example, as early as the third century BCE, Aristotle in his *Politics* proposed a typology of political systems. Another important typology was created by the Swedish botanist Linnaeus in the eighteenth century when he developed the modern scientific classification of plants and animals. But it was Max Weber who, early in the twentieth century, made explicit the procedure of typology for use in the social sciences with his proposal of the "ideal type." An analytical construct, the ideal type is created by combining diverse phenomena and accentuating their essential characteristics.[2] One of Weber's most famous ideal types is his four-fold classification of social actions, or meaningful human behaviors, that are determined by rationality, values, emotions, or habits.[3]

The use of typologies is common today, not only in botany, but in zoology, geography, geology, and other physical sciences. In the area of human behavior, the social scientist attempts to derive types, whether they be types of social organizations, types of occupations, or types of deviants. The use of types in ordering the diversities of observed phenomena has been instrumental in the development of the social sciences.

Types not only reduce phenomena to more systematic observation, but they also assist in the formulation of interrelated concepts and serve as guides for research. The construction of types may lead to a theoretical formulation. The constructed type, as John C. McKinney notes, functions as an analytic element in a more comprehensive theory and also orients empirical research to that theory:

> On the one hand, the type is related to a conceptual scheme and hence is implicated in a theoretical context more broadly conceived than any problem under immediate consideration. On the other hand, it serves as the unit for comparison and probability statement of empirical occurrence.[4]

Thus, the construction of types from a broad range of concrete social phenomena is a necessary stage in the development of specific theories. This process involves theorizing at what Robert K. Merton has called the "middle-range"—intermediate between a comprehensive theory of crime and empirical studies of concrete social phenomena.[5] Middle-range theorizing involves developing specialized theories on various types of crime: a theory of personal violent crime, a theory of occupational crime, a theory of political crime, and so on. Middle-range theorizing from typologies also offers the possibility of formulating a comprehensive theory for the explanation of all the phenomena under observation. Conversely, a typology can be derived from a comprehensive theory of a specified phenomenon. There is, indeed, an interdependence between theory construction and constructed typology. While types may emerge from theory, they also are instrumental in the reformulation and expansion of theory. Typology and its relation to theory construction are essential to the further development of comprehensive theory.

Typologies in Criminology

A diverse and wide range of behaviors is included in the category of crime. The one characteristic that all criminal behaviors have in common is that they have been defined as such by some recognized political authority. Much of the work of criminology is concerned with crime in general. However, because crime refers to a limitless variety of behaviors, criminologists also study particular types of crime. Thus, criminologists consider the identification, classification, and description of types of criminal behavior as defined by politically organized society.

Categories of crime and criminal behavior that are homogenous with respect to a specific explanation have been delineated by criminologists. Considering the wide range of phenomena subsumed under the concept of crime, a theory may be formulated after specific types of crime have been identified. The reciprocal relationship between typology and theory construction is clear: theoretical assumptions are necessary for the formulation of types, and a typology forces the reformulation of theory.

Criminologists have constructed and used many different typologies of crime and criminals. The most common typologies have been the legalistic, the individualistic, and the social.

Legalistic Typologies

The oldest forms of classification are based on the legal definition of the criminal offense. Perhaps the most commonly used legalistic classification is in terms of the seriousness of the offense, as indicated by the kind of punishment provided for the behavior. The most serious offenses, like murder, kidnapping, and arson, are called felonies and are usually punishable by confinement in a state prison for more than 1 year (or by capital punishment in those states that permit it). Less serious offenses, like shoplifting, trespassing, and vandalism, are called misdemeanors and are normally punishable by fines or by confinement in a county jail for up to 1 year. Another legalistic typology of crime, found in the *Model Penal Code* drafted by the American Law Institute, determines the level of culpability based on the defendant's mental state during the commission of the crime. Thus, crime may be committed purposefully, knowingly, recklessly, and negligently.

As classifications of crime, these typologies are not very useful because they are ambiguous and inconsistent. For example, in 2017 possession of any amount of marijuana was a felony in Arizona, possession of 1 ounce was a misdemeanor in Massachusetts, and possession of 1 to 2 ounces carried no penalty in Colorado. As for the *Model Penal Code's* legal classifications, a few states have adopted most of its provisions while other states have adopted only some of them. Consequently, the form of punishment prescribed for given offenses differs from time to time and from state to state.

It is common also to identify the criminal in terms of a legal category. "Crimes against the person" include such illegal acts as murder, assault, and rape; "crimes against property" include burglary, larceny, forgery, and motor vehicle theft; and "crimes against public order" consist of such behavior as prostitution, gambling, drug violations, and driving under the influence. Thus, criminals may be given labels such as "murderer," "rapist," "burglar," "thief," or "prostitute." This method of classifying offenders suffers from a variety of disadvantages. For example: (1) it says nothing about the person and the circumstances associated with the offense, nor does it consider the social context of the criminal act, (2) it creates a false impression of specialization by implying that criminals confine themselves to the kind of crime for which they happen to be arrested or convicted, (3) in order to secure easy convictions, it is a common practice to allow offenders to receive a reduced sentence, and in these cases the final legal status of the original criminal action will bear little resemblance to the actual behavior, (4) because the legal definition of a criminal act varies according to time and place, the legal classification of crime presents problems for comparative analysis, and (5) the use of legal categories in a classification assumes that offenders with a certain legal label are all of the same type or are products of a similar process.

There have been several attempts to overcome some of the problems of legalistic classifications of crime, while still utilizing the legal categories. Although the categories of crime defined in criminal law may not be appropriate for sociological purposes, they may nevertheless be used in forming types of crime. One possibility is that types may be defined *within* specific legal categories. For example, burglars, depending upon their mode of operation, could be divided into housebreakers, smash and grab burglars, professional burglars, and amateur burglars. Another possibility is that related legal categories may be *combined*. For example, the FBI in its National Incident Based Reporting System distinguishes between Group A and Group B offenses based on their severity, frequency, and prevalence as well as on the likelihood and importance of reporting these crimes by law enforcement. Group A incorporates aggravated assault, bribery, counterfeiting, human trafficking, sex offenses, and weapons law violations. Group B integrates writing bad checks, disorderly conduct, liquor law violations, and trespassing.

Criminologists who favor the strategy of defining types according to legal categories claim that doing so is desirable because official data concerning criminal histories appear in terms of legal nomenclature, and because the criminal code contains specific operational definitions of criminal behavior. However, as practical as these procedures of using various legal classifications appear, they have largely resulted in numerous unrelated categories of crime lacking a common conceptual frame of reference. They have not generated comprehensive theories.

An important problem with the construction of legal typologies of crime concerns the controversy over what behaviors and what persons should be regarded as criminal.[6] At what stage of the criminal defining process should persons and behaviors be deemed to be criminal? Is it at the stage of official detection, at the stage of arrest, at the stage of official adjudication, or at the stage of official disposition? Or, to state the extreme, should a typology of crime include persons and behaviors irrespective of official legal action? Indeed, criminologists have long argued that the discipline should go beyond the legal definition of crime to include those actions that cause social harm to the general public. For example, as long ago as 1944, the American criminologist, Edwin H. Sutherland maintained that such actions as antitrust violations, false advertising, and infringements of patents, copyrights, and trademarks—what he called "white-collar crimes"—though not in strict violation of criminal law, should nonetheless be considered crimes because they are socially injurious to business competitors and to consumers.[7]

Even if the criterion of official legal action is dropped in the construction of a typology, there is still the problem of how long a person remains a criminal after they violate the criminal law. Ultimately the selection of the stage of legal action to be used in defining the persons and behavior to be included in a typology of crime depends upon the purpose of the typology and the kinds of research problems that are anticipated. In other words, the needs of the research sometimes dictate the kind of typology employed.

The use of legal categories of crime is valid when the purpose is to understand the process by which behavior becomes defined as criminal.[8] Since criminality is not inherent in behavior but is a quality conferred upon individuals and acts by others, the study of the formulation and administration of the law is important to the criminologist. The legal definition of crime is the best indication of how the category of crime is created as a form of public policy. Any typology could incorporate the legal aspects of criminal offenses. The legal category itself is a constructed category.

Individualistic Typologies

In contrast to the various legal typologies that emphasize the criminal act, there have been typologies based on certain characteristics of individuals. This was the case with the criminologists of the so-called Italian School of Positivist Criminology, founded in the latter part of the nineteenth century, who were instrumental in turning attention to classification and to the use of criteria other than those found in the criminal law.[9] These early criminologists delimited types of offenders in terms of a heterogeneous collection of personal attributes. For example, Cesare Lombroso, in his book of 1878, *The Criminal Man*, identified, to his own satisfaction at least, a "born criminal" with a unique, inferior physique. Later, he recognized other types of criminals, including (1) the insane criminal, (2) the criminal by passion, and (3) the occasional criminal, a type that emphasized the social aspects of the offender as well as individualistic characteristics.

Another member of the Italian School, Raffaele Garofalo, a jurist, maintained that criminals are characterized by psychological anomalies. He divided these "defectives" into four categories: (1) typical criminals, or murderers who kill for enjoyment, (2) violent criminals, (3) criminals deficient in pity and probity, and (4) lascivious criminals. In a similar fashion, Enrico Ferri, of the same School, distinguished between five types of criminals: (1) the insane, (2) the born, (3) the habitual, (4) the occasional, and (5) the passionate.

Criminologists, clinical psychologists, and psychiatrists have subsequently attempted to classify criminal offenders by utilizing either a single personality trait, such as low self-control,[10] or a syndrome or grouping of traits, such as antisocial personality disorder.[11] Accordingly, criminal offenders have been grouped according to whether they are immature, emotionally insecure, dependent, hostile, antisocial, nonconformist, or aggressive. Sometimes a single trait, such as weak or inflated self-esteem, has been applied to a variety of criminal offenders differing in both the nature and seriousness of activity. Consequently, personality trait syndromes by themselves have little meaning for distinguishing types of criminal careers or the behavior of criminals from non-criminals who may also have these traits.

One limited individualistic typology of serial murderers has been developed on the basis of the psychodynamics of criminal motivation and rationalization: (1) the visionary serial killer, (2) the mission serial killer (3) the hedonistic serial killer (4) the power/control serial killer.[12] This typology fails to consider social-structural variables and is overly subjective in its interpretation of offender background characteristics. In terms of individualistic factors, offenders also have been divided according to their gender, age, race, ethnicity, and other personal attributes. Gender is not a very meaningful criterion for classification because, with the exception of prostitution, women in the Western world commit almost as wide a variety of offenses as men, although not as frequently. It is increasingly difficult to distinguish clearly among offenders merely upon the basis of gender.

Age also is a somewhat meaningless classification because all types of crime are committed by persons of varying ages, although at far different rates (for example, rapists are seldom over the age of 60). Offenders committing the most overt serious crimes against the person, however, are more frequently under 25 years of age, while occupational and corporate crimes are generally committed by middle-aged persons. Classification of offenders by age has little merit, for the criminal development of an offender may have little relation to age. An offender may be considered "developed criminally" if they have unfavorable attitudes toward laws, property, and the police; specialized knowledge of techniques to commit crimes and avoid prosecution; and a framework of motives to support their conduct. These qualities can be present in a juvenile offender and be comparatively absent in a middle-aged one, or vice-versa. Classifications by racial and ethnic characteristics have serious negative effects. There is plenty of evidence that racial profiling is used to routinely stop young African American and Latino men by police to search their cars without probable cause,[13] to subject them to higher rates of incarceration,[14] and to expose them to police brutality.[15]

The individualistic approach to criminal classification employs the questionable assumption that individuals with particular personal and physical characteristics commit certain types of crime. In addition, the individualistic approach implies that persons with these characteristics specialize in particular offenses. Finally, while individualistic classifications may offer some diagnostic possibilities for treatment, they have little utility for the construction of sociological theories of criminal behavior.

Social Typologies

If crime is to be studied as a social phenomenon, it is necessary to delineate types of criminal behavior according to the social context of the criminal offender and the criminal act. A number of such types have been developed. Two criminologists of the nineteenth century, the Englishman

Henry Mayhew and the Frenchman Georges Moureau, proposed criminal types based on how crime is related to the various activities of the criminal. Mayhew distinguished between *professional criminals*, who earn their living through criminal activity, and *accidental criminals*, who commit crimes as a result of unanticipated circumstances. Moureau added one other type of criminal to Mayhew's types. Recognizing that many of the offenders who commit crimes against the person cannot be included in either of Mayhew's types, Moureau designated the *habitual criminal* who continues to commit criminal acts for such diverse reasons as a deficiency in intelligence or lack of self-control.

Building on the Mayhew-Moureau criminal types, in 1941 Alfred R. Lindesmith and H. Warren Dunham devised a continuum of criminal behavior ranging from the *individualized criminal* to the *social criminal*.[16] The criminal acts of the individualized criminal are committed for situational and personal reasons, with the behavior finding little cultural support. This would be the case with a murderer who prior to the crime was a law-abiding person. In contrast, the criminal behaviors of the social criminal, such as the racketeer, are supported and prescribed by group norms. The social criminal through criminal behavior achieves status and recognition within a tight and limited group, such as an organized crime group or gang. In addition, although the social criminal uses illegitimate means, the goals he or she seeks, such as economic gain and personal security, are valued by the broader culture. The types of offenders found between the extremes of the individualized criminal and the social criminal share in varying degrees the characteristics of one or the other polar types. Focusing on the relationship between age and criminality, or crime and the life cycle in general, some criminologists have highlighted the vocational aspects of certain forms of crime. Sheldon and Eleanor Glueck may have been the first to examine, during the 1930s, the relationship between age and criminal behavior over the life span.[17] Later criminologists have seen that some crimes are committed by persons who pursue criminal behavior as a *career*.[18]

In a pioneering study, Walter C. Reckless suggested two types of criminal careers: *ordinary* and *professional*.[19] As career crimes, these two types of crime are similar in that they usually involve property offenses for the purpose of gain; the criminals tend to specialize in particular violations; the commission of the offenses requires various degrees of skill and experience; crime is pursued as a way of life; and career criminals continue in crime for a long period of time, possibly for a lifetime. In terms of differences among the career types, ordinary criminals represent the lowest rank of career crime, engaging in conventional crimes such as robbery, larceny, and burglary, that require limited skills. Professional criminals, in contrast, are highly skilled and able to obtain considerable amounts of money, through Ponzi schemes and credit card fraud, for example, without being detected. Whereas Reckless's distinction is important and valid, it is limited to those who make an occupation or career out of crime. Many persons who commit illegal acts are not career criminals.

A more comprehensive typology was developed by Don C. Gibbons that is based on a "role-career model," employing the criteria of "definitional dimensions" and "background dimensions."[20] The definitional dimensions consist of: (1) the nature of the offense behavior, (2) the interactional setting with others in which the offense takes place, (3) self-concept of the offender, (4) attitudes toward society and agencies of social control such as the police, and (5) the steps in role-career of the offender. The background dimensions are (1) social class (by which, presumably, he means socioeconomic status group), (2) family background, (3) peer group associations, and (4) contact with defining agencies such as the police, courts, and corrections. Originally his typology identified 15 adult offender types and 9 juvenile offender types, but he subsequently refined this to 20 types, including both adults and juveniles.

A typology was developed by Ruth Shonle Cavan that gives principal consideration to the public reaction to crime and the criminal's reaction to the public.[21] In an analysis of the interaction between the public and the offender, several types of criminal behavior were delineated. Because societal reaction is crucial to the criminal's self-concept and subsequent behavior, it is an important variable to be included in a typology of crime.

The typological approach continues to be important in criminology, as indicated by the attention devoted to the subject in virtually all contemporary criminology textbooks. Frank E. Hagan, for example, contends that "the real value of criminal typologies is their educational benefit in providing a useful, illustrative scheme, a practical device that, although subject to abstraction and overgeneralization, enables us to simplify and make sense of complex realities."[22] Dean A. Dabney identifies seven categories of criminal behavior: (1) homicide/assault, (2) sexual assault, (3) robbery, (4) burglary, (5) common property crime, (6) public order crime, and (7) crimes within complex organizations. He uses as his unit of analysis for each of these crime types "the criminal event," which he considers in light of behavioral, cognitive, cultural, and societal factors.[23] Terance D. Miethe, et al. also delineate seven similar crime typologies: (1) homicide and aggravated assault, (2) sexual assault, (3) robbery, (4) burglary, (5) motor vehicle theft, (6) occupational and organizational crime, and (7) public order crimes.[24]

Typology construction is far from perfect (all such systems are based on unstated assumptions about what the world is "really like"); nonetheless, without typologies of crime and criminals, theory itself becomes impossible.

The Construction of Typologies

There are several methodological problems in the construction of typologies of crime. These problems themselves serve as the basic principles of criminal typological systems.

Classification and Typology

While not always followed in practice, a distinction can be made between a classification (composed of classes) and a typology (composed of types). A strict *classification* consists of a set of variables or attributes that are linked to form several logically possible classes. A *typology*, in contrast, specifies how the attributes of observable phenomena are empirically connected in the formation of particular types. Thus, for example, we make classifications of insects and typologies of behavior patterns. Moreover, in a classification, there is the assumption that all cases within a class share the properties of that class to the same extent. A type, however, "acts as a point of reference that determines the extent to which any empirical case conforms to it, the principle consideration therefore being degree of approximation."[25] It is the construction of types rather than classes that interests the criminologist.

Ideal and Empirical Typologies

Another distinction is sometimes drawn between two kinds of typologies: the *ideal* and the *empirical*. Following the lead of Weber, an ideal type is an abstraction that does not necessarily describe concrete cases but represents possible or even extreme cases. An ideal type may be conceived of as a distortion of the concrete. All empirical occurrences can then be viewed in terms of this kind of "pure" type. Theoretically, the ideal type never can be found in reality. For example, Weber's ideal type of social action that is rationally-purposeful (that is carefully planned and carried out only after thorough consideration of the goal in relation to other goals), does not describe any actual person's social behavior. Real-life behaviors are not completely rational; they are also influenced by a combination of values, emotions, and habits. The empirical typology, in contrast, is composed of types that describe patterns that exist in the real world. The ideal type is the observer's abstraction; the empirical type is intended to represent what actually exists. In Howard P. Becker's analogy, the ideal type is "like a composite photograph printed from a large number of superimposed negatives," whereas the empirical type "is like a Frans Hals portrait."[26]

The distinction between ideal and empirical types is, however, arbitrary. Moreover, the distinction suffers from a faulty epistemology. The problem is related to the age-old controversy between realism and nominalism. Nevertheless, we cannot naively assume that types are "real." But we can dispense with the question of objective reality and the observer's ability to copy it. "There is no reason to believe in the objective reality of anything. Our concern, rather, is with the formulation of constructs that are meaningful for the purposes at hand."[27] Certainly, we construct types based on our perceptions and experiences. Nothing is either totally *a priori* or completely the result of induction. To conceive of types as developing from either source is to ignore the metaphysical problem of the dual nature of reality and our grasp of it. We construct that which gives meaning to our lives and to the real-world problems that we pose.

Theoretical Assumptions and Underlying Dimensions

No matter how implicit, some assumptions about the nature of crime and society are always present when we construct criminal typologies. In addition, the particular selection of dimensions is guided by the interests of the criminologist. In other words, the purpose at hand determines how the typology is constructed. Also, the level of explanation desired by the criminologist will play a part in the selection of dimensions in the typology. General characteristics for the construction of typologies can be developed in the course of criminological research. With the use of such techniques as factor analysis and regression analysis, and through longitudinal studies, for example, common characteristics of offenders can be found. These dimensions, in turn, can be used in the construction of a typological system. Typologies also can be constructed through the use of findings from other research studies on crime and delinquency. Once such typologies are constructed, and with the addition of interrelated concepts, they can serve as axiomatic theories whereby further statements—in the form of propositions—regarding types of crime can be deduced.

Related to the selection of characteristics underlying typologies is the determination of the phenomena to be included in the typology. The phenomena associated with crime include (1) the formulation and administration of criminal law, (2) the development of persons and behaviors that become defined as criminal, and (3) the social reactions to crime. The distinction between these three subject areas is crucial in the construction of typologies in criminology. For example, if a typology is based on *criminal law*, attention is focused on the process by which criminal definitions are imposed on human behavior by authorized agents of the state. However, if the objective is a typology based solely on *criminals* and their *behavior*, the emphasis is on the process by which persons who are subject to criminal definition acquire their self-conceptions and values, and how they associate with others in social and cultural contexts. Alternatively, a typology could be constructed on the basis of the nature and extent of *social reaction* to crime.

Yet another typology, first proposed by Sutherland, is a *criminal behavior system*, which is characterized by common norms, behaviors, and self-image among participants in the system.[28] A system of criminal behavior could be constructed that would consider all of the three previously mentioned areas of phenomena associated with crime. Such a typology would suggest how persons with certain characteristics and behaviors develop patterns that have a certain probability of becoming defined as criminal and that elicit particular reactions from various segments of society. The development of a multidimensional and integrative typology that considers all three areas of phenomena associated with crime is this book's primary concern.

Comprehensiveness and Homogeneity of Types

There is also the question of whether a typology should include the entire range of crime or be limited in scope. A typology that attempts to be comprehensive must formulate types at a high level of abstraction. When this is done, it is unlikely that many cases will remain outside of the typology. Also, the higher the level of abstraction and the more behavioral phenomena included, the less specificity there is.

Should a typology incorporate both adults and juveniles? Many of the offenses of juveniles are the same as those of adults, as far as the behavior itself is concerned. Therefore, in constructing types, there may be little reason to create separate types for minors and adults. Instead, various forms of juvenile delinquency can be included in a single typology (as we have done). When an offense committed by a minor would be a crime if committed by an adult, it is included within our typology. It is possible to construct a typology based on uniquely juvenile offenses, such as underage purchase or possession of alcohol, but this is not our intent here.

No typology, unless it is on a very low level of abstraction, can contain purely homogeneous types. For every type, several subtypes could be delineated. The level of abstraction of the typology in general and each type, in particular, determines the extent to which subtyping may be appropriate. It is always the *purpose* of the analysis, combined with the desired level of abstraction, that influences the construction of types. Understandably, many of our types could eventually be broken down into subtypes, but this will have to await further work.

The Future of Criminal Typology

Whatever the nature of typology construction, criminology will continue to be concerned with the study of types of crime. In the development of typologies, we cannot expect to achieve a system that all criminologists will agree is the most desirable. Although some classifications will at various times be more popular than others, there are several reasons why we cannot look forward to one unifying typology in criminology.

First, as already mentioned, typologies differ according to the purposes they serve. Since there will continue to be a multitude of purposes and goals, including levels of analysis and degrees of generality, there will always be many, sometimes competing, typologies. Second, there is the fact that crime is relative. The definitions of crime change from time to time and from place to place, depending on the political structure and culture of a community. Therefore, the behaviors and persons to be included in a typology will vary according to historical period and jurisdiction. Third, as criminological theory continues to develop typologies will need to be modified. Finally, theories, theoretical frameworks, and the related typologies will change as the orientations of criminologists change. Inevitably, as with all intellectual and political developments, the interests of criminologists will be attuned to the developments in the larger society.

Theoretical Dimensions of a Typology of Crime and Criminal Behavior

In the typology presented in this book, types of crime are viewed as *systems* of behavior. As heuristic devices, types are necessarily constructed as *systems*. As McKinney noted,

> The constructed type is a special kind of concept in that it consists of a set of characteristics wherein the relations between the characteristics are held constant for the purposes at hand. Hence, the type is a pragmatically constructed "system."[29]

Our *criminal behavior systems* are constructed types that serve as a means by which concrete occurrences can be described and compared within a system of theoretical dimensions that underlie the types.[30]

The theoretical assumptions of our typology are contained in three dimensions:

1. Definition of Behavior as Criminal.
2. Sociology of Criminal Behavior.
3. Social Reaction to Criminal Behavior.

Included in these three dimensions are diverse phenomena associated with crime, that is, the formulation and administration of criminal law, the development of persons and behaviors that may be defined as criminal, and the social reactions to the behaviors. Together these three dimensions with their specific assumptions form the theoretical basis for our typology of criminal behavior systems.

Definition of Behavior as Criminal. Crime, according to most criminologists, is a definition of human conduct that is created by authorized agents in a politically organized society.[31] Criminal laws are formulated by those segments of society that have the power to translate their values, ideologies, and interests into public policy. Criminal laws thus consist of definitions of behaviors that are regarded as threatening to the dominant interest groups. The social history of particular criminal laws reflects changes in the power structure of society.[32]

Sociology of Criminal Behavior. The behavior of the offender is shaped by the extent to which criminally defined norms have become part of the individual's career.[33] The criminal career of the offender includes the social roles they play, as well as their conception of self, progression in criminal activity, and identification with crime. Offenders vary in the degree to which criminally defined behavior has become a part of the organization of their life, usually in the absence of legitimate opportunities. The behavior of the offender is shaped by the extent to which criminally defined norms and activities have become a part of their career.

The behavior of offenders is also supported to varying degrees by the norms of the groups, communities, or subcultures to which they belong.[34] Persons defined as criminals act according to the normative patterns learned in relative social and cultural settings. Group support of criminal behavior varies according to the offender's associations with differential norms and the offender's integration into social groups.

Social Reaction to Criminal Behavior. Criminal behavior patterns are structured in society in relation to legitimate and legal behavior patterns. Within this context, persons develop and engage in actions that have relative probabilities of being defined as criminal. Criminally defined behaviors thus vary in terms of the extent to which they correspond to legitimate patterns of behavior in society. The behavior of the offender is viewed in relation to the norms of the segments of society that have the power to formulate and administer criminal law.

In addition, criminally defined behaviors vary in the intensity and amount of reactions they provoke from different sectors of society. Social reactions range from informal disapproval and censure to the official sanctioning procedures of the criminal justice system. Different policies of punishment and treatment are established and administered for each type of crime. Social reactions are also affected by the visibility of the offense and the degree to which the criminal behavior corresponds to the interests of the power structures of society. Finally, types of criminal behavior vary in the ways that they are processed through the legal system. Patterns of detection, arrest, prosecution, conviction, sentencing, and punishment or treatment exist for each type of crime.

A Typology of Criminal Behavior Systems

Seven types of criminal behavior systems are constructed in relation to the three theoretical dimensions. Further, they are based on a continuum ordered in sequence *from the individual to the structural*. In other words, criminal behavior systems range from crime types in which the individual offender acts alone and with little or no group support, as in the case of personal violent crime, to crime types that involve a collection of offenders colluding in the context of an organizational structure, as in the case of political crime. The types are:

1. Violent Personal Crime.
2. Occasional Property Crime.
3. Public Order Crime.
4. Occupational Crime.
5. Corporate Crime.
6. Organized Crime.
7. Political Crime.

Violent Personal Crime. The criminal laws of homicide, assault, and rape are found in most societies, yet the legal categories are qualified and interpreted in their respective social and historical contexts. Most offenders do not usually conceive of themselves as criminals. They are often persons without previous criminal records who commit a personal offense because of certain circumstances. The offenses are not directly supported by any group, although there may be cultural and subcultural definitions favorable to the general use of violence. There generally is a strong social reaction to these offenses.

Occasional Property Crime. Criminal laws protect the material interests of the propertied classes, specifically prohibiting burglary, larceny, motor vehicle theft, and arson. The offenders do not usually conceive of themselves as criminals and are able to rationalize their criminal behavior. They are usually committed to the general goals of society and find little support for their behavior in group norms. The behaviors violate the value placed on private property in Western culture. Societal reaction is not severe in those cases where the offender has no previous record, and there is leniency in legal processing.

Public Order Crime. Specific criminal laws embody the mores of particular segments of the community. Such offenses as drug violations, gambling offenses, prostitution, and driving under the influence may be seen as crimes without apparent victims, but they are disturbing to some community members. The violators may conceive of themselves as criminals when they are repeatedly defined as criminals by others. There is considerable association with other offenders, and some of the behaviors are supported by rather clearly defined subcultures. There is some correspondence between the illegal behaviors of public order offenders and legitimate patterns of behavior. Some of the behaviors defined as illegal (e.g., prostitution and drug use) are desired by many in legitimate society. There are strong social reactions by some segments of the community and weak reactions by others. Only a small portion of the offenses result in arrest, and many are tolerated as long as they do not become too visible.

Occupational Crime. Criminal laws and administrative laws have been enacted to regulate illegal activities associated with occupations and corporations in the course of their business pursuits. Legal regulation of occupations serves to protect the public and consumers from the vested interests of occupational and professional groups. Occupational offenders violate the law in the course of their occupational activities and do not conceive of themselves as criminal. They are easily able to rationalize their conduct. Some occupations (or groups within occupations) tolerate or even support offenses like money laundering, tax fraud, altering records, and misuse of company property or information. Official penalties have been lenient, often restricted to the sanctions administered by the professional associations themselves. Because such offenses are committed by "respectable" persons, social reaction traditionally has been mild or tolerant.

Corporate Crime. Criminal and civil laws and administrative regulations of corporations have been established to control such behavior as price-fixing, false advertising, misuse of trademarks, insider trading, the manufacture of unsafe foods and drugs, hazardous working conditions, and environmental pollution. Such laws serve to protect honest and socially conscious corporations, the free-market economy, and the consuming public. The criminal behaviors may be an integral part of corporate business operations. Violations are rationalized as being basic to business enterprise. Corporate crime involves a great amount of organization and cooperation among the participants. The offenses are consistent with the prevailing ideology that encourages maximum profits in advanced capitalist societies. Strong legal actions have not traditionally been taken against corporations and their officials. However, negative public reactions and legal actions are increasing as corporate crime becomes more widespread and more costly to the taxpayer.

Organized Crime. Many traditional laws have been used to control organized crime. Special laws also have been enacted to deal with organized criminal activity in legitimate business and racketeering. These offenders pursue crime as a livelihood. In the lower echelons of the organization, they conceive of themselves as criminals and associate primarily with other criminals. In the top levels of the organization, offenders associate with people of legitimate society, reside in the more desirable residential areas, and have access to those in political power. There is considerable correspondence between the criminal activities of organized crime and legitimate society. Organized crime groups provide illegal goods and services, such as gambling, commercial sex, drugs, and weapons, that are desired by legitimate society. The public tolerates organized crime and its activities, largely because of the desired goods and services it provides. Conviction is usually for minor offenses. However, as a result of federal legislation, investigative tools, and extradition treaties with other countries, more major organized crime figures have been successfully prosecuted.

Political Crime. Criminal laws are created by governments to protect themselves and their citizens. Specific criminal laws, such as "conspiracy" laws or laws against terrorism, espionage, and hate speech, are made to control and punish those who threaten citizens' rights and national security. Political offenders, acting out of conscience, do not usually think of themselves as criminals and may see themselves as patriots, freedom fighters, or martyrs. They receive support for their behavior by particular segments of society. Often the behaviors of citizens against the government are consistent with the ideal of political and civil rights and freedoms and basic human rights. Public acceptance of political crime depends on the extent to which the policies of the government are regarded as being legitimate at the time. Crimes of state are distinguished by the nature and extent of the social harm rather than by specific domestic and international criminal laws. State criminal behavior involves crime by a state against its citizens or against other states. Domestic and international laws have been created to protect against violations of human rights, civil rights, and privacy rights. Laws that protect private citizens and civilian populations from governments tend to be weak and ineffectual. States and state actors who engage in genocide, torture, mass surveillance, and police brutality are not likely to criminalize their activities. They see their infringements on civil rights and human rights as justified in the preservation of social and political order. Nondemocratic states support the atrocity crimes of other nondemocratic states as part of the natural order of things. State crime corresponds to the belief in political sovereignty, and governmental authority and prosecutions are rare. Immunity and amnesty are common.

The Organization of the Book

This book's organization is based on the typology of crime constructed above. A separate chapter is devoted to each of the seven criminal behavior systems. Each chapter contains a detailed description of a particular type, an analysis of that type according to each of the three theoretical dimensions (i.e., the definition of behavior as criminal, sociology of criminal behavior, and social reaction to criminal behavior) and a discussion of related research and writings.

Notes

1 John C. McKinney, *Constructive Typology and Social Theory* (New York, NY: Appleton-Century-Crofts, 1966), 3.
2 Max Weber, *Max Weber on the Methodology of the Social Sciences*, trans. and ed. by Edward A. Shils and Henry A. Finch (Glencoe, IL: The Free Press, 1949), 90–91.
3 Max Weber, *Economy and Society*, eds. Guenther Roth and Claus Wittich (Berkeley, CA: University of California Press, 1978), 24–25.
4 McKinney, *Constructive Typology and Social Theory*, 41.
5 Robert K. Merton, "On Sociological Theories of the Middle Range," in *Social Theory and Social Structure*, enlarged edition by R. K. Merton (New York, NY: The Free Press, 1968), 39–72.
6 Richard Quinney and John Wildeman, *The Problem of Crime: A Peace and Social Justice Perspective* (Mountain View, CA: Mayfield Publishing, 1991), Chap. 1.
7 Edwin H. Sutherland, "Is 'White Collar Crime' Crime?" *American Sociological Review* 10, no. 2 (1944): 132–139.
8 Richard Quinney, *The Social Reality of Crime* (Boston: Little, Brown, 1970); Piers Beirne and James W. Messerschmidt, *Criminology: A Sociological Approach*, 6th edition (New York, NY: Oxford University Press, 2014).
9 See Nicole H. Rafter, ed., *The Origins of Criminology: A Reader* (New York: Routledge, 2009); Anthony Walsh and Lee Ellis, *Criminology: An Interdisciplinary Approach* (Thousand Oaks, CA: Sage, 2007), Chap. 3; Thomas J. Bernard, Alexander L. Gerould, George B. Vold, *Vold's Theoretical Criminology*, 7th edition (New York, NY: Oxford University Press, 2015), Chap. 4.
10 Travis Hirschi and Michael Gottfredson, *A General Theory of Crime* (Stanford, CA: Stanford University Press, 1990).
11 American Psychiatric Association, *Diagnostic and Statistical Manual of Mental Disorders*, 5th edition (APA Publishing: Washington, DC., 2013).
12 Ronald M. Holmes and Stephen T. Holmes, *Serial Murder*, 3rd edition (Thousand Oaks, CA: Sage, 2010).
13 Albert J. Meehan and Michael C. Ponder, "Race and Place: The Ecology of Racial Profiling African American Motorists," *Justice Quarterly* 19, no. 3 (2002): 399–430.
14 Ted Chiricos, Kelly Welch and Marc Gertz, "The Racial Typification of Crime and Support for Punitive Measures," *Criminology* 42, no. 2 (2004): 359–389.
15 Malcolm D. Holmes and Brad W. Smith, *Race and Police Brutality: Roots of an Urban Dilemma* (SUNY Press, 2008).
16 Alfred R. Lindesmith and H. Warren Dunham, "Some Principles of Criminal Typology," *Social Forces* 19, no. 3 (1941): 307–314.
17 Sheldon and Eleanor Glueck, *Criminal Careers in Retrospect* (New York, NY: Commonwealth Fund, 1943).
18 Alfred Blumstein, Jacqueline Cohen, Jeffrey A. Roth, and Christy A. Visher, *Criminal Careers and Career Criminals* (Washington, DC: National Academy Press, 1986); Arnold Barnett, Alfred Blumstein, and David P. Farrington, "A Prospective Test of a Criminal Career Model," *Criminology* 27, no. 2 (1989): 373–385; Robert J. Sampson and John H. Laub, *Crime in the Making: Pathways and Turning Points through Life* (Cambridge, MA: Harvard University Press, 1995); John H. Laub and Robert J. Sampson, *Shared Beginnings, Divergent Lives: Delinquent Boys to Age 70* (Cambridge, MA: Harvard University Press, 2006).

19 Walter C. Reckless, *The Crime Problem*, 4th edition (New York, NY: Appleton-Century-Crofts, 1967), 279–298.

20 Don C. Gibbons, *Society, Crime, and Criminal Behavior*, 6th edition (New York, NY: Prentice-Hall, 1991), 206.

21 Ruth Shonle Cavan, *Criminology*, 3rd edition (New York, NY: Thomas Y. Crowell, 1962).

22 Frank E. Hagan, *Crime Types and Criminals* (Thousand Oaks, CA: Sage, 2010), 56.

23 Dean A. Dabney, *Crime Types: A Text Reader*, 2nd edition (New York: Aspen Publishing, 2013).

24 Terance D. Miethe, Richard C. McCorkle, and Shelley J. Listwan, *Crime Profiles: The Anatomy of Dangerous Persons, Places, and Situations* 3rd edition (New York: Oxford University Press, 2005).

25 John K. Rhoads, "The Type as a Logical Form," *Sociology and Social Research* 51, no. 3 (1967): 346–359.

26 Howard P. Becker, "Constructive Typology in the Social Sciences," *American Sociological Review* 5, no. 1 (1940): 40–55, 55.

27 Quinney, *The Social Reality of Crime*, 138.

28 Edwin H. Sutherland, *Principles of Criminology*, 4th edition (Chicago, IL: J.B. Lippincott, 1939), 218–219.

29 McKinney, *Constructive Typology and Social Theory*, 7.

30 Our typology of criminal behavior systems had its beginnings in Marshall B. Clinard, *Sociology of Deviant Behavior* (New York, NY: Rinehart and Winston, 1957), 200–209.

31 This theoretical perspective is developed in Quinney, *The Social Reality of Crime*, 15–23.

32 See, for example, Jerome Hall, *Theft, Law, and Society*, 2nd edition. (Indianapolis: Bobs-Merrill, 1952), Chap. 1; William J. Chambliss, "A Sociological Analysis of the Law of Vagrancy," *Social Problems* 12, no. 1 (1964): 67–77; Joseph R. Gusfield, *Symbolic Crusade: Status Politics and the American Temperance Movement* (Urbana, IL: University of Illinois, 1963).

33 For the theoretical background of this perspective, see Marshall B. Clinard and Robert F. Meier, *Sociology of Deviant Behavior*, 15th edition (Boston, MA: Cengage, 2016), 117–119.

34 Elijah Anderson, *Code of the Street: Decency, Violence, and the Moral Life of the Inner City* (New York: W. W. Norton, 1999); Waverly Duck, *No Way Out: Precarious Living in the Shadow of Poverty and Drug Dealing* (Chicago, IL: University of Chicago Press, 2015).

2

VIOLENT PERSONAL CRIME

Violent crimes against the person include acts in which physical injury is inflicted against one or more others, including criminal homicide, aggravated assault, robbery, rape, and intimate partner violence. What is referred to as murder-suicide where a depressed and distressed person (usually a man) kills his loved ones and himself, falls into the same category. Physician-assisted suicide, which involves a doctor providing a terminally ill patient with the knowledge or means required to commit suicide, is a form of homicide and is illegal in most, but not all, states in the United States. Kidnapping involves the element of physical force, and child abuse sometimes also involves the use of force and personal violence. Armed robbery involves an element of force, such as the use of a dangerous weapon, or threat of violence in obtaining money, jewelry, drugs, or other items of value.

The use of violence and the reaction of society to it can be viewed in an even wider perspective. As Marvin E. Wolfgang noted long ago, the use of personal and institutional violence has played a critical role in human history from riots to wars:

> Not all violence transgresses legal norms, but legal sanction proscribing many types of violence reflect a general societal opposition to violence, the historical concern with it, and the need to regulate its expression. Murder, rape, aggravated assault, armed robbery, and kidnapping are obvious examples of criminal violence. Labor riots, race riots, lynching mobs, fights among delinquent gangs, and attacks by organized criminal syndicates are all forms of collective violence that have punctuated the history of social change.[1]

Wars, civil riots, and violent demonstrations may involve thousands of individual acts of assault, murder, arson, vandalism, and theft.[2] The worst riot in US history since the Watts Riots of 1965 occurred in Los Angeles in May of 1992 in reaction to a police brutality case and the subsequent acquittal of the defendants. Wars offer testimony to the involvement of hundreds of thousands in mass violence. As these are forms of collective violence, however, their origin and nature are quite different from individual violent personal acts like homicide, assault, and rape. Collective acts of violence will be discussed in Chapter 8, on political crime.

This chapter deals with criminal homicide, aggravated assault, robbery, rape, and intimate partner violence, inasmuch as there is significant research and empirical data on these offenses.

Although arson can result in violent death, it is excluded from the typology because it is chiefly directed toward the destruction of personal property (it will be discussed in Chapter 3). Child molestation is not included here, because only a relatively small percentage of child sexual abuse involves force to gain the compliance of the child.

Definition of Behavior as Criminal

For most of human history, generally, the murder of or assault on a person was considered to be a private wrong for which the relatives of the deceased or assaulted person either took vengeance or demanded compensation. Such individual acts of violence were usually of minor concern to the tribal or political state and in fact, required retribution beyond the capacity of existing law enforcement institutions. But in contemporary societies, minimizing crimes of violence is the stated goal of the legal order. The distinction between criminal and noncriminal homicides required many centuries of development under English common law (upon which American law had largely been modeled). Excusable homicides include killings by misadventure and, under certain circumstances, self-defense. Whereas excusable homicides were never considered felonies in common law, they required the king's pardon and generally resulted in the confiscation of the offender's property (although this practice was later eliminated).

Further, the difference between murder and manslaughter can be traced to the Norman Conquest of England in 1066. Originally, murder (*murdrum* in medieval Latin) applied both to the killing of a Norman and the fine levied by the king on a district if the offender was not brought to justice. This distinction between the killing of Normans and English people was not eliminated until the fourteenth century when murder acquired the meaning of willful homicide. At this point, pardonable homicides were differentiated from those committed with "malice aforethought." Early English law did not discriminate between degrees of homicide; all were considered murder. Distinctions in modern law have their roots in statutes enacted in the late fifteenth and sixteenth centuries that excluded "murder upon malice aforethought." Thus, a second category was created: all criminal homicides that were not murder were *manslaughter*. Before that, in the old common law of England, one who inadvertently killed another while committing some other felony was guilty of murder.

The type of *criminal homicide* that will be referred to here as "murder" consists of *murder*, first- or second-degree; *nonnegligent manslaughter*, excluding justifiable homicide or attempts or assaults to kill; and *negligent manslaughter* other than manslaughter connected with the operation of motor vehicles. Murder is the unlawful killing of a human being with "malice aforethought." Malice aforethought represents a "guilty mind," or *mens rea*, but not necessarily premeditation and planning. In many jurisdictions of the United States, there are degrees of murder, first-degree and second-degree, often dependent on the situation or the means used. This constitutes a legal situation that affects the length and type of sentence. This distinction is of great importance, for it can mean the difference between imprisonment (for second-degree murder) or capital punishment (for first-degree murder in states that have the death penalty).

The concept of malice aforethought eventually took on a meaning under criminal law quite different from its original usage. Today a killing may be said to have malice aforethought when the accused (1) intended to kill either the victim or another, (2) intended to inflict serious bodily injury on the victim, (3) did not intend to kill but engaged in conduct of extreme recklessness, (4) killed another in the course of committing some other felony, or (5) killed a police officer while resisting arrest. Some of these acts are treated as first-degree murder and others as second-degree murder, depending on the jurisdiction's legal code. Under present-day law, one may legally kill an assailant when there is a reasonable belief of imminent danger of loss of life or of suffering serious bodily injury. In those states with "stand-your-ground" laws, the defendant has no legal duty to retreat from threats or perceived threats. One report found that the stand-your-ground defense was 17 times more successful when used by whites in the shooting of a black person than when the defense was used by blacks in the shooting of a white person.[3] Generally, a person may also use deadly force to save a third party who is a member of the person's household or to whom the person has special commitments.

Manslaughter is unlawful or criminal homicide without malice aforethought, that is, without *mens rea*. It covers a wide range of acts, including those that result in accidental death. A person might attack another without the intention of causing death or severe bodily harm, but death may be the outcome. The unlawful killing may be in a sudden heat of rage or anger and without premeditation. The element of provocation by the victim is often considered an element in manslaughter. In many cases of intimate partner violence, provocation by the victim is taken into account. One study found that in cases of domestic violence, provocation by a wife (victim) toward a husband (perpetrator) attributed more responsibility to the wife than to the husband and less sympathy for the wife.[4]

All such manslaughter is termed voluntary or nonnegligent manslaughter. Involuntary manslaughter is death arising from unintentional killing, primarily from negligence, such as death resulting from the collapse of an improperly constructed building. This is death attributable to the negligence of some person other than the victim.

In general, murder and aggravated assault are similar, for both involve the use of physical force to settle a dispute. In aggravated assault, there is an attempt to cause a person injury or kill him or her. Nearly all murders thus represent some form of aggravated assault, the chief difference being whether the victim died. Serious assaults are invariably considered felonies as they cover such behavior as an attempt to inflict severe injury or to kill. These include assault with a deadly weapon, assault to commit murder, or assault by shooting, cutting, sticking, stabbing, maiming, and so forth. Whether the behavior results in injury or is only an attempt to cause injury, it is still aggravated assault. In most cases, it is probably the element of chance that prevents the offense from crossing over into criminal homicide by the death of one of the participants.

Compared to other crimes, homicide is fairly accurately reported and recorded so that it is possible to make cross-national comparisons. The United States homicide rate is higher than in many countries in Western Europe. The homicide rates in Sub-Saharan Africa are extremely high as a result of rapid social change, intertribal strife, and civil wars. The highest homicide rates are in Latin America and the Caribbean, largely because of armed conflicts, drug trafficking, and gang violence. It is generally accepted that there is a strong positive relation between the degree of social inequality in a country and the levels of homicide.

According to the United Nations' *Global Study on Homicide 2013*, the United States homicide rate per 100,000 population was 3.9, Canada 1.5, Australia 1.0, and the United Kingdom 0.9. Even tiny Liechtenstein, with the most homicides in Western Europe, had a rate of only 2.7.[5] Nevertheless, since the mid-1990s, the violent crime rate in the US has generally been dropping. Psychologist Steven Pinker has even argued that, in the broad sweep of human history, violence has steadily declined.[6]

Despite the relatively low rate of violent crime in the US, the country has the highest ratio of citizens behind bars or under some sort of correctional supervision. This mass incarceration has been directed primarily toward poorly educated African American men[7] who have been disproportionately subjected to tough-on-crime measures, such as longer sentences and aggressive police tactics.[8] The United States is also alone among the advanced industrial nations still to execute offenders. Penal policies in the US have, by and large, failed to control violent crime. Peacemaking and restorative justice alternatives are sought by many criminologists and criminal justice professionals.[9] The driving idea behind these alternatives is that state violence against offenders only provokes more violence on the part of citizens and fails to have any positive effect on the offender. If we examine homicide rates in large cities, a complex picture emerges. Contrary to popular belief, it is not city size, but population density, that is correlated with homicide rates. Another key factor in violent crime rates is the degree of income inequality that characterizes a country. In other words, high levels of income inequality correlate with high rates of violent crime.[10]

Robbery, by legal definition means the actual use or threat of violent force against the victim. It involves the additional element of direct confrontation between criminal and victim. Despite this, only about 35 percent of all robberies result in physical injury to the victim.[11] Robbery is regarded as aggravated larceny. It consists of taking property from another with an element of force, placing the victim in a state of fear and intimidation. The fear and intimidation may be induced by a gun, knife, iron pipe, fist, or other instrument (even a toy gun).

In the past, the common law defined rape as sexual penetration by a man of a woman without her consent. It involved the use of force. This definition has been abandoned. Most states now address forcible penetration of another person, *whether a man or a woman*, without that person's consent. In 2013, the Federal Bureau of Investigation, in its reporting system, removed the term "forcible" and revised the definition of rape to refer to any "penetration, no matter how slight, of the vagina or anus with any body part or object, or oral penetration by a sex organ of another person, without the consent of the victim."[12] This also includes attempts to commit rape. Though the definition of rape varies widely between individual states, some now use the term sexual assault, which may or may not involve the use of force.

Problems of underreporting sexual violence have diminished somewhat as a result of four factors: (1) an increased willingness of victims to report their attacks, particularly those involving known assailants, to the police, (2) an increasing tendency among district attorneys to accept and vigorously pursue rape charges instead of, as in the past, discouraging the victim from pressing charges, (3) the establishment of special rape investigation units made up of female police officers, and (4) increased media attention, especially in reference to sexual assaults on university campuses, and public awareness through social movements, especially of sexual assault and harassment in the workplace. The pressures of organized advocacy groups for the empowerment of women, like those that make up the #MeToo movement, have secured these progressive steps.

Sociology of Criminal Behavior

Murderers, assaulters, and rapists generally do not have criminal careers. In the case of homicides, it is rare to find a person arrested for this crime who has previously committed such an offense, although the individual may have arrests for other offenses, violent as well as nonviolent. One study found that only about 30 percent of murderers who killed multiple victims during a criminal episode, had criminal careers.[13]

Few people make careers out of assaulting others. Only a small percentage of those arrested for aggravated assault have been arrested previously for this same offense. These statistics tend to remain remarkably stable over time with regard to using actual or threatened violence in the form of assault and even homicide as part of their careers in crime. The exceptions are organized criminals who will be discussed in Chapter 7.

Most murderers and assaulters do not think of themselves as being real criminals; they seldom identify with crime, and criminal behavior is not a significant part of their life organization. The situation is somewhat different with rapists; they are reported by some to have an extensive criminal record for other offenses, particularly against property. While youth tend to be persistent or frequent violent offenders,[14] they usually exhibit only a small degree of specialization in violence.[15] However, among adults, one study found substantial levels of specialization in violence as well as considerable stability in specialization over time.[16] In other words, violent offenders often have a pattern of violence, and hence, past violence is a predictor of future violence.

Another study based on cluster analysis methodology concluded that (1) the number of offender's prior violent crimes is strongly associated with that offender's number of nonviolent crimes, (2) offenders with psychiatric histories display a greater tendency than other offenders toward violent crime, (3) offenders addicted to alcohol and drugs are more likely to be convicted of burglary than of violent personal crime, (4) offenders with no psychiatric history who are convicted of homicide are more likely to do so with a gun, away from their own residence, and to choose a friend or acquaintance as their victim, whereas offenders with psychiatric histories tend to slay spouses or relatives, within their own homes, and not use a gun as their weapon.[17]

Many rapists appear to have had a record of arrests for criminal offenses. One study found that rapists remain at risk of re-offending long after their release, in some cases 15–20 years after release.[18] Much of violent behavior is linked to differences in power that people have over one another. Nevertheless, there are some people who react with violence in a variety of situations and circumstances. It is likely that such people have extensive criminal records and a long history of antisocial conduct in other areas of their lives, such as at school and in the family. One study found that offenders experience an increasing sense of violence as a solution to some provocation such as feeling disrespected or "pushed around" and in so doing come to see themselves as violent individuals.[19] According to criminologist Lonnie H. Athens, dangerous offenders generally go through a series of five stages in their socialization into violence. First, the subject is forced into engaging in acts of brutalization by others in their primary group. Second, the subject repeats the belligerency as an act of defiance. Third, the subject continues to engage in violent dominative encounters. Fourth, the subject acquires a violent personality. Finally, the subject becomes a violent predator.[20]

Some continue perpetrating such acts of violence, meanwhile learning from the way others react in the wake of such actions. These individuals perceive themselves and are perceived by others as dangerous and powerful. The unpredictability of their violence is also a potent factor. In short, others bestow the mantle of power on the person, and that reinforces the use of violence.

The general cultural and subcultural pattern seems to determine the frequency of crimes of violence. Acceptance of the use of violence varies from country to country, region to region, and state to state. It also varies by neighborhood (within a city), social class, race, gender, and age. The existence of *subcultures of violence*, normative systems of a group or groups smaller than the total society, has been advanced as a concept, primarily by Marvin E. Wolfgang and Franco Ferracuti, to explain these variations.[21] According to this view, specific populations, such as social classes, ethnic groups, and so forth, have different attitudes toward the use of violence. Favorable attitudes toward violence are organized into a set of norms that are culturally transmitted. Subcultural groups exhibit norms about the importance or lack of importance of human life in the scale of values, and the kinds of reactions to certain types of social stimuli, in the evaluation of such stimuli and in the socialization process in general. A subculture of violence represents values that stand apart from the dominant or mainstream culture of society. For example, sociologist Elijah Anderson found that poor, inner-city black communities develop a "code of the street," which is a set of informal rules that govern interpersonal violence and aggression.[22] The code of the street informs inner-city residents how to respond to, and survive, violent confrontations. Introduction to the code of the street begins early in life:

> In the street, through their play, children pour their individual life experiences into a common knowledge pool, mixing, negating, affirming, confirming, and elaborating on what they have observed in the home and matching their skills against those of others. They also learn to fight; in particular, they learn the social meaning of fighting. In these circumstances, even small children test one another, pushing and shoving others, and they seem ready to hit other children over matters not to their liking. In turn, they are readily hit by other children, and the child who is the toughest prevails.[23]

It should be pointed out, however, that the proponents of a "subculture" of violence base the existence of the theory of differences on *rates* of violence between various groups or communities. This does not, of course, mean that *all* persons in any group share the values supposedly reflected in a subculture of violence or, conversely, in a subculture of nonviolence. Indeed, Anderson found families with "street" values and families with "decent" values in the same community.

Different segments of society define different social situations as violence-appropriate. Some males "must" defend their mothers' honor, often to the point of violence. For some, a sneer, a "dis," or simply being stared at is considered enough to call for a violent response, while for others, being taken advantage of monetarily is what merits a violent response. Many American adolescents (males, in most cases) consider violence an appropriate response to being denied a request for money or even use of the family car from parents or relatives.

It has been argued by criminologists, philosophers, and social scientists that state-mandated executions constitute powerful support and reinforcement for violence in the minds of many citizens. The reasoning is, "if it is legitimate for the state to punish a wrong by killing the wrongdoer, why is it not legitimate for me to do the same when I am wronged?" The reasoning, of course, is flawed, but the conclusion is suggested and not entirely unreasonable.[24]

In general, American popular culture encourages and nurtures violence. From the sports industry, there is ice hockey, stock car racing, mixed martial arts, and football. The case is perhaps worse in Europe where violence is engaged in by the spectators. Football hooliganism, destructive and violent behavior by football (soccer) fans, takes place before, during, and after matches.

> Football-hooligan confrontations take a number of different forms and they can take place in a variety of contexts beside the football ground itself. They can, for example, take the form of hand-to-hand fighting between just two rival supporters or between two small groups of them. Alternatively, they can involve up to several hundred fans on either side. In the most serious incidents weapons are sometimes used. Football-hooligan confrontations can also take the form of aerial bombardments using as ammunition missiles that range from innocuous items to dangerous, even potentially lethal, ones such as darts, metal discs, coins (sometimes with their edges sharpened), broken seats, bricks, slabs of concrete, ball bearings, fireworks, smoke bombs and, as has happened on one or two occasions, crude incendiary devices.[25]

There is also some evidence that violent song lyrics, common in various music genres, may lead to violent behavior in the short run.[26] There is, however, no conclusive evidence that playing violent video games is related to violent crime. On the whole, there is little in American culture that encourages peacemaking and nonaggression.

The greater the degree of integration of an individual into a subculture of violence, in terms of appropriate reactions to certain types of stimuli and the importance of human life, the more likely that that individual will resort to violence in a dispute to gain an objective. Child-rearing practices and peer group associations that employ violence are part of this subculture. One controversial report argues that the spanking of children, a practice prevalent in American culture, teaches them that violence is to be used to correct wrongs.[27]

There are many cultural and subcultural socialization patterns that lead to social interactions and personal decisions that produce people who are ready to inflict serious physical harm with only minor provocation. One ethnographer who studied a Chicago neighborhood troubled by gang violence found that injury was a compelling motivation for retaliation.

> Once out of the hospital, Marcus received a visit from his friends, who wanted to plot an assault on members of the rival gang who had jumped Marcus. "Inside my head, I'm like, 'Do I really want to go with them?'" Marcus says. "Or do I wanna listen to my mother?" His main concern was appearing weak if he chose not to retaliate. It wasn't simply Marcus's reputation that was one the line, his friends argued—the whole set's was.[28]

Another ethnographer discovered that in a poor African American community where drug dealing was prevalent, there had arisen an "interaction order." This was a lifestyle that involved personal interactions that differed sharply with those of the dominant culture. The interaction order helped community residents avoid trouble by accurately interpreting what was meant by a particular gaze, a way of walking, or a way of dressing.[29]

Violence is defined as an appropriate response to provocation among poor, disenfranchised male adolescents and young adults in inner-city neighborhoods. Violent crimes are more closely linked to males, particularly young males, partly because of the felt need to display toxic masculinity. This toxic masculinity has been equated with the view of violence as manly, the perception of danger as exciting, and callous behavior toward women.[30] Often these young males have no other way to assert themselves or to prove their worth.

Subcultural settings with a ceremonial expression of toxic masculinity, such as in some sports clubs, college fraternities, and preparatory boarding schools, can be prime environments for sexual violence and rape. In these subcultures, sexual aggression is socially approved, and there are rituals (such as the Senior Salute) where young men are expected to make sexual conquests and score sexual "points."

Regional, National, and International Differences

In general, homicide rates in various countries and regions of the world are related to cultural differences regarding the use of violence rather than to laws or individual personality characteristics. Overall, the Americas have the highest rates of homicide, followed by Africa, Asia, Europe, and Oceania. In looking at the sub-regional picture, Southern Africa and Central America are the sub-regions with the most homicides, followed by South America, Middle Africa, and the Caribbean. The countries with some of the highest rates in Eastern Europe include Russia, Moldova, Bulgaria, and the Czech Republic.

Globally the highest numbers of homicide are found in Central and South America, particularly in Honduras, Venezuela, Belize, El Salvador, Columbia, and Mexico.[31] Many of the murders in these countries are linked to armed political conflicts, warring gang factions, organized criminal groups, and drug trafficking.

In El Salvador, Honduras, and Guatemala, the so-called northern triangle countries of Central America, gang-related violence has contributed to some of the highest homicide rates in the world. The major gangs operating in the northern triangle region are the "18th Street" gang (also known as M-18), and its main rival, the *Mara Salvatrucha* (MS-13).

> Gang-related murders occur when gangs discipline their members or punish those who attempt to leave, dispute territory, confront law enforcement and their families, and punish those who fail to comply with their orders. Gangs have also targeted witnesses to crimes.[32]

In Mexico, tens of thousands of people have been murdered since the mid-2000s in drug-related killings. The violence there is the result of drug-trafficking organizations competing for control of the cocaine, marijuana, and methamphetamine transportation routes. The drug cartels have engaged in fierce gun battles with Mexican military and police. They have corrupted police departments and assassinated honest police commanders. In northern Mexico, and along the Mexico-US border, drug traffickers and drug trafficking are celebrated in ballads called *narco-corridos*. These *narcocorridos* often glamorize the subculture of violence.[33]

The importance of cultural definitions in criminal homicide was revealed as long ago as the 1930s when wide regional differences in the United States were found.[34] Even today, homicide rates in the South are considerably higher than those of other regions. The difference is due largely to the fact that cultural definitions demand personal violence in certain situations. Moreover, the pattern of Southern violence cannot be explained by the rural nature of the population, relative poverty, or backwardness or underdevelopment. One study showed that, contrary to the general pattern of other offenses, murder and aggravated assault are negatively correlated with most socioeconomic variables, whether they occur in rural, urban, or standard metropolitan statistical areas.[35] "Offenses against the person regardless of the population area may become institutionalized and perceived by people in these structures as the most appropriate solutions to interpersonal problems."[36] Several scholars have suggested that the high prevalence of homicide in the US South originates from the historical settlement of that area by Scots-Irish. It is said that they brought with them an exaggerated "culture of honor," whose purpose is the defense of a reputation. This way of life demands that any personal slight or insult is to be answered by violence.[37]

The Use of Firearms

The possession of firearms is part of the subculture of violence as are the norms for their use. For example, in 2007 the United States had in its possession 270 million firearms. The US estimate of civilian gun ownership was between 83 to 97 per 100 people, while in Canada it was between 25 and 38 and in England and Wales between 3.3 and 7.8. With less than 5 percent of the world's population, the United States is home to roughly 35–50 percent of the world's civilian-owned guns. Of some 8 million new firearms manufactured annually around the world, roughly 4.5 million are purchased by Americans.[38] Looked at another way, 45 percent of Americans report having a gun in their home.[39]

In the United States, firearms, usually handguns, are commonly involved in crimes involving violence. This is the case in 71 percent of homicides, 24 percent of aggravated assaults, and 41 percent in robberies.[40] Firearms allow greater range, provide more concealment, and permit attacks by persons either unwilling or unable to overpower a victim by other means.

In 2015, over 13,000 people were murdered with a firearm.[41]

The intent of the persons, the nature of their interaction and relationships, the availability of firearms to them, and the level of law enforcement are critical in explaining when and why firearm violence occurs.[42]

Most of the states in the US have right-to-carry laws that allow qualified adults to carry concealed handguns. Some studies find that these laws deter crimes against individuals, others that the effects are negligible, and still others that such laws increase violent crime.[43]

Federal law prohibits the purchase and possession of firearms by people who fall within certain categories, such as convicted felons, domestic abusers, and people with specific kinds of mental health histories. Despite background checks on people desiring to purchase handguns, they are nevertheless widely available.

The United States does not have a comprehensive national system of gun registration. Some states require registration of some firearms, but only a handful of states require the registration of all firearms. Although the domestic production and sale of firearms can be known with a fair degree of accuracy, it is impossible to know the number imported and sold, either legally or illegally. Some people make their own improvised guns, usually for self-protection. A steel pipe, a trigger mechanism, and a cartridge chamber are all that is needed. Three-dimensional (3D) printing technology can also be used to make parts for a fully functional firearm.

Demographics

Characteristics of nearly all homicide and aggravated assault offenders and their victims have been found to be similar, indicating that they represent basically similar behavior.

> In all nations where they have been recorded, rates of homicide and serious assault are higher among men and the young than women and older persons. In the United States, the prevalence of homicide and serious assault is greater among African Americans and Hispanics than non-Hispanic whites. In all groups, firearm use greatly increases the risk that a violent encounter results in the victim's death. Large fractions of victims are acquainted with the perpetrator in homicide and aggravated assault, sometimes intimately. Women are more likely than men to be killed or injured in attacks by an intimate partner.[44]

Despite similarities in the type of homicide and assault, they vary a great deal by community, race, social class, gender, and age. This fact illustrates the role of demographic characteristics in criminal violence. While we examine each of these characteristics in turn, it is important that an *intersectionality* approach is also considered to see the interconnection between these factors.[45]

Community. Violence occurs primarily in large urban areas. For example, in 2015, the rate of violent crime in US metropolitan statistical areas was 402 per 100,000 population, compared to nonmetropolitan counties where it was 194 per 100,000 population. As far as the area of the city is concerned, violent crime is more frequent in communities that have exceptionally high rates of unemployment, overcrowding, and housing decay, and that are characterized by considerably substandard schools, drug dealing, and poverty. These communities have extremely high levels of income inequality, and income inequality is an indicator of the level of violence. One study found that over half of urban crimes can be explained by the presence of more female-headed households in cities, a phenomenon that itself may be related to poverty.[46] The use of interpersonal violence as a means of settling disputes has become common in the inner-city subculture.

A great deal of urban violence is the result of the drug trade, gang warfare, and retaliation. Often, members of gangs and organizations that deal in drugs kill each other in the competition for customers and marketing territory, even when they are not personally acquainted. Drive-by shootings involve innocent victims who happen to be in the wrong place at the wrong time. In these incidents, the victims are unknown to the killers.

In 2015, Chicago had the highest rate of violent crime among larger US cities. This included 478 murders; 1,432 rapes; 9,649 robberies; and 13,104 aggravated assaults.[47] According to the Chicago Police Department, gangs were responsible for over half of the murders in Chicago.[48]

Despite gang activity, it remains true that in crimes of violence it is more common that the offender and the victim were on some level of intimacy or acquaintance at the time of the offense. Some indication of the relationship between criminal homicides and the pattern of life in certain areas of the city is suggested in Wolfgang's classic study in which he found that 65 percent of all criminal homicides in Philadelphia occur during weekends, particularly on Saturday night.[49] Robert J. Sampson found that neighborhood characteristics such as structural density, residential mobility, and female-headed families, have strong positive effects on rates of personal criminal victimization.[50] Another study found that concentrated disadvantage and extreme poverty produced high levels of crime in local areas of Columbus, Ohio.[51] In a later study of Columbus, the same researchers found that communities may reduce violent crime by developing local institutions, such as recreation centers and libraries, that provide organized activities for community members.[52]

Race. Racial disparity is greatest in arrest rates for crimes of violence. The national United States rate in 2015 showed, for example, an African American arrest rate for murder and non-negligent manslaughter of 51 percent as compared to 46 percent for whites. This contrasts with crimes against property where the burglary arrest rate was 30 percent for African Americans and 68 percent for whites.[53] Racial disparity also shows up in the rate of violent victimization with 23 percent of victims being African American and 17 percent being white.[54] Criminal homicide was ranked 8th as the leading cause of death for blacks and 19th for whites. It contributed to 2.6 percent of total deaths in the black population compared to 0.3 percent in the white population.[55] Moreover, African American communities experience violent crime at a rate five times greater than white communities.[56]

One explanation for the disproportionate representation of African Americans as offenders and victims in violent crime is the so-called racial invariance thesis proposed by Robert J. Sampson and William Julius Wilson.[57] The thesis explains the black–white disparities in violence as a result of the racial segregation that exposes blacks to violence-inducing and violence-protecting neighborhood factors. A violence-protecting factor involves neighborhoods with an above average proportion of people in professional or managerial jobs and with higher concentrations of immigrants. A violence-inducing factor pertains to the fact that African American neighborhoods tend to be located near environments characterized by social and economic disadvantage.[58] Another study found that because African American communities have such extremely high levels of concentrated disadvantage (measured as poverty, female-headed families, and male joblessness), other factors have little effect in explaining the high rates of criminal violence in those communities.[59]

Other criminologists point to the disproportionate representation of African Americans in violence as stemming from racial conceptions by the public, such as the "criminalblackman" stereotype, that generally depicts black men as violent criminals.[60] As Richard Quinney has noted, the social reality of crime is basically constructed from the criminal conceptions.[61] Moreover, racial profiling by police has resulted in African Americans being more likely than whites to experience face-to-face contact with police, arrest, and the use or threat of force by police.[62]

Social Class. Violent crime is found to be concentrated among the lower classes. As John Braithwaite succinctly put it, "lower-class people, and people living in lower-class areas, have higher official crime rates than other groups."[63] One study showed that levels of *absolute* poverty (severe conditions of material disadvantage) but not of *relative* poverty (inequality in the distribution of wealth or income) are significantly associated with higher rates of violent criminal activity.[64] Another study concluded that homicide and assault may be more closely associated with absolute and relative poverty, than rape and robbery.[65] Aside from the differences in types of poverty and offenses, it is clear that there exists a relationship between socioeconomic conditions and violent criminal behavior, whether at the neighborhood, city, or country level.

For example, a neighborhood study of St. Louis found that retaliatory killings—defined as those involving retribution for an offense committed by the victim against the offender in a previous interaction—were concentrated in socioeconomically disadvantaged neighborhoods. While in low-poverty neighborhoods 12.6 percent of homicides were retaliatory, in neighborhoods with extreme poverty, 19 percent of homicides were retaliatory. One of the reasons for these high rates is that poor neighborhoods often lack adequate police protection.[66] Researchers have also found that intimate partner violence (IPV) is more prevalent and severe in disadvantaged neighborhoods. Indeed, one study found that women living in disadvantaged neighborhoods were more than twice as likely to be the victims of intimate violence compared with women in more advantaged neighborhoods.[67] The same study concluded that IPV also occurs more in households facing economic distress (being unemployed or not making enough money to meet family needs and thus worrying about finances). The prevalence of intimate partner violence jumps dramatically, however, when the economically distressed household is in a disadvantaged neighborhood.

As for violence in urban areas, a study of 236 US cities found that cities with high levels of poverty clustering also have high rates of homicide.[68] And at the country level, one study found that relative poverty has a significant and positive effect on the incidence of homicide and robbery rates within and between countries.[69]

As Alice Goffman states in her ethnography of a lower-class neighborhood in Philadelphia, which she nicknamed "6th Street": "Crime and violence are undeniable problems in poor urban communities. . . . around 6th Street the street trade in drugs, neighborhood rivalries, and their potential for violence are all deeply woven into community life."[70]

This is not to say that criminal violence does occur among the middle and upper classes. But it is relatively rare, even in regions with high homicide rates such as the US South and countries in Latin America. When homicide is committed among the higher socioeconomic groups, it is likely to be more rational and planned. Deterrence likely operates with these groups more than with the lower groups, for the consequences can be potent and meaningful to their lives. In general, however, the cultural phenomenon of interpersonal violence does not pervade the middle- and upper-class strata of industrial societies.

> The infrequency of known homicides committed by persons of middle or upper-class status supports the conventional sociological wisdom concerning the powerful taboo against violence in the value systems of the middle and upper-class subcultures. When there is a resort to violence, the *modus operandi* more often resembles the fictional conception of the calculated murder than the impulsive alcohol-stimulated passionate outburst of lower-class violence. Premeditation, uncommon in lower-class violence, is a feature of more than three-fourths of upper-class homicides. The wish for pecuniary gain motivates the upper-class killer more than any other single desire; while in studies of lower-class cases, it appears only in connection with murders committed in the course of robberies. Mental depression,

the next most frequently ascribed motive in upper-class homicide, does not even appear as a category of analysis in the lower-class studies.[71]

Gender. Criminologists agree that men are always and everywhere more likely than women to engage in violent criminal behavior. In the United States, nearly 9 in 10 persons arrested for murder and nonnegligent manslaughter are male. Over three-fourths of arrests for aggravated assault are of men. As would be expected, rape is almost exclusively a male crime, with 97 percent of those arrested being men. The overall arrest rate for males for all violent offenses is almost 80 percent.[72]

Aside from these numerical differences, there are also gender-role differences that determine the method and outcome of violent crime committed by women. For example, when women do participate in acts of violence, they result in fewer and less serious injuries. This is largely because of the way in which they enact the crime. For example, in the case of street robbery, males typically target other males, and their robberies often involve direct confrontation, physical violence, and guns. Females most often target other females and seldom use a weapon. When women do rob men, they always carry a gun, but they are more likely to soften the target with sex than with actual violence.[73]

Although both men and women are victims of domestic violence, women are more likely to be raped and sexually assaulted by their intimate partners. There are also important gender differences in the motivations to use violence. Whereas men are more likely to use violence when they perceive themselves losing control of the relationship or when they believe their partner is challenging their authority, women are more likely to use violence in self-defense, when they believe they are in imminent danger of being attacked, or in retaliation for being attacked.[74]

Age. "As long as records have been kept," Michael Gottfredson and Travis Hirschi contend, "in all societies in which records are available, it appears that crime is an activity highly concentrated among the young."[75] Indeed, urban violence generally is higher among the younger age groups. Urban arrest rates for homicide in the United States are much higher among the 18–24 male group. Over half of all robberies (56 percent) are committed by persons under the age of 25.[76] By the same token, violent offending prior to ages 12 to 14 is relatively rare, and most individuals terminate serious violent offending by age 25.[77] This means that crime rates peak during the adolescent years. According to Robert Agnew, the peak stems from several effects resulting from the fact that adolescents in industrialized societies are extended some, but not all, of the privileges and responsibilities of adults. These effects include a reduction in supervision; an increase in social and academic demands; participation in a larger, more diverse, peer-oriented social world; an increased desire for adult privileges; and a reduced ability to cope in a legitimate manner, and increased disposition to cope in a criminal manner.[78]

Several longitudinal studies reveal that desistance from violent criminal behavior occurs with age.[79] This is due to life-course transitions such as marriage, employment, entry into the military,[80] and changing patterns of peer relations.[81] There is also evidence that offenders generally follow a sequence from participation in minor offending at young ages and involvement in violent crimes later in the life course. A Pittsburgh study found that males progress from shoplifting at age 10, to property damage at age 12, to fighting and violence at age 13.[82]

Situational Interaction and the Use of Violence

Most murder and aggravated assault represents a response growing out of social interaction between one or more parties in which a situation comes to be defined as requiring the use of violence.

Generally, for such an act to take place, all parties must come to perceive the situation as one requiring violence. If only one responds in a dispute, it is unlikely to become violent; likewise, if only one of the disputants is accustomed to the use of violence, the dispute is likely to end only in a verbal argument. However, when a cultural norm is defined as calling for violence by a person in interaction with another who harbors the same response, serious altercations—fist fights, physical assaults with weapons, and violent domestic quarrels, all of which may end in death—may well be the result. In the process of an argument, person A and person B both define the initial situation as a serious threat, B then threatens A physically, A threatens B, and B then threatens A. By circular reaction, the situation can rapidly build to a climax in which one takes serious overt action, partly because of fear. Consequently, the victim, by being a contributor to the circular reaction of an argument increasing in its physical intensity, may precipitate his or her own injury or death.

Violence may result from a single argument or dispute. Other cases may result from a series of arguments, sometimes extending over a period of years, between intimate partners, neighbors, or fellow employees. Increasingly, verbalization in these arguments declines, while emotional reactions increase, until in a final argument, a climax is reached. With the use of a weapon, one of the parties may be injured or killed.

Many cases of violence grow out of what some people might regard as trivial disputes. What is considered "trivial" is related to judgments derived from age, social class, gender, and other background factors. To an outside observer of a different social class (psychiatrist, prosecutor, judge, middle-class jury member, researcher), such slights or insults leading to homicide among the lower classes may not justify such acts of violence. Homicides and assaults may involve the nonpayment of "very small" debts, "minor" disputes, or "petty" jealousies, but these may be very important to the person involved.

Research indicates that these "senseless" interpersonal conflicts that erupt seemingly over almost nothing—a parking space, an insult, a dirty look—are actually attempts to establish respect, status, and power.[83] They occur primarily when a power hierarchy in the social relationship between opponents is ambiguous. The following violent altercation ensured as a result of the loss of a valued social relationship:

> We went over to my friend's house to get his stuff, and his girlfriend thought I was his new girlfriend, so she attacked me. We fought. She jumped at me and grabbed me by my hair and tried to punch me. I was punching and kicking her and dragged her across the lawn back into the house. I told her to stay in there because I thought the cops were going to come, and she did. She was screaming out the window, calling us names, and carrying on.[84]

From this point of view, violent personal criminal behavior must be studied as an interactional and situational event

As are most human behavior patterns, homicide is a situational transaction. Because of this, in many homicide incidents the victim is a partial contributor to his or her own death. This has been called "victim precipitated homicide." For example:

> During an argument in which a male called a female many vile names, she tried to telephone the police. He grabbed the phone from her hands, knocked her down, kicked her, and hit her with a tire gauge. She ran to the kitchen, grabbed a butcher knife, and stabbed him in the stomach.[85]

Sociologist Erving Goffman referred to a "character contest" in which the homicide is the peak of the escalation of a confrontation.[86] He also made a distinction between a "situated transaction," which is a chain of interactions between two individuals during the time they are in one another's immediate physical presence, and a "social occasion," which consists of many situated transactions over a period of time. Social transactions ending in a situated transaction that ends with homicide occur mainly during leisure hours and in leisure settings such as at home, at a bar, or in the car.

The domestic setting, in particular, produces a high percentage of victim precipitated homicides. For example, a study that compared domestic and non-domestic contexts found that 84 percent of the domestic killings could be considered victim precipitated, while only 49 percent of non-domestic killings were victim precipitated.[87] Moreover, most of the victim precipitated domestic homicides were perpetrated by women as indicated by one Detroit study of martial homicides. It revealed that 81 percent of domestic homicides committed by wives were victim precipitated, while only 10 percent of those committed by husbands fell into this category.[88]

David F. Luckenbill[89] identified five stages of situated interactions that involve a series of "moves"—challenges and counterchallenges—between victim and offender that end in homicide. Stage One consists of three events: (1) the victim makes some direct, verbal expression, (2) the victim refuses to cooperate or comply with the offender's requests, (3) the victim makes some physical or nonverbal gesture. In Stage Two, the offender interprets the victim's previous move as purposive and intentional. In Stage Three, the offender retaliates verbally or physically in order to restore their reputation and demonstrate strong character. In Stage Four, the victim stands up to the challenge by continuing the activity that the offender deems offensive. Finally, in Stage Five, the victim and offender commit to resolving the conflict through violence and the victim is killed with a weapon. Consider the case in which Mike starts an argument with Gabe as they board a train:

> In this account, the opening move, . . . is made when the young man Mike, tells the solider, Gabe, to find another seat. Stage Two follows when Gabe interprets the move as offensive, and then Stage Three occurs when Gabe, rather than looking for a seat elsewhere, challenges Mike by attempting to take the seat. Mike in moving to Stage Four then "must stand up to the challenge" which he does by springing up, fists ready, which then leads to the actual fight (Stage Five), and then Gabe's fatal stabbing.[90]

One violent crime that criminologists have recently avoided designating as victim precipitated, is rape. In the 1960s and 1970s, it was not uncommon for criminologists and the public to believe that the victim of forcible rape often appeared to have much to do with the fact that she was raped. For example, a controversial Philadelphia study first published in 1968 designated 19 percent of forcible rapes as victim precipitated in the sense that (1) the victim actually, or so it was interpreted by the offender, agreed to sexual relations but retracted before the actual act or (2) did not resist strongly enough when the offender made the suggestion to have sex.[91] The study also reported that the victim's role was crucial when she entered a situation in which sexual stimulation was pervasive or made what could be interpreted as an invitation to sexual relations. The researcher further noted that 33 percent of the victims of victim precipitated rape previously had "bad" reputations.

The phenomenon of "victim-blaming" casts rape victims as deserving of their misfortune. Research has found that men attribute higher levels of blame to rape victims than do women and that women who are raped are blamed more if they violate traditional gender roles (for example, by wearing provocative clothing) or if they consume alcohol prior to their attack.[92]

Personal Relationships in Violent Crime

Many studies have revealed that there are close relationships between offenders and victims in crimes involving violence. Homicide and assault often occur between relatives, friends, or acquaintances, and typically involve spontaneous altercations, family quarrels, and jealous rages. Although people are often concerned about physical assaults from strangers on city streets, personal violence is less likely to be perpetuated by a stranger according to the US Bureau of Justice Statistics which found that the percentage of stranger violence reported to police (42 percent) was lower than the percentage of domestic violence (58 percent) and lower than intimate partner violence (54 percent).[93] In the case of homicide, 54 percent of victims were killed by someone they knew (acquaintance, neighbor, friend, boyfriend, etc.) and 25 percent were slain by family members. Thirty-seven percent of females were murdered by their husbands or boyfriends. Forty-three percent of victims were murdered during arguments (including romantic triangles).[94] In the case of rape, of state prison inmates imprisoned for a crime against their son or daughter in 1997, 79 percent had raped or sexually assaulted the child. Data also show that between 1998 and 2002, twice as many rapes were committed by family members as by strangers.[95] Robbery is the only violent crime that is committed more often by a stranger rather than by someone known to the victim.

These rates have remained remarkably consistent over time. For example, Wolfgang's statistical analysis of criminal homicide in Philadelphia for the years 1948 to 1952 found that approximately one-third of homicides resulted from general altercations. Family and domestic quarrels accounted for 14 percent, jealousy 12 percent, altercation over money 11 percent, and robbery only 7 percent. Close friends and relatives accounted for over half (59 percent) of all homicides and four-fifths of the female victims. In 28 percent of the cases, the victim was a close friend of the murderer, in 25 percent a family relative, in 14 percent an acquaintance. In only one out of eight was the victim a stranger. In contrast to men, a much larger proportion of women kill someone in their own families. It was concluded that when a woman committed a homicide, the victim was more likely to be her partner; and when a man was killed by a woman, he was most likely to be killed by his partner.[96] In those cases in which a woman kills her husband or boyfriend, it is likely that she has herself been the victim of violent physical abuse over a long period of time.

A vivid description of deadly assaults between relatives and close acquaintances is conveyed in the following newspaper account of 1992:

> A Fourth of July family gathering in a Queens park turned deadly early yesterday morning when a dispute ended with knives drawn, one man dead and six people wounded. The victims, all related by blood or marriage, were among 10 people slain and 22 people wounded in New York City during an eight-hour period over Saturday night and Sunday morning. In addition to the death in Queens, the police reported two other stabbing deaths, also the result of disputes among relatives or acquaintances. The overnight toll also included three children who were wounded by random gunfire. One of the children was a 5-year old who was watching fireworks with his mother in Brooklyn. In the incident in the Queens park, one man was stabbed to death and six others wounded during what police called "a family get-together for the Fourth of July that went bad." In the Bronx another man was stabbed once in the back with a screwdriver when he intervened in a dispute between his sister and her husband. On the Upper East Side of Manhattan a man was fatally stabbed in the chest and abdomen during a dispute in his apartment building. His roommate was arrested. Two children were the victims of stray gunshots in the Bronx late Saturday evening.[97]

Most crimes of violence involve male offenders and female victims who are involved in an intimate relationship. Women are much more likely than men to experience physical injury and death from domestic violence. They are also more likely to experience multiple forms of violence compared to men.[98] While women hit more often, they cause less physical damage than men.[99]

Social Reaction to Criminal Behavior

Both the criminal law and the religious teachings of Judaism, Christianity, Islam, and Buddhism expressly forbid violence, seeing it as antithetical to organized society. The fact is that the use of violence on other human beings is often sanctioned both by religion and organized society. The killing and other acts of violence directed at enemy soldiers and even enemy civilians is sanctioned by the political state in wartime. Those persons killed or injured under wartime conditions exceeds by tens of millions all those persons ever killed by civilian murder and assault. For a civilian willfully to kill 10 persons may warrant the death penalty or life imprisonment; for a soldier to do the same to the enemy warrants a medal or other form of reward for heroism.

The total cost to the principal belligerents during World War I was an estimated 17 million military personnel killed or missing in battle, to which must be added some 20 million civilian deaths. During World War II, 10 million military personnel were killed or missing and 43 million civilians were killed. While estimates of casualties from the Iraq War vary widely, it is believed that between 2003 and 2017 there were upwards of 194,000 civilian deaths and nearly 5,000 US service member deaths. The US War in Afghanistan resulted in over 26,000 civilian deaths during 2001 and 2014, with over 2,000 US military deaths. All of this makes the civilian killing of other human beings, often in connection with higher moral principles than those involved in war, somewhat of a logical anachronism. Thus, it is in the name of the political state that large numbers of civilians have been killed for reasons regarding state, religion, class, and ethnic characteristics. Probably the most brutal extermination of this type was the killing and torture deaths of 6.5 million Jews during the Nazi control of Germany and its occupied territories. Yet the various killing sprees and mass shootings that have occurred in the US since the 1980s seem to provoke more horror than the great number of deaths in wartime or the many politically incited civilian deaths like the Guatemalan genocide of the early 1980s (with over 42,000 killed) and the Bosnian ethnic cleansing campaign of the 1990s (with over 8,000 killed). Although society says that human life should not be willfully taken, if a state, which represents certain power interests, does it, the situation may be regarded as of quite a different nature.

State-mandated execution is the ultimate violence against citizens of which the state is capable. Although about half of Americans approve of it and 31 states use capital punishment as a legal penalty, it has been abolished in all European countries (except Belarus) and in Canada and Mexico. All European countries, as well as Canada and Mexico, prohibit extradition of offenders to countries where they might face the death penalty.[100] The countries that execute the most prisoners are China, Iran, Pakistan, Saudi Arabia, and the United States. In fact, it is estimated that about 16,000 people have been put to death in the US since the first recorded execution in 1608.

Between 1977 and mid-2017 there were 1,455 prisoners executed in the US. Over one-third of these were in Texas and 80 percent in the Southern states. The largest death row in mid-2016 was in California, with nearly 741 inmates, followed by Florida (396) and Texas (254).[101] There are isolated, but not infrequent, instances of botched executions that seriously threaten and erode the public's general support of capital punishment. Consider the 2014 execution, by lethal injection, of Clayton Lockett. Condemned to die by the state of Oklahoma, the executioners used the wrong drugs, syringes, and tubing on Lockett. They tried, but failed repeatedly, to insert the needle into Lockett's arms, biceps, jugular, collar bone, foot, and groin. Lockett struggled violently, began writhing and was observed twitching and convulsing. He attempted to rise from the execution table despite having been declared unconscious. Lockett died 43 minutes after the first execution drug was administered.

One scholar estimates that 3 percent of all executions carried out in the US from 1890 to 2010 were botched.[102] Several American and European pharmaceutical companies have prohibited the distribution of their drugs for use in lethal injections.

All violence is by no means harmful or dysfunctional to a society. As the sociologist Lewis S. Coser pointed out, violence may perform a useful social function.[103] It may help groups of individuals in a society achieve certain goals that otherwise are difficult or impossible for them to achieve; it may serve as a danger signal of political and economic dislocation in a society, and it may serve as a catalyst for change. Consider the urban riots of the late 1960s and the social changes that followed as well as the positive responses in the form of financial aid and social improvements to the 1992 Los Angeles riots.

Violence has frequently been employed, even on a large scale, to attain certain idealistic moral goals or to reverse the social and political power of interest groups or social classes. For example, the achievement of the right of labor to organize for collective action was a long and violent struggle in most countries. In the United States, "beginning in the 1870s, workingmen attempting to organize for collective action engaged in more than a half century of violent warfare with industrialists, their private armies, and workers employed to break strikes, as well as with police and troops."[104] In addition, American women used militant, violent action to secure their right to vote in 1920. The historian Richard Maxwell Brown referred to all of this as "positive violence." Surveying the development of the United States Brown stated:

> American life has been characterized by continuous and often intense violence. It is not merely that violence has accompanied such negative aspects of our history as criminal activity, political assassination, and racial conflict. On the contrary, violence has formed a seamless web with some of the most positive events of US history: independence (Revolutionary violence), the freeing of the slaves and the preservation of the Union (Civil War violence), land settlement (white-Indian wars), the stabilization of frontier society (vigilante violence), the social elevation of the farmer and laborer (agrarian and labor violence), and the preservation of law and order (violent law enforcement). The patriot, the humanitarian, the nationalist, the pioneer, the landholder, the farmer, and the laborer (and the capitalist) have used violence as a means to a higher end.[105]

Historically, the United States has been characterized by violence. In general, historical evidence suggests that during the 1960s—with race riots, protests against the Vietnam War, the assassinations of political figures and civil rights leaders—Americans were more violent toward one another than in the past. In fact, between 1964 and 1974 the country witnessed doubling rates of criminal homicide and more than doubling of robbery and rape.[106]

In the nineteenth century, immigrant and racial groups were thrown into fierce competition with one another and with the dominant Anglo-American white Protestant group in their quest for economic security and acceptance. There were, for example, bloody anti-Catholic, anti-Irish, anti-German, anti-Chinese, and anti-Italian riots. The anti-Irish riots of 1844 in Philadelphia resulted in over 20 deaths. In 1891, 11 Italians were lynched by a mob in New Orleans.

The twentieth century saw riots in which violence was directed against other racial and ethnic minorities. For example, the anti-Asian Pacific Coast race riots of 1907 directed violence at Asian immigrants and in the Los Angeles Zoot-Suit riots of 1943 US servicemen physically assaulted hundreds of Mexican American youth. However, it is African Americans who have historically borne the brunt of racial violence in the US.

From 1882 to 1903, 1,985 blacks were lynched. From 1900 to 1949 there were about 40 white-on-black race riots that occurred in many cities including Atlanta (1906), Chicago (1919), and Tulsa (1921). The latter left over 300 dead when a white mob rampaged through the black community, killing men and women, burning and looting stores and homes. The twenty-first century has witnessed frequent and recurrent police killings of unarmed black men, such as Michael Brown, Jr (2014), Eric Garner (2014), Freddie Gray (2015), Philando Castile (2016), and others. Perhaps the most visible hate crime against African Americans was perpetrated in 2015 by white supremacist Dylann Roof who shot to death nine black worshipers in a church in Charleston, South Carolina.

In addition, America's long history of violence and vigilantism on the western frontier was easily adapted to a form of "neo" vigilantism in which various persons (representing religious groups, ethnic minorities, unions, political factions, civil liberties advocates, alternative lifestyles) have become victims of violent attacks. More recently, there have been vicious assaults—hate crimes—committed against persons because of their race/ethnicity/ancestry, gender, religion, sexual orientation, gender identity, and disability.

Some forms of violence are legally sanctioned within a society while others are not. For a soldier, killing and wounding another person is an approved behavior; in fact, a soldier may be severely punished if he or she does *not* use violence when it is expected or commanded. Similarly, the use of force by law enforcement officers (providing it is not excessive) has generally met with public approval. Additionally, situations of real or perceived self-defense are considered appropriate for violent behavior. The celebrated case of African American teen, Trayvon Martin, who in 2012 was shot to death by George Zimmerman, is a telling illustration of the extent of public approval of violence perpetrated in one's own defense.

Finally, the social values involved in homicide and aggravated assault among intimates are similar to that of nonviolent persons. People assault, and sometimes kill, for the same reasons people live—pride, preservation of honor, to blot out shame, to avenge one's self, to settle an argument, or as a reaction to an insult. Persons who do not use violence utilize other methods to deal with such important values. Since the 1990s, there has been a turning to processes of peacemaking and restorative justice in place of violence.

The middle and upper socioeconomic groups of most societies have codified legal rules that prohibit the use of violence. The powerful segments of society denounce violence in part to discourage attacks against established political power. Generally, the criminal laws and courts do not recognize the existence of separate subcultural norms among certain groups that deem as legitimate the use of force to settle disputes. However, the courts have permitted rare exceptions to this. Although these same groups would generally not approve of murder, at the same time, in sanctioning violence that may lead to murder, there is an inconsistency in their value system. Middle- and upper-class persons (those in positions of social and political power) react strongly to the use of violence as seen in the severe legal penalties for murder, manslaughter, and rape.

Such offenses as murder, rape, and aggravated assault are punished severely not because they constitute a serious threat to the larger political and economic order, but because of the injury to the individual. Severe punishment is thought to work as a deterrent to help avoid retaliation by relatives and friends of the victims and serves to reinforce the religious beliefs and secular values held by many in the larger society about the sanctity of life and the sexual conduct of individuals.

Penalties in the law generally do not recognize the close relationship between criminal homicide and aggravated assault. In some jurisdictions, while aggravated assault may result in a short prison sentence or even probation, if the victim dies the penalty may be death or at least life imprisonment, which is greater than for most other criminal offenses. Serial killers and mass murderers are most likely to receive the death penalty in those states where it is a legal sanction. Likewise, manslaughter and forcible rape are normally punished by an unusually long period of imprisonment. The last year anyone was executed in the United States for rape was 1964; the number executed for rape that year was six. Penalties for all offenses against children are much harsher than laws prohibiting essentially the same offense with adults. This is because this population is seen as the most vulnerable and defenseless.

In 2009, 0.7 percent of defendants in the largest US counties were charged with murder. Most of them, 82 percent, were detained until case disposition. Bail amount in excess of $50,000 was set in 95 percent of the cases. Ultimately, 70 percent were convicted, and all of them were incarcerated with 20 percent sentenced to life in prison.[107]

That same year, 1 percent of defendants were charged with rape. Forty-eight percent of them were detained until a final settlement was reached. Fifty-nine percent of defendants had bail of $50,000 or over. Conviction occurred in 68 percent and incarceration in 89 percent of the cases. The average sentence was 12 years.

In 2009, 12 percent of defendants were charged with assault. In addition, 37 percent were detained until case disposition. The highest bail was set in 30 percent of the cases. While only 56 percent of the cases resulted in conviction, 81 percent received prison or jail time, with most being sentenced to 1 to 2 years.

Regarding social reaction to and legal processing of violent crime there has been deep frustration:

> Let us begin with a fundamental realization: No amount of thinking and no amount of public policy have brought us any closer to understanding and solving the problem of crime. The more we have reacted to crime, the farther we have removed ourselves from any understanding and any reduction of the problem. In recent years, we have floundered desperately in reformulating the law, punishing the offender, and quantifying our knowledge.[108]

Thus, since the 1990s a couple of alternatives to conventional criminal justice, whose focus is *criminal* justice, are the peacemaking approach and the restorative justice approach, both of which focus on *social* justice. Peacemaking contends that crime is connected to human suffering and that to reduce crime, suffering in its various forms—poverty, racism, sexism—must be reduced. Because "crime is a reflection of something larger and deeper,"[109] the societal conditions that contribute to suffering must be addressed. Further, contrary to the conventional criminal justice system that perpetuates violence through repressive tactics and proposals—warlike policies, aggressive policing, retributive sentences like the death penalty and lengthy prison terms—peacemaking criminology considers how the principles and values of peace can be applied to doing justice. Ultimately it requires that offenders be reintegrated into society. This is a transformative approach that advocates a nonviolent justice system based on service, connectedness, awareness, understanding, forgiveness, and compassion.[110]

Restorative justice (RJ), focuses on victim–offender reconciliation and is involved in righting the wrong caused by crime. It involves the victim, the offender, and the community—the latter can include "anyone who feels connected emotionally, physically, or in other ways to the victim(s), or the event itself."[111] Together these stakeholders participate in holding offenders to account and determining the appropriate punishment for the crime. Through this cooperative process, the needs and interests of the victim and the offender are satisfied. Restorative justice programs underscore connectedness, compassion, and forgiveness with the goal of repairing the individual, relational, and social harm caused by the crime.

One well-publicized case of personal violent crime in which restorative justice was used occurred in 2011 in Florida. It involved the murder of a young woman, Ann, who was killed by her 19-year-old boyfriend, Conor. Ann's parents, along with Conor, his parents, and the prosecutor, all agreed to participate in a pre-plea RJ conference. Typically, the charge of first-degree murder in Florida carries either a life sentence or the death penalty. Conor accepted a plea deal of 20 years in prison and 10 years of probation based on both the recommendations of Ann's parents and the prosecutor's evaluation of the case. Ann's parents said they didn't forgive Conor for his sake but for their own.

> Everything I feel, I can feel because we forgave Conor . . . Because we could forgive, people can say [Ann's] name. People can think about my daughter, and they don't have to think, Oh, the murdered girl. I think that when people can't forgive, they're stuck. All they can feel is the emotion surrounding that moment. I can be sad, but I don't have to stay stuck in that moment where this awful thing happened. Because if I do, I may never come out of it. Forgiveness for me was self-preservation.[112]

The use of restorative justice for violent crimes remains controversial. It has been criticized in cases of intimate partner violence and sexual assault. Opponents maintain that RJ unwittingly undermines the safety, and fails to respond to the unique needs, of women who have experienced domestic violence.[113] Nevertheless, it has been argued that restorative justice, particularly the practice of victim–offender mediation and dialog, can be successfully applied in crimes of severe violence, including sexual assault, attempted murder, and murder. Preliminary data indicate exceptionally high levels of satisfaction with the outcome of victim–offender mediation and dialog in crimes of severe violence.[114]

A study of randomized controlled trials of restorative justice programs conducted in the UK and Australia concluded that they do better than conventional criminal justice at repairing the harm that crime causes to victims. The restorative justice conferences in this study involved face-to-face meetings among offenders, their victims, and their respective family and friends as supporters. Results showed that from a victim's perspective, RJ conferences created a renewing commitment to group morality. Offenders were many times more likely than those not involved in restorative justice to admit that they breached their moral obligations, and by apologizing to the victims reaffirmed their commitment to those obligations. These face-to-face conferences also succeed in "normalizing" victim contact with an offender.[115] The same researchers found that seven of seven restorative justice programs worked at least as well as conventional criminal justice in regard to repeat offending; two of the programs did better at preventing repeat offending. This reduction also included a reduction in crimes of vengeance committed by victims.[116]

Notes

1 Marvin E. Wolfgang, "A Preface to Violence," *The Annals of the American Academy of Political and Social Science* 364 (1966): 1–7, 2.
2 Ted Robert Gurr, *Violence in America: Protest, Rebellion, Reform*, 2 vols. (Thousand Oaks, CA: Sage, 1989); James F. Short, Jr. and Marvin E. Wolfgang, eds., *Collective Violence*, revised edition (Piscataway, NJ: Aldine

Transaction, 2009); James Gilligan, *Violence: Reflections on a National Epidemic* (New York, NY: Vintage, 1997); Neil Alan Weiner, Margaret A. Zahn, Rita J. Sagi, *Violence: Patterns, Causes, and Public Policy* (Belmont, CA: Wadsworth, 1990); Terry H. Anderson, *The Movement and The Sixties: Protest in America from Greensboro to Wounded Knee*, 5th edition (New York, NY: Oxford University Press, 1995); Paul Arn Gilje, *Rioting in America* (Bloomington, IN: Indiana University Press, 1999).

3 John K. Roman, *Race, Justifiable Homicide, and Stand Your Ground Laws: Analysis of FBI Supplementary Homicide Report Data* (Washington, DC: Urban Institute, 2013).

4 Maria Pavlou and Ann Knowles, "Domestic Violence: Attributions, Recommended Punishments and Reporting Behavior Related to Provocation by the Victim," *Psychiatry, Psychology and Law* 8, no. 1 (2001): 76–85.

5 United National Office on Drugs and Crime, *Global Study on Homicide, 2013* (Vienna: United Nations Publication, 2014).

6 Steven Pinker, *The Better Angels of Our Nature: Why Violence Has Declined* (New York, NY: Viking, 2011).

7 Michelle Alexander, *The New Jim Crow: Mass Incarceration in the Age of Colorblindness* (New York, NY: The New Press, 2010).

8 James Forman Jr., *Locking Up Our Own: Crime and Punishment in Black America* (New York, NY: Farrar, Straus and Giroux, 2017).

9 Harold E. Pepinsky and Richard Quinney, eds., *Criminology as Peacemaking* (Bloomington, IN: Indiana University Press, 1991); Michael Braswell, John Fuller, and Bo Lozoff, *Corrections, Peacemaking, and Restorative Justice* (Cincinnati, OH: Anderson, 2001), Dennis Sullivan and Larry Tifft, *Restorative Justice: Healing the Foundations of Our Everyday Lives* (Monsey, NY: Willow Tree Press, 2001); Carolyn Boyes-Watson, *Peacemaking Circles and Urban Youth: Bringing Justice Home* (St. Paul, MN: Living Justice Press, 2008).

10 Pablo Fajnzylber, Daniel Lederman, and Norman Loayza, "Inequality and Violent Crime," *The Journal of Law and Economics* 45, no. 1 (2002): 1–39.

11 Leah E. Daigle, *Victimology: The Essentials* (Thousand Oaks, CA: Sage, 2013), 42.

12 Federal Bureau of Investigation, *Crime in the United States: Rape, 2015, Uniform Crime Reports*, accessed April 17, 2017, https://ucr.fbi.gov/crime-in-the-u.s/2015/crime-in-the-u.s.-2015/offenses-known-to-law-enforcement/rape

13 Matt Delisi and Aaron M. Schereer, "Multiple Homicide Offenders: Offense Characteristics, Social Correlates, and Criminal Careers," *Criminal Justice and Behavior* 33, no. 3 (2006): 367–391.

14 Rolf Loerber, David P. Farrington, and Daniel A. Waschbusch, "Serious and Violent Juvenile Offenders," in *Serious and Violent Juvenile Offenders: Risk Factors and Successful Interventions*, ed. by Rolf Loeber and David P. Farrington (Thousand Oaks, CA: Sage, 1998): 13–29.

15 David P. Farrington, "Predictors, Causes, and Correlates of Male Youth Violence," *Crime and Justice* 24 (1998): 421–475; Alex R. Piquero, "Frequency, Specialization, and Violence in Offending Careers," *Journal of Research in Crime and Delinquency* 37, no. 4 (2000): 392–418.

16 D. Wayne Osgood and Christopher Schreck, "A New Method for Studying the Extent, Stability, and Predictors of Individual Specialization in Violence," *Criminology* 45, no. 2 (2007): 273–312.

17 Hans Toch and Kenneth Adams, *The Disturbed Violent Offender* (Hyattsville, MD: American Psychological Association, 1994).

18 Robert A. Prentky, Austin E S. Lee, Raymond A. Knight, and David Cerce, "Recidivism Rates among Child Molesters and Rapists: A Methodological Analysis," *Law and Human Behavior*, 21, no. 6 (1997): 635–657.

19 Lonnie H. Athens, *The Creation of Dangerous Violent Criminals*, 2nd edition (Piscataway, NJ: Transaction, 2017).

20 Ibid.

21 Marvin E. Wolfgang and Franco Ferracutti, *The Subculture of Violence: Toward an Integrated Theory in Criminology* (London: Tavistock, 1967); Franco Ferracuti, Renato Lazzari, and Marvin E. Wolfgang, eds. *Violence in Sardinia* (Rome: Mario Bulzoni, 1970).

22 Elijah Anderson, *The Code of the Street: Decency, Violence, and the Moral Life of the Inner City* (New York, NY: W. W. Norton, 1999).

23 Ibid., 69.

24 Harold E. Pepinsky and Richard Quinney, eds., *Criminology as Peacemaking* (Bloomington, IN: Indiana University Press, 1991).

25 Eric Dunning, Patrick J. Murphy, and John Williams, *The Roots of Football Hooliganism: An Historical and Sociological Study* (New York, NY: Routledge, 1988), 6.

26 Craig A. Anderson, Nicholas L. Carnagey, and Janie Eubanks, "Exposure to Violent Media: The Effects of Songs with Violent Lyrics on Aggressive Thoughts and Feelings," *Journal of Personality and Social Psychology* 84, no. 5 (2003): 960–971.

27 Murray A. Straus, *Beating the Devil Out of Them: Corporal Punishment in American Families* (New York, NY: Lexington Books, 1994).

28 Laurence Ralph, *Renegade Dreams: Living through Injury in Gangland Chicago* (Chicago, IL: University of Chicago Press, 2014), 132.

29 Waverly Duck, *No Way Out: Precarious Living in the Shadow of Poverty and Drug Dealing* (Chicago, IL: University of Chicago Press, 2015).

30 Matt Zaitchik and Donald Mosher, "Criminal Justice Implications of the Macho Personality Constellation," *Criminal Justice and Behavior* 20, no. 3 (1993): 227–239.

31 United National Office on Drugs and Crime, *Global Study on Homicide, 2013*.

32 Clare Ribando Seelke, *Gangs in Central America* (Washington, DC: Congressional Research Service, 2016), 5.

33 Mark C. Edberg, "Drug Traffickers as Social Bandits: Culture and Drug Trafficking in Northern Mexico and the Border Region," *Journal of Contemporary Criminal Justice* 17, no. 3 (2001): 259–277.

34 Harrington Cooper Brearley, *Homicide in the Unites States* (Chapel Hill, NC: University of North Carolina Press, 1932).

35 Richard Quinney, "Structural Characteristics, Population Areas, and Crime Rates in the United States," *Journal of Criminal Law, Criminology and Police Science* 57, no. 1 (1966):45–52.

36 Ibid, 49.

37 Dov Cohen and Richard Nisbett, *Culture of Honor: The Psychology of Violence in the South* (Boulder, CO: Westview Press, 1996); Bertram Wyatt-Brown, *The Shaping of Southern Culture: Honor, Grace, and War, 1760s–1880s.* (Chapel Hill, NC: University of North Carolina Press, 2001); Pauline Grosjean, "A History of Violence: The Culture of Honor and Homicide in the U.S. South," *Journal of the European Economic Association* 12, no. 5 (2014):1285–1316.

38 *Small Arms Survey 2007: Guns and the City* (New York, NY: Cambridge University Press, 2007).

39 *Sourcebook of Criminal Justice Statistics Online*. www.albany.edu/sourcebook/pdf/t2602011.pdf

40 Federal Bureau of Investigation, *Crime in the United States: Violent Crime, 2015*. https://ucr.fbi.gov/crime-in-the-u.s/2015/crime-in-the-u.s.-2015/offenses-known-to-law-enforcement/violent-crime/violentcrimemain_final

41 Federal Bureau of Investigation, *Crime in the United States: Violent Crime, 2015*. Murder Victims by Weapon, 2011–2015. https://ucr.fbi.gov/crime-in-the-u.s/2015/crime-in-the-u.s.-2015/tables/expanded_homicide_data_table_8_murder_victims_by_weapon_2011-2015.xls

42 Charles F. Wellford, John V. Pepper, and Carol V. Petrie, eds., *Firearms and Violence: A Critical Review* (Washington, DC: The National Academies Press, 2005), 12.

43 Ibid., 7.

44 Richard Rosenfeld, "Homicide and Serious Assaults," in *The Oxford Handbook of Crime and Public Policy*, ed. by Michael Tonry (New York: Oxford University Press, 2009), 26–27.

45 Hillary Potter, ed., *Intersectionality and Criminology: Disrupting and Revolutionizing Studies of Crime* (New York, NY: Routledge, 2015).

46 Edward L. Glaeser and Bruce Sacerdote, "Why Is There More Crime in Cities?" *Journal of Political Economy* 107, no. S6 (1999): S225–S258

47 Federal Bureau of Investigation, *Crime in the United States: Violent Crime, 2015*. Illinois: Offenses Known of Law Enforcement by City. https://ucr.fbi.gov/crime-in-the-u.s/2015/crime-in-the-u.s.-2015/tables/table-8/table-8-state-pieces/table_8_offenses_known_to_law_enforcement_illinois_by_city_2015.xls

48 Chicago Police Department, *Chicago Murder Analysis Report* (Chicago: Research and Development Division, 2011), 27.

49 Marvin E. Wolfgang, *Patterns in Criminal Homicide* (Philadelphia: University of Pennsylvania Press, 1958), 106–107.

50 Robert J. Sampson, "Neighborhood and Crime: The Structural Determinants of Personal Victimization," *Journal of Research in Crime and Delinquency* 22, no. 1 (1985): 7–40.

51 Lauren J. Krivo and Ruth D. Peterson, "Extremely Disadvantaged Neighborhoods and Urban Crime," *Social Forces* 75, no. 2 (1996): 619–648

52 Ruth D, Peterson, Lauren J. Krivo and Mark A. Harris, "Disadvantage and Neighborhood Violent Crime: Do Local Institutions Matter?" *Journal of Research in Crime and Delinquency* 37, no. 1 (2000): 31–63.

53 Federal Bureau of Investigation, *Crime in the United States: Arrests by Race and Ethnicity, 2015*. https://ucr.fbi.gov/crime-in-the-u.s/2015/crime-in-the-u.s.-2015/tables/table-43

54 US Department of Justice, "Criminal Victimization, 2015," *Bulletin: Bureau of Justice Statistics* (October 2016), 9.

55 Melonie Heron, "Deaths: Leading Causes for 2014," *National Vital Statistics Reports* 65, no. 5 (Centers for Disease Control and Prevention, 2016), 12.

56 Ruth D. Peterson and Lauren J. Krivo, *Divergent Social Worlds: Neighborhood Crime and the Racial-Spatial Divide* (New York, NY: Russell Sage Foundation, 2010).

57 Robert J. Sampson and William Julius Wilson, "Toward a Theory of Race, Crime, and Urban Inequality," in *Crime and Inequality*, ed. by John Hagen and Ruth D. Peterson (Stanford: Stanford University Press, 1995), 37–54.

58 Robert J. Sampson, *Great American City: Chicago and the Enduring Neighborhood Effect* (Chicago: University of Chicago Press, 2012), 248–251.

59 Lauren J. Krivo and Ruth D. Peterson, "The Structural Context of Homicide: Accounting for Racial Differences in Process," *American Sociological Review* 65, no. 4 (2000): 547–559.

60 Katheryn Russell-Brown, *The Color of Crime: Racial Hoaxes, White Fear, Black Protectionism, Police Harassment, and Other Macroaggressions*, 2nd edition (New York, NY: New York University Press, 2009), 71.

61 Richard Quinney, *The Social Reality of Crime* (Boston, MA: Little, Brown & Co., 1970).

62 US Bureau of Justice Statistics, *Police-Public Contact Survey* (Washington, DC: US Department of Justice, 2011).

63 John Braithwaite, *Inequality, Crime, and Public Policy* (London: Routledge and Kegan Paul, 1979), 32.

64 E. Britt Patterson, "Poverty, Income Inequality, and Community Crime Rates," *Criminology* 29, no. 4 (1991): 755–776.

65 Ching-Chi Hsieh M. D. Pugh, "Poverty, Income Inequality, and Violent Crime: A Meta-Analysis of Recent Aggregate Data Studies," *Criminal Justice Review* 18, no. 2 (1993): 182–202.

66 Charis E. Kubrin and Ronald Weitzer, "Retaliatory Homicide: Concentrated Disadvantage and Neighborhood Culture," *Social Problems* 50, no. 2 (2003): 157–180.

67 US Department of Justice, *When Violence Hits Home: How Economics and Neighborhood Play a Role* (Washington, DC: US Department of Justice, 2004).

68 Paul B. Stretesky, Amie M. Schuck, and Michael J. Hogan, "Space Matters: An Analysis of Poverty, Poverty Clustering, and Violent Crime," *Justice Quarterly* 21, no. 4 (2004): 817–841.

69 Pablo Fajnzylber, Daniel Lederman, and Norman Loayza, "Inequality and Violent Crime," *The Journal of Law and Economics* 45, no. 1 (2002): 1–39.

70 Alice Goffman, *On the Run: Fugitive Life in an American City* (Chicago, IL: University of Chicago Press, 2014), 201.

71 Edward Green and Russell P. Wakefield, "Patterns of Middle and Upper-Class Homicide," *Journal of Criminal Law and Criminology* 70, no. 2 (1979): 172–181, 180.

72 Federal Bureau of Investigation, *Crime in the United States: Arrests by Sex, 2015*. https://ucr.fbi.gov/crime-in-the-u.s/2015/crime-in-the-u.s.-2015/tables/table-42

73 Jody Miller, "Up It Up: Gender and the Accomplishment of Street Robbery," *Criminology* 36, no. 1 (1998): 37–66.

74 Ola W. Barnett, Cheok Y. Lee, and Rose E. Thelan, "Gender Differences in Attributions of Self-Defense and Control in Interpartner Aggression," *Violence Against Women* 3, no, 5 (1997): 462–481; Russell P. Dobash, Rebecca E. Dobash, Kate Cavanagh, and Ruth Lewis, "Separate and Intersecting Realities: A Comparison of Men's and Women's Accounts of Violence against Women," *Violence Against Women* 4, no. 4 (1998): 382–414; Susan L Miller, *Victims as Offenders: The Paradox of Women's Violence in Relationships* (New Brunswick, NJ: Rutgers University Press, 2005); Mekha Rajan and Kathy A. McCloskey, "Victims of Intimate Partner Violence: Arrest Rates Across Recent Studies," *Journal of Aggression, Maltreatment, and Trauma* 15, nos. 3–4 (2007): 27–52.

75 Michael Gottfredson and Travis Hirschi, "The True Value of Lambda Would Appear to be Zero: An Essay on Career Criminals, Criminal Careers, Selective Incapacitation, Cohort Studies, and Related Topics," *Criminology* 24, no. 2 (2006): 213–234.

76 Federal Bureau of Investigation, *Crime in the United States: Arrests, Cities, Persons Under 15, 18, 21, and 25 Years of Age, 2015*. https://ucr.fbi.gov/crime-in-the-u.s/2015/crime-in-the-u.s.-2015/tables/table-47

77 Delbert S. Elliot, "Serious Violent Offenders: Onset, Developmental Course, and Termination," *Criminology* 32, no. 1(1993): 1–21; David P. Farrington, "Developmental and Life-Course Criminology: Key Theoretical and Empirical Issues," *Criminology* 41, no. 2 (2003): 221–255.

78 Robert Agnew, "An Integrated Theory of The Adolescent Peak in Offending," *Youth & Society* 34, no. 3 (2003): 263–299.

79 Robert J. Sampson and John H. Laub, "Life-Course Desisters? Trajectories of Crime Among Delinquent Boys Followed to Age 70," *Criminology* 41, no. 3 (2003): 555–592.

80 Robert J. Sampson and John H. Laub, *Crime in the Making: Pathways and Timing Points Through Life* (Cambridge: Harvard University Press, 1993).

81 Mark Warr, "Life-Course Transitions and Desistence from Crime," *Criminology* 36, no. 2 (1996): 183–216.

82 Barbara Tatem Kelley, Rolf Loeber, Kate Keenan, and Mary DeLamatre, *Developmental Pathways in Boys' Disruptive and Delinquent Behavior* (Washington, DC: US Department of Justice, 1997).

83 Elizabeth Griffiths, Carolyn Yule, and Rosemary Gartner, "Fighting over Trivial Things: Explaining the Issue of Contention in Violent Altercations," *Criminology* 49, no.1 (2011): 61–94.

84 Ibid., 75.

85 Marvin E. Wolfgang, *Patterns of Criminal Homicide* (Philadelphia, PA: Pennsylvania University Press, 1958), 253.

86 Erving Goffman, *Interaction Ritual: Essays on Face-to-Face Behavior* (Garden City, NY: Doubleday, 1967).

87 Coramae Richey Mann, "Getting Even? Women Who Kill in Domestic Encounters," *Justice Quarterly* 5, no. 1 (1988): 33–51.

88 Ann Goetting, "Patterns of Marital Homicide: A Comparison of Husbands and Wives," *Journal of Comparative Family Studies* 20, no. 3 (1989): 341–354.

89 David F. Luckenbill, "Criminal Homicide as a Situated Transaction," *Social Problems* 25, no. 2 (1977): 176–186.

90 Kenneth Polk, *When Men Kill: Scenarios of Masculine Violence* (New York, NY: Cambridge University Press, 1994), 86.

91 Menachem Amir, "Victim Precipitated Forcible Rape," *Journal of Criminal Law and Criminology* 58, no. 4 (1968): 493–502.

92 Amy Grubb and Emily Turner, "Attribution of Blame in Rape Cases: A Review of the Impact of Rape Myth Acceptance, Gender Role Conformity and Substance Use on Victim Blaming," *Aggression and Violent Behavior* 17, no. 5 (2012): 443–452.

93 US Department of Justice, "Criminal Victimization, 2015," *Bulletin: Bureau of Justice Statistics* (October 2016), 6.

94 Federal Bureau of Investigation, *Crime in the United States: 2011, Expanded Homicide Data*. https://ucr.fbi.gov/crime-in-the-u.s/2011/crime-in-the-u.s.-2011/offenses-known-to-law-enforcement/expanded/expanded-homicide-data

95 US Department of Justice, "Family Violence Statistics Including Statistics on Strangers and Acquaintances," Bureau of Justice Statistics (June 2005).

96 Wolfgang, *Patterns in Criminal Homicide*, 325.

97 George James, "10 are Slain are 22 Hurt in New York over Holiday," *New York Times*, July 6, 1992. www.nytimes.com/1992/07/06/nyregion/10-are-slain-and-22-hurt-in-new-york-over-holiday.html

98 National Center for Injury Prevention and Control, *National Intimate Partner and Sexual Violence Survey, Summary Report* (Atlanta: Centers for Disease Control and Prevention, 2010).

99 John Archer, "Sex Differences in Aggression Between Heterosexual Partners: A Meta-Analytic Review," *Psychological Bulletin* 126, no. 5 (2000): 651–680.

100 Roger Hood and Carolyn Hoyle, *The Death Penalty: A Worldwide Perspective*, 5th edition (New York, NY: Oxford University Press, 2015), 35–38.

101 Death Penalty Information Center, *Death-Row Prisoners by State*. https://deathpenaltyinfo.org/death-row-inmates-state-and-size-death-row-year?scid=9&did=188

102 Austin Sarat, *Gruesome Spectacles: Botched Executions and America's Death Penalty* (Stanford: Stanford University Press, 2014).

103 Lewis S. Coser, "Some Social Functions of Violence," *The Annals of the American Academy of Political and Social Science* 364, no. 1 (1966): 8–18.

104 Jerome H. Skolnick. *The Politics of Protest*, revised edition (New York, NY: New York University Press, 2010), 14.

105 Richard Maxwell Brown, "Historical Patterns of Violence in America," in *Violence in America*, vol 2, ed. by Ted Robert Gurr (Thousand Oaks, CA: Sage, 1989), 48.

106 Franklin E. Zimring, *The City that Became Safe: New York's Lessons for Urban Crime and its Control* (New York, NY: Oxford University Press, 2012), ix.

107 US Bureau of Justice Statistics, *Felony Defendants in Large Urban Counties, 2009—Statistical Tables* (Washington, DC: US Department of Justice, 2013).

108 Richard Quinney, "The Way of Peace: On Crime, Suffering, and Service," in *Criminology as Peacemaking*, ed. by Harold Pepinsky and Richard Quinney (Bloomington, IN: Indiana University Press, 1991), 3.

109 Richard Quinney, "Socialist Humanism and the Problem of Crime: Thinking about Erich Fromm in the Development of Critical/Peacemaking Criminology," in *Erich Fromm and Critical Criminology:*

Beyond the Punitive Society, ed. by Kevin Anderson and Richard Quinney (Urbana, IL: University of Illinois, 2000), 21.

110 Pepinsky and Quinney, *Criminology as Peacemaking*.

111 Mara Schiff, "Satisfying the Needs and Interests of Victims," in *Handbook of Restorative Justice*, ed. by Gerry Johnstone and Daniel Van Ness (Portland, OR: Willan Publishing, 2007), 235.

112 Paul Tullis, "Can Forgiveness Play a Role in Criminal Justice?" *New York Times Magazine*, January 4, 2013.

113 Julie Stubbs, "Beyond Apology? Domestic Violence and Critical Questions for Restorative Justice," *Criminology and Criminal Justice* 7, no. 2 (2007): 169–187.

114 Mark S. Umbreit, William Bradshaw, and Robert B. Coates, "Victims of Severe Violence Meet the Offender: Restorative Justice Through Dialogue," *International Review of Victimology* 6, no. 4 (1999): 321–343.

115 Lawrence W. Sherman and Heather Strang, "Effects of Face-to-Face Restorative Justice on Victims of Crime in Four Randomized, Controlled Trials," *Journal of Experimental Criminology* 1, no 3 (2005): 367–395.

116 Heather Strang and Lawrence W. Sherman, "Repairing the Harm: Victims and Restorative Justice," *Utah Law Review* 2003, no. 1 (2003): 15–42.

3

OCCASIONAL PROPERTY CRIME

Offenses against property were among the first to be punished under legal systems. Because the importance of various forms of property has changed with developments in society, such as the prevalence of cars and electronic devices as well as power interests, the penalties for crimes against property have also changed. Theft is the term encompassing most property crimes, but the basic theft offense in English common law was larceny. This act consists of taking and carrying goods away from the possession of another without the owner's consent. Originally, the goods had to be in possession, but later the concept was expanded to cope with the problems of an industrial, commercial society with the addition, in the eighteenth century, of embezzlement and obtaining money under false pretenses. Other additions have included shoplifting, motor vehicle theft, and employee theft. Richard Quinney calls these offenses against property, "predatory crimes" because they are frequently pursued out of the need to survive in a society that will not provide for people's basic needs.[1]

As we saw in Chapter 1, the characteristics of a fully developed career criminal include identification with crime and a conception of the self as a criminal. There is group support for criminal activity in the form of extensive association with other criminals and with criminal norms and practices. Criminality progresses to the use of more complex techniques, the employment of more sophisticated technology, and ever-more frequent offenses. Ultimately, crime may become a sole means of livelihood. Those with such highly developed criminal careers generally engage in some type of theft of money or other valuable commodities, such as expensive technology, drugs, inventory, or store merchandise.

Occasional property criminals are the opposite of career criminals. While they may commit nonviolent offenses similar in type to those committed by career criminals, they do so only infrequently and irregularly. Valuables may be taken, checks forged, and motor vehicles stolen, but in a comparatively crude manner. It has been estimated that the majority of all check forgeries are committed by persons with no previous patterns of such behavior. An even larger proportion of shoplifting is committed by noncareer offenders who take items of relatively small value. Similarly, the destruction of public or private property through vandalism is a sporadic, age-specific offense; one could hardly visualize a person making a career out of vandalism. We will not consider in this chapter property crimes that represent a career pattern.

Definition of Behavior as Criminal

Laws to protect private property were established in England. The change from an agricultural to an industrial economy required laws to protect the interests of the powerful. Before the fifteenth century, there was no legal conception of theft. During that century, in England, the modern law of theft was officially formulated into criminal law. To this day a large portion of criminal law in the United States is devoted to protecting the interests of the propertied class.[2]

Anyone who periodically steals or damages another's property may be classified as an occasional property offender. Among the occasional property offenses that have been researched extensively are check forgery, shoplifting by adults, employee theft, burglary, some types of motor vehicle theft, vandalism, and arson.

Legally, forgery is the false signing of a legal instrument that creates a liability. Under the old common law of England, forgery was "the fraudulent making, or altering, of a writing to the prejudice of another's rights." In medieval times, priests and monks had a virtual monopoly on writing, so other people used seals to authenticate documents. Forgery of the seal of another person is still an offense. Forgery can take many forms, such as forgery of wills and other documents, check forgery, and counterfeiting. The US Federal Reserve System identifies seven forms of check fraud: (1) forged signatures, (2) forged endorsements, (3) counterfeit checks, (4) altered checks, (5) check kiting, (6) third-party bill paying services, and (7) demand drafts.[3] Check forgery is extensive in the United States. Because check forging and check kiting constitute bank fraud, these offenses can sometimes be prosecuted as federal felonies. The maximum federal penalty for bank fraud is $1,000,000 and/or no more than 30 years in prison.

Forging checks seldom involves the formerly popular methods of changing the value of the check, falsifying signatures, or tampering with negotiable instruments. Checks are widely used and are cashed outside of banks, often with only perfunctory methods of identification. Rather than checks being written on someone else's account, they may be written on a non-existent account with a nonexistent name or on one's own account without sufficient funds in the bank. The practice of "kiting" involves writing a check drawn on one's own depleted account in anticipation of a future deposit. Little training is necessary for fraudulent check writing and the skills required are elementary. The learning of writing bad checks has been described as follows:

> He was first a check writer, which is a craft requiring little to no tutelage. It takes no great flash of wisdom to realize that people will give you money for a slice of paper or to realize that if you are going to depend on that for your livelihood, it might be more pleasant to use names other than your own. Highly skilled craft aspects, such as check raising, are now fairly rare. The problem in check passing is handling the person with the money you want, and that is dependent on personal style rather than technical skill.[4]

Due to the increased use of credit cards, debit cards, and online payments, people are writing fewer checks. Nevertheless, checks remain one of the most popular methods of payment. The number of checks written in the United States in 2015 was over 17 billion with a total value of nearly $29 trillion.[5] By industry estimates, while debit card fraud accounts for 66 percent of financial losses to the nation's banks, check fraud accounts for 32 percent of losses.[6]

Given the popularity of mobile check deposit, where the bank account holder takes a picture of a check with a smartphone or tablet camera, digital check forgery has increased. Here, the offender, using image processing tools, extracts the check image and replaces it with a digitally modified one before it reaches the bank's servers, or else generates a fake check digitally from scratch.[7] When a forged check is paid, any mistake by the bank will result in the bank's bearing the loss unless the forger can be found and successfully prosecuted. Most shoplifting and employee thefts, which are closely related in nature, involve the stealing of relatively small and inexpensive articles; professionals, on the other hand, may steal things like diamond jewelry or artwork, and electronics, like laptops, gaming systems, and tablets. The total value of shoplifting and employee thefts may be quite large. Over $13 billion worth of goods are stolen from retailers in the US each year. The average dollar loss per shoplifting incident in 2017 was $798.48. Retailers estimated that 36.5 percent of their inventory shrinkage (merchandise only) was due to shoplifting. The specialty apparel sector attributed 41 percent of their merchandise shrinkage to shoplifting.[8] In the grocery store and supermarket sector, nearly a quarter of their inventory shrinkage was due to shoplifting. Grocery stores and supermarkets experienced an average dollar loss of $100.17 per shoplifting incident.[9]

Some further indication of the extent of shoplifting is revealed by several accounts. According to FBI statistics, shoplifting had been on the rise since 2011. However, in 2016 there was a 6.7 percent decrease over the previous year. The decrease may have been due to the greater use of uniformed guards but also of sophisticated technologies such as microwave and electronic security tags as well as live customer visible closed-circuit television cameras. Despite these prevention strategies, there were still over 1 million shoplifting cases reported in 2016. These cases constituted 20.9 percent of all larceny-thefts nationwide.[10] One study found that about 11 percent of the US population shoplifted. The people most likely to engage in shoplifting were US-born, never married, and between the ages 18 of 29.[11]

One expert on the problem of employee theft defined it as, "any unauthorized appropriation of company property by employees either for one's own use or for sale to another."[12] Retailers estimate that 30 percent of their inventory shrinkage is due to employee theft. The men and women's specialty apparel industry loses 35.5 percent of their merchandise to employee theft.[13] Employee theft is 10 times costlier than the nation's street crime and accounts for approximately 30–50 percent of all business failures.[14]

Another property crime that involves theft with a long history under the common law is burglary. Under the old common law, burglary was breaking and entering the dwelling of another at night with the intent to steal. This has now been expanded to include buildings other than houses and the night element has been eliminated. Thus, burglary is the unlawful entry of a house, apartment, business, or other structure with the intent to commit an offense, usually a theft. In 2016, more than 1.5 million burglaries were reported to law enforcement. These accounted for about 19 percent of all property crimes.[15] That same year, over 3 million household burglaries were attempted or completed.[16] Professional burglars are specialists who have prior knowledge of their targets and use considerable skill and planning. Occasional burglars, by contrast, engage in minimal preparation and are likely to burgle when the opportunity arises. They usually do so out of a perceived need for cash. Here is how one offender explains his decision to commit a residential burglary:

> Well, it's like, the way it clicks into your head is like, you'll be thinking about something and, you know, it's a problem. Then it, like, all relates. "Hey, I need some money! Then how am I going to get money? Well, how do you know how to get money quick and easy?" Then there it is. Next thing you know, you are watching [a house] or calling to see if [the occupants] are home.[17]

Because many burglars are addicted to drugs, they often steal money to finance their drug habit.[18] Most burglars seem to target residences on weekdays during daylight hours when most occupants are at work[19] and that are close to where the burglars live.[20]

The law generally distinguishes two types of motor vehicle theft. One is where auto thieves deprive the owner of the car permanently. The car is either kept, sold, or stripped of batteries, global positioning system, grilles, airbags, engine parts, in a chop shop. The individual body and dismantled parts are then sold. The Motor Vehicle Theft Law Enforcement Act of 1984 requires that manufacturers stamp cars and major replacement parts with identification numbers to make it easier to trace stolen parts or vehicles.

The other type of auto theft, committed mostly by teenage males, is stealing the car for a joy-ride in which the car is eventually returned to the owner, although in many cases it is damaged. Cars are stolen or "borrowed" for the entertainment of one's adolescent peers. In this case, it is regarded simply as a way to have fun. Since joyriding usually involves no intent to deprive the legal owner permanently of the car, the offense is usually designated as "operating a motor vehicle without the owner's permission."

In 2016, auto thefts accounted for 9.7 percent of all property crimes reported to police. The average dollar value per motor vehicle stolen was $7,680.[21] Because cars are such an integral part of American culture and so vital for transportation in the absence of any well-developed systems of public transportation, vehicular theft is widespread. Due to increasingly sophisticated built-in security designs, cars are harder to steal. However, these target-hardening measures have encouraged the use of keys to steal cars. While the exact number of vehicles stolen using keys is not known, according to one British study, theft of keys accounts for a relatively large proportion of auto thefts.[22] More recently, thieves have used high-tech relay devices that are able to trick the vehicle into believing its electronic keys were nearby.

Other occasional property crimes such as vandalism and arson do not involve theft; they involve destruction. Legally, vandalism involves "malicious mischief" or the willful destruction, damage, or defacement of property; it can be committed by a juvenile or an adult, although most of it is perpetrated by juveniles and youths. Marshall B. Clinard and Andrew L. Wade have defined juvenile vandalism as "the deliberate defacement, mutilation, or destruction of private or public property by a juvenile or group of juveniles not having immediate or direct ownership in the property so abused."[23] It is said that the term "vandalism" was used in 1794 by a writer who, attempting to cast blame for the willful destruction of works of art during the French Revolution, likened such destruction to the behavior of the Vandals, the Germanic tribe that sacked Rome in the fifth century.[24]

While the juvenile arrest rate for vandalism fell 75 percent between 1994 and 2015,[25] vandalism continues to be widespread in the United States. It constitutes one of the largest categories of juvenile delinquency offenses, although it can be committed by persons of all ages. It is associated with affluence in industrialized societies, for it rarely occurs in developing countries, where the willful destruction of goods in limited supply is inconceivable except during riots, civil wars, or demonstrations. Property destruction, as a form of protest, is one of the few ways that the poor and disenfranchised segments of affluent societies can bring attention to their civil cause.

Studies of complaints made by citizens and public officials reveal that hardly any property is safe from this form of aggression. Vandalism occurs in a wide range of settings including public transportation, private residences, public housing, schools, stores, parks, and libraries. It has been suggested that vandalism is more prevalent in residential areas with a shopping mall, high schools, large proportions of rental property, and where unemployment rates are high.[26] One study considered exposure to potential offenders and the suitability of property for damage and destruction, in understanding vandalism victimization risks. Findings indicated that persons living near a park have greater risks for vandalism because parks are places with a higher percentage of unsupervised youth hanging around. Another finding was that persons who have vandalized are more likely to themselves be victims of vandalism. Other conditions of vandalism victimization risk include frequently going to community festivals, primarily using one's own vehicle for transportation, and being around others who are using or preparing to use drugs.[27]

Public property of all types appears to offer a peculiar allurement to teens bent on destruction. Parks, playgrounds, and highway signs are frequently defaced or destroyed. Trees, shrubs, flowers, benches, and other equipment suffer in like manner. Car owners often report the slashing of tires, the keying (scratching) of paint, the smashing of windows and side mirrors, and the theft of accessories. Golf course owners complain that benches, markers, flags, and even expensive and difficult-to-replace putting greens are defaced, broken, or uprooted. Libraries report the theft and intentional mutilation of books and the destruction of equipment. Railroads complain of the graffiti marking of boxcars, the destruction of freight car seals, theft of property, willful and deliberate throwing of stones at passenger car windows and tampering with rails and switches. Moreover, gangs use graffiti to challenge rival gangs and to identify members and mark territory, which is called "tagging."

Additionally, vandalism is frequently associated with hate crimes, as when offenders desecrate Jewish cemeteries or paint racist slurs and other hateful messages on Islamic centers. Vacant houses seem to be the particular delight of young people seeking outlets for destructive instincts; windows are broken and plumbing and hardware is stolen, destroyed, or rendered unusable. Gas station operators report damage to credit card readers and that fuel pumps and other service equipment are stolen, broken, or destroyed. Theater managers complain of the slashing of seats, willful damaging of toilet facilities, even the burning of rugs, carpets, and more.

Fires pose a major and prevalent vandalism problem. But fire-setting also constitutes the property crime of arson, defined as the willful or attempted malicious burning of a structure, vehicle, aircraft, or property of another. German scientists in the late 1700s were the first to study arson, believing that fires were intentionally set mostly by young peasant women suffering from a mental illness.[28] A medical textbook from 1815 describes one such case:

> A servant girl in the country, happy in her situation and liked by her master and mistress, one day while making a toast for the tea was overcome with the propensity to set fire to the barnyard—instantly went out and committed the act, for which she was hanged.[29]

Today the criminal charge of arson no longer depends on gender but on the age of the fire-setter. In the United States, children beneath the statutory minimum age of jurisdiction will generally not be charged with arson because they are considered to be mentally incapable of forming the intent needed to constitute malice.

In 2015, a total of 41,376 arsons were reported to law enforcement. More than 45 percent of these offenses involved residential, storage, and public structures.[30] Besides vandalism, other motives for arson include: (1) to destroy evidence from a crime, (2) revenge, (3) profit, and (4) bias against a particular group. As an example of the latter, one report explained the burning of more than 200 black and multi-racial churches between 1989–1996 as due to the competition of political and economic resources between the more powerful ethnic group (whites) and subordinate groups (African Americans).[31] One study examined the relationship between property target location and motives of arson. It found that arsonists motivated by emotional factors travel shorter distances from their homes to the location where they commit the crime than those motivated by goal-directed gain.[32]

Sociology of Criminal Behavior

Most occasional property offenders commit only infrequent theft of some kind. Such criminal behavior is incidental to their way of life. The offenses are so rare that offenders in no way make a living out of crime. Occasional property offenders do not identify with crime or conceive of themselves as criminals. Their offenses show little sophistication in the techniques of crime. Most of them have little real knowledge about criminal activities or of the specialized vocabulary of crime, nor do they have contact with other offenders. Adult occasional shoplifters, as contrasted with "boosters" or professional shoplifters, do not, in general, define themselves as criminals. They often are "respectable" professionals or middle-class women. In the mid-1800s, Henry Mayhew wrote about these respectable shoplifters:

> There is a class of women who visit shops in various parts of the metropolis, sometimes two and at other times three together. They vary their dress according to the locality they visit. Sometimes you find them dressed very respectably, like the wives of people in good circumstances in life. . . . They generally call into shops at busy times when there are many persons standing around the counter and will stand two or three together. They ask to look at certain articles, and will possibly say, after they have inspected them, that they do not suit them; they will say they are too high in price, or not the article they want, or not the proper color. They will likely ask to see some other goods and keep looking at the different articles until they get a quantity on the counter. When the shopman is engaged getting some fresh goods from the window or from the shelves, one of them generally contrives to slip something under her cloak or shawl, while the other manages to keep his attention abstracted they will get some article and lay it down behind their basket, such as a roll of ribbons, or a half-dozen of gloves, or other small portable goods. While the shopman's back is turned or his attention withdrawn, it is hidden under their shawl or cloak. We frequently find the skirt of their dress lined from the pocket downward, forming a large repository all along the dress, with an opening in front, where they can insert a small article, which is not observed in the ample crinoline. . . . We find ladies in respectable position occasionally charged with shoplifting.[33]

Cesare Lombroso, writing in the 1890s, explained why he thought women were motivated to shoplift:

> Shoplifting, which has become common since the establishment of huge, fashionable department stores, is a form of occasional crime in which women specialize. The temptation stems from the immense number of articles on display; these excite the dreams of women who can afford only a few of them, an excitement made all the easier in that, as we have seen, for women ornaments are not luxury items but rather necessities, powerful tools of seduction.[34]

While shoplifting is a serious offense, it has sometimes been treated as a relatively minor one, and sometimes not a legal offense at all. In the late nineteenth century, when much attention was given to the "epidemic" of shoplifting, particularly when committed by affluent women, it came to be regarded as a mental condition.

> Therefore, the diagnosis of kleptomania was socially constructed by key decision-makers to deal with these sensitive cases, thus "legitimatizing" the actions of the stores and courts to dismiss or acquit those afflicted with this "women's disease."[35]

An early study of the occasional or "naive" check forger showed that such persons perceive their offenses as relatively minor acts of crime because large sections of the public do not think they fit the criminal stereotype. Check forgery has low visibility as a crime because of the peculiar interaction with the victim who accepts the check. As one criminologist has pointed out, forgery for them emerges "as behavior which is out of character or 'other than usual' for the persons involved."[36]

Naive check forgers may commit such offenses in the face of a financial problem when other alternatives are blocked. The offense is a product of occasional difficult social situations in which the offender finds himself or herself, a certain degree of social isolation, and a process of "closure" or "constriction of behavior alternatives subjectively held as available to the forger."[37]

> Assuming we have established situational isolation as the more general prerequisite for the commission of naive check forgery, it is still necessary to factor out more specific situational factors conducive to the crime. These we believe are found in certain dialectical forms of social behavior—dialectical in the sense that the person becomes progressively involved in them. These behaviors are further distinguished in that they make imperative the possession of money or money substitutes for their continuance or fulfillment. They are objective and identifiable and once a person is committed to them the impetus to "follow through" with them is implicit. A quick example is that of a man away from home who falls in with a small group who have embarked upon a 2- or 3-day or even a week's period of drinking and carousing. The impetus to continue the pattern gets mutually reinforced by the interaction of the participants and tends to have an accelerated beginning, a climax and a terminus. If midway through such a spree a participant runs out of money, the pressures immediately become critical to take such measures as are necessary to preserve the behavior sequence.[38]

Because shoplifters commit their crimes in public places, they must "act normal" to minimize unwanted attention before, during, and after completing their crimes. Shoplifters employ behaviors that are perceived as engaging in normal shopping and not seen as stealing:

> "I already knew that the electric tape was in the corner, but I just, when I saw it right there, I just needed something to ask her [an employee] about, just to give her something to do because I figured that she was trying to keep a close eye on me. . . I worked at [a sporting goods store], so. . . you know how you're supposed to act when people come around. You just want to keep constant communication with the employees, so then they won't think you're trying to do something mysterious . . ."

> "I think that I play it off [like I'm a shopper]. When you watch those hidden videos on shows of people stealing and stuff like that, they look so sketchy on camera; they're looking like this [nervous] and slipping stuff in their pocket. Just the way that my facial reactions [are]. . . like I'm reading the back [of the product label as if] I don't know if this is good. . . . Then I'll put it in [my pocket] like that; make it kinda so the box wouldn't stick out. Then I kinda look [at the product on the shelves], I look again; then I just kinda shake my head like nothing here is good."

> "[I left the store] in a meandering way. Just kinda act like I was looking for things but wasn't a hundred percent sure on what I wanted, making it look like they didn't really have exactly what I was interested in. . . I'm kinda just walking, kinda looking around the store, making it look like I just, not really sure what I want to buy, if I want to buy anything."[39]

During holiday periods in which gift-giving is customary, retailers commonly display vast quantities of commodities in conspicuous view in order to stimulate sales. It comes as no surprise, then, that during these periods, shoplifting—particularly of the amateur variety—is most prevalent. In this sense, it may be argued that the retailers bring about their own inventory losses, for a culture founded on commercialism activates its own peculiar brand of deviance. This is particularly true in countries such as the United States, where there exists a wide gap between the rich and the poor, and where the mass media displays the same commodities for all to desire equally.

A large proportion of those who commit vandalism are likely to have a noncriminal view of themselves and their actions. The fact that often nothing is stolen tends to reinforce the vandal's conception of self as prankster rather than delinquent or criminal. Generally, acts of vandalism are committed by persons who have no special criminal orientation toward themselves or what they do. Some writers consider this a distinguishing characteristic of the vandal when compared with other property offenders. The adolescent considers property defacement as entertaining, rebellious, and exciting, as well as a protest against his or her role and status in an unequal society. For example, graffiti, which is sometimes considered vandalism, is seen by marginalized urban adolescents, not as a crime, but as an expression of resistance to legal and political authority. Graffiti, which includes the tagging of subcultural nicknames on city walls and the creation of large illegal murals,

> reclaims public space for at least some of those systematically excluded from it, and thus resists the confinement of kids and others within structures of social and spatial control.[40]

The same is true for arson, which is sometimes seen as a means of rebellion, resistance, and defiance. As one criminologist put it:

> To understand why "fire" has become such a "burning issue" at this particular moment, then politicians, policy-makers, and criminologists need to understand the everyday experience of a life lived within the constraints and constrictions of policies created by one group to make rational another. In other words, policies that make, for politicians, an ordered world—neat, tidy but unbearable to those who live within it. Fire is a response to the unbearable nothingness of contemporary life and brings fun, meaning, and resistance to the meaninglessness of the political, rational world.[41]

The youth crime of joyriding, the stealing of a car for the fun of driving it, is not a career type of offense. It is usually done by young men and the offenses committed are sporadic. Aside from enhancing an offender's self-esteem, self-identity, and status in the eyes of his friends, one British study found that joyriding may be a potentially addictive behavior in which the offender experiences high levels of arousal:

> I used to get dead excited, then—and as we were getting close to it man (phew) you know what I mean, and then we'd see a car and that, and that's it. . . put some screwdrivers in the door, sweating and that, you know what I mean, and used to get that much of an adrenaline rush, when I'd be sitting at traffic lights, when I'd just took a car and be sat at lights. Me foot was like that [demonstrates] shaking on the clutch, you know what I mean?[42]

The usual patterns are quite simple—either stealing a car that has readily accessible keys, using a duplicate key or jumping or hot-wiring the car. With sophisticated anti-theft devices in many cars, this is becoming progressively more difficult. The theft of a car is more like "borrowing" it and does not involve techniques commonly associated with conventional career offenses, such as selecting a special type of car, finding fences for the sale of the car or its parts, or stripping the car. Moreover, the occasional car thief, or joyrider, does not usually progress in techniques and skills.

Of particular significance among occasional offenders is their ability to rationalize their criminal behavior. Adult shoplifters, for example, tend to take relatively inexpensive items of merchandise just a little above the level of that which they would purchase; therefore, they view their acts as somewhat reprehensible but not "really criminal." One exploratory study found that because shoplifters saw stealing as morally wrong, they engaged in widespread use of neutralizations to justify their crime to others. Respondents in the study gave such neutralizations as,

> "I don't know what comes over me. It's like, you know, is somebody else doing it, not me?" . . . "I'm really a good person. I wouldn't ever do something like that, stealing, you know, but I have to take things sometimes for my kids. They need stuff and I don't have any money to get it" . . . "I wanted the item and could not afford it . . . Stores charge too much for stuff. They could sell things for half of what they do and still make a profit. They're just too greedy."[43]

The occasional property offender generally has little group support for his or her criminal behavior. However, burglars and juvenile arsonists do sometimes commit their crimes with co-offenders. One study found that burglars' decision to commit a crime in informal groups was encouraged by three interactional dynamics.[44] The first, "incremental signaling," occurs when someone in the group indirectly suggests the need for money, someone else proposes a possible target, then someone talks up the need for committing the burglary. "Target convergence" happens when group members decide on a target with only gestures, nods, and a few words between them. "Establishing identity" happens when group members recognize that other group members have reputations as burglars; they then see themselves as a burglary group and are encouraged to commit the offense. These three spontaneous styles of group interaction explain why people who are not motivated to engage in burglary quickly see an opportunity for doing so.

Likewise, a Swedish study revealed that youth play different roles or positions in their interactions with co-offenders during the planning, preparation, and execution of their arson crime. Some of these positions included the "motivator" who supplies the incentive, the "resource-keeper" who brings the material resources needed to set the fire, and the "fire-setter" who sets the fire. It is, however:

> possible for a single person to act in all five positions proposed in this study as characterizing the planning and preparatory phases of the fire-setting events, and in the final phase only the position of a fire-setter is necessary for the crime to be completed.[45]

Similarly, in acts of simple wanton vandalism several individuals may be involved:

> Acts of vandalism seldom utilize or even require prior sophisticated knowledge. They grow out of collective interaction of the moment; few are deliberately planned in advance. Participation in acts of vandalism gives status and group interaction to each member; through direct involvement, the individual avoids becoming a marginal member of the group. Vandalism is spontaneous behavior and the outgrowth of social situations in which group interaction takes place. Each interactive response by a participant builds upon the

action of another participant until a focus develops and the group act of vandalism results. In the typical act of vandalism there are usually five stages: (1) waiting for something to turn up, (2) removal of uncertainty about what to do, resulting in an "exploratory gesture" to the act, (3) mutual conversion of each member of the group to participation, (4) joint elaboration of the vandalism, and (5) aftermath and retrospect.[46]

Mutual excitation is particularly important in vandalism. A primary function of this element is the tendency for the individual to lose his or her feeling of self-identity in the prevailing group interaction. This temporary loss of identity is especially significant because it helps make possible the participation in vandalism and any resulting elaboration of the act. The very fact that property destruction is generally a group act reduces individual feelings of fear and guilt. The dilution of such feeling in the peer association operates as a sort of "guilt insurance." The peer group inadvertently furnishes a sense of security in numbers, which curtails feelings of individuality and responsibility. Further, the belief is that when the act is committed by a group, the authorities will find it difficult, if not impossible, to single out the specific instigators. The feeling of security is enhanced by the additional belief that vandalism is one of the less serious delinquencies. This is particularly the case when the adolescent interprets his or her destructive behavior as a prank or "just having fun." This interpretation also helps to neutralize whatever guilt feelings the offender may have from participation in vandalism.

The fact is that most occasional property criminal behavior is more the result of spontaneous group interaction than the product of a criminal subculture or subculture of burglary, arson, or vandalism. Naive check forgery is also usually carried out alone. Shoplifting by adults is generally done alone as well. Shoplifting by juveniles tends to be a group activity, although not group-coordinated beyond setting up a lookout. More typically, a group of adolescents will disperse throughout a store, meeting later at another location to see who has stolen the most goods and the most valuable commodities. Afterward, what has been shoplifted is either used, sold, or discarded.

The main reason occasional property crimes need little group or peer support is because they are relatively easy to commit in that few skills are called for and a social network of facilitators is not necessary. This suggests the relative unimportance of criminal associations in crimes of this type. Most persons in their everyday lives have occasion to cash personal checks and need no one's help to do so. Likewise, the mass display of merchandise in stores makes training in techniques of theft largely unnecessary. To some who illegally "borrow" an automobile, it involves no more than driving away an unlocked car. Naive check forgeries generally are committed by persons who have had no previous criminal record and no previous contact or interaction with delinquents and criminals. Amateur shoplifters have no special preparation. They seem to not give much thought to what they steal, taking items they will not use or sell:

> The amateur shoplifter takes ill-fitting blouses or high-heeled sandals she doesn't like or other unusable or unsellable items—a piece of gum, a pencil, or a marble. These shoplifted souvenirs languish in a closet or the desk drawer.[47]

Marshall B. Clinard reported a similar lack of commitment to crime in his study of young rural offenders who occasionally engaged in property offenses.[48] He found that their law-violating behavior did not start early in life, they exhibited little knowledge of criminal techniques, such activity was not pursued as a means of livelihood, and they did not conceive of themselves as criminals. Rather than identifying with crime, the offenders considered themselves "reckless" and saw their law-violating activity as an adventure.

Social Reaction to Criminal Behavior

Most conforming behavior is evaluated and judged from the rational choice perspective. Research has shown, however, that occasional property offenses such as petty theft and vandalism are not sufficiently explained by the rational choice model.[49] For example, one study revealed that because most persistent property offenders are motivated by the constant pursuit of a partying lifestyle (consuming drugs, enjoying luxury items and activities), they give little thought to the risk of arrest in their decisions to commit a crime.[50]

The same may be said with regard to public support for this form of criminal behavior. Occasional property offenders find little support for their criminal behavior in the legitimate behavior patterns of society. In general, all of the offenses represent a violation of the values placed on private property. In most cases, offenders are expressing frustration or attempting to obtain something that they consider to be necessary and important. In any event, this points to the fact that they are unable to acquire valuables or status through legitimate channels. For example, according to Leon F. Fannin and Marshall B. Clinard, lower-class youth who live in high crime areas may be more likely to use arson due to a perceived lack of other methods for achieving goals.[51]

Most Americans obey most of the laws most of the time because they think that the legitimate authorities should be respected and because most law-abiding people want to think of themselves as moral persons.[52] This being the case, it is not difficult to see the lack of fit between criminal and legitimate behavior in the case of occasional property offenses.

While these offenders tend to be committed to the general goals of society, at least in their own minds their behavior stands in occasional contradiction to this self-image. Naive check forgers "appear to have acquired normal attitudes and habits of law observance."[53] Adult department store pilferers are generally "respectable" citizens with little or no contact with criminal groups.[54] Despite engaging in employee theft hospital nurses nevertheless see themselves "as caregivers whose job is to help their patients at any cost."[55] It is only in their criminal acts that there is little correspondence between the offender and the nonoffender. The extent to which occasional property crime represents a rejection of legitimate behavior patterns, as incorporated in middle-class norms, is open to question. Much destruction of property through vandalism, and sometimes arson, seems to occur as a way of challenging the values associated with the emphasis placed on private property. Graffiti writing—painting or writing on property belonging to another without permission—has been regarded as malicious destruction by irresponsible adolescents. But it has also been seen as an attempt to call public attention to oneself as well as a desire for peer recognition. For example, a study of graffiti writers in Australia found that recognition by other writers was an important motivating factor in the behavior:

> I don't know, it's just getting to have your name well-known all around the place . . . They'll be like, they'll see your tag and they'll be like, that's good . . . and they'll be like, I know who writes that, I'm his friend . . . he's heaps cool.[56]

In many other cases graffiti writing appears to be an attempt merely to have some fun:

> If I'm pleased with it it's . . . a pretty good feeling really, like I've gone home a few times with big smiles on my face, it's just, oh yeah, I'm hell chuffed cos I've just done this, like, big thing that looks pretty cool.[57]

Graffiti has been variously interpreted as "street art," "spray can art"[58] and "subway art."[59] There is, however, no clear line that divides art from vandalism:

Oh, yeah, it's obviously both [art and vandalism] isn't it? In some forms it's vandalism. Some guys probably don't even differentiate between the two . . . They do graffiti, [they go] bombing or trashing or whatever, [and] they want to label it as [art]. Obviously, murals are seen as art. [But] if I don't like it I might just think it's rubbish—then that wouldn't be art to me. If you can appreciate it, then I think . . . it is art. Probably within the right confines it always is art.[60]

Perhaps it is all these things. Evidence seems to indicate that middle-class legitimate behavior patterns are not equally internalized by all persons and groups and that many law violators are relatively isolated from the behavior patterns of the dominant power segments of society. Others theorize that both criminal and middle-class legal norms are internalized and that crime is a product of the offender's relations with an illegal "code of the street"[61] or a "precarious interaction order" that differs sharply from the American mainstream.[62] In any event, as Richard Quinney has noted, the problem for criminology is "explaining the development of behavior patterns that have relative probabilities of being defined as criminal."[63]

With all forms of occasional property crime, the behaviors that may become defined as criminal are pursued for a variety of reasons, with variations occurring according to the location of the participants in the social structure. In the study of criminal behavior, criminologists must be careful not to impute their own motives and values to those that underlie the behavior of the offenders.

Societal reaction toward occasional property crime is often not severe. Because the offender is unlikely to have any (or at most a minor) previous criminal record, and because these types of offenses do not represent a serious personal threat to the average person, the criminal charge is likely to be dismissed or the offender given probation, a fine, or a suspended sentence or warning. Minor property crimes like vandalism, petty theft, and joyriding are usually considered misdemeanors and are usually punished by little, if any, jail time. In most cases, the illegal behavior is carried out in isolation from the supporting values of a criminal subculture or group, and largely in a system of noncriminal relationships. The criminal behavior of the occasional offender is likely to be unstable, and when confronted with legal action in the form of an arrest, which defines the behavior as actually being "criminal," the offender is usually deterred from continuing such activity.

The effect of this societal reaction generally holds true whether it is shoplifting, simple check forgery, or vandalism. Persons can behave, for example, as thieves without defining themselves as thieves. Arrests by security guards or the police are crucial in helping to redefine a shoplifter's conception of his or her behavior as being merely "antisocial" or "bad" to being "criminal." Considerable leniency is allowed the occasional property offender by law enforcement and judicial agencies because such offenders are not likely to progress into a criminal career.

There are several reasons why relatively few shoplifters are arrested and prosecuted. There is difficulty in getting court action; suspects refuse to confess; the thefts are not usually of large, expensive items; and often the suspects are respectable, employed persons and the companies do not wish to appear to be "picking on" the individual. One final consideration looms large: the more shoplifting losses a retail outlet reports to the police, the more its insurance rates will increase. Another reason for the mild reaction to occasional property crime is the fact that the offenders often come from the same socioeconomic and cultural backgrounds as those responsible for enforcing the law. In many localities, the offenders are an integral and important part of the community. In such cases, much of the criminal behavior of residents is ignored by the local law enforcement agencies. Through their own legal agencies, local communities are able to establish the limits to which they will tolerate certain forms and amounts of deviance.

This lack of official reaction to occasional property crimes has led businesses to turn to alternative approaches to the public criminal justice system: private justice initiatives and restorative justice programs. For example, a study of the largest US corporations with hundreds of retail stores found that there was a private justice system complete with investigative, adjudicatory, and sentencing powers to deal with shoplifters.[64] No need to turn the suspect over to the police or to risk higher insurance rates. This study found that among the factors determining private justice for shoplifters were such variables as the retail value of the item taken, and the neighborhood, social class and degree of physical resistance of the suspect.

Many major retail stores resort to private justice when they routinely send a "civil demand letter" to customers they catch shoplifting, seeking a payment for hundreds of dollars.

> Technically these letters are simply offers to settle a potential civil lawsuit; if the alleged perpetrator does not pay, the store will simply sue him for damages under tort law. . . . Supporters of the program note that the shoplifter benefits from the procedure because by participating, he "avoids criminal prosecution." . . . Stores that send out these letters no doubt have no intention of bringing criminal charges against the recipients. Instead, these stores are indirectly using the public criminal law as a threat to coerce the recipients into paying a civil settlement. If the accused pays up, the store gets some amount of restitution—but even if not, there is some deterrent effect on the alleged shoplifter, thus helping to prevent further crime against the store.[65]

Restorative justice (RJ) programs have also been used with occasional property offenders. One study examined the effects of RJ conference proceedings on juveniles, many of whom had been involved in shoplifting.[66] The results indicated that most of the teens who experienced RJ conferences were significantly more likely to perceive that they were able to repay the victim and repay society than those who had experienced traditional court processing. Moreover, those who experienced RJ conferences were significantly more likely to feel repentance for their crime. It appears that occasional property offenders who are exposed to restorative justice approaches are more likely to perceive that their future offending is reduced than those who go through the retributive criminal justice system.

In sum, occasional property crime is inevitable in a society that values acquisition of property but is structured on economic inequality. As the Dutch criminologist, Willem Bonger, noted over a century ago:

> The greater the care to maintain existence, or often simply to procure daily bread, the greater is the number of offenses against property. When need appears, at the same time comes the instinct impelling a man to seize the property of another, better situated than himself.[67]

Criminal behavior patterns may develop to solve the problem of a society that both values property and limits possibilities for obtaining it.

Notes

1   Richard Quinney, *Class, State, and Crime: On the Theory and Practice of Criminal Justice* (New York: Longman, 1977), 54.
2   Richard Quinney, *Criminology*, 2nd edition (Boston: Little, Brown, 1979), 84–86.
3   Federal Reserve System, *Check Fraud*. www.checkcomposer.com/Downloads/CheckFraud.pdf
4   Bruce Jackson, *A Thief's Primer* (New York: Macmillan, 1969), 23.

5 The Federal Reserve, *Payments Study: 2017 Annual Supplement*. www.frbservices.org/assets/news/research/2017-payments-study-supplement.pdf

6 2015 ABA Deposit Account Fraud Survey. www.aba.com/Products/Surveys/Pages/2015DepositAccount.aspx

7 Rigel Gjomemo, Hafiz Malik, Nilesh Sumb, V.N. Venkatakrishnan, and Rashid Ansari, "Digital Check Forgery Attacks on Client Check Truncation Systems," in *Financial Cryptography and Data Security 18th International Conference, FC 2014, Christ Church, Barbados, March 3–7, 2014, Revised Selected Papers*, ed. by Nicolas Christin and Reihaneh Safavi-Naini (New York, Springer, 2014), 3–20.

8 *2017 National Retail Security Survey*. https://nrf.com/system/tdf/Documents/NRSS-Industry-Research-Survey-2017.pdf?file=1&title=National%20Retail%20Security%20Survey%202017

9 *2016 National Retail Security Survey*. https://nrf.com/system/tdf/Documents/retail%20library/NRF_2016_NRSS_restricted-rev.pdf?file=1&title=National%20Retail%20Security%20Survey%202016

10 Federal Bureau of Investigation, *Crime in the United States: Offense Analysis, 2016*. https://ucr.fbi.gov/crime-in-the-u.s/2016/crime-in-the-u.s.-2016/tables/table-15

11 Carlos Blanco, Jon Grant, Nancy M. Petry, H. Blair Simpson, Analucia Alegria, Shang-Min Liu, and M.S. Deborah Hasin, "Prevalence and Correlates of Shoplifting in the United States: Results from the National Epidemiologic Survey on Alcohol and Related Conditions (NESARC)," *American Journal of Psychiatry* 165, no 7 (2008): 905–913.

12 Jerald Greenberg, "Employee Theft," in *Blackwell Encyclopedic Dictionary of Organizational Behavior*, ed. by Nigel Nicholson (Cambridge, MA: Wiley, 1995), 154.

13 *2017 National Retail Security Survey*.

14 P.D. Bullard and A.J. Resnick, "SMR Forum: Too Many Hands in the Corporate Cookie Jar," *Sloan Management Review* 24, no. 3 (1983): 51–56.

15 Federal Bureau of Investigation, *Crime in the United States: Burglary, 2016*. https://ucr.fbi.gov/crime-in-the-u.s/2016/crime-in-the-u.s.-2016/topic-pages/burglary

16 US Department of Justice, Office of Justice Programs, Bureau of Justice Statistics, *Criminal Victimization, 2016*. www.bjs.gov/content/pub/pdf/cv16.pdf

17 Richard T. Wright and Scott H. Decker, *Burglars on the Job: Streetlife and Residential Break-ins* (Boston: Northeastern University Press, 1994), 36.

18 Paul F. Cromwell, James N. Olson, and D'Aunn W. Avary, *Breaking and Entering: An Ethnographic Analysis of Burglary* (Thousand Oaks, CA: Sage, 1990).

19 Timothy Coupe and Lawrence Blake, "Daylight and Darkness Targeting Strategies and the Risks of Being Seen at Residential Burglaries," *Criminology* 44, no. 2, (2006):431–464.

20 Wim Bernasco and Paul Nieuwbeerta, "How Do Residential Burglars Select Target Areas? A New Approach to the Analysis of Criminal Location Choice," *British Journal of Criminology* 45, no. 3 (2005): 296–315.

21 Federal Bureau of Investigation, *Crime in the United States: Property Crime, 2016*. https://ucr.fbi.gov/crime-in-the-u.s/2016/crime-in-the-u.s.-2016/topic-pages/property-crime

22 Heith Copes and Michael Cherbonneau, "The Key to Auto Theft: Emerging Methods of Auto Theft from the Offenders' Perspective," *British Journal of Criminology* 46, no. 5 (2006): 917–934.

23 Marshall B. Clinard and Andrew L. Wade, "Toward the Delineation of Vandalism as a Sub-Type in Juvenile Delinquency," *Journal of Criminal Law and Criminology* 48, no. 5 (1958): 493–499.

24 Andrew Merrills and Richard Miles, *The Vandals* (Malden, MA: Wiley-Blackwell, 2010), 9.

25 US Department of Justice, Office of Juvenile Justice, *Delinquency Prevention Statistical Briefing Book, 2017*. www.ojjdp.gov/ojstatbb/crime/JAR_Display.asp?ID=qa05212

26 Teresa C. Lagrange, "Routine Activities and Vandalism" (master's thesis, University of Alberta, 1994).

27 Richard Tewksbury and Elizabeth Ehrhardt Mustaine, "Routine Activities and Vandalism: A Theoretical and Empirical Study," *Journal of Crime and Justice* 23, no. 1 (2000): 81–110.

28 Monica Hesse, *American Fire: Love, Arson, and Life in a Vanishing Land* (New York, NY: W.W. Norton, 2017).

29 Ibid., 44–45.

30 Federal Bureau of Investigation, *Crime in the United States: Arson, 2015*. https://ucr.fbi.gov/crime-in-the-u.s/2015/crime-in-the-u.s.-2015/offenses-known-to-law-enforcement/arson

31 Sarah A. Soule and Nella Van Dyke, "Black Church Arson in the United States, 1989–1996," *Ethnic and Racial Studies* 22, no. 4 (1999): 724–742.

32 Katarina Fritzon, "An Examination of the Relationship between Distance Travelled and Motivational Aspects of Firesetting Behavior," *Journal of Environmental Psychology* 21, no. 1 (2001): 45–60.

33 Henry Mayhew, *The London Underworld in the Victorian Period: Authentic First-Person Accounts by Beggars, Thieves and Prostitutes* (Mineola, NY: Dover Publications, 2005), 171–172.

34 Cesare Lombroso and Guglielmo Ferrero, *Criminal Woman, the Prostitute, and the Normal Woman*, trans., Nicole Hahn Rafter and Mary Gibson (Durham, NY: Duke University Press, 2004), 197.

35 Lloyd Klemke, *The Sociology of Shoplifting: Boosters and Snitches Today* (Westport, CT: Praeger, 1992), 19.

36 Edwin M. Lemert, "An Isolation and Closure Theory of Naive Check Forgery," *Journal of Criminal Law and Criminology* 44, no. 3 (1953): 296–307, 300.

37 Ibid., 297.

38 Ibid., 302.

39 Nicole Lasky, Scott Jacques, and Bonnie S. Fisher, "Glossing Over Shoplifting: How Thieves Act Normal," *Deviant Behavior* 36, no. 4 (2015): 293–309, 300, 303.

40 Jeff Ferrell, "Urban Graffiti: Crime, Control, and Resistance," *Youth & Society* 27, no. 1 (1995): 73–92, 75.

41 Mike Presdee, "Burning Issues: Fire, Carnival, and Crime," in *Questioning Crime and Criminology*, ed. by Moira T. Peelo and Keith Soothill (Portland, OR: Willan Publishing, 2005), 82.

42 Sue Kellett and Harriet Gross, "Addicted to Joyriding? An Exploration of Young Offenders' Accounts of their Car Crime," *Psychology, Crime & Law* 12, no. 1 (2006): 39–59, 47.

43 Paul Cromwell and Quint Thurman, "'The Devil Made Me Do It': Use of Neutralizations by Shoplifters," *Deviant Behavior* 24, no. 6 (2003) 535–550, 541–542.

44 Andy Hochstetler, "Opportunities and Decisions: Interactional Dynamics in Robbery and Burglary Groups," *Criminology* 39, no. 3 (2001): 737–764.

45 Sara Uhnoo, "Starting a Fire Together: The Dynamics of Co-offending in Juvenile Arson," *European Journal of Criminology* 13, no. 3 (2016) 315–331, 326.

46 Andrew L. Wade, "Social Processes in the Act of Juvenile Vandalism," in *Criminal Behavior Systems: A Typology*, ed. by Marshall B. Clinard and Richard Quinney (New York, NY: Holt, Rinehart, Winston, 1967), 268.

47 Rachel Shteir, *The Steal: A Cultural History of Shoplifting* (New York: Penguin, 2011), 105–106.

48 Marshall B. Clinard, "Rural Criminal Offenders," *American Journal of Sociology* 50, no. 1 (1944): 38–45.

49 Raymond Paternoster, "Decisions to Participate in and Desist from Four Types of Common Delinquency: Deterrence and the Rational Choice Perspective." *Law & Society Review* 23, no. 1 (1989): 9–40.

50 Neal Shover and David Honaker, "The Socially Bounded Decision Making of Persistent Property Offenders," *The Howard Journal of Crime and Justice* 31, no. 4 (2009): 276–293.

51 Leon F. Fannin and Marshall B. Clinard, "Differences in the Conception of Self as a Male Among Lower and Middle-Class Delinquents," *Social Problems* 13, no. 2 (1965): 205–214.

52 Tom R. Tyler, *Why People Obey the Law* (New Haven, CT: Yale University Press, 1990).

53 Lemert, "An Isolation and Closure Theory of Naive Check Forgery," 298.

54 Mary Owen Cameron. *The Booster and the Snitch: Department Store Shoplifting* (New York: Free Press, 1964), xii.

55 Dean Dabney, "Neutralization and Deviance in the Workplace: Theft of Supplies and Medicines by Hospital Nurses," *Deviant Behavior* 16, no. 4 (1995): 313–331, 329.

56 Mark Halsey and Alison Young, "'Our Desires are Ungovernable': Writing Graffiti in Urban Space," *Theoretical Criminology* 10, no. 3 (2006): 275–306, 280.

57 Ibid., 281.

58 Henry Chalfant and James Prigoff, *Spraycan Art* (London: Thames & Hudson, 1987).

59 Henry Chalfant and Martha Cooper, *Subway Art* (London: Thames & Hudson, 2016).

60 Halsey and Young, "Our Desires are Ungovernable," 284–285.

61 Elijah Anderson, *The Code of the Street: Decency, Violence, and the Moral Life of the Inner City* (New York: W.W. Norton, 1999).

62 Waverly Duck, *No Way Out: Precarious Living in the Shadow of Poverty and Drug Dealing* (Chicago, IL: University of Chicago Press, 2015).

63 Richard Quinney, *The Social Reality of Crime* (Boston, MA: Little, Brown & Co., 1970), 213.

64 Melissa G. Davis, Richard J. Lundman, and Ramiro Martinez, Jr., "Private Corporate Justice: Store Police, Shoplifters, and Civil Recovery," *Social Problems* 38, no. 3 (1991): 395–411.

65 Ric Simmons, "Private Criminal Justice," *Wake Forest Law Review*, 42 (2007): 911–990, 939–940.

66 Hee Joo Kim and Jurg Gerber, "The Effectiveness of Reintegrative Shaming and Restorative Justice Conferences: Focusing on Juvenile Offenders' Perceptions in Australian Reintegrative Shaming Experiments," *International Journal of Offender Therapy and Comparative Criminology* 56, no. 7 (2012): 1063–1079.

67 Willem Adriaan Bonger, *Criminality and Economic Conditions*, trans. by Henry P. Horton (Boston, MA: Little, Brown, 1916), 76.

4
PUBLIC ORDER CRIME

No one knows for certain which crimes are committed with the greatest frequency, but with the possible exception of fraud, public order crimes are the most numerous. Public order crimes include prostitution, drunkenness, substance abuse, gambling, traffic offenses, disorderly conduct, and exhibitionism.

Public order crimes, like other types of crimes, are deeply embedded in the society's organization and operation. These are produced by a contradiction: if a society cannot provide a humane and unifying existence, it must deal with behaviors that are defined as criminal. These crimes are at the same time a threat to the society and also furnish goods and services to its citizens.[1]

Much of the behavior in public order offenses provides an economic commodity for both those who offer the service or product and the dominant culture that receives it. For example, prostitution is closely related to regular market transactions: "prostitution is not merely a criminalized sexual activity but also an economic exchange."[2] Likewise, substance abusers engage in an elaborate social and economic arrangement that consists of a system of supply and demand in which they must continually search for dealers to sell them drugs to support their habit.

All crimes that fall into a criminal behavior system have similar and distinct characteristics. In one sense, public order crimes are alike in that they all break some penal law. In another sense, each individual crime is situationally unique. There are obviously some striking differences in the behavior systems of the more important public order offenses of prostitution, public intoxication, and the use of controlled substances. Still, because of the many similarities, all the offenses in this group will be discussed together under the three dimensions of our typology: definition of behavior as criminal, sociology of criminal behavior, and social reaction to criminal behavior. In each case, when pertinent and reliable data exist, the differences between these types of offenses will also be indicated and discussed.

Definition of Behavior as Criminal

Much of US criminal law has been formulated for the purpose of publicly enforcing moral principles. Thus, it is that criminal laws regulate various kinds of sexual conduct, prostitution, abortion, public intoxication, drug use, and certain public behaviors defined variously as public nuisance, loitering, and trespassing.

To be moral in America is to be sexually discreet. Just as the Puritan heritage has affected many aspects of crime, it has also made the criminal law a moral device for the control of a wide range of sexual conduct. The Puritans of Massachusetts Bay Colony restricted sexual activity to the marriage bond. Adultery was made a crime punishable by death. Prostitution—"the oldest profession"—has been defined in some way as a crime in most states. Although prostitution and sex work continue to flourish, the criminal laws regulating it serve their purpose of providing a sense of public morality.

Drinking, while not a crime itself, is also subject to criminal arrest when it takes place excessively in public view. Criminal laws are available to handle persons who openly disturb the community's sense of order. Intoxicated persons may be apprehended simply because of their condition, or they may be arrested because their condition leads to other acts of public nuisance or disturbance. But essentially, public intoxication violates the Puritanical standard of moral strength and personal discipline.

Similarly, the use of any type of illicit drug—whether a narcotic, marijuana, a psychedelic drug, addictive or nonaddictive—produces a public response that almost certainly leads to further legislation and increased arrests. To a large extent, the criminalization of drug use is tied to the American tendency to fear that which may restrict processes of rational thought. To lose control over oneself is also to make oneself available to immoral pleasures.

The acts involved in crimes against public order are quite different from crimes committed against a person, such as murder, sexual assault, or the theft and vandalism of a person's property. In fact, many so-called public order crimes do not involve any real injury to another person or destruction of their property. Rather, they disturb the moral sense of some members of the community, as in the case of prostitution and gambling, or they may be judged to be injurious to the individual engaging in them, as in drunkenness, or the abuse of controlled substances. Since the participants in illegal gambling are willing associates, and the act of using controlled substances is—outside of addiction—voluntary, they are frequently called "victimless crimes."[3] The same might be said for acts of prostitution in which both parties are consensual partners who stand to gain something from the exchange.

All the forms of conduct mentioned above are subject to criminalization because they violate a sense of public morality. And yet the dilemma involved in the criminalization of such conduct is that the activities have not been diminished by the application of criminal sanction. Furthermore, the morality behind the laws has not been noticeably strengthened in the attempt to enforce the laws. Some of the laws have actually perpetuated the behaviors they have sought to control.

Prostitution

The history of prostitution in the Western world is characterized by a history of ambiguity. This remains true today. In the Middle Ages prostitution was widespread and regarded as a necessary evil; it was not usually considered a criminal act. The demand for prostitution from all segments of society was great; therefore, in Europe, it was often not simply tolerated but even protected and regulated by law and was a source of public revenue.

In some areas of Europe, the Catholic Church was involved in the maintenance of houses of prostitution, particularly in France. The Protestant Reformation, with its extreme concern for personal morals, initiated a reaction against extramarital relations of any type. At the same time, many were concerned about the increasing spread of sexually transmitted diseases such as syphilis, thought to have been brought from the New World, in which prostitutes were heavily involved. As a result, statutes enacted against prostitution in the fifteenth and sixteenth centuries were enforced to a considerable degree. In England, when prosecution passed from the ecclesiastical courts to the common law after 1640, prostitution was not regarded as a criminal offense but rather as a public nuisance.

From its beginnings in France and Germany, state regulation of prostitution spread across Europe, and in 1871 at the International Medical Congress in Vienna an international law was proposed to make regulation uniform throughout the world. The goal was social reform and improved health conditions. Prostitution itself was not questioned. In England, the Contagious Diseases Acts were implemented between 1864 and 1869.

Victorian social reformer Josephine Butler of Liverpool, England, radically changed how people thought about prostitution. Butler tried to end the human trafficking of young girls and women into prostitution on the Liverpool docks. She eventually built her campaign from a single-city movement to a national, and then international, crusade against state-controlled and state-protected prostitution.[4] In the US today, there are laws criminalizing prostitution, variously targeting pimps, customers, and prostitutes themselves. Most of this legislation draws a clear distinction between females under and over certain ages.

Prostitution takes a variety of forms including (1) the "call girl," (2) the "streetwalker," (3) the brothel prostitute, and (4) the massage parlor prostitute. In the 1970s, a social movement arose in the United States that challenged the traditional definitions of prostitution as a social problem, regarding it instead as the occupation of "sex work" and advocating its decriminalization. Centered around an organization called COYOTE (an acronym for "Call Off Your Old Tired Ethics"), the campaign seeks to sever prostitution from its historical association with sin, crime, and illicit sex, and "place the social problem of prostitution firmly in the discourse of work, choice, and civil rights."[5]

Drunkenness

Under English common law, intoxication itself was not a crime; it was tolerated, whether in a public place or not, unless it resulted in some breach of the peace or disorderly conduct charge. It was not until 1606 that intoxication in public first became a criminal offense. Intoxication in public remains a criminal offense in some states.

Laws against public drunkenness have their origin in religious values and attitudes (particularly Protestant) toward personal morality, that is, ideas about the individual's lack of moral control and his or her inability to carry out effectively the will of God in his or her work and family relationships. Another facet is the protection of citizens from bothersome disorderly public behavior. Laws against public intoxication reflect the power structure in that lower-class persons are most likely to be drunk in public places, having few resources to protect their private behavior from public view.

According to the FBI, more than 376,000 people were arrested in 2016 for public drunkenness alone, excluding drunken driving offenses and other alcohol-related crimes.[6] Many states do not have laws against public drunkenness. Those that do, consider it as a misdemeanor, usually punishable by a fine. Others use laws stating that drunkenness that causes a breach of the peace is punishable, while still others deal with drunkenness under a disorderly conduct provision. Laws provide maximum jail sentences ranging from 30 days to 180 days, and depending on the state, a fine of between $250 and $1,000. Operating a motor vehicle under the influence of alcohol or other drugs, is severely punished where not only may the offender be fined and imprisoned, but his or her driver's license will almost certainly be revoked for a year or even permanently (and this is generally with even the *slightest* amount of alcohol in the blood). In 2016, over 10,400 people in the United States were killed in alcohol-impaired vehicle crashes.[7]

Drug Use

Drug use in the United States and other countries is pervasive. This includes the use of substances that are "controlled" by the state, such as heroin, LSD, and Ecstasy, as well as opioids, also controlled, that are usually prescribed by a physician for pain relief, like Demerol, OxyContin, and Fentanyl. According to the National Institute on Drug Abuse, every day, more than 115 Americans die after overdosing on opioids, and the economic cost is $78.5 billion a year, including the costs of healthcare, lost productivity, addiction treatment, and criminal justice involvement.[8]

Substances that have not been criminalized by penal law are also extensively used. By far the greatest costs to a nation in economic and health terms accrue from the use of noncontrolled substances: nicotine in tobacco; caffeine in coffee and energy drinks; and alcohol in beer, wine, and liquor. Alcohol addiction is a drug problem that affects the largest number of people. *Drug abuse* is the willful misuse of either legal or illegal drugs for recreation or convenience. *Drug misuse* is the unintentional or inappropriate use of either prescribed or "over-the-counter" drugs. *Drug dependence* involves compulsive drug use and drug-seeking behaviors despite harmful consequences; it produces physical and psychological changes in the user.

The US government defines a controlled substance as any of the substances listed in the schedules of the Controlled Substances Act of 1970. The schedules are classified into five categories:

Schedule I—These substances have no currently accepted medical use and have a high potential for abuse. Examples include heroin, LSD, marijuana, and Ecstasy.

Schedule II—These narcotics and stimulants have a high potential for abuse and may lead to severe psychological or physical dependence. Examples include methadone, Demerol, OxyContin, Percocet, morphine, opium, codeine, amphetamine (Dexedrine, Adderall), and methamphetamine.

Schedule III—These drugs have a moderate to low potential for physical and psychological dependence. They include Vicodin, Codeine, and anabolic androgenic steroids.

Schedule IV—These substances have a low potential for abuse and low risk of dependence. They include Xanax, Soma, Darvon, Darvocet, Valium, Ativan, Versed, Restoril, and Ambien.

Schedule V—These consist primarily of preparations that contain limited quantities of narcotics, including cough syrups that contain codeine.

Although marijuana (or cannabis) is classified as a Schedule I drug, most states have legalized it to varying degrees for medical use. Further, despite the fact that marijuana remains illegal under federal law, several states have legalized it for recreational purposes. A number of states have also decriminalized the possession of small amounts of marijuana. Marijuana use is high among Americans. According to one poll, over half of American adults have tried marijuana at some point in their lives, 22 percent said they currently use marijuana, and 63 percent of those said they use it regularly.[9]

Ecstasy, also a Schedule I drug, is considered a "club drug" commonly taken by young people to enhance their emotional and physical experiences at nightclubs and dance parties. The intense rush from Ecstasy (or X), referred to as "blowing up" or "rolling," is described by two people as follows:

> When you're blowing up it is like your fucking skin is going to come undone. Just imagine an orgasm, but 20 or 50 times better and intense. That's the lure of X.
>
> I felt like I was coming undone from inside. You can feel every inch of your skin, even the tiny little hairs on your arms and legs . . . feels that good.[10]

Methamphetamine, classified as Schedule II, is a synthetic drug that is produced in clandestine laboratories by "cooks" who hold the highest position of privilege and prestige within the meth-producing group:

> If you are a cook, you are all set. I mean, like, you could have anything you wanted. You want other drugs? You got 'em. You want a stereo? You got it. It might be hot, but you got it. Everyone in every group I saw was, like, tuned-in to the cook. [What do you mean, "tuned-in"?] Well, like the cook is the top dog. Without the cook you'd have to buy meth on your own—or schmooze [persuade] it outa somebody else.[11]

Anabolic androgenic steroids (AAS), listed as Schedule III substances, have garnered attention due to their illicit use by athletes seeking a competitive advantage in various professional sports and in the Olympics. Known as "performance-enhancing" drugs, AAS use has spread to other groups like amateur weightlifters and to people wanting to "lose weight, lengthen life span, heal more quickly from injuries, or simply feel and look younger."[12] This demand has resulted in the rise of an illicit drug market that is largely internet-based.

During the eighteenth and nineteenth centuries in the US, the sale and use of uncontrolled patent medicines flourished. Morphine and heroin were widely used by middle- and upper-class women who took them in patent medicines for "female disorders." At that time, these and other drugs could be easily and legally purchased. Any legislation regarding these medicines was concerned solely with protecting the secret, patented ingredients, which ranged from alcohol, through opium, morphine and cocaine, to heroin.

Several sociohistorical forces gradually led to the dawning of a new consciousness in the country, to the effect that patent medicines were often ineffective, frequently harmful, and usually led to addictive dependence. A series of articles in *Collier's* magazine in 1905, under the title "The Great American Fraud," alerted the public to the abuse of patent medicines. These articles coined the term "dope fiend" from "dope," which was an African word meaning "intoxicating substance."[13] The American Medical Association quickly joined in the attack. Opium smoking was found among large segments of the so-called fringe society of Chinese immigrants, prostitutes, and drifters. Nevada became the first state, in 1877, to criminalize retail sales of smokable opium, the so-called Chinese scourge.

The first real milestone in federal regulations controlling the marketing of drugs was the Pure Food and Drug Act of 1906, concerned mainly with addiction to patent medicines. This was followed by the 1912 Sherley Amendment, which criminalized false or fraudulent claims on drug labels. However, the history of true drug abuse laws on the federal level began in 1914 with the Harrison Act, which made the sale of opiates and cocaine illegal without a doctor's prescription. There followed the Narcotic Drugs Import and Export Act of 1922, the Heroin Act of 1924, the Federal Narcotics Hospitals Act of 1928, the Marijuana Tax Act of 1937, the Opium Poppy Control Act of 1942, and the Narcotic Drug Control Act of 1956. The effect of these acts was to impose stiff penalties for the importation, sale, distribution, possession and/or use of what eventually came to be known as controlled substances.

The Comprehensive Drug Abuse Prevention and Control Act of 1970 established a series of education, research, and rehabilitation programs, and divided drugs into the five "schedules" according to their actual or relative potential for abuse. The War on Drugs, declared by President Richard M. Nixon, resulted in the repressive drug enforcement-oriented Anti-Drug Abuse Act of 1988 advocated by the George H.W. Bush Administration.

In considering the mandatory minimum penalties for cocaine offenses, the Act distinguished powder cocaine and crack cocaine and established significantly higher penalties for crack cocaine offenses.

Under the Act, a person convicted of possession with intent to distribute *5 grams* or more of crack cocaine was subject to a mandatory minimum sentence of 5 years in federal prison. By contrast, only if a person was convicted of possession with intent to distribute at least *500 grams* of powder cocaine were they subject to a 5-year mandatory minimum sentence. This meant that the penalty for the possession of crack cocaine was 100 times harsher than the penalty for possession of powder cocaine. A problem with distinguishing between crack and powder cocaine in this way is that crack cocaine tends to be used and sold largely by African Americans and powder cocaine largely by whites. The result of the crack/powder cocaine punishment differential was that blacks were sent to prison in unprecedented numbers and kept there longer than whites.[14] In *The New Jim Crow*, legal scholar Michelle Alexander demonstrates that, due to the War on Drugs the disproportionate imprisonment of African American men, even those convicted of minor drug offenses, has produced a "racial caste system" that denies them basic rights and opportunities that would allow them to become productive, law-abiding citizens.[15]

As for regulation on the state level, historically the states were the first to pass laws regulating the abuse or misuse of drugs. Federal legislation usually followed.

> Today, state law enforcement of drug statutes does not always reflect federal regulations, although, for the most part, the two statutory levels are harmonious. An example of where the two differ is marijuana, which has been approved for medicinal use [in many states] and more recently has been legalized by state referenda . . . Despite these state actions, marijuana is still considered a Schedule I substance by federal regulatory agencies.[16]

European countries take a different approach; most of them treat drug use not as a criminal matter, but as an issue to be handled in a way that minimizes adverse effects to both the individual and society. While each country in Europe has its own policy regarding illicit drug use, the Frankfurt Resolution of November 1990, which focuses on harm reduction rather than on criminality, has been influential. It states in part that combating drug addiction solely by criminal law has failed; that illegality is the main factor that contributes to the misery, death, and criminalization of addicts; that criminalization is not only a barrier to assistance and therapy but also forces the police and the courts to perform a task they cannot fulfill.

Sociology of Criminal Behavior

Many public order offenders do not regard their behavior as criminal *per se*, nor do they believe that criminal behavior is part of their life organization. The ambivalence of general social norms toward much of this behavior accounts, in part, for the fact that most offenders do not have a clearly defined criminal career. It is most important that we make the distinction between the status of *being* a certain kind of person and the acts of *doing* certain things.

Prostitution

The extent of prostitution and the reaction of society to it has fluctuated throughout history, but its definition has basically remained the same. Prostitution, a form of "sexual labor," is defined as sexual intercourse or the rendering of other "services," such as oral sex, usually with emotional detachment, on a promiscuous and mercenary basis. While both males and females may be prostitutes, the majority are females. Their number, however, is not known. There are several reasons why reliable statistics on the number of prostitutes are difficult to obtain including the fact that there is a high turnover rate of workers who are highly mobile.[17] What is more, many people engage in prostitution for a period and then return to legitimate lifestyles; some work full-time, others part-time.

Prostitution is legal and regulated in some countries in Latin America, Europe, in New Zealand, and in parts of Australia. Prostitution is legal but unregulated in several African countries as well as in the United Kingdom and India. Nevada is the only state in the US that since 1971 has allowed legal prostitution in the form of regulated brothels. The Swedish *Kvinnofrid* ("protection of women") Law of 1999, which criminalized the buying but not the selling of sexual services, has influenced legislation in several countries including Norway and Iceland. The Swedish government justifies the law in that,

> By prohibiting the purchase of sexual services, prostitution and its damaging effects can be counteracted more effectively than hitherto. . . . The government considers, however, that it is not reasonable to punish the person who sells a sexual service. In the majority of cases at least, this person is a weaker partner who is exploited by those who want only to satisfy their sexual drives.[18]

Mere sexual experiences do not make a person a prostitute, but the cash nexus does. Historically, persons who enter prostitution have lived in local communities, such as inner cities or well-delineated areas, where sexual promiscuity has been approved or at least condoned. For example, Amsterdam has one of the most famous red-light districts in the world, with brothels, sex shops, window prostitutes, peep shows, strip clubs, sex theaters, a Museum of Prostitution, and a Museum of Erotism. Other cities—including Bangkok, Brussels, Hamburg, The Hague, Singapore, and Tokyo—have similar areas that attract large numbers of tourists.

Although clients greatly outnumber prostitutes, it is the latter who are most often arrested. In the United States, the number of arrests for prostitution dropped steadily from a peak of 125,600 in 1983 to 56,600 in 2009. In 2016 over 38,000 arrests were made for prostitution.[19] The number of American men saying they have bought sex has remained stable at about 15–18 percent. But given the stigma of prostitution, the real figures are likely higher.[20]

Prior to entering into prostitution, most people have had personal contact with someone professionally involved in such activities: pimps, other prostitutes, or those seeking sexual activities in exchange for payment. One call girl tells of how she first made contact with people already involved in the sex industry:

> I worked at a nonprofit organization one summer in college and the vice president was someone who said, "Don't tell your parents, I'm a masseuse." And I was like, "I don't know what that is, and I don't know why I shouldn't tell them," but in retrospect [I understand what she was saying]—if you want to work full-time at some of the unpaid, important work, then [prostitution] is probably a really good job to have. And I didn't realize it at the time [I began working as a call girl], but I had already met people who were in the business so, upon reflection, when I finally figured out what it was they were talking about I [thought] "Oh, that's a really good role model."[21]

A prerequisite for most streetwalkers is to have a male sponsor who can protect them from other men, and to whom they must turn over their earnings. One streetwalker explains the necessity of a pimp:

You really can't walk the streets for yourself unless you got a man—not for a long length of time . . . 'cause the other pimps are not going to like it because you don't have anybody to represent you. They'll rob you, they'll hit you in the head if you don't have nobody to take up for you. Yeah, it happens. They give you a hassle . . . [The men] will say, "Hey baby, what's your name? Where your man at? You got a man?"[22]

A sort of "quasi-prostituting" experience may lead to prostitution as in the case of waitresses who accept money from customers in return for sexual intercourse. One woman explains how bartending led to her becoming a prostitute:

When I worked in bars, or waitressing, you'd get these comments [from customers, like], "Hey, baby, if you took off your bra you'd make better tips," and I was like, "Shut up, I'm a bartender." And finally, I thought, "Why don't I go somewhere else where I can take off my damn top and I will make better tips?" You're gonna have to deal with sexism anywhere you go. As a woman you're gonna have to put up with all this bullshit—you might as well be compensated for it. But. . . I think I get more respect for doing this [prostitution] from my clients than I did for other jobs.[23]

The mechanics of developing a career in prostitution involve a series of progressive stages: entrance into the career, apprenticeship under other prostitutes or pimps, and the cultivation and development of a stable clientele. Training and the establishment of contacts are essential in building a career in prostitution as is the learning of the requisite emotional distancing from clients. This is why a subculture must be entered into, one that provides the proper milieu for learning, practicing, and executing the behaviors necessary for success as a prostitute.[24] Less training, skill, and apprenticeship experience are required for the relatively simple role of a streetwalker, than for that of a call girl or elite prostitute. However, because different occupational hazards arise from selling sex for money, prostitutes of all types need to manage risk. Even call girls must take safety precautions and negotiate with their clients in ways that minimize their chances of being physically and emotionally harmed while at the same time maximizing profit. Because women are frequently alone with the client while performing the sexual service, this increases their vulnerability.[25]

It is difficult to generalize about the self-attitudes of prostitutes. Because the prostitute encounters a duality of social values, there is a tendency to justify or rationalize commercial sex behavior by emphasizing certain legitimate values of society, such as financial success or taking care of persons who are financially dependent on them. One study of sex workers in Mexico City found that they lead a double life that puts them in a constant double bind as mothers and prostitutes. These women justify their work at night as a better-paying employment opportunity for women, as a necessary evil, and as a type of social service, while at the same time they hide their profession from their families and create myths about their actual "jobs." They experience a type of "social schizophrenia" with their selves as divided between the mother/"saint" and the traitor/"prostitute" archetypes.[26]

The net negative experiences that prostitutes, especially streetwalkers, endure—"the accumulation of violent encounters, elevated levels of exhaustion, heightened stigma and broken relationships with family members, increased drug addiction as a way to cope with the difficulties of the work, and multiple arrests and jail sentences"[27]—compel many of them to leave the profession. There are several pathways out of prostitution.

Scholars who explain the process of desisting from the sex trade tend to employ a multi-stage model. For example, Baker, Dalla, and Williamson formulated an integrated six-stage model of exiting street-level prostitution that consists of: (1) *immersion*, wherein the woman is totally immersed in prostitution and has no thoughts of leaving or any conscious awareness of the need to change, (2) *awareness*, wherein the woman experiences uneasy feelings and thoughts about prostitution and then verbalizes them, (3) *deliberate planning*, wherein the woman begins assessing both formal and informal support resources, (4) *initial exit*, wherein the woman begins actively using informal (e.g., moving in with a family member) and formal (e.g., attending counseling, entering detox) support services, (5) *reentry*, wherein the woman transitions back into street-based prostitution and then recycles through the previous stages, (6) *final exit*, a difficult stage to define adequately.[28]

In addition, there are several non-governmental programs, "prostitute-serving organizations," (PSOs) that provide direct services to local prostitute populations with the intention of improving the quality of their lives.[29] One such PSO is New Friends New Life in the Dallas area that provides long-term support for trafficked teen girls and for women working as streetwalkers and escorts, in massage parlors, and strip clubs. Their mission statement says:

> New Friends New Life restores and empowers formerly trafficked teen girls and sexu-ally exploited women and their children. By providing access to education, job training, interim financial assistance, mental health and spiritual support, New Friends New Life helps women and their children overcome backgrounds of abuse, addiction, poverty and limited opportunities.[30]

Sometimes a person engaged in prostitution eventually marries a former customer, but this is rare. Some financially successful prostitutes—those who have been able to achieve and maintain a high standard of living—eventually establish their own business. These "madams" then employ others either in brothels or in escort agencies.

Previous arrest records, however, may make leaving the profession more difficult; and for those affected by HIV/AIDS or other sexually transmitted infections, alcoholism and drug addiction, the end is a derelict life, punctuated by arrests and jail sentences. From there it seems to be an easy step to petty stealing, street corner drug sales, and shoplifting. Because the illegality of prostitution forces prostitutes into a world of police, courts, and correctional institutions—thus keeping them from exiting sex work—law enforcement efforts generally fail to reduce prostitution. Contacts with legal authorities often become complicated by arrests for alcoholism, drugs, and petty theft, returning to the way of life the person likely left behind to enter into prostitution. The individual's position makes her vulnerable to blackmail by law enforcement and other political and legal forms of corruption. Often the person is forced by the police into the highly dangerous role of an informer on thefts and drug dealing.

Focusing only on women's involvement as prostitutes ignores both the economic transactions that make up the sex market and the interpersonal relationships between the male client and female prostitute. Though the male clients have not been studied as extensively as the sex work-ers, more data on their involvement are emerging. For example, in considering the "demand" side of prostitution, it is evident that male client participation is high based on the sex industry's economic profitability. One British study estimated that annual earnings in the escort and massage parlor markets in the UK (which are legal) were £534 million—this was on par with the amount that Briton's spent on going to the movies during the same year as the study.[31]

As for the attitudes and social characteristics of men who purchase sexual services, one study in Scotland found, among other things, that the age range for these men's first use of women in prostitution was 14 to 49 years of age, with 37 percent of them first buying sex between ages 18 and 20.

The men interviewed in the study most frequently bought sex indoors in a brothel or a private flat that functioned as a brothel (61 percent), a massage parlor (52 percent), a sauna (44 percent), or a lap dance club (31 percent). Other locations where men bought sex were bars (28 percent), private flats (19 percent), escort agencies (16 percent), and private clubs/hotels (9 percent).[32]

Concerning the issue of violence against prostitutes by male clients, the above-mentioned study found that the men who frequently used prostitutes were most likely to have committed sexually aggressive acts against nonprostituting women compared with the less frequent users. A Canadian study found that only a relatively small proportion of very violent men prey on the marginalized social and situational position of street prostitutes. In this survey of self-reported offenses, the researchers concluded tentatively that many sex buyers to not assault, rob, rape, or murder sex workers, and the majority of them claim not to verbally abuse them.[33] Yet, another study of information that was also obtained by self-report concluded that, compared to men who did not buy sex, sex buyers were more likely to report sexual aggression and likelihood to rape. It was revealed that men who patronized prostitutes scored higher on measures of impersonal sex and hostile masculinity; they had less empathy for prostitutes and tended to deny their humanity. When compared with non-sex-buyers, the study's findings indicated that men who buy sex share certain key characteristics with men at risk of committing sexual aggression.[34]

Drunkenness

Alcohol, a chemical substance, has been produced throughout the world for centuries, either through a process of fermentation or distillation, in the form of distilled spirits such as whiskey or gin, or in the form of fermented beverages such as wine or beer. As alcohol is consumed, it increasingly acts as a depressant and an anesthetic; it is not a stimulant as is commonly believed. Under the influence of alcohol, a person may become aggressive, silent, or even fall into a stupor as a result of the reduction of cortical control rather than as a result of stimulation. With increasing intoxication, there is a dulling of sensory and motor functions and the impairment of thinking, reasoning, and muscle coordination.

Alcoholism is a disease, not a crime, but public drunkenness and driving under the influence (DUI) are crimes. Extreme use of alcohol sets the stage for arrest for public drunkenness and drunk driving. Alcohol has both short-term and long-term effects. Among the former are disinhibition, or the loss of conditioned reflexes due to depression of inhibitory centers of the brain, and the "hangover," the morning-after effect of fatigue, nausea, upset stomach, headache, and ill temper. Among the long-term effects are hallucinations, tremors, muscle (heart) disease, and cirrhosis of the liver, which often leads to death.

There is considerable evidence that a large proportion of those arrested for drunkenness are alcoholics with a long history of prior drunkenness arrests. Recidivism runs very high among this group of offenders; becoming the virtual "career alcoholic," some individuals are arrested for drunkenness up to 20 times a year. In 2016, at a national level, of all the arrests for alcohol-related offenses, 1,017,808 were for driving under the influence, 234,899 were for liquor law violations, 376,433 were for drunkenness, and 369,733 were for disorderly conduct.[35] The majority of these arrests, particularly of those arrested for driving under the influence, were repeat offenders.

Statistics concerning alcohol and violent crimes reveal the following patterns: alcohol is a factor in between 19 percent and 37 percent of violent crimes; alcohol-related crime is more likely to result in injury and to take place in the evening hours and on weekends; a large proportion of alcohol-related violence occurs in and around residences; alcohol-related violence is more likely to involve intimates than other types of violence.[36]

Several studies have been conducted on the aggression and violence that people expect to experience as a result of drinking. For example, one study focusing on the motivation of some offenders for using alcohol before offending found that drinking may be a means for carrying out violent acts. This was particularly the case with heavy drinkers who had high alcohol-aggression expectancies.[37] A similar study looking at alcohol-aggression proneness also found that some offenders may drink heavily before violent offending either to give them courage or to excuse their behavior.[38]

Yet another study, this one looking at ecological factors, found that neighborhoods in Baton Rouge, Louisiana with a large number of taverns and bars seemed to have little impact on arrest rates for robbery and aggravated assault. By contrast, those neighborhoods with a large number of package-only outlets (liquor stores, 24-hour convenience stores, etc.) did have high arrest rates for these violent crimes. Relying on a routine activities argument, the researchers speculate that three conditions in the neighborhoods with a high density of package-only stores explained the high rates of robbery and assault. First, because customers go to package-only stores with the intention of making a purchase, and thus have money on them, they become *suitable targets* of violent crime. Second, because customers often frequent liquor stores alone and at odd hours, there is, in those circumstances, the *absence of guardianship* that can prevent their victimization. Third, package-only outlets tend to attract people who are uninhibited by the effects of alcohol consumption and are thus likely to be *motivated offenders*.[39]

The effects of driving while drunk include impaired perception, difficulty steering, and reduced ability to maintain lane position and brake appropriately. Drunk driving is the most common form of "violent crime." Approximately one-third of all traffic crash fatalities in the United States involve drunk drivers accounting for over 10,000 deaths per year, and around $44 billion in damages.[40]

Tough enforcement of drunk-driving laws has been a major factor in reducing drunk-driving deaths since the 1980s. Charges range from misdemeanors to felony offenses, and penalties for impaired driving can include fines, jail time, community service, vehicle impoundment, and alcohol education and treatment. Most states have administrative license revocation laws that suspend a driver's license prior to conviction for DUI. Some states require drunk-driving offenders to install, at their own expense, an ignition interlock device, which is a breath test device connected to a vehicle's ignition. The vehicle will not start unless the driver blows into the interlock and has a blood alcohol concentration (BAC) that is usually below 0.02 grams of alcohol per deciliter of blood. Many states use sobriety checkpoints that allow law enforcement officers to identify and assess drivers for the possibility of alcohol impairment.

Public opinion has shown strong support for most measures that target drinking and driving. The most support for alcohol control policies has been for mass media campaigns that warn of the dangers of drunk driving. Public awareness campaigns such as "Drive Sober or Get Pulled Over," and "Buzzed Driving is Drunk Driving" basically attempt to persuade individuals to either take personal steps to avoid drinking and driving or try to prevent others from drinking and driving. One study found that the median decrease in alcohol-related car crashes resulting from such campaigns was 13 percent.[41]

Religious values play a complex role in alcohol use. Drunkenness is seen as a lack of moral strength, willpower, and devotion to the goals of personal discipline and work. Religious communities differ in their attitudes and teachings with regard to the use of alcohol. Islam and the more "fundamentalist" Christian denominations take an abstemious approach to alcohol consumption. The more "mainstream" religions permit the use of alcohol, sometimes even in their liturgy. Whatever their religion, Americans in general take a moral view of drunkenness. For example, 61 percent think drinking alcohol excessively is morally wrong. On a list of 10 behaviors, having "one too many" drew the third most disapproval, behind having an affair and not reporting income taxes. More people said excessive drinking was morally wrong than said the same for having an abortion, and twice as many condemned drinking as did overeating.[42]

Societal reaction to drunkenness may be expressed through the spouse, employer, work associates, parents, friends, neighbors, or church members. Societal reaction to drunkenness is also dependent on structural inequalities that are based on race and gender. For example, in a US study in which female and male, black and white college undergraduates were interviewed, three general findings were revealed. First, women who appeared to drink "excessively" were stigmatized as having lost their feminine identity. This sentiment is articulated by a black male student as follows:

> For me (a woman who is) drunk is a very total turn off. They (women) are sloppy obnoxious and it is a turn off. I think that if a female is tanked, I don't think that she is at all attractive. I'm not being like sexist but there is something about a woman chugging back a beer that looks so masculine, you know what I mean?[43]

Second, women who appeared to be intoxicated risked being subject to both violent and sexual victimization. As one white female student explained:

> That is a reason why I don't drink too much. I'm afraid of going to bars and having something put into my drink. Or you know, if I, see, one time I was really drunk and the thought occurred "what if I passed out what would happen?" I have heard lots of stories and I don't want to become one of the statistics.[44]

Finally, African American men who used alcohol were more likely than their white counterparts to have their behavior controlled formally, usually by the police. A black female student observed:

> I have never seen a whole bunch of Black guys walking on campus and I think that the police have something to do with it. Even if they weren't drunk, you see five Black guys and you think something is up; but if they were drunk that would worsen the scenario for them. I think for their safety they don't do that.[45]

Repeated arrests and incarcerations for drunkenness may serve to reinforce the deviance rather than correct it. Finally, excessive drinking and alcoholism may be perceived by others as an extreme deviation. Excessive drinkers may eventually come to think of themselves as problems, and even as alcoholics, but not as criminals even though their drinking may result in frequent arrests. They may come to refer to themselves as "drunks" and "drunken bums" but not as criminals; increasingly, the more persistent excessive drinkers come to conceive of themselves as alcoholics or persons with an illness requiring medical intervention, clinical treatment, and rehabilitation, or a 12-step program like Alcoholics Anonymous.

Drug Use

Drug addiction is learned just as any other behavior is learned, primarily from association with other addicts or through knowledge of its use. An addict must learn the techniques of drug use, how to acquire the drug, and how to recognize and appreciate its effects. The reasons and motivations for the initial use of an opiate may be quite different from the motivation to continue to use it. In the case of the opioid analgesics like oxycodone, codeine, and meperidine, people may use them for pain relief under medical supervision or abuse them for recreation purposes without a prescription.

A study intended to determine adolescents' motivations for engaging in the illicit (nonmedical) use of prescription opioid pain medications found that, in the case of sleeping pills, 75 percent of the teens used them only for help sleeping. However, in the case of pain medications, 69 percent used them for pain control and 11 percent used them to get high. Twenty-one percent of those who used stimulants did so to get high, to concentrate, and to increase alertness. The most frequently cited reasons for using sedatives were to help with sleep, to decrease anxiety, and to get high.[46]

According to the Substance Abuse and Mental Health Services Administration misuse of prescription psychotherapeutic drugs is second only to marijuana as the most prevalent illicit drug use issue in the US. In 2015, it was estimated that 44.5 percent of the US population aged 12 or older *used* prescription psychotherapeutic drugs. About 36 percent used pain relievers, 14.7 percent used tranquilizers, 6.4 percent used stimulants, and 6.9 percent used sedatives. In 2015, 7.1 percent of people aged 12 or older *misused* prescription psychotherapeutic drugs in the past year. This included 4.7 percent who misused pain relievers, 2.3 percent who misused tranquilizers, 2 percent who misused stimulants, and 0.6 percent who misused sedatives. However, most people (84.1 percent) who used prescription drugs in the past year did not misuse them.[47]

Drug use and misuse are one thing; dependence is another. Drug dependence, as a generic term, is defined as "a state that produces psychophysiological changes in the user and is characterized by compulsive drug use and drug-seeking behaviors despite harmful consequences."[48] Under closer inspection, the term has a variety of meanings. It is often employed to refer to addiction, whether physiological or psychological, or it may be utilized synonymously with the term *drug abuse*. The traditional addictive drugs are the opiate narcotics: opium, morphine, codeine, and heroin. Many people consume these drugs over extended periods of time and do not become addicted; others become addicted in a very brief time. Addiction to the narcotics class of drugs is a product of the physical qualities of the drugs and the recognition of the association of the drug with the distress that accompanies sudden cessation of its use.

The elements of drug dependence or addiction generally follow a pattern. If the initial drug experience is unrewarding or aversive, there normally is no further use. A rewarding experience, on the other hand, leads to many trials and consequent positive reinforcement, resulting in primary psychological dependence. Next comes intermittent and chronic abuse of the potent psychoactive drugs: the stimulants—cocaine and its derivative crack, and amphetamines; the hallucinogens—LSD, marijuana, or mescaline; the depressants—alcohol, barbiturates, or the opium derivatives, heroin and morphine. Withdrawal from drug dependence can be physical and psychological agony for the addict. In his ethnography of homeless heroin users, Philippe Bourgois describes an addict's withdrawal of "dopesickness":

> Felix tried to urinate into the plastic water bottle that he kept next to his blankets, but his body was shaking too hard. He stood up, but his leg muscles spasmed and he fell down the highway embankment. He had to drag himself on his hands and knees to get back up to his mattress, pausing twice to retch. . . . "First I'm cold; then poof! Heat flashes, and I'm ripping the covers off. But it's cold out here, so I get like freezing, 'cause I'm covered with wet sweat. I try to spit, and all this green stuff comes out. Then I'm just squirtin' out my guts. My heart feels like it's going to stop. I can't pick up my bones. My knees hurt; my legs are locked; I can't breathe; I can't even think; I feel every nerve in my fingertips, every single one. I can't stand still. I can't lie down."[49]

In becoming an addict, the individual changes his or her conception of self and of the behavior he or she must engage in as a "drug addict." The more the individual associates with other drug addicts and the drug subculture, the more he or she withdraws from prior social and family relationships. Moreover, the more the person finds that it is impossible to achieve freedom from drug dependence, the more he or she comes to adopt the self-concept and play the social role of an addict.[50] One study found that the drug-using role was salient with three types of heroin addicts. *The using dealer/runner* had no other social role than a drug user. However, these addicts maintained enough control over their drug use to be able to supply themselves with heroin or money for heroin. Like the using dealer/runner, *the using sex worker* had no other social role; however, they had some control over their drug use, at least during those times when they needed to complete the sex service. The street *junkie*, for whom life revolved around drug use, occupied the lowest status level; they had no other social role than drug user and had no control over drug use. "Lack of any social routines or activities other than drug use is the most evident characteristic of the junkie."[51]

Endeavoring to answer the general question, "Why do people use heroin and other drugs?" sociologist Richard C. Stephens developed a "general role theoretic explanation of heroin use" composed of five propositions:

> (1) There is a subculture of street addicts; (2) Within this subculture, a master role exists, the components of which are organized about the expected use of heroin; (3) This master role is highly valued by members of the subculture, and the more one's behavior approximates the role, the higher one's status is in the subculture; (4) The street addict role provides meaningful social and personal rewards to those who play it; (5) Several secondary roles (dealer, tout, steerer, etc.) function to maintain the subculture, especially the status of the master role.[52]

Stephens claims that street addicts hooked on heroin are rational in that most of them have chosen to take on the role appropriate to their way of life. These addicts are products of environments where there are few opportunities to be successful in the outside world. People living in such neighborhoods see heroin use as an expressive lifestyle that gives dignity, a sense of belonging, and success to the alienated and disenfranchised. Stephens contends that the street addict role consists of a "cool cat syndrome" characterized by a favorable attitude toward conning or trickery and an antisocial attitude toward conventional society. The "cool cat" shows little concern or guilt for his or her actions. Instead, he or she values signs of material success, such as possessing heroin and other drugs. He or she admires and practices an ability to communicate easily in street language and to experience its excitement. The role eschews long-range planning, condemns snitching and minimizes the use of violence. Since the role is influenced by street culture, the heroin addict places a high premium on an ability to con or trick others into providing drugs, cash, food, or lodging. Finally, the street addict role involves feelings of persecution in a world largely inhabited by persons who cannot be trusted. Stephens's role theoretic explanation contradicts the common belief that heroin addiction is rooted in physiological or genetic factors, or in personality adjustment problems.

Addicts may engage in serious larceny, burglary, petty theft, or prostitution to support their habit. Even when crime is associated with securing funds to maintain the drug habit, it does not become an end in itself. Those addicts, juvenile or adult, who engage in other crimes do so chiefly to obtain the means with which to purchase illicit drugs. There is little evidence to indicate that crimes of violence are associated with obtaining drugs. There is, however, some confirmation of the "crimes cause drugs" hypothesis; in other words, that increased criminal income enhances drug availability which then facilitates drug consumption. As one hard-core heroin addict remarked, "The better I got at crime, the more money I made; the more money I made, the more drugs I used." She went on to explain:

> I think that most people that get high, the reason it goes to the extent that it goes—that it becomes such a high degree of money—is because they make the money like that. I'm saying if the money wasn't available to them like that, they wouldn't be into drugs as deep as they were.[53]

This is in contrast to violent crimes committed while under the influence of one or more substances. Violence is rampant, however, among competing groups of illegal drug sellers, street gangs, and drug cartels.

Heroin and crack addicts from the lower classes live in inner-city neighborhoods where most drugs are generally acceptable and easily obtainable, and where drug dealing is pervasive. In the book, *In Search of Respect: Selling Crack in El Barrio*, Philippe Bourgois details how difficult it was for some of the Puerto Rican residents of Spanish Harlem to completely leave the drug trade:

> Their poverty remains their only constant as they alternate between street-level crack dealing and just-above-minimum-wage legal employment. The working-class jobs they manage to find are objectively recognized to be among the least desirable in U.S. society. . . . [Most of the dealers] were usually fired from these jobs, but they treated their return to the world of street dealing as a triumph of free will and resistance on their part. A straightforward refusal to be exploited in the legal labor market pushes them into the crack economy and into substance abuse.[54]

This situation differs considerably from the community that Patricia A. Adler studied during the late 1970s of predominantly white, middle-class residents involved in the upper-level drug dealing and smuggling of marijuana and cocaine. One dealer in this Southern California community recounts how he became involved with the drug world clique:

> I used to be in real estate making good money. Through my property management and investment services, I started meeting some rich people. I was the only person at my firm renting to longhairs and dealing with their money. They all paid me in cash from a giant wad of bills. They never asked for a receipt and always had cash, 24 hours a day. I slowly started getting friendly with them, although I didn't realize how heavy they were. I knew ways of buying real estate and putting it under fictitious names, laundering money so that it went in as hot cash and came out as spendable income. I invested their money in gems, metals, cars. But the whole time I never asked any questions. I just took my commission and was happy. Then one guy asked me to clear some checks for him through my bank account—said he was hiding the money from his ex-wife and the Treasury people. This was the beginning. I slowly got more and more involved with him until I was neglecting my real estate business and just partying with him all the time. My spending went up, but my income went down, and suddenly I had to look around for another way to make money fast. I took the money I was cashing for him, bought some [marijuana] bricks from another dealer friend of his and sold them out of state before I gave him back the cash. Eventually I started to deal with him too, on a front basis. Within six months I was turning 100 [one-kilo] bricks at a time.[55]

This drug scenario also differs from the use and production of methamphetamine, which is especially prevalent among white rural populations in the United States. One study conducted in three rural areas—the Arkansas-Mississippi Delta, western Kentucky, and western Ohio—found that meth users were almost exclusively white—about 99 percent of them.[56]

As for college undergraduates, heavy alcohol consumption has been a normative practice for many generations, particularly among first-year students, fraternity members, and athletes. More recently, the consumption of flavored alcoholic beverages and alcohol mixed with energy drinks has become common on college campuses. While marijuana use among this group is relatively infrequent and only somewhat prevalent, other drugs have gained popularity. For example, according to a national survey, illicit use of prescription stimulants (Ritalin, Dexedrine, Adderall) was more prevalent among college students who were male, white, members of fraternities, and earned lower grade point averages. Rates were higher at colleges located in the northeastern region of the US and colleges with more competitive admission standards. Nonmedical prescription stimulant users were more likely to report use of alcohol, cigarettes, marijuana, Ecstasy, cocaine, and other risky behaviors.[57]

Once addicted to a drug like heroin or cocaine, an individual must depend upon a continuous supply; this demand usually becomes the most important single aspect of the person's daily life. These addicts originally took the drug for pleasure or an effect, and many started using heroin as a less expensive opioid substitute after their prescription painkillers (such as OxyContin) became too costly. However, as tolerance increases and larger and more frequent dosages are needed, the cost may be as high as $100 or $200 a day to support the addiction. Such a daily expenditure involves finances that are greater than most addicts earn or have legitimate access to, which forces them to engage in theft or other crimes simply to maintain an adequate supply. Many such addicts begin street corner dealing to support their habits, thus "hooking" still others so that the cycle grows exponentially.

In the case of the street corner dealer and other low-echelon suppliers, it is common for them to "cut" the drug, that is, to add adulterants or diluents before selling it down to the next in line. Some dealers dilute the drug with sugars, starch, and talc to increase volume and maximize profits. Others add adulterants either to give the impression of a better-quality drug or to mask a poor-quality product. Thus, heroin dealers frequently add Fentanyl, a painkiller that is 25 to 50 times more powerful than heroin, to enhance the high. A serious problem arises when street buyers assume the drug is diluted and adjust their dose accordingly. Sometimes, however, it has not been diluted but adulterated, and the user overdoses.

According to the Centers for Disease Control and Prevention, between 2010 and 2015, drug overdose deaths increased from 38,329 to 52,404. The largest increase in deaths was for heroin overdose that rose from 8 percent to 25 percent during that 5-year period.[58] Also, from July 2016 through September 2017, there was a rise in opioid overdoses so that emergency department visits increased by 30 percent in all parts of the US; opioid overdoses went up 30 percent in 52 areas in 45 states, the Midwestern region had a 70 percent rise of such overdoses, and in large cities they increased by 54 percent in 16 states. What is more, every demographic group saw a substantial increase in opioid overdose rates, including men (30 percent), women (24 percent), people ages 25 to 34 (31 percent), 35 to 54 (36 percent), and 55 or older (32 percent).[59]

A person smoking marijuana for recreation must conceive of the drug as producing pleasurable sensations. For most people, the first use of cannabis is unrewarding; it is a *learned* high.[60] The individual must learn (1) to smoke the drug in a way that will produce certain effects, (2) to recognize the effects and associate the drug with these effects, and (3) to enjoy the felt sensations. When people first smoke marijuana, they do not ordinarily get high. This may be because they do not know the proper technique of drawing on the joint and holding the smoke in the lungs. Even after learning the technique they do not always form an immediate conception of smoking as being related to enjoyment. Even though there are pleasurable sensations, the first-time cannabis smoker may not be sufficiently aware of their specific nature to become a regular user. People learn to experience being high as defined by others. With more frequent use, they begin to appreciate the drug's effects. Finally, a further step is necessary to continue the use of marijuana. The person must learn to enjoy the sensations being experienced. Feeling dizzy, being thirsty, misjudging distances, having a sudden desire for food, or finding ordinary objects and conversations very amusing may not of *themselves* be pleasurable experiences. The person must learn to define these sensations in this way. Associations with other cannabis users help to turn sensations that may have been initially frightening into something pleasurable and to be looked forward to. These learned techniques also largely apply to the "vaping" and "dabbing" (inhaling and exhaling of vapor) of marijuana from a vaporizer, vape pen, or e-cigarette. There are, however, more straightforward ways of consuming the drug that include eating, drinking, sipping, sucking on lozenges, chewing on gum, applying unguents, and administering a cannabis-infused tincture under the tongue.

The Substance Abuse and Mental Health Services Administration's *National Survey on Drug Use and Health* released several findings about marijuana use for 2013 (before most states legalized its recreational use). That year, marijuana was the most commonly used illicit drug. There were almost 20 million past month users, and marijuana was used by over 80 percent of current illicit drug users. Over 8 million people used marijuana daily or almost daily. The rate of use among youths aged 12 to 17 was 7 percent. It was the most commonly used illicit drug by underage drinkers in combination with alcohol. Over 70 percent of drug initiates reported that marijuana was their first drug. About half (48.6 percent) of youths aged 12 to 17 reported that it would be "fairly easy" or "very easy" for them to obtain marijuana if they wanted some.[61]

Most drug users, whether of hard drugs or marijuana, do not think of themselves as criminals, for they deny the validity of drug laws and consider as wrong the punishment of what should be a matter of individual choice. Widespread support for their views is found among fellow users of the drug and even among segments of the population of nonusers, particularly in the case of marijuana and opioids. Persons who use narcotics seldom think of themselves as real criminals because they tend to regard themselves as being in a unique situation when under the influence of a drug. They feel it is because of necessity that they violate the law by using the controlled substances or committing offenses to support their habit. Some indication that drug dependence need not be associated with self-regarding criminal attitudes is the fact that throughout the United States there is a high incidence of addiction to opioids among "respectable," white, middle-class individuals who first started taking them as prescription pain relievers.

Public order offenses such as prostitution and drug use grow out of and are deeply immersed in clearly defined deviant subcultures. Others, such as drunkenness, have group support in the drinking patterns of certain social classes and ethnic groups and in the general norms of society that support the drinking of alcoholic beverages.

Prostitution

Prostitutes can generally be classified according to their methods of operation. Call girls and escorts command high fees for their sexual services, which means that they tend to have affluent clients. Many of them work at their home or come to the client's house, or more likely hotel room. The call girl often depends on some organization for recruiting her clients, although she may operate independently; the more experienced call girls have an established base of clientele who call on them directly. More frequently, clients are secured through fliers, ads in sex tabloids, or the internet. Escorts usually work for agencies. These agencies

> range from a single booker operating with a cellphone to an established office where escorts wait during their shift to be sent to clients. Some agencies even offer temporary housing to escorts and become informal social spaces for escorts to network, discuss clients, and give and receive social support.[62]

One woman described the pros and cons of working for an agency:

> I still work for an agency just to supplement, because they have more volume of calls and they're a little more consistent. Of course, I get paid less, but it's good to have that fall-back in case I don't have a call for two weeks. I still do that sometimes . . . usually they take a 50/50 split. . . . Sometimes they try to make you work when you don't want to work . . . You don't know who you're going to. They tell you his name, they tell you all the information, but ultimately you don't get to speak to the client before you get to them. So, you don't know what they're like. They could be someone who you normally would not have made an appointment with. I've had few bad situations with that. . . . So, I have that on the downside. You have to sort of trust the person on the phone too, so I only work with certain phone girls [booking agents].[63]

Street-level prostitutes drift into sex work for several reasons including poor interactions with conventional society, a stressful home life, a desire for new experiences, and financial gain. Streetwalkers are the most likely of prostitutes to be arrested, to be victims of violence, and to be at higher risk of contracting sexually transmitted diseases such as HIV. Many streetwalkers suffer beatings and sexual assaults at the hands of their patrons, partners, and pimps. It is common for street prostitutes to get high on drugs, crack cocaine specifically, as a coping strategy to engage in sex work; after a period of time, they become addicted. This puts them in a vicious cycle of using drugs to perform sex work and performing sex work to obtain the money to purchase drugs.

Unlike street prostitutes who are frequently subjected to physical harms, prostitutes who work in brothels, especially in brothels that are legally-regulated like those in Nevada, have a reduced risk of particular forms of violence and sexually transmitted diseases. "A safe, conflict-free transaction that protects the laborers as well as the customers is built into the operating structure of brothels as a means to sustain the economic and social viability of the legalized prostitution industry."[64] Finally, prostitutes who work in saunas and erotic (illicit) massage parlors, ostensibly offering relaxation and physical therapy, tend to be mostly immigrant women from Asia seeking a better life in the US. Massage parlors, which are usually operated in houses or storefronts, are subject to undercover stings by the police and are frequently raided. The sex workers and owners are usually charged with prostitution, promoting prostitution, and performing massage therapy without a license.

In each of these cases there is an elaborate network of support systems to teach, foster, and nourish the proper values, attitudes, and techniques. These provide a steady supply of customers and collect and equitably distribute the fees. In many cases, there is also the need for go-betweens to pay off local law enforcement officials.

In the early twentieth century, prostitution was mainly conducted in organized establishments variously called bordellos, whorehouses, cathouses, and houses of ill repute. Since prostitution is a business wherein money is made illegally and its sex workers and operators are not likely to go to the police for aid and assistance, these houses were vulnerable targets for extortion by organized crime bosses. Crime syndicates, like the Mafia, controlled most of the brothel trade at that time, moving the prostitutes from house to house and city to city as the market dictated. The term "white slave trade" came to be used to designate this practice. In the 1960s, this organizational form was largely replaced by call girls and streetwalkers. Because these forms of the trade are decentralized, organized crime found extortion costly and ceased to view prostitution as a major income-generating business.

Prostitution has a continual turnover of workers as prostitutes grow old, contract diseases, drop out of "the game," or move to new locations. As a result, sex workers are constantly being recruited. New personnel in brothels and escort agencies are introduced to the rules and regulations, and each new worker learns various sex techniques during what amounts to a probationary period. She learns how to handle large numbers of customers without running the risk of losing them as patrons, how to deal with different types of customers, and above all, how to protect herself against HIV/AIDS and other sexually transmitted infections. Escort agencies advertise in magazines and newspapers, and on their own websites, thus giving the business an air of legitimacy. Massage parlors advertise in internet classified ad listing services such as Backpage and Craigslist. Even streetwalkers advertise on social network sites like Twitter. Some prostitution is not strictly organized but is tolerated and may even be encouraged through legitimate, but often disreputable, businesses such as bars, gentlemen's clubs, strip clubs, and night clubs. Prostitutes are often introduced to the profession by someone closely associated with it. Usually coming from lower-class backgrounds, they seldom develop a high degree of organization within their occupational group. Its very nature is competitive, each prostitute attempting to build and maintain her own clientele; hence, the personal group solidarity that may exist is mainly for protection from the police and abusive clients.

Drunkenness

There is evidence that excessive drinking and alcoholism are associated with a culture where there is conflict over its use, where children are not introduced to it early in life, and where drinking is largely done outside meals for personal reasons and not as part of a ritual, ceremony, or family celebration. The general pattern of drinking in the United States seems to support this relationship given that over one-quarter of American adults report that they engage in binge drinking as do 38 percent of college students. Indeed, approximately 20 percent of college students meet the criteria for Alcohol Use Disorder, which is a chronic relapsing brain disease characterized by an impaired ability to stop or control alcohol use despite adverse social, occupational, or health consequences.[65]

Social drinking is common in most Western countries, including the United States. The excessive use of alcohol leading to arrests for drunkenness and for driving under the influence appears to be learned from others, group associations and cultural factors playing an important role. Differences exist not only in the drinking customs of societies but in those of subgroups within a society. People learn to drink excessively because of the type of drinking behavior of their companions, social class, occupation, or ethnic identity. Group associations determine the individual's attitude toward excessive drinking, the kind of beverage and the amount consumed, the time of drinking, the location at which drinking occurs, and the individual's behavior during and after excessive drinking. Of adolescents and young adults surveyed, for example, nearly all drank in the company of others rather than alone: 10 percent usually drank with a family member or other adult, and 73 percent usually drank with a friend. As for drinking location and behavior, those who usually drank in public locations were significantly more likely to experience physical altercations after drinking than those who usually drank in private homes.[66]

An individual's drinking norms and patterns appear to conform closely to those of family, friends, and intimate partners. There is a strong association between alcohol consumption and intimate partner violence.[67] Children whose parents define adolescent alcohol use as unacceptable have relatively more conservative alcohol-use norms for themselves.[68] Customs and attitudes toward drinking vary by socioeconomic status; lower SES groups drink larger quantities while higher SES groups drink more frequently.[69] Work environment plays a role on workplace drinking norms and employee drinking patterns. One study found that the type of organizational culture in industrial plants influences norms regarding drinking before or during work shifts and higher workplace drinking rates.[70] Heavy and problem drinking is found among certain types of workers including managerial and professional workers, lumber workers, bus and railway drivers, physicians, teenage fast-food workers, military personnel, and assembly workers.[71]

Likewise, around the world, men drink more often and more heavily than women.[72] In regard to religion in the US, those who are Mormon, Church of God, Muslim, and Assembly of God have the highest rates of abstention; Jews, Lutherans, and Presbyterians are most likely to engage in moderate drinking; Catholics make up the highest percentage of heavy drinkers.[73] American whites are more likely to drink than blacks, but blacks have the highest volume of intake and frequency of heavy drinking. American whites of Southern and Eastern European origin drink more moderately than those of Northern or Central European origin. Hispanics and Native Americans are less likely to drink but consume more alcohol when they do drink.[74]

The role of group factors in creating and perpetuating public intoxication is seen, for example, at tailgating parties, which usually occur in the parking lots of stadiums before and sometimes after sporting events. Consuming alcohol has become part of sports-fan culture and is seen as complementary to "enjoying the game." Alcohol is available to fans through in-stadium sales, allowing them to bring in alcohol, and tailgating parties. Sometimes violent behavior erupts because of public drunkenness at college football games. It is known that college football fans drink significantly more on game day than they do during other parties and social activities.[75] One study of college students found that those who participated in tailgating and pregaming (drinking before a social event) drank alcohol more frequently, engaged in heavy drinking more frequently, and engaged in binge drinking more than those who did not participate in these activities.[76] Another study found that there were higher arrest rates during football game days than there were during traditional "drinking holidays" (New Year's Eve, St. Patrick's Day, Memorial Day, the 4th of July, Labor Day, and the night before Thanksgiving). Arrests during game days included alcohol possession by a minor, driving under the influence, open container violation, alcohol possession at the stadium, and nonviolent resisting of arrest.[77] Alcohol consumption and aggression are not limited to American football fans. A Welsh study of male rugby fans found that their aggression increased when their team won or drew a tie, but not when their team lost. Moreover, aggression, not celebration, drove these fan's post-game alcohol consumption.[78] The fact is that most people consume alcohol, and consume vast quantities of it, almost exclusively in social contexts and in groups.

Drug Use

When we consider the nature and degree of group support for the use of illicit drugs such as marijuana and cocaine, we find that it is powerful and resistant to change from the outside. Indeed, research has consistently demonstrated a relationship between peoples' drug use and the drug use of members in their social network. Perhaps no other form of criminal behavior has the same intense degree of group support. This generalization is true not only of the marginalized segments of US society but of the upper classes as well. In fact, this is one of the most frequently advanced arguments for the decriminalization and legalization of drugs like cannabis. Laws making the use of certain drugs a crime make it more difficult to obtain those drugs, thus throwing those who use them into a highly bonding mutual dependency in order to obtain them. As anthropologist Merrill Singer has noted:

> In response to laws banning the use of some drugs, and of their evermore stringent police enforcement, there emerged an underground drug subculture that functioned to enable addicts to gain access to drugs and drug use equipment (e.g., syringes, crack pipes) and to avoid arrest. It also created mechanisms to recruit and socialize new drug users.[79]

The use of drugs is learned primarily from association with others who also use them. Most persons are initiated into the use of controlled substances by friends, siblings, significant adult role models, and intimate partners. In these close relationships, people not only learn how to use drugs and appreciate them; they also learn a set of positive beliefs about the benefits of drugs that others help to reinforce constantly. Perhaps most important, they learn how to *obtain* the controlled substances—at the lowest risk. What sociologist Erich Goode reported in the late 1960s regarding the use of marijuana as a group activity lending itself to friendships and participation in a group setting, remains true today:

> (1) It is characteristically participated in a group setting; (2) the others with whom one smokes marijuana are usually intimates, intimates of intimates, or potential intimates, rather than strangers; (3) one generally has long-term continuing social relations with the others; (4) a certain degree of value consensus will obtain within the group; (5) a value convergence will occur as a result of progressive group involvement; (6) the activity maintains the circle's cohesion, reaffirms its social bonds by acting them out; (7) participants view the activity as a legitimate basis for identity—they define themselves, as well as others, partly on the basis of whether they have participated in the activity or not.[80]

Belongingness—or the degree to which one identifies with particular persons or groups—is influential in the initiation of drug use. Four elements found in drug subcultures give users a strong sense of belongingness. First, as people form stronger ties with other users in the drug subculture, they become increasingly alienated from mainstream society. Second, strong social ties emerge among drug users as they engage in the locating, purchasing, and consuming of drugs, the latter becoming a bonding ritual for them. Third, the drug subculture provides users with shared feelings of excitement and of the pleasurable effects that come from using the drug. Finally, as people become entrenched in the drug subculture, they derive a sense of mastery from success in finding drugs, making money through illicit sources, avoiding being caught by authorities, and so on.[81]

Although the drug use street scene is frequently "brutal, exploitative, and cruel," there also exists a sense of social responsibility, support, caring, and shared values, that make the drug subculture a community. One addict told of an act of generosity with the most coveted of resources:

> [The building we used to get high in is] empty. I'll never do something like that where people live. I respect kids. . . . When we go there, everybody got their own stuff [drugs and drug paraphernalia]. But, one time I split a bag with a guy because that guy was real sick and

I don't like to see that. If I can, I give you a little bit because I know and [can] imagine how you feel when you're sick. . . . I put like ten [units of liquified drugs] in my cooker and the other half I gave to him. So, he do it and I do mine.[82]

That social ties among drug-using friends tend to remain strong is exemplified in a study of inner-city addicts with a history of injecting illicit drugs. It found that associating with drug-using friends and partners was the strongest predictor of continuing use of heroin and cocaine among the addicts.[83]

One study investigated whether the gay neighborhood drug subculture led to greater risk for drug use among homosexual men living in the neighborhood. It found that the use of methamphetamine and Ecstasy was related to residence in gay neighborhoods. These drugs are associated with the club drug phenomenon, and a significant number of these dance clubs are found in gay communities. The study also revealed that homosexual men in gay neighborhoods who have social networks that are both gay-centric and non-gay-centric are less likely to engage in methamphetamine and polydrug use.[84]

It has long been known that homeless youth are more likely to engage in drug use and have more favorable attitudes toward drugs as compared to their non-homeless peers. Use of cocaine, amphetamine, and marijuana among homeless adolescents is significantly higher than among their non-homeless counterparts. Drug-using street youths are marginalized from the larger society because of the stigmas associated with drug use. Peer networks become a refuge from the social exclusion they suffer. A study of newly homeless young people in Los Angeles and Melbourne, Australia, found that drug-using peer networks increased these youth's cocaine use, amphetamine use, and injection drug use, thus adding to their social exclusion.[85]

The concepts of "social network" and "subculture" have been important tools in ethnographic research, particularly in studying heavy drug use among marginalized populations. One scholar, however, has argued that the term "subculture" is not very useful in researching people who use drugs recreationally. An ethnographic study of two drug-using groups—one whose members had little in common aside from using drugs, the other consisting of people living in group homes—reported that the concepts of drug "scene" and "pathways" (established drug practices) are more helpful than "subculture" in researching certain contexts of drug use.[86]

Another study that eschewed the notion of a drug subculture drew on interviews from patrons of a youth drop-in center.[87] It found that young peoples' initiation to and continued use of drugs was not based on peer pressure to belong to a drug subculture. Rather, it was influenced by friendship—affective relationships of trust and intimacy, belonging and sharing. Disadvantaged and homeless young people stated that drugs furnish them with a relatively inexpensive pastime to share with friends, introducing opportunities for intimacy. Through "borderwork" these young adults constructed boundaries between what they regarded as acceptable and dangerous drug use and drug users. This borderwork allowed them to justify and solidify the bonds they shared with the people they preferred to use drugs with.

In the United States, the role of advertising drugs provides further evidence of powerful group support for drug use, if not necessarily for the use of *controlled* drugs. But people are not always aware of the distinctions and differences between, (1) *over-the-counter (OTC) drugs* or medicines sold to consumers with no prescription required. These include medicines—intended to treat aches, pains, headaches, fever, allergies, upset stomach, and skin rashes—that are sold in pharmacies, supermarkets, and gas stations, (2) *prescription drugs* that require a prescription from a healthcare professional (physician, psychiatrist, physician assistant). These are dispensed in pharmacies and include analgesics (painkillers), antibiotics, cholesterol-lowering statins, barbiturates, benzodiazepines, and sleep medications, (3) *illegal drugs*, which include those listed as Schedule I drugs.

Pushing one subtly fosters use of the other. Consumers are saturated with advertisements for OTC drugs that promise relief from whatever illness or discomfort they may experience. There are ads for drugs that will induce sleep or stave off sleep, for treating indigestion, headaches, tension, constipation, diarrhea, depression, energy levels, and so on. The message is clear but subtle, thus making it more insidious: if experiencing undesirable physical or emotional symptoms, taking drugs is acceptable.

A trend among teenagers in the US is the nonmedical abuse of OTC and prescription cough and cold medications, called "pharming." These are taken alone or in combination with other substances, usually alcohol, to obtain a high. Adolescents have easy access to these and other medications from medicine cabinets in their own homes and the homes of their friends. A National Survey on Drug Use and Health report found that in 2006 over 3 million people aged 12 to 25 (5.3 percent of this age group) had used an OTC cough and cold medication to get high at least once in their lifetime. More than 70 percent had obtained the medications from a friend or relative.[88]

Later in this book, we will be looking more closely at the drug industry—both legal and illegal—under the headings of other criminal behavior systems. For now, in connection with group support of drug use, it is important to bear in mind that the illegal drug trade in the US has higher yearly earnings than the Fortune 500 companies of Apple, J.P. Morgan Chase, and Berkshire Hathaway combined. Between 1988 and 2010 Americans spent over $100 billion on cocaine, heroin, marijuana, and methamphetamine.[89] This fact serves as proof of the extensive, albeit illegal, support of the use of controlled substances in the country. It is a system wherein addicted persons as well as casual users continually recruit new members to both sell and obtain drugs. Multiple layers of drug dealers connect street dealers to users. The street-level dealers buy from higher-level dealers and re-sell in smaller quantities at the next lower market level. There are also defensive communication systems with their own argot for drugs, suppliers, and drug users and various warning systems by which addicts and sellers are protected by others. The support of drug habits requires a complex distribution network of controlled substances. Controlled substances can be imported or produced domestically, either in clandestine laboratories, greenhouses, on in open fields. This supply chain is largely run through both legitimate and illegitimate groups—drug cartels, online black markets, pill mills, prescribing physicians, as well as other highly organized and legitimate structures. This constitutes group support at the highest level, for it is a support system that provides the addict with what he or she needs. A crystal meth addict tells about the additives and equipment needed in the production of the drug:

> Angie used to be a [crystal meth] cooker so we hold her in high regard even as we resent the fact that she made and sold the poison we lived for. In her little trailer outside Hot Desert Springs, Angie had performed the filthy alchemy that produces crystal from a twisted recipe: Sudafed pills, the iodine used to treat diseased horse hooves, and red phosphorous derived from the strike pads of thousands of matchbooks. These rare ingredients were transformed into a toxic brew with the catalytic agents of Coleman's gas, muriatic acid, Methanol, and Red Devil lye. Because each step of the process is combustible and Angie loves to smoke, it occurs to me that Angie may not have plucked out her eyelashes but burned them off when she blew up her trailer.[90]

Social Reaction to Criminal Behavior

Except for those who are highly involved in their way of life, prostitutes, users of illegal drugs, and excessive drinkers are probably not much different in their attitudes toward the general goals of society from those who are not so engaged. Where the behavior becomes more fully an important part of the individual's life organization, and there is a degree of isolation from conventional society, however, such offenders may become more committed to the goals of a deviant subgroup, such as the subculture of drug addicts or sex workers, and less to mainstream values.

Much of the behavior of public order offenders is consistent with legitimate behavior patterns. The prostitute's behavior is a commercial occupation with the same goal as most other occupations: making money. A drunken person is participating in a generally approved behavior for adults, that is, the drinking of alcoholic beverages.

The use of drugs such as heroin and cocaine, while legally and officially disapproved of, has its counterparts in the frequent use of legitimate drugs such as alcohol, anti-anxiety medications, antidepressants, and other minor drugs such as aspirin. Coffee, tea, and energy drinks are also drug stimulants that can have a considerable effect when consumed regularly in large quantities. Some idea of the widescale use of the more accepted drugs is indicated by the fact that 300 tons of barbiturates are legally produced every year in the United States.

Criminologist George B. Vold indicated that in many of these public order offenses, as in the United States, there are economic and cultural considerations common to the general society.[91] In such offenses as drunkenness, narcotic addiction, and prostitution, commercial gain plays a prominent role. Prostitution is an economic commodity: the sale of sex. A huge economic interest enters the production and sale of alcoholic beverages and liquid nicotine for vaporizers and e-cigarettes, and there are large financial profits resulting from the illegitimate sale of opioids. The illegal behavior represents an occupation for many of the offenders in this group. Sex work is a "job" as much as any other. There are even opportunities to develop a degree of professional skill with resulting status among one's associates.

In sum, it may be argued that public order criminal offenses are a subterranean acting out of so-called conventional behavior. As such, public order criminal behavior is not much different from what most people do.

As was pointed out at the beginning of this chapter, public order offenses are numerous. They constitute behavior defined by law as contrary to the system of morals or the standards of proper conduct for an individual. Yet, for the most part, the condemnation is not strong. Prostitutes, when arrested, typically are booked, held overnight, and released the following day with a small fine. Only when specific interest groups press for the enforcement of the law are they driven from an area. Some police departments target the men who buy sex and try to help the women who sell it. Apart from drunk driving, public intoxication is widely tolerated, and in the event of an arrest, the penalties are mild. And drug addiction is no longer thought of as calling primarily for a law enforcement response, but rather for prevention and treatment. In the past, drug addiction—for example, during the crack cocaine epidemic of the 1980s that disproportionately affected lower-class people of color—was treated as a War-on-Drugs criminal issue that contributed to mass incarceration. Today, the opioid epidemic that affects large numbers of middle-class whites, is instead seen as a public health issue. The use of marijuana for recreational purposes is seldom a matter for individual arrest, even in those states that criminalize its use. The possession or sale of substantial amounts of narcotics, and the combination of drug use and the commission of other, more serious, crimes, however, does elicit a strong public and law enforcement response.

Values and moral standards change through time. The behavior involved in public order offenses reflects, in part, the changing definitions of what is and what is not proper behavior, and also the extent to which the political state can intervene to support the morals and practices of some and condemn those of others. As Vold pointed out, blasphemy and heresy were once condemned in the interest of private and public morality and were severely prosecuted as criminal offenses.

Both of these have disappeared from the categories of crimes calling for police control in the world of today, though both types of behavior persist in the community. But ideas and events in the world at large have changed, and we no longer seek to make men religious by law and police action. Could it be that we may be in the process of a similar transformation in the matter of control of personal habits and morality represented by these categories of petty crime, as they appear in the American world of today?[92]

In many parts of the world, these public order offenses are not considered crimes, while in other cultures they are severely punished. For example, depicting images of the Prophet Muhammad or desecrating the sacred Qur'an merit death in those countries under Sharia law.

Public order crimes represent efforts to control certain moral and personal behavior through laws. Undoubtedly, only a small proportion of those who commit these offenses are ever apprehended. Indeed, there is a dilemma between criminal action as opposed to no action at all against such behavior as prostitution, public intoxication, and drug use.

After many years of penalizing these areas of behavior as crime, we still have the problem behavior with us, and we have as well a large number of officially designated criminals convicted under such procedure. Furthermore, there is widespread recognition of the fact that the behavior is much more prevalent than that researched by criminal prosecution and conviction. Penalizing behavior in these areas as crime does not seem to have been particularly successful in controlling or eliminating the problem behavior. It is entirely possible that we have a larger proportion of our population involved in these behaviors than is the case in some of the countries that do not include them under the criminal law. Behavior in these several areas is criminal because we so define it, but if we should not penalize it as criminal, would the behavior become rampant and without control?[93]

There is also the question of the economic costs of criminalizing public order behaviors. First, there is the tremendous expense incurred by the state in enforcing laws that seek to control these behaviors. Second, there is the loss of tax revenues that would occur if selected controlled substances or sexual services were decriminalized and a tax levied on their purchase. Third, there is the $80 billion a year that is spent to incarcerate 2.4 million people in the US, the majority of whom are incarcerated for nonviolent drug offenses.

This mass incarceration for drug offenses also has human costs. Paternal incarceration is associated with behavior problems and delinquency, especially among boys. It deprives thousands of children of important economic and social support from their fathers. Greater unemployment and poverty exist in communities where most of the men are in prison or jail. Dealing with an incarcerated relative places a financial and social strain on the rest of the family.

Prostitution

Commercialized sex—including pornography, prostitution, and the use of sex and female bodies in media and marketing—is omnipresent in everyday life.

In modern society, sex as a commodity on the market is usually regarded as undesirable and immoral, and in most cultures buying and selling sex is controlled or criminalized.[94]

Nevertheless, prostitution evokes a deep ambivalence. Attitudes toward prostitution have varied historically, and today they differ widely by country and region of country. Some Americans are willing to tolerate it as a necessity. They believe that if certain urban districts or zones are set aside specifically for sex work, prostitutes could be subject to health checks and regularly inspected for HIV/AIDS and other sexually transmitted infections. Feminists basically see prostitution in one of two ways:

> First, women working as prostitutes are exploited by those who manage and organize the sex industry (mostly men). Moreover, prostitution and the wider sex industry serve to underpin and reinforce prostitution as a patriarchal institution that affects all women and gendered relations. Second, in contemporary society, prostitution for many women is freely chosen as a form of work, and women working in the sex industry deserve the same rights and liberties as other workers, including freedom from fear, exploitation, and violence in the course of their work. Additionally, sex work or erotic labor can actually be a "liberatory terrain for women."[95]

One scholar lists 10 reasons for *not* legalizing prostitution. According to her, legalizing prostitution would: (1) be a gift to pimps, traffickers, and the sex industry, (2) promote sex trafficking, (3) expand the sex industry, (4) increase illegal, clandestine, and street prostitution, (5) increase child prostitution, (6) not protect the women in prostitution, (7) encourage men to buy women for sex in a wider and more permissible range of socially acceptable settings, (8) not promote women's health, (9) not enhance women's choice, and finally, (10) women in prostitution do not want the sex industry legalized.[96] Other scholars support the legalization of prostitution on several grounds: (1) prostitutes who are themselves victims of abuse and exploitation would not be punished, (2) it would address public health issues more effectively given that prostitutes would be subject to routine medical screenings for diseases, (3) sex workers will more likely go to the police for help or to report a crime, thus possibly deterring their customers from becoming abusive, (4) it stops penalizing prostitutes from doing sex work which they enjoy, (5) lower-level street prostitutes would not be targeted, (6) it will lessen the stigma that prostitutes bear, which makes them more susceptible to hate crimes, discrimination, and harassment. In short, they maintain that legalizing prostitution,

> has the potential to protect society, protect prostitutes, and protect social order. It could help solve the practical problems of sexually transmitted diseases (STDs) and violence against a vulnerable population and potentially help poverty-stricken communities clean up.[97]

One nationally representative study found that 18 percent of Americans favor the legalization of prostitution and that public support for its legalization was strongest with men, Catholics, residents from the western states, and whites.[98] A study on attitudes toward prostitution found that male college undergraduates were significantly more accepting than were the female students of "prostitution myths"—beliefs that justify prostitution, promote misinformation about it, and that contribute to a social climate that exploits and harms women. Because of these findings, the researchers hypothesized that:

> More men than women might support prostitution because men are more likely to believe that male sexual urges are an imperative and that prostitution should exist as an institution to meet men's sexual needs. On the other hand, fewer women might support prostitution because they identify with the situation of prostituted women and view prostitution as exploitation.[99]

Public support for prostitutes and prostitution is not limited to the US or Western societies. For example, it is much more acceptable in Sub-Saharan Africa than in the West,[100] and in Thailand there appears to be a relative lack of severe or lasting social stigma for prostitutes.[101]

Laws against sex work are efforts to control private moral behavior by punitive social control. In most countries, the enforcement of these laws has been sporadic and largely unsuccessful. During the late-1950s, a study commissioned by the British government popularly known as *The Wolfenden Report* contained recommendations for laws governing sexual behavior. What it said about prostitution back then continues to apply to today:

> It has persisted in many civilizations throughout many centuries, and the failure of attempts to stamp it out by repressive legislation shows that it cannot be eradicated through the agency of the criminal law. It remains true that without a demand for her services the prostitute could not exist and that there are enough men who avail themselves of prostitutes to keep the trade alive. It also remains true that there are women who, even when there is no economic need to do so, choose this form of livelihood. For so long as these propositions continue to be true there will be prostitution, and no amount of legislation directed toward its abolition will abolish it.[102]

Drunkenness

The use of alcohol has its material basis in the growth of the advanced political economy in the United States. Manufacture and sale of alcohol have become big business. Moreover, the recreation and night-club industry profits and a large part of the consuming population is pacified in its daily existence. Drinking and drunkenness are an integral part of American society.

Although the consumption of alcohol may bring pleasure and relaxation to many, its social role is perceived by different observers as either a blessing or a curse. Despite the vast amount of research that has shown the involvement of alcohol in countless injuries, diseases, and crimes, the precise nature of the relationship remains problematic and unpredictable. In research dealing with diseases, accidents, or criminal violence, all that is known for certain is that only in a variable proportion of cases is alcohol involved. The proportion of involvement is often quite high, however.

Of further consideration here is the empirical evidence that there are important cross-national, regional, and situational variations in the role of alcohol in casualties. Different sectors of any population run different risks of alcohol-related casualties. Studies have shown that young adult males have a high proportion of drinking-related accidents and violent crime; older people have drinking and falls; chronic heavy drinkers have drunken driving accidents; middle-aged men and women have suicides. But the relative risk based on the frequency of the activity in relationship to consumption of alcohol may reveal different findings.

Studies are mixed in demonstrating a positive relationship between acute alcohol consumption and the risk of injury. Some show no association while others do. One cross-national meta-analysis examined the relationship between alcohol consumption and the severity of injury in hospital emergency departments in six countries (United States, Canada, Mexico, Australia, Spain, and Italy). Findings generally supported a relationship between acute alcohol consumption and injury severity.[103]

As for alcohol-related crime, one study of Worcester, England, found that though alcohol was a contributing factor in only 8 percent of crimes overall, its role was far higher in certain types of offenses: 48 percent of all harassment crimes; 36 percent of violent crime, and 16 percent of criminal damage. Considering spatial and temporal factors, it found that around midnight, alcohol-related crime and disorder was clustered in the city center by the pubs and clubs. After the closure of pubs and clubs, the crime and disorder followed the night-time revelers out along key routeways to residential areas.[104] A similar study, this one of Madison, Wisconsin, found a link between high-risk student drinking in that college community and crime. Results indicated that serious crimes peaked between 2 and 3am, coinciding with bar closing time. Less serious crimes peaked between 11pm and midnight.[105]

It is well-known that alcohol plays an important part in intimate partner violence (IPV). One study reported that 30 to 40 percent of the men and 27 to 34 percent of the women who perpetrated violence against their partners were drinking at the time of the event. Despite the close association between alcohol consumption and IVP, its role is nonetheless difficult to explain:

> Alcohol's role in partner violence may be explained by people's expectations that alcohol will have a disinhibitory effect on behavior or by alcohol's direct physiological disinhibitory effect. It is also possible that people consciously use alcohol as an excuse for their violent behavior or that alcohol appears to be associated with violence because both heavier drinking and violence have common predictors, such as an impulsive personality.[106]

Alcohol plays different and complex roles in different levels of violent offending. For example, average drinking behavior has a moderating role in the prevalence of assault. This means that average alcohol consumption facilitates a person to become a violent offender, *but only if* that person is characterized by deviant and violent inclinations.[107]

If excessive drinking is continued over long periods of time the individual may increasingly become involved in difficulties that arise from the drunkenness itself. People may lose intimate partners and jobs. They may be ostracized by neighbors and friends. The Protestant ethic may play an important role in the attitudes of others because drunkenness is regarded as a lack of moral strength, of devotion to the goals of personal discipline, of willpower, and of dedication to work. The excessive drinker who becomes an alcoholic is sometimes the chronic drunkenness offender before the courts, especially in cases of driving under the influence. Such a person may, with increasing frequency, be arrested and jailed. The irony is that drinking may become a way of getting away from the societal reaction to problems caused by the drinking itself: problems caused by drinking can be faced only through more excessive drinking, which in turn leads to more arrests for public order disturbances. Final rejection is taking up a life of social ostracism.

Aside from DUI convictions, drinking and drunkenness are no longer treated primarily through criminal law. This movement away from criminalizing these behaviors in part extends the forces that repealed the Eighteenth Amendment to the US Constitution in 1933. That was the end of the "great experiment" known as prohibition, which had been established by the Volstead Act and ratified by the Eighteenth Amendment in 1920. It has been observed that the movement to ban drinking and the liquor trade was an assertion of the rural Protestant mind against the urban culture that grew up at the end of the nineteenth century and the beginning of the twentieth. For a significant portion of the population, prohibition meant stamping out sin in an evil society. The rural element was temporarily successful in enacting prohibition legislation but succumbed within 13 years to the inevitable.

Amid resentment against drinking and what it represented, specific interest groups were active in the movement that led to prohibition legislation. The Prohibition party was founded in 1869 as a third political party to deal with the problem of drinking. Later, such organizations as the Anti-Saloon League and the Women's Christian Temperance Union crusaded against alcohol and the saloon. Their lobbying brought about state and local temperance legislation. The "dry" interest groups exerted great pressure against legislators and brought about formal enactment of prohibition. But prohibition was to fail both as law and as a noble experiment. An outdated morality could not be enforced by criminal law.[108]

Though the production, transport, and sale of alcohol are today no longer illegal, its distribution and sale are nonetheless controlled by the states. With some exceptions, most states have laws against public drinking, do not allow open containers of alcohol inside moving vehicles, and limit alcohol sales in grocery stores and gas stations to beer. But the national attempt at regulating the buying and possessing of alcohol has been based on age.

In 1984, the US Congress passed the National Minimum Drinking Age Act, which was intended to encourage a uniform minimum drinking age across all states. With the goal of deterring drunk-driving fatalities, the Act made it illegal for persons below 21 years of age to purchase and publicly possess alcoholic beverages. Though the Act did not prohibit furnishing alcoholic beverages to minors, each state and county has its own regulatory system for the provision and selling of alcohol to minors.

Despite these regulations, only a very small number of violations of the drinking age law result in an arrest or other action. For example, the results of one study showed that youthful looking buyers were able to purchase alcohol without age ID in about half of all purchasing attempts.[109] It has been found that, on average, only 2 of every 1,000 occasions of illegal drinking by youth under 21 result in an arrest, and only 5 of every 100,000 youth drinking occasions result in an administrative action against an alcohol outlet.[110] In addition, although many youth purchase alcohol themselves, most obtain it through friends, siblings, parents, coworkers, and strangers approached outside of alcohol establishments.

Commercial establishments licensed to sell alcohol as well as social sources face potential criminal penalties, fines, license suspensions, and lawsuits for selling or providing alcohol to minors. However, the rate of enforcement of the legal minimum drinking age is very low.[111] One study found that counties with the higher rates of enforcement of the drinking age shared three ecological characteristics: high general crime arrest rates, high proportions of unoccupied housing, and smaller populations.[112] A study of alcohol outlets in Minnesota showed that those that tended not to sell alcohol to minors shared the following three characteristics: they are more likely to be bars (compared to liquor stores), have a manager on the premises at all times, and have a formally trained bar staff.[113] A similar study, this one of off-premise alcohol outlets in Oregon, found that the underage-looking decoys who did not carry IDs were able to purchase alcohol at 34 percent of the outlets approached. Purchase rates were highest at convenience (38 percent) and grocery (36 percent) stores but were relatively low (14 percent) at liquor stores. Alcohol purchases by minors were less likely at stores with the following characteristics: those participating in the state's responsible vendor training program, those where salesclerks asked for age identification, and those that posted a sign warning against alcohol sales to minors.[114]

Drug Use

Prior to the passage of the Harrison Act in 1914 outlawing the use of certain drugs without a physician's prescription, there was considerable public tolerance for the use of drugs, which was regarded as a personal problem. By this law and others passed by the states, drug users became "criminals" and drugs something mysterious and evil. State penalties became more severe and the possession, sale, or transfer of narcotics was often made a felony instead of a misdemeanor.

The War on Drugs campaign was launched under the administration of Richard Nixon in the early 1970s. The strategy consisted of a set of drug policies and practices intended to stem the production, distribution, and consumption of illegal drugs. In 1986 the US Congress passed the Anti-Drug Abuse Act, and cocaine eradication received top priority. Even though between 1979 and 1985 the number of young adults who had ever used marijuana and cocaine decreased by 12 percent and 11 percent respectively, the policy rhetoric of the Reagan Administration created a moral panic leading Americans to believe that drug use was increasing.[115] President Reagan's use of common-good calls to action like those made in the following public statements rallied support for an aggressive War on Drugs. Appearing on national television with her husband, Mrs. Regan stated:

> Today, there's a drug and alcohol abuse epidemic in this country, and *no one* is safe from it—not you, not me, and certainly not our children. . . . Now you can see why drug abuse concerns every one of us, *all the American family.*[116]

In another television appearance President Regan said:

> My generation will remember how America swung into action when we were attacked in World War II. Now, we're in another war for our freedom, and it's time for all of us to pull together again. . . . As we mobilize for this national crusade, please remember this when your courage is tested: you are Americans. You're the product of the freest society mankind has even known.[117]

Statistics on the War on Drugs reveal the following for the year 2016:

1. Over $50 billion was spent annually in the US on the War on Drugs.
2. Over 1.5 million arrests were made in the US for drug law violations, 84 percent of which were for possession only.
3. The number of Americans incarcerated in federal, state, and local prisons and jails was 2,157,000, which was the highest incarceration rate in the world.
4. Over half—57 percent—of people incarcerated for a drug offense in state prison were black or Latino, although these groups use and sell drugs at similar rates as whites.[118]

About 90 percent of police agencies regularly perform drug enforcement functions. Eighteen percent of departments had officers assigned full-time to a special unit for drug enforcement with about 12,000 officers assigned to such duty nationwide. In 2013, about half of the departments were participating in a multi-agency drug task force, including almost all departments serving a population of 100,000. The average number of officers assigned to drug units ranged from 233 officers in jurisdictions with 1 million or more residents to 1 officer in those jurisdictions with fewer than 2,500 residents.[119]

At the federal level, the Drug Enforcement Administration (DEA) has authority for the control of illicit drugs, controlled pharmaceuticals, and listed chemicals. With a budget of $3 billion, it has over 9,000 employees assigned to 221 domestic offices and 86 foreign offices in 67 countries. In 2014, the DEA made over 30,000 domestic drug arrests and seized more than 33,000 kilograms of cocaine, 1,000 kilos of heroin, 74,000 kilos of marijuana, nearly 3,000 kilos of methamphetamine and almost 49,000 dosage units of hallucinogens. There were also 9,338 seizures of meth labs, dumpsites, and chemical and glassware in the US.[120]

Through the 1980s and 1990s, extreme measures were employed in the War on Drugs. But the effort was largely seen as a failure by many experts in the field. An entire arsenal of weapons was thrown into the fight: eradication of marijuana and cocaine crops in Colombia and Bolivia through aerofumigation with the deadly pesticide paraquat and other chemical herbicides; border interdiction of illegal drug shipments to the United States from foreign countries; seizure of assets ranging from yachts to automobiles even when as little as one marijuana "roach" was found; the involvement of immigration and customs officials; the use of US troops to assist and train antinarcotic forces in Bolivia, Mexico, and Colombia; and even the 1990 invasion of Panama in order to bring its *de facto* ruler, Manuel Noriega, to trial in the United States on charges of drug trafficking. The frenzy of these efforts led some critics to label the War on Drugs a transnational crime of broad scope that can be called "ecobiogenocide."[121]

During the 1980s and 1990s, legal sanctions for those involved in the international drug traffic were severe. So were sanctions for importers, distributors, and sellers of controlled substances within the territorial borders of the United States harsh and unyielding. As a result, the demand for more and more prison cells exploded across the country. For example, in New York State alone, the percent of overcapacity of its prisons rose dramatically from 6.1 percent overcapacity in 1984 to 19.6 percent overcapacity in 1991. The percentage of all inmates convicted on drug charges rose correspondingly from 15.3 percent in 1984 to 44.7 percent in 1991.

The Fourth Amendment to the Constitution deals with the rights of people to be secure in their persons, houses, papers, and effects "against unreasonable searches and seizures." Such searches and seizures can be legalized only through the issuance of a warrant if the searches involved "probable cause." The latter, in the enforcement of drug laws, often goes well beyond the real legal interpretation to illegal search and seizure. Some of these involve frequent routine searches on the street and the search of private premises. One of the most controversial of these practices has been New York City's stop-and-frisk program, which involves detaining, questioning, and searching civilians on the street for weapons and drugs. The practice has raised concerns over racial profiling, illegal stops, and privacy rights. In 2017, New Yorkers were stopped by the police 10,861 times. Black and Latino communities were the overwhelming target of these tactics. For example, African Americans were stopped 58 percent of the time, Latinos 32 percent, and whites 9 percent. In 67 percent of these stops, the people were innocent of any wrongdoing.[122] Indeed, War on Drugs policing strategies—particularly, stop-and-frisk and Special Weapons and Tactics (SWAT) teams—have not only eroded specific legal protections originally designed to curtail police powers, but they also appear to increase police brutality targeting black communities, even as they make little progress in reducing street-level drug activity.[123] One study found that race differences in drug offending, nondrug offending, and residing in neighborhoods with high police presence did not fully explain racial disparities in drug arrests. Instead, it concluded that it was *racial bias* in law enforcement that was more likely responsible for African American's higher probability of drug arrests.[124]

The problem of public order crimes has become so difficult that there has been serious discussion of eliminating or decriminalizing public drunkenness, gambling, the use of controlled substances, and prostitution, on the grounds that these crimes constitute an overreach of the criminal law. These offenses, however, would remain crimes if committed against persons under a certain age, if more than a certain quantity of drugs were possessed (presumably for sale), and if an injury to someone has taken place in connection with intoxication. The arguments for the elimination of public order offenses can be summarized as follows: (1) such acts should not be the concern of the state, (2) the interference of the political state makes matters worse, for

> where the supply of goods and services is concerned, such as narcotics, gambling, and prostitution, the criminal law operates as a "crime tariff" which makes the supply of such goods and services profitable for the criminal by driving up prices and at the same time discourages competition by those who might enter the market were it legal,[125]

(3) little is accomplished by such crime control because it is ineffective against people who are favorably disposed to the behavior, and (4) the legal processing of the offenses seriously interferes with a justice system that is already insufficient and overburdened. According to estimates by the Federal Bureau of Investigation, the estimated number of arrests in 2016 for public order crimes in the United States was 3,243,730.[126] Arrests for public order crimes in this context include prostitution and commercialized vice, drug abuse violations, gambling, public drunkenness, violations of liquor laws, and driving under the influence. All this effort has proven largely impotent in the elimination of such behaviors. In fact, it may even be counterproductive.

The inclusion of public order offenses in the criminal code has other important consequences of a negative nature. Many persons are driven into associations with others who are already well-established in the subculture of criminality. It is particularly in the areas of prostitution, controlled substances, and gambling that police and political officials are corrupted. Organized crime gains enormous profits from drugs, and to a lesser extent, from gambling and prostitution.

Two alternatives to the criminalization and the legalization of public order crimes are problem solving approaches and harm reduction approaches. *Problems solving approaches* use specialized courts that are dedicated to cases involving specific public order offenses. These specialized courts include drug courts, gambling courts, DUI courts, and prostitution courts. The problem solving model uses various components of the criminal justice system and the service and treatment systems to promote abstinence and prosocial behavior. The typical adjudication process results in probation or short sentence, along with community-based treatment and frequent monitoring and supervision.

> Diversionary [court] programs typically enroll offenders in a drug treatment program and dismiss charges upon graduation from the treatment program. Post-adjudication programs defer or suspend sentences in exchange for successful completion of the treatment program but reserve the right to reimpose the initial sentence if the offender does not comply.[127]
>
> Problem solving courts ask judges and attorneys to do more than just apply the law correctly. Problem solving courts demand that everyone attached to the court broaden their scope to see the real-life consequences of courtroom decisions. And they insist that courts use data to make more informed decisions about where to target resources and how to craft effective sanctions. Those who practice problem solving justice are committed to seeing each individual case in the context of the life of victims, communities, and defendants.[128]

In 2008, there were more than 2,500 problem solving courts in the US. The most popular are the drug courts designed to increase the likelihood that drug-addicted offenders seek and persist longer in drug treatment. One experimental design study found that severely drug-addicted chronic offenders who were processed through drug court were less likely to re-offend compared to those not so processed. The threat of future punishment along with drug treatment proved to be successful in reducing recidivism. Results showed that during the 2-year follow-up, 66.2 percent of the drug court subjects and 81.3 percent of the control subjects were re-arrested and the number of new arrests was 30 percent lower for the treatment than for the control subjects.[129] A meta-analytic review of drug court evaluations found similar results. The majority of the participants to adult drug courts had significantly lower rates of recidivism (38 percent) compared with non-participants (50 percent). This also seemed to be the case with DUI courts, though more evaluations are needed. However, drug courts for juveniles appeared to have smaller effects on recidivism (43.5 percent).[130]

Harm reduction approaches are intended to help people manage their high-risk and illegal behaviors—particularly drug abuse and sex work—and divert them away from the criminal justice system. It also involves reducing damage to their families and communities. In the case of drug abuse, a policy, program, or intervention is one of harm reduction if,

> (1) the primary goal is the reduction of drug-related harm rather than drug use per se; (2) where abstinence-oriented strategies are included, strategies are also included to reduce the harm for those who continue to use drugs; and (3) strategies are included which aim to demonstrate that, on the balance of probabilities, it is likely to result in a net reduction in drug-related harm.[131]

Harm reduction measures have included the implementation of programs involving needle exchange, drug education and information, and methadone treatment.

Some of the harms associated with sex work include sexually transmitted infections, drug addiction, sexual abuse, violence, reduced self-esteem, and negative mental health. Sexual risk reduction efforts include peer education, training in condom-negotiating skills, safety tips for street-based sex workers, male and female condoms, the prevention–care synergy, occupational health and safety guidelines for brothels, self-help organizations, and community-based child protection networks.[132] In short,

> Harm reduction drives towards re-humanizing the dehumanized, de-demonizing the demonized, normalizing and welcoming back to the human fold the outcast person, and the outcast behavior and reclaiming them as part of our humanity, so we can confront and deal with them in properly human ways.[133]

Notes

1 Richard Quinney, *Criminology*, 2nd edition (Boston, MA: Little, Brown, 1979), 251.
2 Monica Prasad, "The Morality of Market Exchange: Love, Money, and Contractual Justice," *Sociological Perspectives* 42, no. 2 (1999): 181–214, 182.
3 Edwin M. Schur, *Crimes without Victims* (Englewood Cliffs, NJ: Prentice-Hall, 1965).
4 Jane Jordan, *Josephine Butler* (London: John Murray Publishers, 2001).
5 Valerie Jenness, "From Sex as Sin to Sex as Work: COYOTE and the Reorganization of Prostitution as a Social Problem," *Social Problems* 37, no. 3 (1990): 403–420, 403.
6 Federal Bureau of Investigation, *Crime in the United States: Estimated Number of Arrests, 2016*. https://ucr.fbi.gov/crime-in-the-u.s/2016/crime-in-the-u.s.-2016/topic-pages/tables/table-18
7 National Highway Traffic Safety Administration, *Traffic Safety Facts, 2016 Data*. https://crashstats.nhtsa.dot.gov/Api/Public/ViewPublication/812450
8 National Institute on Drug Abuse, *Opioid Overdose Crisis, 2018*. www.drugabuse.gov/drugs-abuse/opioids/opioid-overdose-crisis#one
9 Marist College Institute for Public Opinion, *Weed & The American Family*, April 17, 2017. http://maristpoll.marist.edu/wp-content/misc/Yahoo%20News/20170417_Summary%20Yahoo%20News-Marist%20Poll_Weed%20and%20The%20American%20Family.pdf
10 Wilson R. Palacios and Melissa E. Fenwick, "'E' is for Ecstasy: A Participant Observation Study of Ecstasy Use," in *In Their Own Words: Criminals on Crime*, 6th edition, ed. by Paul Cromwell and Michael L. Birzer (New York: Oxford University Press, 2014), 372.
11 Robert Jenkot, "'Cooks are Like Gods': Hierarchies in Methamphetamine-Producing Groups," *Deviant Behavior* 29, no. 8 (2008): 667–689, 674.
12 Peter B. Karska, Charles R. Bussard, and John J. Brent, "Trafficking in Bodily Perfection: Examining the Late-Modern Steroid Marketplace and Its Criminalization," *Justice Quarterly* 27, no. 2 (2010): 159–185, 161.
13 Glen R. Hanson, Peter J. Venturelli, and Annette E. Fleckenstein, *Drugs and Society*, 13th edition (Burlington, MA: Jones & Bartlett Learning, 2017), 254.

14 Susan Guarino-Ghezzi and A. Javier Treviño, *Understanding Crime: A Multidisciplinary Approach* (Cincinnati, OH: Anderson Publishing, 2005), 48–49.

15 Michelle Alexander, *The New Jim Crow: Mass Incarceration in the Age of Colorblindness* (New York, NY: The New Press, 2010).

16 Hanson, et al., *Drugs and Society*, 660.

17 Hendrik Wagenaar, Sietske Altink and Helga Amesberger, *Designing Prostitution Policy: Intention and Reality in Regulating the Sex Trade* (Bristol, UK: Policy Press, 2017), 60–61.

18 Gunilla Ekberg, "The Swedish Law That Prohibits the Purchase of Sexual Services: Best Practices for Prevention of Prostitution and Trafficking in Human Beings," *Violence Against Women* 10, no. 10 (2004): 1187–1218, 1188.

19 Federal Bureau of Investigation, *Crime in the United States: Estimated Number of Arrests, 2016.* https://ucr.fbi.gov/crime-in-the-u.s/2016/crime-in-the-u.s.-2016/topic-pages/tables/table-18

20 Ronald Weitzer, *Legalizing Prostitution: From Illicit Vice to Lawful Business* (New York, NY: New York University Press, 2012), 4–5.

21 Ann M. Lucas, "The Work of Sex Work: Elite Prostitutes' Vocational Orientations and Experiences," *Deviant Behavior* 26, no. 6 (2005): 513–546, 528.

22 Kim Romenesko and Eleanor M. Miller, "The Second Step in Double Jeopardy: Appropriating the Labor of Female Street Hustlers," *Crime & Delinquency* 35, no.1 (1989): 109–135, 30.

23 Lucas, "The Work of Sex Work," 518.

24 James H. Bryan, "Apprenticeships in Prostitution," *Social Problems* 12, no. 3 (1965): 287–297.

25 Teela Sanders, *Sex Work: A Risky Business* (Devon, UK: Willan Publishing, 2005).

26 Xóchttl Castañeda, Víctor Ortíz, Betania Allen, Cecilia García and Mauricio Hernández-Avila, "Sex Masks: The Double Life of Female Commercial Sex Workers in Mexico City," *Culture, Medicine and Psychiatry* 20, no. 2 (1996): 229–247.

27 Sharon S. Oselin, *Leaving Prostitution: Getting Out and Staying Out of Sex Work* (New York, NY: New York University Press, 2014), 36.

28 Lynda M. Baker, Rochelle L. Dalla, and Celia Williamson, "Exiting Prostitution: An Integrated Model," *Violence Against Women* 16, no. 5 (2010): 579–600.

29 Sharon S. Oselin and Ronald Weitzer, "Organizations Working on Behalf of Prostitutes: An Analysis of Goals, Practices, and Strategies," *Sexualities* 16, nos. 3/4 (2013) 445–466.

30 New Friends New Life. *Mission Statement.* www.newfriendsnewlife.org/what-we-do/

31 Peter G. Moffatt and Simon A. Peters, "Pricing Personal Services: An Empirical Study of Earnings in the UK Prostitution Industry," *Scottish Journal of Political Economy* 51, no. 5 (2004): 581–720.

32 Melissa Farley, Jan Macleod, Lynn Anderson and Jacqueline M. Golding, "Attitudes and Social Characteristics of Men Who Buy Sex in Scotland," *Psychological Trauma: Theory, Research, Practice, and Policy* 3, no. 4 (2011): 369–383.

33 John Lowman and Chris Atchison, "Men Who Buy Sex: A Survey in the Greater Vancouver Regional District," *Canadian Review of Sociology* 43, no. 3 (2006): 281–296.

34 Melissa Farley, Jacqueline M. Golding, Emily Schuckman Matthews, Neil M. Malamuth, and Laura Jarrett, "Comparing Sex Buyers with Men Who Do Not Buy Sex: New Data on Prostitution and Trafficking," *Journal of Interpersonal Violence* 32, no. 23 (2017): 3601–3625.

35 Federal Bureau of Investigation, *Crime in the United States: Estimated Number of Arrests, 2016.* https://ucr.fbi.gov/crime-in-the-u.s/2016/crime-in-the-u.s.-2016/topic-pages/tables/table-18

36 US Department of Justice, Office of Justice Programs, Bureau of Justice Statistics, *Alcohol and Crime: Data From 2002 To 2008*, www.bjs.gov/content/acf/ac_conclusion.cfm

37 Lening Zhang, John W. Welte, and William W. Wieczorek, "The Role of Aggression-Related Alcohol Expectancies in Explaining the Link between Alcohol and Violent Behavior," *Substance Use & Misuse* 37, no. 4 (2002):457–471.

38 Mary McMurran, "The Relationships between Alcohol-Aggression Proneness, General Alcohol Expectancies, Hazardous Drinking, and Alcohol-Related Violence in Adult Male Prisoners," *Psychology, Crime & Law* 13, no. 3 (2007): 275–284.

39 S. E. Costanza, William B. Bankston, and Edward Shihadeh, "Alcohol Availability and Violent Crime Rates: A Spatial Analysis," *Journal of Crime and Justice* 24, no. 1 (2001): 71–83.

40 National Highway Traffic Safety Administration, *Drunk Driving.* www.nhtsa.gov/risky-driving/drunk-driving

41 Randy W. Elder, Ruth A. Shults, David A. Sleet, James L. Nichols, Robert S. Thompson, and Warda Rajab, "Effectiveness of Mass Media Campaigns for Reducing Drinking and Driving and Alcohol-Involved Crashes: A Systematic Review," *American Journal of Preventive Medicine* 27, no.1 (2004): 57–65.

42 Pew Research Center, *St. Patrick's Day Drinking, 2009* www.pewresearch.org/fact-tank/2009/03/09/st-patricks-day-drinking/

43 Robert L. Peralta, "Raced and Gendered Reactions to the Deviance of Drunkenness: A Sociological Analysis of Race and Gender Disparities in Alcohol Use," *Contemporary Drug Problems* 37, no. 3 (2010): 381–415, 393.

44 Ibid., 396.

45 Ibid., 401.

46 Carol J. Boyd, Sean Esteban McCabe, James A. Cranford, and Amy Young, "Adolescents' Motivations to Abuse Prescription Medications," *Pediatrics* 118, no. 6 (2006): 2472–2480.

47 Substance Abuse and Mental Health Services Administration, *Prescription Drug Use and Misuse in the United States: Results from the 2015 National Survey on Drug Use and Health*. www.samhsa.gov/data/sites/default/files/NSDUH-FFR2-2015/NSDUH-FFR2-2015.htm

48 Carrie B. Oser, "Drugs," in *Investigating Social Problems*, ed. by A. Javier Treviño (Los Angeles: Sage, 2019), 295.

49 Philippe Bourgois and Jeff Schonberg, *Righteous Dopefiend* (Berkeley, CA: University of California Press, 2009), 80.

50 Alfred R. Lindesmith, *Addiction and Opiates* (Chicago, IL: Aldine, 1968).

51 Miriam Williams Boeri, "'Hell, I'm An Addict, But I Ain't No Junkie': An Ethnographic Analysis of Aging Heroin Users," *Human Organization* 63, no. 2 (2004): 236–245, 241.

52 Richard C. Stephens, *The Street Addict Role: A Theory of Heroin Addiction* (Albany, NY: State University of New York Press, 1991), 42.

53 Charles E. Faupel, *Shooting Dope: Career Patterns of Hard-Core Heroin Users* (Gainesville, FL: University Press of Florida, 1991), 73.

54 Philippe Bourgois, *In Search of Respect: Selling Crack in El Barrio*, 2nd edition (New York, NY: Cambridge University Press, 2003), 115.

55 Patricia A. Adler, *Wheeling and Dealing: An Ethnography of an Upper-Level Drug Dealing and Smuggling Community*, 2nd edition (New York: Columbia University Press, 1993), 125.

56 Brenda M. Booth, Carl Leukefeld, Russel Falck, Jichuan Wang and Robert Carlson, "Correlates of Rural Methamphetamine and Cocaine Users: Results from a Multistate Community Study," *Journal of Studies on Alcohol* 67, no. 4 (2006): 493–501.

57 Sean Esteban McCabe, John R. Knight, Christian J. Teter, and Henry Wechsler, "Non-Medical Use of Prescription Stimulants among US College Students: Prevalence and Correlates from a National Survey," *Addiction* 100, no. 1 (2005): 96–106.

58 Holly Hedegaard, Margaret Warner, and Arialdi M. Miniño, *Drug Overdose Deaths in the United States, 1999–2015, February 2017*. www.cdc.gov/nchs/data/databriefs/db273.pdf

59 Centers for Disease Control and Prevention, *Vital Signs: Opioid Overdoses Treated in Emergency Departments, 2018*. www.cdc.gov/vitalsigns/opioid-overdoses/

60 Howard S. Becker, "Becoming a Marihuana User," *American Journal of Sociology* 59, no. 3 (1953): 235–242.

61 Substance Abuse and Mental Health Services Administration, *Results from the 2013 National Survey on Drug Use and Health: Summary of National Findings*. www.samhsa.gov/data/sites/default/files/NSDUHresultsPDFWHTML2013/Web/NSDUHresults2013.pdf

62 Janet Lever and Deanne Dolnick, "Call Girls and Street Prostitutes: Selling Sex and Intimacy," in *Sex for Sale: Prostitution, Pornography, and the Sex Industry*, 2nd edition, ed. by Ronald Weitzer (New York, NY: Routledge, 2010), 209.

63 Ibid., 210.

64 Barbara G. Brents and Kathryn Hausbeck, "Violence and Legalized Brothel Prostitution in Nevada: Examining Safety, Risk, and Prostitution Policy," *Journal of Interpersonal Violence* 20, no. 3 (2005): 270–295, 277.

65 National Institute on Alcohol Abuse and Alcoholism, *Alcohol Facts and Statistics, 2015*. https://pubs.niaaa.nih.gov/publications/AlcoholFacts&Stats/AlcoholFacts&Stats.htm

66 Samantha Wells, Kathryn Graham, Mark Speechley, and John J. Koval, "Drinking Patterns, Drinking Contexts, and Alcohol-Related Aggression among Late Adolescent and Young Adult Drinkers," *Addiction* 100, no. 7 (2005): 933–944.

67 Raul Caetano, Carol B. Cunradi, John Schafer and Catherine L. Clark, "Intimate Partner Violence and Drinking Patterns Among White, Black, and Hispanic Couples in the U.S.," *Journal of Substance Abuse* 11, no. 2 (2000): 123–138.

68 Gene H. Brody, Xiaojia Ge, Jennifer Katz, and Ileana Arias, "A Longitudinal Analysis of Internalization of Parental Alcohol-Use Norms and Adolescent Alcohol Use," *Applied Developmental Science* 4, no. 2, (2000): 71–79.

69 Taisia Huckle, Ru Quan You, and Sally Casswell, "Socio-Economic Status Predicts Drinking Patterns but Not Alcohol-Related Consequences Independently," *Addiction* 105, no. 7, (2010): 1192–1202.

70 Genevieve M. Ames, Joel W. Grube, and Roland S. Moore, "Social Control and Workplace Drinking Norms: A Comparison of Two Organizational Cultures," *Journal of Studies on Alcohol* 61, no. 2 (2000): 203–219.

71 Ibid., 203.

72 Richard W. Wilsnack, Sharon C. Wilsnack, Arlinda F. Kristjanson, Nancy D. Vogeltanz-Holm, and Gerhard Gmel, "Gender and Alcohol Consumption: Patterns from the Multinational GENACIS Project," *Addiction* 104, no. 9 (2009): 1487–1500.

73 Laurence Michalak, Karen Trocki, and Jason Bond, "Religion and Alcohol in the U.S. National Alcohol Survey: How Important is Religion for Abstention and Drinking?" *Drug and Alcohol Dependence* 87, nos. 2–3 (2007): 268–280.

74 Deborah A. Dawson, "Beyond Black, White and Hispanic: Race, Ethnic Origin and Drinking Patterns in the United States," *Journal of Substance Abuse* 10, no. 4 (1998): 321–339.

75 Tavis Glassman, Chudley E. Werch, Edessa Jobli, and Hui Bian, "Alcohol-Related Fan Behavior on College Football Game Day," *Journal of American College Health* 56, no. 3 (2007): 255–260.

76 John T.P. Hustad, Nadine R. Mastroleo, Rachel Urwin, Suzanne Zeman, Linda LaSalle, and Brian Borsari, "Tailgating and Pregaming by College Students with Alcohol Offenses: Patterns of Alcohol Use and Beliefs," *Journal Substance Use & Misuse* 49, no. 14 (2014): 1928–1933.

77 Lisa J. Merloa, Jisu Honga, and Linda B. Cottler, "The Association between Alcohol-Related Arrests and College Football Game Days," *Drug and Alcohol Dependence* 106, no.1 (2010): 69–71

78 Simon C. Moore, Jonathan P. Shepherd, Sam Eden, and Vaseekaran Sivarajasingam, "The Effect of Rugby Match Outcome on Spectator Aggression and Intention to Drink Alcohol," *Criminal Behaviour and Mental Health* 17, no. 2 (2007): 118–127.

79 Merill Singer, "What is the 'Drug User Community'?: Implications for Public Health," *Human Organization* 65, no. 1 (2006): 72–80, 74.

80 Erich Goode, "Multiple Drug Use among Marijuana Smokers," *Social Problems* 17, no. 1 (1969): 48–64, 54.

81 Samantha J. Moshier, R. Kathryn McHugh, Amanda W. Calkins, Bridget A. Hearon, Anthony J. Rosellini, Meara L. Weitzman, and Michael W. Otto, "The Role of Perceived Belongingness to a Drug Subculture among Opioid-Dependent Patients," *Psychology of Addictive Behaviors* 26, no. 4 (2012): 812–820.

82 Singer, "What is the 'Drug User Community'?" 75–76.

83 Jennifer R. Schroeder, Carl A. Latkin, Donald R. Hoover, Aaron D. Curry, Amy R. Knowlton and David D. Celentano, "Illicit Drug Use in One's Social Network and in One's Neighborhood Predicts Individual Heroin and Cocaine Use," *Annals of Epidemiology* 11, no. 6 (2001): 389–394.

84 Richard M. Carpiano, Brian C. Kelly, Adam Easterbrook, and Jeffrey T. Parsons, "Community and Drug Use among Gay Men: The Role of Neighborhoods and Networks," *Journal of Health and Social Behavior* 52, no. 1 (2011): 74–90.

85 Eric Rice, Norweeta G. Milburn, Mary Jane Rotheram-Borus, Shelley Mallett, Doreen Rosenthal, "The Effects of Peer Group Network Properties on Drug Use Among Homeless Youth," *American Behavioral Scientist* 48, no. 8 (2005):1102–1123.

86 David Moore, "Beyond 'Subculture' in the Ethnography of Illicit Drug Use," *Contemporary Drug Problems* 31, no. 2 (2004):181–212.

87 Karen Foster and Dale Spencer, "'It's Just a Social Thing': Drug Use, Friendship and Borderwork Among Marginalized Young People," *International Journal of Drug Policy* 24, no. 3 (2013): 223–230.

88 Substance Abuse and Mental Health Services Administration. The NSDUH Report: *Misuse of Over-the-Counter Cough and Cold Medications among Persons Aged 12 to 25* (Rockville, MD: Office of Applied Studies, 2008).

89 National Drug Control Strategy. *Data Supplement, 2015.* https://obamawhitehouse.archives.gov /sites/ default/files/ondcp/policy-and research/2015_data_supplement_final.pdf

90 Patrick Moore, *Tweaked: A Crystal Meth Memoir* (New York, NY: Kensington Books, 2006), 2–3.

91 George B. Vold, *Theoretical Criminology* (New York, NY: Oxford University Press, 1958), 151–154.

92 Ibid., 148.

93 Ibid., 156.

94 Pekka Räsänen and Terhi-Anna Wilska, "Finnish Students' Attitudes towards Commercialised Sex," *Journal of Youth Studies* 10, no. 5 (2007): 557–575, 558.

95 Maggie O'Neill, *Prostitution and Feminism: Towards a Politics of Feeling* (Cambridge: Polity Press, 2001), 16.

96 Janice G. Raymond, "Ten Reasons for *Not* Legalizing Prostitution and a Legal Response to the Demand for Prostitution," *Journal of Trauma Practice* 2, nos. 3–4 (2003–2004): 315–332.

97 Rebecca Hayes-Smith and Zahra Shckarkhar, "Why is Prostitution Criminalized? An Alternative Viewpoint on the Construction of Sex Work," *Contemporary Justice Review* 13, no. 1 (2010): 43–55, 44.

98 David C. May, "Tolerance of Nonconformity and its Effect on Attitudes toward the Legalization of Prostitution: A Multivariate Analysis," *Deviant Behavior* 20, no. 4 (1999): 335–358.

99 Ann Cotton, Melissa Farley, and Robert Baron, "Attitudes Toward Prostitution and Acceptance of Rape Myths," *Journal of Applied Social Psychology* 32, no. 9 (2002): 1790–1796, 1793.

100 John C. Caldwell, Pat Caldwell, and Pat Quiggin, "The Social Context of AIDS," *Population and Development Review* 15, no. 2 (1989): 185–234.

101 Sara Peracca, John Knodel, and Chanpen Saengtienchai, "Can Prostitutes Marry? Thai Attitudes toward Female Sex Workers," *Social Science & Medicine* 47, no. 2 (1998): 255–267.

102 *The Wolfenden Report*. Report of the Committee on Homosexual Offenses and Prostitution. (New York, Stein and Day, 1963), 143–144.

103 Rachael A. Korcha, Cheryl J. Cherpitel, Yu Ye, Jason Bond, and Gabriel Andreuccetti, "Alcohol Use and Injury Severity among Emergency Department Patients in Six Countries," *Journal of Addictions Nursing* 24, no.3 (2013):158–165.

104 Rosemary D.F. Bromley and Amanda L. Nelson, "Alcohol-Related Crime and Disorder Across Urban Space and Time: Evidence from a British City," *Geoforum* 33, no. 2 (2002): 239–254.

105 Aaron M. Brower and Lisa Carroll, "Spatial and Temporal Aspects of Alcohol-Related Crime in a College Town," *Journal of American College Health* 55, no. 5 (2007): 267–275.

106 Raul Caetano, John Schafer, and Carol B. Cunradi, "Alcohol-Related Intimate Partner Violence Among White, Black, and Hispanic Couples in the United States," in *Domestic Violence: The Five Big Questions*, ed. by Mangai Natarajan (New York, NY: Routledge, 2016), 153.

107 Lening Zhang, William F. Wieczorek, and John W. Welte, "The Nexus between Alcohol and Violent Crime," *Alcoholism: Clinical & Experimental Research* 21, no. 7 (1997): 1264–1271.

108 Quinney, *Criminology*, 151–152.

109 Jean L. Forster, David M. Murray, Mark Wolfson and Alexander C. Wagenaar, "Commercial Availability of Alcohol to Young People: Results of Alcohol Purchase Attempts," *Preventive Medicine* 24, no. 4 (1995): 342–347.

110 Alexander C. Wagenaar and Mark Wolfson, "Enforcement of the Legal Minimum Drinking Age in the United States," *Journal of Public Health Policy* 15, no. 1 (1994): 37–53.

111 Traci L. Toomey, Carolyn Rosenfeld and Alexander C. Wagenaar, "Minimum Legal Drinking Age: History, Effectiveness and Ongoing Debate," *Alcohol Health and Research World* 20, no. 4 (1996): 213–218.

112 Alexander C. Wagenaar and Mark Wolfson, "Deterring Sales and Provision of Alcohol to Minors: A Study of Enforcement in 295 Counties in Four States," *Public Health Reports* 110, no. 4 (1995), 419–427.

113 Mark Wolfson, Traci L. Toomey, Jean L. Forster, Alexander C. Wagenaar, P. G. McGovern and Cheryl L. Perry, "Characteristics, Policies and Practices of Alcohol Outlets and Sales to Underage Persons," *Journal of Studies on Alcohol* 57, no. 6 (1996):670–674.

114 Mallie J. Paschall, Joel W. Grube, Carol Black, Robert L. Flewelling, Christopher L. Ringwalt, and Anthony Biglan, "Alcohol Outlet Characteristics and Alcohol Sales to Youth: Results of Alcohol Purchase Surveys in 45 Oregon Communities," *Prevention Science* 8, no. 2 (2007):153–159.

115 James E. Hawdon, "The Role of Presidential Rhetoric in the Creation of a Moral Panic: Reagan, Bush, and the War on Drugs," *Deviant Behavior* 22, no. 5 (2001): 419–445.

116 As cited in ibid., 428.

117 As cited in ibid., 429.

118 Drug Policy Alliance, *Drug War Statistics, 2016*, www.drugpolicy.org/issues/drug-war-statistics

119 Dennis J. Stevens, *An Introduction to American Policing*, 2nd edition (Burlington, MA: Jones and Bartlett Learning, 2018), 268.

120 Drug Enforcement Administration, *Statistics & Facts, 2014*, www.dea.gov/resource-center/statistics.shtml#arrests

121 Rosa del Olmo, "Aerobiology and the War on Drugs: A Transnational Crime," *Crime and Social Justice* 30 (1987): 28–44.

122 New York Civil Liberties Union, *Stop-and-Frisk Data, 2018*, www.nyclu.org/en/Stop-and-Frisk-data.

123 Hannah L.F. Cooper, "War on Drugs Policing and Police Brutality," *Substance Use & Misuse* 50, nos. 8–9 (2015): 1188–1194.

124 Ojmarrh Mitchell and Michael S. Caudy, "Examining Racial Disparities in Drug Arrests," *Justice Quarterly* 32, no. 2 (2015): 288–313.

125 Norval Morris and Gordon Hawkins, *The Honest Politician's Guide to Crime Control* (Chicago, IL: University of Chicago Press, 1970), 5.

126 Federal Bureau of Investigation, *Crime in the United States: Estimated Number of Arrests, 2016.* https://ucr.fbi.gov/crime-in-the-u.s/2016/crime-in-the-u.s.-2016/topic-pages/tables/table-18

127 Denise C. Gottfredson, Stacy S. Najaka, and Brook Kearley, "Effectiveness of Drug Treatment Courts: Evidence from a Randomized Trial," *Criminology & Public Policy* 2, no. 2 (2003):171–196, 172.

128 Greg Berman and John Feinblatt, *Good Courts: The Case for Problem-Solving Justice* (New Orleans LA: Quid Pro Quo Books, 2015), np.

129 Gottfredson, Najaka, and Kearley, "Effectiveness of Drug Treatment Courts."

130 Ojmarrh Mitchell, David B. Wilson, Amy Eggers, and Doris L. MacKenzie, "Assessing the Effectiveness of Drug Courts on Recidivism: A Meta-Analytic Review of Traditional and Non-Traditional Drug Courts," *Journal of Criminal Justice* 40, no. 1 (2012): 60–71.

131 Simon Lenton and Eric Single, "The Definition of Harm Reduction," *Drug and Alcohol Review* 17, no. 2 (1998): 213–220.

132 Michael L. Rekart, "Sex-Work Harm Reduction," *The Lancet* 363, no. 9503 (2005–2006): 2123–2134.

133 Richard Pates and Diane Riley, eds., *Harm Reduction in Substance Use and High-Risk Behavior: International Policy and Practice* (Oxford: Wiley-Blackwell, 2012), ix.

5
OCCUPATIONAL CRIME

Edwin H. Sutherland, the "dean" of American criminology, first formulated the concept of *white-collar crime* and introduced it in his presidential address to the American Sociological Society in 1939.[1] In his original formulation, Sutherland used the term to refer to a violation of legal codes in the course of occupational activity by persons who are "respectable" and "of high social status." The concept turned the attention of criminologists to the study of offenses that had not been included within the scope of criminology. Traditionally criminologists had studied the conventional offenses, such as murder, robbery, and larceny, largely to the exclusion of those offenses in violation of the laws that regulate the numerous occupations. Then in 1949 Sutherland published *White Collar Crime* and wrote:

> The thesis of this book, stated positively, is that persons of the upper socio-economic class engage in much criminal behavior; that this criminal behavior differs from the criminal behavior of the lower socio-economic class principally in the administrative procedures which are used in dealing with the offenders; and that variations in administrative procedures are not significant from the point of view of causation of crime. . . . White collar crime may be defined approximately as a crime committed by a person of respectability and high social status in the course of his occupation.[2]

Of note is that in his original formulation of white-collar crime, Sutherland uses the term "person" rather than "business" or "corporation."

The realization that middle- and upper-class persons commit their own forms of crime was by no means limited to Sutherland.[3] Earlier sociologists had criticized unscrupulous behaviors by individuals in business that occurred in the course of achieving the American Dream. The sociologist Edward A. Ross, in particular, directed his attention to what he labeled "criminaloids," a term that predated white-collar crime by over 30 years. During the 1930s, criminologist Albert Morris called attention to "criminals of the upperworld." But it was with Sutherland's work that such crime began to be taken seriously as an object of study by criminologists.

Sutherland's concept of white-collar crime turned the attention of criminologists to a consideration of the relation of crime to the pursuit of one's legitimate occupation. Gradually the concept was expanded to include the violations that occur in all occupations, irrespective of social class. In his critique of white-collar crime, one criminologist, for example, suggested that, farmers, repairmen, and others in essentially nonwhite collar occupations, could through such illegalities as watering milk for public consumption, making unnecessary "repairs" on TV sets, and so forth, be classified as white-collar violators.[4]

In his research on wartime black market violations, Marshall B. Clinard included gasoline station operators and those of any other occupations, regardless of their social status.[5] Consequently, Richard Quinney suggested that an expansion of the concept of white-collar crime to account for all violations that occur in the course of occupational activity—regardless of the social status of the offender—would increase the utility of the concept.[6] Thus, occupational crime can be defined as a violation of the criminal law in the course of activity in a legitimate occupation.

There is, however, a need for further refinement and reformulation, because the concept of white-collar crime is multidimensional and requires greater specification. Even if Sutherland's original concept is expanded by considering all occupations, there remain the questions of the structural context within which the violation takes place and the nature and motivation of the offender. Sutherland added considerable ambiguity to the concept by referring to occupational activity but then engaging in research on the infractions that take place in the context of large corporations. Furthermore, rather than regarding the corporations per se as the violators, he studied the policy-making officials of corporations. In this typology, we take the position that corporations themselves are violators and should be set apart from individual occupational criminals.

For the purpose of our typology of criminal behavior systems, we are dividing white-collar crime into two distinct types: occupational crime and corporate crime. *Occupational crime* consists of offenses committed by individuals for themselves in the course of their occupations. *Corporate crime* consists of the offenses committed by corporate officials on behalf of their corporations and the offenses of the corporations themselves. The general public or the consumer may be exploited in the course of both occupational and corporate crime. When consumer fraud is committed by the individual businessperson or the professional, such crime will be included in occupational crime; when consumer fraud is committed by corporations or corporate officials, it will be included in corporate crime. The discussion in this chapter will be limited to occupational crime. Corporate crime will be discussed in the following chapter.

Definition of Behavior as Criminal

Law-breaking is often divided into two categories: *conventional crimes*, such as larceny, burglary, and robbery, which are usually punished under the criminal law; and *white-collar crimes*, which consist of *occupational crimes* and *corporate crimes*, which are not usually punished under the criminal law but rather through civil law and administrative law. Punishment by the government through civil law includes injunctions, treble damage suits, and license suspension suits. Administrative sanctions include license suspensions, seizure of illegal commodities, monetary payments, and so on.

Research on occupational crime has concentrated on offenses committed by businesspersons, politicians, government employees, labor union officials, doctors, pharmacists, and lawyers. Such violations include infringements of law by businesspersons and business employers, restraint of trade (through monopoly, illegal rebates, infringements of patents, trademarks, and copyrights), misrepresentation in advertising, unfair labor practices, financial manipulations, and wartime crimes such as black marketeering. Embezzlement is a common form of occupational crime committed by businesspersons of various kinds and in different settings, especially banks, casinos, and charitable organizations. In developing countries violations by businesspeople of the income tax laws, import and export regulations, and currency control measures are often common. Indeed, corruption, fraud, and embezzlement have achieved crisis levels in many developing countries.

It is important to recognize, however, that fraud, forgery, and embezzlement are not always occupational crimes. For example, one study examined arrests rates for four offenses—larceny, fraud, forgery, and embezzlement (LFFE)—that are typically regarded as occupational crimes. It found that, contrary to common belief, most LFFE offending is not committed in an occupational setting. This is especially the case for females whose arrests are disproportionately for shoplifting, bad checks, and welfare/benefit fraud. Male arrests tend to be for theft from motor vehicles, transportation fraud (e.g., jumping subway turnstiles), and counterfeiting (e.g., street vending of counterfeit goods). The conclusion is that arrestees for larceny, fraud, and forgery overwhelmingly represent minor, conventional property crime offenders, not occupational offenders. Indeed, LFFE offenses may be poor indicators of occupational crime and instead involve more mundane frauds (e.g., bad checks, credit card or benefit fraud) and embezzlements involving persons in low-ranking financial or service positions.[7]

This notwithstanding, these types of crimes *are* extensive among persons in many occupations and in business. For example, e-commerce transactions are a growth area for fraudulent activities. There is a significant level of fraud aimed at buyers of items and services on online auction websites such as eBay. However, only a fraction of these swindles is ever reported.

> Many fraud cases are situations in which the defrauded person/s considers the amount in question to be too low to warrant spending his time reporting and/or going after the swindler or cases in which the defrauded person is protected by insurance. In such cases, he does not have the incentive to report the swindling activity.[8]

Another example of occupational crime is insurance fraud. One experimental study of insurance fraud in the auto body repair business investigated whether repair estimates were related to insurance coverage. The study used a statewide representative sample of nearly 100 auto body repair shops in Massachusetts. It was found that in the case of drivers covered by insurance, the repair cost estimates were about one-third higher regardless of type of car, extent of damage, gender of driver, and location of shop. The implication of these results is that the automobile insurance industry is very susceptible to fraudulent or illegal practices that take unfair advantage of insurance companies and the consumer.[9]

In the investment business, brokers sell fraudulent securities, misrepresent asset statements, and illegally use customer assets. Stockbrokers may themselves engage in "insider trading," where they gain illegal profits based on information about possible mergers or corporate takeovers that they obtain before the public has information about them. One widely publicized criminal case of insider trading involved businesswoman and celebrity chef, Martha Stewart, who in 2004 was convicted of charges related to securities fraud. Stewart sold all her shares of stock in a biopharmaceutical company after receiving "insider," or confidential, information from her broker. The day following her sale, the stock value fell 16 percent and she avoided a loss of over $45,000. Stewart served a sentence of 5 months in prison, and 5 months of home arrest.

As early as 1909, the US Supreme Court ruled that the director of a company must either disclose the inside information or abstain from buying or selling shares. In 1934, the Securities and Exchange Commission (SEC), an independent agency of the United States federal government, was established to prohibit undisclosed trading of securities (stocks, bonds, and debentures) based on inside information. However, these and other measures have not prevented brokers and investment bankers from engaging in insider trading. Indeed, one comprehensive global study found that insider trading laws have not been very effective. On the contrary, their enforcement has increased both the incidence and the profitability of insider trading. Harsher laws with tougher penalties work better at reducing the profitability, but not the incidence, of insider trading.[10]

In prosecuting occupational crime, there are problems on several levels: first, the detection of the suspected crime; second, its investigation; third, regulation aimed at preventing future malfeasance; and finally, how to go about prosecuting the criminal. There is a wide variety of behaviors involved in occupational crime, ranging from fraud and the misuse of entrusted funds to illegal electronic transfers of money, stock, and bonds, or the violation of copyright law.

It is often difficult or impossible to establish the actual monetary cost resulting from occupational crime, but it is high. For example, every year investors lose billions of dollars to scams such as Ponzi schemes and pyramid schemes. In 2009, investment advisor, Bernie Madoff was convicted of operating the costliest and longest-running Ponzi scheme in history, and of perpetrating the largest stock and securities fraud in US history. Prosecutors estimated the size of the fraud to be $65 billion, based on the amounts in the accounts of Madoff's clients, which numbered nearly 5,000.

In 2010, about 45,000 cases of insurance fraud were opened for investigation resulting in more than 4,200 arrests and 2,000 civil actions.[11] The extent of injury to the victim is usually vague and tenuous, subject to a variety of definitions. In addition, it is sometimes difficult to distinguish the perpetrator from the victim. As criminologist Jock Young noted:

> Let us take, for example, the Palm Beach Country Club in Florida, which was ravaged by [Madoff's] Ponzi scheme. This is an island of wealth, with an initiation fee of more than $300,000 and a long waiting list; one assessment of its worth is that one third of club members had invested a collective $1 billion with Madoff by 2008. It has to be remembered that it was the cupidity of Madoff's clients that was the real motor behind the scheme and that it was they who benefitted year in and year out until the final collapse. Anyone with an ounce of sense, particularly the big players, must have been only too aware that it was impossible to keep a level rate of return in a fluctuating stock market and that the rate of payment was extremely unlikely. Yet, once Madoff was arrested, his greedy Palm Beach investors considered themselves, with breathtaking hypocrisy, victims. It was this transformation of their greed into the mantle of victimization, once Madoff was arrested, that was the greatest act of hypocrisy.[12]

Labor union officials may engage in such criminal activities as misappropriating or misapplying union funds, defying the government by failure to enforce laws affecting their unions, colluding with employers to the disadvantage of their own union members, or using fraudulent means to maintain control over the union. Forms of union corruption include bribery, extortion, embezzlement, and frauds committed either by union officials or by employers. For example, employers may bribe union officials to obtain sweetheart contracts. Extortion may occur when employers pay union officials to avoid being assigned only unqualified or incompetent workers. Embezzlement happens when union officers pay themselves extravagant "consulting" fees. Vote fraud in union elections occurs with the stuffing of ballot boxes or the miscounting of ballots in union elections.

Physicians may illegally prescribe narcotics, make fraudulent reports or give false testimony in accident cases, and split fees. Fee splitting, the practice of a doctor paying a fee to another health professional in exchange for a referral, is illegal in many places in the United States because of the danger that such referrals might be based on the fee rather than on the doctor's ability. The majority of states have laws that prohibit fee splitting, stating that referral to facilities in which the physician has a financial interest must be accompanied by disclosure and allow the patient the option of choosing an alternative physician.

Lawyers engage in such illegal activities as misappropriating funds in receiverships and securing perjured testimony from witnesses. Many personal-injury lawyers engage in aggressive solicitation and advertisement in billboard, television, and radio advertisements, usually to collect fraudulent damage claims arising from an accident. Lawyers frequently defraud their clients by double billing, padding hours, and overcharging. Double billing happens, for example, when the lawyer, traveling on behalf of one client, does work for another client during that travel time. Padding hours involves invoicing clients for work not performed, for unnecessary work, or for inflating the amount of time spent working on the case. While many of these practices are not criminal offenses, they are nonetheless considered unethical by the American Bar Association. Bankers, investment brokers, politicians, and others may also violate the law in various ways.

The legal regulation of occupations has a long and varied history. The beginnings are found in the development of licensure practices among the medieval guilds, toward the end of the feudal period in Europe. These practices sought to protect the economic interests of the guild members and to protect the community from harmful economic and trade activities. By the beginning of the nineteenth century, the tradition of professional and occupational licensing was well-established in the US, especially in the case of law and medicine. Later in the century, the laws were greatly modified, and in many instances repealed, following the laissez-faire doctrine of industrial capitalism. But with the eventual founding of national and state occupational associations, regulations were once again established. The founding of these associations promoted the interests of the particular occupations.

By 1900, all the established professions had laws, due to pressure from their respective associations. Hence, occupational associations in areas such as medicine and law have been responsible for many of the laws that regulate occupations or professions. To this day, the statutes and administrative codes that regulate occupations and professions are largely influenced by the occupations and professions themselves, which represent their own narrow interests. This is known as professional self-discipline and is open to widespread abuse.

Sociology of Criminal Behavior

A major characteristic of occupational crime is the way the offender conceives of himself or herself. The lack of a conception of self as a "criminal" can be as significant as the presence of such a self-concept. Since these offenses take place in connection with a legitimate occupation or profession and offenders generally regard themselves as respectable, they do not regard themselves as criminals. At most, the self is defined as perhaps a lawbreaker, or one who "skirts the edge" of the law (but with ample justification). The attitude of such an offender is similar to that of those convicted of such crimes as nonsupport of dependents or driving under the influence.

Because the occupational offender is a member of a legitimate occupation or profession, it is difficult for the public to conceive of that person as being a real criminal, even though the offending behavior itself may be condemned. This social definition of others is reflected in the offender's self-image. In fact, many people may secretly admire offenders who are sent to prison for crimes like insider trading, who may make millions or even billions of dollars out of the swindle. A large crowd of admirers stood outside the courthouse and applauded Michael Milken, a prominent figure in the investment business, and a notorious inside trader in the 1980s, after he was convicted of and sent to prison for white-collar felonies that netted hundreds of millions of dollars. Martha Stewart also had her supporters. As *The New York Times* reported:

Outside the courthouse, an upbeat Ms. Stewart, 62, was greeted by a crowd of sympathizers wearing sandwich signs and chef hats who chanted "Save Martha!" Ms. Stewart, who had faced as much as 16 months in prison, told them: "I'll be back. I will be back. I'm used to all kinds of hard work, as you know, and I'm not afraid. I'm not afraid whatsoever."[13]

In his landmark study of white-collar embezzlers, Donald R. Cressey argued that the maintenance of a noncriminal self-concept by the offender is one of the essential elements in the process leading to occupational crime. He found that three interrelated steps were present in all the cases: (1) a "non-sharable" financial problem, (2) knowledge of how to violate, and an awareness that the problem could be secretly resolved by violating their position of trust, and (3) rationalizations about the violations.[14] Typical occupational criminals are able to reconcile their concept of themselves as trusted, decent persons with their concept of themselves as illegal users of entrusted funds or property. Potential trust violators normally define the situation through rationalizations that enable them to regard their criminal behavior as essentially noncriminal. Cressey found that the behavior of his sample was rationalized either as merely "borrowing," as justified, as part of the "general irresponsibility" for which the offenders were not completely accountable, or as due to unusual circumstances.

Occupational offenders frequently regard the law they are breaking as unfair and unjust and thus deserving of violation. As such, occupational offenders are able to rationalize their law-violating behavior. Similar rationalizations are found among criminal telemarketers who solicit funds or sell products based on false assertions or enticing claims. Goods or services are either not delivered or they are substantially inferior to what was promised. One study of telemarketers who had been convicted of fraud found that most rejected the labels of "criminal" and "crime" as descriptions of them and their activities. They employed several explanations and excuses for their offenses. For example, some former owners of telemarketing businesses stated,

> that they set out to maintain a legitimate operation, emulated the operations of their previous employers and assumed, therefore, that their activities violated no laws. Others said they are guilty only of expanding their business so rapidly that they could not properly oversee day-to-day operations. Some said that indulgence in alcohol and illicit drugs caused them to become neglectful of or indifferent toward their businesses. Most claimed that the allure of money caused them to "look the other way." Those who owned or managed firms are prone also to blame rogue sales agents for any fraudulent or deceptive activities. As one put it: "The owners are trying to do the right thing. They're just attracting the wrong people. It's the salesmen." Another subject likewise suggested: "I guess I let the business get too big and couldn't watch over all of the agents to prevent what they were doing." For their part, sales agents charge that their owners and managers kept them in the dark about the business and its criminal nature.[15]

Telemarketing criminals who defraud their "customers" frequently blame the customers for their own victimization. They see their customers as greedy or ignorant and deserving of what befalls them:

> If these people can't read, so be it. Screw them, you know. It [doesn't say] everybody's gonna get the diamond and sapphire tennis bracelet. They're dumb enough not to read, dumb enough to send me the money, I really don't care, you know. I'm doing what I have to do to stay out of jail. They're doing what they have to do to fix their fix. They're promo

junkies, and we're gonna find them and get them, and we're gonna keep getting them. And they're gonna keep buying. And, you know what I used to say, "They're gonna blow their money in Vegas, they're gonna spend it somewhere. I want to be the one to get it."[16]

A similar instance of rationality in the violations of occupational offending is found in a study of white-collar offenders who develop justifications and excuses to explain their involvement in the criminal activities.[17] Though the white-collar offenders did not deny engaging in the criminal behavior for which they were convicted, they *did* deny criminal intent. For example, one offender convicted of antitrust violations involving the building and contracting industry compared his crimes with conventional or "real" crimes that directly and purposely victimize people at a particular time and place:

> It certainly wasn't a premeditated type of thing in our case as far as I can see. . . . To me its different than [name] and I sitting down and we plan, well, we're going to rob this bank tomorrow and premeditatedly go in there. . . . That wasn't the case at all. . . . It wasn't like sitting down and planning, I'm going to rob this bank type of thing. . . . It was just a common everyday way of doing business and surviving.[18]

Another offender convicted of fraud and making false statements stated that his violations were mere technical matters and that on one was harmed:

> First of all, no money was stolen or anything of that nature. The bank didn't lose any money. . . . What I did was a technical violation. I made a mistake. There's no question about that, but the bank lost no money.[19]

Contrary to common assumptions, white-collar criminals are often repeat offenders. The data also suggest that these offenders normally begin their criminal careers in occupational crime when they are well into their legitimate careers, but that they offend less frequently than do criminals convicted of street crimes.[20] The "slippery slope" metaphor applies here. The occupational offender begins transgressing the law well into his or her professional or occupational career, and once the first step is taken, it is relatively easy to move further down the "slope" and commit more offenses without actually defining oneself as a "real criminal." In addition, because white-collar crimes are committed for utilitarian purposes rather than for purposes of emotional expression (as are crimes of violence), the threat of punishment has a powerful deterrent effect on occupational criminals.

Embarrassment and shame typically accompany the public degradation that follows upon conviction of occupational crime. Such emotional reactions, however, are often matched by anger and rage, which tends to render the justice system counterproductive. One study of white-collar offenders convicted for occupational crimes found that the degradation ceremonies of conviction fuel anger and techniques of neutralization such as condemning the condemners.

> When offenders feel anger toward a society that stigmatizes them, they also may feel less respect for the legitimacy of law. This feeling in turn may strengthen the cohesion of subcultures of noncompliance in the business world.[21]

Further, the high social status and respect of most occupational offenders, compared to that of violent offenders and other conventional criminals, makes it difficult for the general public to conceive of occupational offenders as being involved in "real" criminality; this in turn also influences the noncriminal self-conception of occupational criminals.[22] It seems clear that the life organization of the occupational offender is not built around a criminal role. Such a person plays a variety of roles, the most prominent one being that of respected citizen. In Marshall B. Clinard's classic, *The Black Market*, in which he examined the most flagrant cases of price and rationing violations during World War II, those in which criminal prosecution was instituted, it was noted that less than 1 violator in 10 was reported to have had any criminal record.[23] In Richard Quinney's study of pharmacists who engaged in prescription violation, he found that the majority of them resided in the most desirable areas of the city.[24] In terms of career lifestyle, the occupational offender can hardly be distinguished from the occupational nonoffender.

Occupational crime has expanded along with (1) the expansion of techniques of doing business, (2) the social structure of the economy, and (3) the contraction of governmental control and regulation on the federal and state levels. No longer is occupational crime "nickel and dime" behavior; it has expanded into the billions of dollars. Indeed, the economic costs for frauds, identity theft, and employee theft are in the hundreds of billions of dollars annually. As David O. Friedrich's puts it:

> Whether the economic losses due to white-collar crime are more than 50 times greater than those due to conventional crime or only 10 times greater, most of those who have studied this issue would agree that they are certainly significantly greater.[25]

To the concept of group support—meaning the support of one's fellows and the support of a network of people facilitating and approving of the offense—must be added to the concept of organizational structure and the changing nature of production itself. As the US has shifted from a manufacturing economy to a finance economy, so the nature of group support of this type of offense has also changed.

Ever since Sutherland introduced the concept of white-collar crime, most studies of occupational crime viewed the behavior in terms of the group attachments and associations of the offender. Occupational crimes were generally explained according to the principle of differential association, whereby criminal behavior is learned from others who define the behavior favorably and in isolation from those who do not. While this is still the case, the nature of occupational crime, and thus the nature of group support for it, has changed perceptibly. The issue of group support is not as important as the issue of organizational structure, external regulation, and—most important of all—the shift from a manufacturing to a finance economy.

Nevertheless, it remains true that in some occupations members may learn specific techniques by which the law can be violated and build up such rationalizations as "business is business" or "good business demands it." This diffusion of illegal practices is spread from a person already in the occupation to persons new to it, and from one business establishment, political machine, or white-collar group to another. Although many forms of occupational crime can be satisfactorily explained by a theory of differential association (it would seem obvious where there has been continuous and intimate association with unethical and illegal norms and isolation from other norms), this theory has several limitations as an explanation for *all* cases of occupational crimes. Many individuals do not engage in these illegal practices, even though they are familiar with the techniques and rationalizations of violation and frequently associate with persons similarly familiar. A business or professional person could hardly remain in a business or profession for any length of time without acquiring a complete knowledge of the wrongdoing involved. This is true in some occupations and professions more than in others. For example, an accountant is quite likely to be well acquainted with the illegal practices of some of his or her professional colleagues. Persons appear to accept or reject opportunities for occupational crime according to their orientations toward their roles and their attitudes toward general social values like honesty and integrity. Some of the other factors leading to law-violating or law-abiding behavior are attitudes toward other persons in general; the relative importance attached to the status symbol of money; the importance of law observance in general; and the relative importance attached to personal, family, or business reputations.

Each occupational or work situation contains its own set of group norms concerning the possibility of illegal behavior. This has been borne out in the study of police officers' views on excessive force.[26] Over 3,000 sworn personnel in 30 departments in the US were administered questionnaires that included a hypothetical scenario on the use of excessive force that was worded as follows:

> Two police officers on foot patrol surprise a man who is attempting to break into an automobile. The man flees. They chase him for about two blocks before apprehending him by tackling him and wrestling him to the ground. After he is under control both officers punch him a couple of times in the stomach as punishment for fleeing and resisting.[27]

The results showed that while 72 percent of police officers stated that the violence depicted in the scenario was highly serious, a significant proportion (about one in seven) did not view this sort of excessive force as particularly grave. What is more, almost one-third of respondents indicated that it was unlikely that they would report a fellow officer's use of excessive force as depicted in the scenario. The number of years of experience in policing showed the difference in how the respondents saw the police misconduct. As compared with novice officers and senior veterans, those with intermediate levels of experience were more likely to view the depicted offense as less serious and were more likely to indicate a low likelihood of reporting fellow officers for the use of excessive force. The difference was explained by the fact that the intermediate group is most likely to be strongly integrated into and affected by the occupational values, norms, and beliefs of the street cop subculture. "The street cop subculture supports the belief that excessive force can be an appropriate, or at least an understandable, response to threatening or disrespectful actions by certain groups of people."[28]

Another study on the influence of work group norms on the attitudes of employees, this one of registered nurses, concerned the reporting or not reporting of a coworker's wrongdoing.[29] Such wrongdoing included narcotic use by colleagues while on the job, patient abuse, negligence, incompetence, consistent errors, and lack of respect for the patient. Organizational reasons for the nurse respondents not reporting wrongdoing included the workplace culture of the organization being retaliatory. For example, a staff hospital nurse expressed this sentiment as follows:

> Patient placed on bed pan and forgotten for 1 hr. Cups of medication left at bedside and patient forgot to take—wrong medication given. Patient left up in wheel chair and not assisted to bed till late at night. In our organization if you want to keep your job the less said the better.[30]

It would be expected that nonprofit church organizations that instill ethical values of accountability in their employees would have little or no occupational crime. Yet one report suggests that not only is embezzlement not uncommon in religious organizations, they also tend to deal with it rather leniently. These organizations can be too trusting, believing that their employees abide by its ethical, religious values. In addition, their humanitarian attitude of forgiveness may distort the reality and severity of occupational crime and even encourage it.

> Religious organizations that have controls and guidelines in place often overlook them in favor of the qualities and limitations of mercy and trust which must be tempered with justice.[31]

Some forms of occupational crime are related to the structure of the occupation in which the offender is engaged and to the roles played by the offender within the occupation. The importance of the occupational structure and occupational roles of the offender has been shown in Richard Quinney's study of prescription violation among retail pharmacists.[32] He found that violations occur more frequently among business pharmacists and least often among professional pharmacists, with professional–business pharmacists and indifferent pharmacists (those not oriented to either role) being intermediate in the frequency of violations. Quinney concluded that prescription violation is related to the structure of the occupation and the "differential orientation" of retail pharmacists to the roles within the occupation. Thus, group support for occupational crime can be in the form of diffuse and subtle processes. Each occupation contains its own supports both for and against the violation of occupational laws.

Kitty Calavita and Henry N. Pontell introduced the concept of "collective embezzlement," which is the siphoning off of corporate funds for personal use by top management.[33] This criminal activity, an occupational crime, is carried out by individuals within an economic structure that is centered on the management and manipulation of money itself. Drawing on data from government documents, congressional hearings, and news media accounts, Calavita and Pontell were able to "isolate the forces facilitating crime and fraud in these industries, and to link those forces to their base in the industries' structure."[34] Here the group support comes not from other individuals but from the very structure of the savings and loan, banking, and insurance industries. "Different from the traditional embezzlers described by Sutherland and Cressey, the perpetrators of collective embezzlement are not lone lower-level employees but institutions' owners and operators, acting within networks of co-conspirators inside or outside the institutions."[35]

Group support for occupational crime comes from what one scholar calls "criminogenic organizational structures and processes."[36] The same holds true for group support of insider trading, or violation of securities laws by individuals. Likewise, group support for occupational crimes such as fraudulent billing of Medicaid and Medicare in the medical health industry comes as much from the structure of payment bureaucracies as it does from other professionals in the industry who support such criminal actions with the "everyone does it" argument.

Social Reaction to Criminal Behavior

Occupational crime cannot be fully understood without reference to the structure and values of the general society. The values involved in the regulation of commercial transactions may conflict with those of free enterprise, individualism, supply and demand, trickle-down economics, or the "open market." An individual's attitude toward selective obedience to a "good" or "bad" law becomes the key to compliance. "The demand of law arises out of the conflicts in cultures, and because there is conflict in cultures, the law is not effective as a deterrent upon other groups that did not at first demand the law."[37]

One of the most important reasons for the high degree of correspondence between some forms of occupational crime and patterns of legitimate behavior is that many of the activities are only defined gradually over time as they surface and attract official attention. What happens as a result is that public opinion gradually comes to define them as criminal. In a highly and increasingly differentiated and segmented society, the ambivalence of average citizens, businesspeople, and lawyers reflects structured conflicts in social roles and the larger social system. Additional studies are continually giving us some idea of the conditions that lead to the definition of behavior as criminal and of the ways in which legal norms intersect and are integrated with the norms of other institutional structures. Values, norms, and other aspects of middle- and upper-class cultures may help explain occupational crime in much the same way that knowledge of the culture of the lower class is necessary to understand street crime.

Donald R. Cressey suggested that the extent of correspondence between some occupational crime and legitimate patterns is indicated in our everyday language. This language can easily provide the offender with appropriate verbalizations. Furthermore, these verbalizations may actually be "vocabularies of motive" for the offender. As in the case of embezzlers:

> Vocabularies of motive are not something invented by embezzlers (or anyone else) on the spur of the moment. Before they can be taken over by an individual, these verbalizations exist as group definitions in which the behavior in question, even crime, is in a sense *appropriate*. There are any number of popular ideologies that sanction crime in our culture: "Honesty is the best policy, but business is business"; "It is all right to steal a loaf of bread when you are starving"; "All people steal when they get in a tight spot." Once these verbalizations have been assimilated and internalized by individuals, they take a form such as: "I'm only going to use the money temporarily, so I am borrowing, not stealing," or "I have tried to live an honest life but I've had nothing but troubles, so to hell with it."[38]

A symbiotic relation exists between occupational crime and the very organization of legitimate society. This is evident, for example, in the number of physicians engaged in health care fraud, which includes such activities as billing for services not rendered or not medically necessary; "unbundling," or billing each stage of a procedure as if it were a separate treatment; "upcoding," or billing more costly services than those actually performed; and double billing for services provided. Whatever the illegalities, physicians generally view their fraudulent behavior—exaggerating severity of illness, changing billing diagnosis, or reporting symptoms a patient did not have in order to obtain coverage for care that physicians perceived to be necessary—as essential to ensure high-quality care for their patients. Indeed, there sometimes occurs a type of "collusion" between physician and patient:

> A series of studies have made it clear that a sizeable percentage of physicians are willing to deceive insurers in order to obtain insurance benefits for their patients. A rich list of words (stretching, fudging, gaming, advocacy, exaggerating, lying) has been employed to describe such conduct, and many patients request their physicians to perform these acts. Many physicians seem to believe such behavior is necessary (if not ethically required) if their patients are to receive appropriate care, and they have deep-seated ethical objections to many of the cost-containment strategies currently employed by MCOs. When physicians believe that the manipulation of reimbursement rules is "the only feasible way to provide high quality care," the shame a physician might feel for violating program requirements is significantly muted.

Remarkably enough, the prospect of being prosecuted for health care fraud does not substantially affect physician willingness to commit such conduct.[39]

Occupational crime is not far removed from the legitimate realm of US society. It is simply the reverse side of the coin, the darker side. It is not uncommon that individuals convicted of occupational crimes such as insider trading, computer hacking, or insurance fraud are the objects of widespread popular admiration for their ingenuity. Or, at least in the case of physicians, patients are willing to give them the benefit of the doubt:

> In one recent case in New York, a prominent obstetrician–gynecologist was prosecuted for submitting claims for infertility treatments that were not covered by the patient's insurance. In order to obtain coverage, the physician mischaracterized the services he had rendered. His patients rallied to his defense and insisted that the physician was behaving appropriately since the patients actually required the uncovered services and petty insurance restrictions were of no real importance.[40]

In discussing "our criminal society," Edwin M. Schur described the relation between criminal behavior and certain values, drawing upon the criminogenic character of American society:

> Of course, this undercurrent of values conducive to business crimes and related offenses is not surprising, given the extensive influence of the "business spirit" in our society. Indeed, certain of the values that help promote criminality in America are far from being subterranean in character. Thus, sociologist Donald Taft has cited the following "characteristics of American society" as having possible significance in the causation of crime: "its dynamic quality, complexity, materialism, growing impersonality, individualism, insistence upon the importance of status, restricted group loyalties, survivals of frontier traditions, race discrimination, lack of scientific orientation in the social field, tolerance of political corruption, general faith in law, disrespect for some law, and acceptance of quasi-criminal exploitation." . . . These are clearly dominant values or characteristics of American life, and they seem in some sense to have very real bearing on at least some types of criminality.[41]

Perhaps there is no need to look for individual pathologies when parts of the American Dream can help us understand crime. As Steven F. Messner and Richard Rosenfeld have noted,

> the American Dream itself and the normal social conditions engendered by it are deeply implicated in the problem of crime. . . . The American Dream has a dark side that must be considered in any serious effort to uncover the social sources of crime. It encourages an exaggerated emphasis on monetary achievements while devaluating alternative criteria of success; it promotes a preoccupation with the realization of goals while deemphasizing the importance of the ways in which the goals are pursued; and it helps create and sustain social structures incapable of restraining criminogenic cultural pressures.[42]

Occupational crime differs from conventional crime not only in its unique form of activity but in the toleration and support it receives from the public at large as well as from the courts, both on the federal and state level. Punishments given for occupational offenses normally differ in severity and harshness from the punishments given for offenses such as burglary, auto theft and, particularly, those (such as robbery) that involve the threat or actual use of violence. This is because the public had previously not seen white-collar crimes as being as serious as crimes of violence or property.[43]

However, this perception is changing. One study found that students from a mid-sized Midwestern university rated white-collar offenses as less serious than violent crime, but more serious than property crime. The same finding held when examining the wrongfulness and harmfulness of the acts.[44] A national survey examining perceptions of crime seriousness between select street and white-collar crimes revealed that the majority of individuals perceived that white-collar crimes were as serious—if not more so—than street crimes. However,

> it is difficult to know whether the public's perception about the seriousness of white-collar crime will translate into a willingness among public officials and policy makers to impose harsher sanctions.[45]

Neither of the studies of perceived seriousness between white-collar crime and street crime distinguished between occupational and corporate crime. One Norwegian study, however, examined the differences in sentence length for occupational and corporate offenders. It found that although the seriousness of the crime committed was greater among corporate criminals, they still received shorter prison sentences compared to occupational criminals. The longer sentences imposed on the occupational offenders may be because they committed crime for their own purposes or enrichment, while this is generally not the case among corporate criminals.[46]

The policing of occupational crime has increased. Many large-city police departments have a White-Collar Crimes (or Financial Crimes) Unit that investigates occupational crimes. For example, the San Antonio Police Department's White-Collar Unit

> is responsible for investigating embezzlement, elder fraud, intellectual property crimes (fake merchandise), barratry, and other complex financial crimes. As financial technology becomes more elaborate, criminals devise increasingly complicated schemes in an attempt to defraud individuals, businesses, and entities. White-Collar detectives train continuously to stay on top of crime trends and communicate with businesses and individuals in an attempt to minimize risk and loss.[47]

The Federal Bureau of Investigation is also active in investigating white-collar crime, including various forms of occupational crime. According to its *Financial Crime Report*, at the end of FY 2011, the FBI was investigating 1,846 cases of securities and commodities fraud and had recorded 520 indictments and 394 convictions. Nearly 2,700 cases of health care fraud were investigated resulting in 1,676 indictments and 736 convictions. In addition, there were 521 indictments, and 429 convictions of financial institution fraud, which includes insider fraud (embezzlement and misapplication), check fraud, counterfeit negotiable instruments, check kiting, and fraud contributing to the failure of financial institutions.[48]

While investigations of occupational crime have increased, there are still two major issues of enforcement to overcome: (1) many police agencies lack resources and training needed in dealing with certain types of occupational crime and (2) much occupational crime goes unreported to the police. For example, many local police departments find it difficult to keep pace with "technocriminals" who engage in internet fraud that includes identity theft, credit/debit card fraud, general merchandise sales, and auction fraud. A nationwide survey of 700 US police departments and sheriff's agencies found, among other things, that respondents did not believe that judges and elected officials perceived internet fraud as being a major problem and that respondents reported a lack of staff and overall resources in their attempts to address internet fraud.[49]

An Australian study of crime against small businesses revealed that while most business proprietors tended to report such conventional crimes as armed robbery, burglary, and owner/employees assaulted or threatened, they tended *not* to report occupational crimes such as check/credit card fraud, bribery/extortion, and employee theft. Though the reasons for choosing not to report occupational crime to the police are numerous and complex, many of the victimized business proprietors indicated that reporting would not achieve anything, that the incident was not serious enough to report, that the police could not do anything, and that the chance of a successful solution of the matter was slight.[50]

The "saving grace" of occupational crime is that it usually does not involve violence. This, however, is not always the case. As criminologist David O. Friedrichs notes regarding medical crime:

> The performance of unnecessary surgery is arguably the single most disturbing form of medical crime, insofar as it can be considered violent occupational crime. Most operations (perhaps 80 percent) are elective procedures. Some studies have suggested that up to 15 or 20 percent of the several million operations performed annually in the United States may be unnecessary, and the percentage of unnecessary operations has increased in recent years. . . . By one account, some 16,000 patients die annually in the United States from unnecessary operations. . . . The most common forms of unnecessary surgery have involved the removal of tonsils, hemorrhoids, appendixes, and uteruses; heart-related surgery (e.g., coronary bypasses, pacemaker implants); and caesarian section deliveries—all at an annual cost of billions of dollars and many lives. . . . In at least some cases, surgeons performing clearly unnecessary operations have caused paralysis, blindness, and other forms of permanent injury.[51]

Along these lines, some have called for the criminalization of nontherapeutic cosmetic surgery that carries a high risk of long-term harm. One legal scholar has argued that procedures such as breast augmentation and nontherapeutic labiaplasty, are a form of physical harm, not a form of medicine. He maintains that,

> The consenting victims of nontherapeutic harmful cosmetic surgery may not feel wronged because they consent, but they are wronged and harmed. They are wronged and harmed because the surgeon uses them as a means to an end, that is, as an object for making money. The issue is not about criminalizing the consenter (the putative patient); instead, it is about criminalizing the harm-doer, the surgeon. A criminal offense would not limit the self-harmer's freedom to self-harm; her freedom would be limited only to the extent that others will be deterred from harming her.[52]

Despite the harms that may occur with unnecessary surgery, most occupational crime does not involve any form of physical force. Thus, aside from the relative absence of violence, other reasons for the public's toleration of occupational crime is the fact that occupational crime is usually more complex, and diffused over a longer period of time, than conventional crime, and this fact obscures the essential criminality of the acts. The truism seems to be "steal a little from a great many over time rather than a lot from a few in a short time." In addition, the type of publicity given to occupational crime by the media seldom creates much public resentment or fear, as contrasted to the depiction of more overt crimes like burglary or assault.

Another study involved an inspection of the socioeconomic status of the occupational offender and the severity of the sentence received. It concluded that, while the majority of occupational criminals come from the broad middle segment of the socioeconomic status range, judges normally tend to punish offenders of higher status much more harshly than their less socially and economically privileged fellow occupational offenders.[53] In a related vein, a study conducted in the late 1980s of eight types of occupational offenders (perpetrators of bank embezzlement, postal fraud, credit fraud, false claims, tax fraud, bribery, antitrust violations, and securities fraud) summarized the findings as follows:

> The results show that a minority of men but only a handful of women fit the image of a highly placed white collar offender. Most employed women are clerical workers, and most employed men were managers or administrators. Women were more likely to be nonwhite, less likely to have completed college, and owned less in economic assets. Men were more likely to work in crime groups and to use organizational resources in carrying out crimes, and their attempted economic gains were higher. Occupational marginality, not mobility, better explains the form of women's white collar crime. *The results raise questions about white collar arrest data and the nature of the crime and offenders in white collar sentencing samples.* They compel an investigation of the multiple influences of gender, class, and race relations in generating varieties of white collar crime and in being caught and prosecuted for white collar crime.[54]

Thus, in the laws directed at the illegal behavior of offenders—particularly those in the medical, legal, and clerical professions—there has been a tendency to enact lenient statutes and to enforce them in a similar fashion, showing favoritism to offenders of high social status.

> Their specialized knowledge puts professionals in a different position from that of entrepreneurs, retailers, and salespeople. As patients, clients, and students people typically defer to the judgments of professionals much more readily than they do as consumers or customers because they perceive they have less reason to be confident in their own judgment.[55]

Many laws provide no criminal sanctions for these "trusted criminals," and where criminal sanctions are included, they have been used hesitantly. Thus, the laws outlawing occupational crime differ from laws of conventional crime not only in their origin, but also in philosophy, in the determination of responsibility or intent, in enforcement and prosecution procedures, and in the sanctions used to punish the violators.

The enforcement and administration of occupational laws depend largely on specially created agencies rather than on police and prosecutors. The administrative process of hearing cases, rather than undertaking criminal trial procedures, closely approximates juvenile court procedures. The actions are often remedial in nature, as in the use of cease-and-desist orders, rather than consisting of direct punishment of the offender through imprisonment or stiff fines. This becomes apparent when one considers that an apprehended burglar or robber is punished by a jail or prison sentence, a fine or probation, whereas a physician may be punished by a government warning or injunction, the levying of civil damages or the suspension of his or her license to practice medicine.

Regulation of the medical profession provides an excellent example of how occupational laws are enforced and administered. Responsibility for the regulation of the medical profession lies with each state's board of medical examiners. These boards are composed of physicians who are usually appointed by the governor on the recommendation of the state medical society. The boards of medical examiners devote most of their time to granting licenses to new physicians, but they are also charged with taking disciplinary actions against incompetent or unethical practitioners.

> Medical examiners generally maintain high standards for the granting of a medical license; once a license is issued, however, it is rarely revoked. Once admitted to the fellowship of

physicians, incompetent or even criminal practitioners are apt to be given the protection of their colleagues.[56]

It is a similar situation with the police passing administrative judgments through their internal affairs divisions that investigate cases of police misconduct including corruption, harassment, or the use of excessive force.

The physician, thus, is virtually a free agent. Once licensed, he or she has a lifetime certificate to practice largely at his or her own discretion. When infractions of medical practice laws are detected, the state board is rarely quick to act. Thus, self-discipline among medical practitioners may be more illusory than real. One physician who has examined the corruption prevalent among his colleagues when they take payoffs from big drug companies and other medical suppliers, states the following:

> In medicine there is little policing and virtually no sanctions for physicians with financial conflicts [of interest]. Professional associations must no longer look away from this issue. If they wish to retain the trust of the public, they must develop far more high-minded policies, indeed ones that would embarrass physicians who collaborate with industry's marketing goals and would reward doctors who keep free of such conflicts. I challenge the ACP [American College of Physicians] and the AMA [American Medical Association] and other major professional organizations to upgrade the standards for their members and show the public that they intend to take a much higher ground on the issue of conflict of interest.[57]

Several factors, then, may explain the lenient treatment of occupational offenders by the legal system: (1) the absence of interpersonal violence, (2) the latitude of the general public, (3) the social status of the offender, and (4) the protection afforded by a professional organization.

There are, however, several forms of societal reaction and legal processing that may reduce occupational crime. One, *occupational disqualification*, involves,

> laws providing that a felony conviction renders one either permanently or temporarily ineligible to pursue certain licensed vocations such as pharmacist, barber, and liquor store or pawn shop owner. And many convicted persons are barred from holding public office and public employment. . . . Perhaps most importantly, it is a severe enough sanction to be appropriate to many different egregious legal violations committed in the course of occupation.[58]

Another societal reaction, *reintegrative shaming*, condemns the occupational offender's wrongdoing but does so without stigmatization.[59] In this way, offenders understand and recognize their wrongdoing and shame themselves. They are then able to be reintegrated back into the community of respectables. Occupational offenders are highly deterrable by public disapproval because they have much to lose in social status and respectability by having their reputations sullied. A survey of taxpayers in Australia who had been caught and punished for engaging in illegal tax avoidance schemes assessed the relationship between disapproval, shame-related emotions, and recidivism. An important finding in this study was that those offenders who perceived their treatment as being reintegrative, and consequently less stigmatizing, were less likely to report that they had evaded their taxes in the years following their enforcement experience.[60]

In sum, most occupational crime consists of both exploiting others and surviving within the system. People in many occupations and professions survive and profit from their work by taking part, in small ways or massively, in criminal activities, some of them harming those who receive their services. The small businessperson who shortchanges the customer is committing an illegal and harmful act against the public. The failing lawyer who arranges to fix a case engages in a criminal act in attempting to survive in the profession.

Occupational crime must be understood as part of the economic system's structure and culture. The norms and values that prevail in the pursuit of economic gain also regulate the activity by members of occupations and professions. A symbiotic relationship or close association connects occupational crime and the organization of capitalist society. Thus, to engage in business or professional life in the United States is to follow the basic patterns of capitalist society. An economy of competition and success, as well as economic gain, promotes a form of life emphasizing the rightness of any activity pursued in the interest of one's business or occupation.[61] This form of life is deeply ingrained in the US political economy, thus making it difficult to articulate, much less challenge those abstract financial forces. As one criminologist has observed about the news media's coverage of the 2008 financial crisis that was partly associated with Bernie Madoff's fraudulent schemes:

> Media discourses about Madoff's crime have focused on his individual, egregious behavior and the mistakes or ethical lapses of other individuals. . . . What was painfully lacking was a positioning and discussion of Madoff's place within the overall culture of modern capitalism and the conditions that led—and will lead again—to economic collapse. In other words, our cultural scripts, embedded in the logic of capitalism, proved ultimately impermeable to change and reproduced themselves through the Madoff case.[62]

Notes

1 Edwin H. Sutherland, "White-Collar Criminality," *American Sociological Review* 5, no. 1 (1940): 1–12.
2 Edwin H. Sutherland, *White Collar Crime* (New York, NY: Dryden Press, 1949), 9.
3 See Gilbert Geis, ed., *White-Collar Criminal: The Offender in Business and the Professions* (New York, NY: Atherton Press, 1968): 1–19.
4 Donald J. Newman, "White Collar Crime," *Law and Contemporary Problems* 23, no. 4 (1958): 735–753, 737.
5 Marshall B. Clinard, *The Black Market: A Study of White Collar Crime* (New York, NY: Holt, Rinehart & Winston, 1952).
6 Richard Quinney, "The Study of White Collar Crime: Toward a Reorientation in Theory and Research," *Journal of Criminal Law, Criminology, and Police Science* 55, no. 2 (1964): 208–214.
7 Darrell Steffensmeier, Casey T. Harris, and Noah Painter-Davis, "Gender and Arrests for Larceny, Fraud, Forgery, and Embezzlement: Conventional or Occupational Property Crime Offenders?" *Journal of Criminal Justice* 43, no. 3 (2015): 205–217.
8 Bezalel Gavish and Christopher L. Tucci, "Fraudulent Auctions on the Internet," *Electronic Commerce Research* 6, no. 2 (2006): 127–140, 128.
9 Paul E. Tracy and James Alan Fox, "A Field Experiment on Insurance Fraud in Auto Body Repair," *Criminology* 27, no. 3 (1989): 589–603.
10 Arturo Bris, "Do Insider Trading Laws Work?" *European Financial Management* 11, no. 3 (2005): 267–312.
11 National Association of Insurance Commissioners, *Insurance Fraud, 2018*. www.naic.org/cipr_topics/topic_insurance_fraud.htm
12 Jock Young, "Bernie Madoff, Finance Capital, and the Anomic Society," in *How They Got Away with It: White Collar Criminals and the Financial Meltdown*, ed. by Susan Will, Stephen Handelman, and David C. Brotherton (New York, NY: Columbia University Press, 2013), 77.
13 Constance L. Hays, "Martha Stewart's Sentence: The Overview; 5 Months in Jail, and Stewart Vows, 'I'll Be Back,'" *New York Times*, July 17, 2004, www.nytimes.com/2004/07/17/business/martha-stewart-s-sentence-overview-5-months-jail-stewart-vows-ll-be-back.html
14 Donald. R. Cressey, *Other People's Money: A Study in the Social Psychology of Embezzlement* (New York, NY: The Free Press, 1953).

15 Neal Shover, Glenn S. Coffey, and Dick Hobbs, "Crime on the Line: Telemarketing and the Changing Nature of Professional Crime," *British Journal of Criminology* 43, no. 3 (2003): 489–505, 499.

16 Ibid., 500.

17 Michael L. Benson, "Denying the Guilty Mind: Accounting for Involvement in White-Collar Crime," *Criminology* 23, no. 4 (1985): 589–599.

18 Ibid., 592–593.

19 Ibid., 598.

20 David Weisburd, Elin Waring, with Ellen F. Chayet, *White-Collar Crime and Criminal Careers* (New York, NY: Cambridge University Press, 2001).

21 Michael L. Benson, "Emotions and Adjudication: Status Degradation among White Collar Criminals," *Justice Quarterly* 7, no. 3 (1990): 515–528, 526.

22 James William Coleman, *The Criminal Elite: Understanding White-Collar Crime*, 6th edition (New York, NY: Worth Publishers, 2006).

23 Clinard, *The Black Market*.

24 Richard Quinney, "Retail Pharmacy as a Marginal Occupation: A Study of Prescription Violation," (PhD dissertation, University of Wisconsin, 1962), 261.

25 David O. Friedrichs, *Trusted Criminals: White Collar Crime in Contemporary Society*, 4th edition (Belmont, CA: Wadsworth, 2010), 50.

26 Anthony J. Micucci and Ian M. Gomme, "American Police and Subcultural Support for the Use of Excessive Force," *Journal of Criminal Justice* 33, no. 5 (2005): 487–500.

27 Ibid., 492.

28 Ibid., 489.

29 Granville King III and Amy Hermodson, "Peer Reporting of Coworker Wrongdoing: A Qualitative Analysis of Observer Attitudes in the Decision to Report versus Not Report Unethical Behavior," *Journal of Applied Communication Research* 28, no. 4 (2000): 309–329.

30 Ibid., 320.

31 Marilynn P. Fleckenstein and John C. Bowes, "When Trust Is Betrayed: Religious Institutions and White-Collar Crime," *Journal of Business Ethics* 23, no. 1 (2000): 111–115.

32 Richard Quinney, "Occupational Structure and Criminal Behavior: Prescription Violation by Retail Pharmacists," *Social Problems* 11, no. 2 (1963): 179–185.

33 Kitty Calavita and Henry N. Pontell, "'Other People's Money' Revisited: Collective Embezzlement in the Savings and Loan and Insurance Industries," *Social Problems* 38, no. 1 (1991): 94–112.

34 Ibid., 95.

35 Ibid., 91.

36 Gary S. Green, *Occupational Crime*, 2nd edition (Belmont, CA: Wadsworth Publishing, 1996).

37 Albert K. Cohen, Alfred Lindesmith, and Karl Schuessler, eds., *The Sutherland Papers* (Bloomington, IN: Indiana University Press, 1956), 102.

38 Donald R. Cressey, "The Respectable Criminal," *Trans-action* 2, no. 1 (1965): 12–15, 14.

39 David A. Hyman, "Health Care Fraud and Abuse: Market Change, Social Norms, and the Trust 'Reposed in the Workmen,'" *Journal of Legal Studies* 30, no. S2 (2001): 531–567, 542.

40 Ibid., 547.

41 Edwin M. Schur, *Our Criminal Society: The Social and Legal Sources of Crime in America* (Englewood Cliffs, NJ: Prentice-Hall, 1969), 185–186.

42 Steven F. Messner and Richard Rosenfeld, *Crime and the American Dream*, 5th edition (Belmont, CA: Wadsworth Publishing, 2012), 6, 11.

43 Stanton Wheeler, Kenneth Mann, and Austin Sarat, *Sitting in Judgment: The Sentencing of White Collar Offenders* (New Haven, CT: Yale University Press, 1988).

44 Sean P. Rosenmerkel, "Wrongfulness and Harmfulness as Components of Seriousness of White-Collar Offenses," *Journal of Contemporary Criminal Justice* 17, no. 4 (2001): 308–327.

45 Nicole Leeper Piquero, Stephanie Carmichael, and Alex R. Piquero, "Assessing the Perceived Seriousness of White-Collar and Street Crimes," *Crime & Delinquency* 54, no. 2 (2008): 291–312, 307.

46 Petter Gottschalk and Torbjørn Rundmo, "Crime: The Amount and Disparity of Sentencing—A Comparison of Corporate and Occupational White-Collar Criminals," *International Journal of Law, Crime, and Justice* 42, no. 3 (2014): 175–187.

47 San Antonio Police Department, *White Collar Unit, 2018*. www.sanantonio.gov/SAPD/About/Financial Crimes#161111713-white-collar

48 Federal Bureau of Investigation, *Financial Crimes Report 2010–2011*. www.fbi.gov/stats-services/publications/financial-crimes-report-2010-2011

49 Ronald G. Burns, Keith H. Whitworth, and Carol Y. Thompson, "Assessing Law Enforcement Preparedness to Address Internet Fraud," *Journal of Criminal Justice* 32, no. 5 (2004): 477–493.
50 Natalie Taylor, "Under-Reporting of Crime Against Small Businesses: Attitudes Toward Police and Reporting Practices," *Policing and Society* 13, no. 1 (2003): 79–89.
51 Friedrichs, *Trusted Criminals*, 103.
52 Dennis J. Baker, "Should Unnecessary Harmful Nontherapeutic Cosmetic Surgery be Criminalized?" *New Criminal Law Review: In International and Interdisciplinary Journal* 17, no. 4 (2014): 587–630, 589.
53 David Weisburd and Stanton Wheeler, *Crimes of the Middle Classes: White-Collar Offenders in the Federal Courts* (New Haven, CT: Yale University Press, 1991).
54 Kathleen Daly, "Gender and Varieties of White Collar Crime," *Criminology* 27, no. 4 (1989): 769–794, 769.
55 Friedrichs, *Trusted Criminals*, 102.
56 Coleman, *The Criminal Elite*, 141.
57 Jerome P. Kassirer, *On the Take: How Medicine's Complicity with Big Business Can Endanger Your Health* (New York, NY: Oxford University Press, 2005), 199.
58 Green, *Occupational Crime*, 246, 251.
59 John Braithwaite, *Crime, Shame and Reintegration* (Cambridge: Cambridge University Press, 1989).
60 Kristina Murphy and Nathan Harris, "Shaming, Shame, and Recidivism: A Test of Reintegrative Shaming Theory in the White-Collar Crime Context," *British Journal of Criminology* 47, no. 6 (2007): 900–917.
61 Richard Quinney, *Criminology*, 2nd edition (Boston: Little, Brown, 1979), 193–197.
62 Colleen P. Eren, *Bernie Madoff and the Crisis: The Public Trial of Capitalism* (Stanford, CT: Stanford University Press, 2017), 175.

6

CORPORATE CRIME

Corporate crime refers to the illegal activities of large business organizations; generally the larger industrial companies (the Fortune 500 or 1,000) and the executives acting on their behalf. It involves violations of laws, statutes, and regulatory standards affecting corporations for corporate profit and not for the sake of personal gain by an individual (or groups of individuals) working for the corporation. As organizations, large corporations vary in the way in which their social structure generates unlawful behavior.

Today's corporations are multinational conglomerates with assets that total billions of dollars. In 2017, the annual combined sales of the largest United States companies, the Fortune 500, totaled $12.8 trillion in revenues, with profits of $1 trillion. Walmart's sales of $500,343 billion and Exxon Mobil's sales of $244, 363 billion made them two of the world's largest and most profitable corporations. In 2018, Apple became the first American public company to exceed $1 trillion in earnings. Although these giant conglomerates have one or more leading lines of business, most have acquired a variety of other product lines. For example, CVS Health, the retail pharmacy and health care company with over $6.5 billion in profits and 203,000 employees is involved in retail pharmacy, benefit management, and insurance.[1] Consequently, these conglomerates have amassed political and economic power that extends beyond that of the traditional large corporation operating in a single product line. Although they may have other goals (such as lobbying clout or increased power and prestige) along with their corporate growth and stability, their paramount objectives remain the maximization of corporate profits and the general financial success of the corporation, whether through sales, market shares, or increased assets.

Along with the large corporations' greatly increased productive power, they "are also responsible for a wide range of harmful effects, including the use of technologies with deleterious consequences for human health and the production of environmental hazards that threaten the planet."[2] There have been many extensive violations of law, as revealed by government investigative committees, both state and federal, that have looked into banking institutions, mining, and the oil, auto, pharmaceutical, and defense industries, among others. Widespread corporation payoffs, domestic and foreign, and illegal political contributions also have been exposed by investigations.

As Marshall B. Clinard stated, corporate crime covers a variety of serious misbehavior:

Among these violations are accounting malpractices, including false statements of corporate assets and profits; occupational safety and health hazards; unfair labor practices; the manufacture and sale of hazardous products and misleading packaging of products; abuses of competition that restrain trade such as antitrust and agreements among corporations to allocate markets; false and misleading advertising, environmental violations of air and water pollution, and illegal dumping of hazardous materials; illegal domestic political contributions and bribery of foreign officials for corporate benefits.[3]

Despite the limited number of government investigative and prosecutory staffs available, between 1990 and 2004 35 of the Fortune 500 industrial and manufacturing companies were charged with violations of corporate law; the size of fine or settlement for 18 of these companies was $1 to $5 million, for 10 of them it was $5 to $10 million, and for 4 of the companies it was over $1 billion.[4] Marshall B. Clinard and Peter C. Yeager had previously found that 115 corporations of the Fortune 500 had been convicted of at least one major crime between 1970 and 1980 or had paid civil penalties for serious illegal behavior. The largest of these corporations were the chief violators.[5] They had also received a widely disproportionate share of the sanctions for serious and moderate violations.[6]

The estimated annual rate of corporate crime is difficult to estimate given that there is not much dependable data like there is with street crime. There are several reasons for this lack of data. First, most victims of corporate crime (e.g., price-fixing) often do not realize they have been victimized and thus cannot report the offense to survey takers or the police. Second, there is no large-scale survey of those in corporate positions asking them to anonymously report on the offenses in which they have been involved.[7] Third, when executives and organizations are both charged and convicted of corporate crime, determining the number of offenders and offenses becomes problematic. Fourth, there is no centralized agency responsible for recording instances of corporate crime. Fifth, corporate crime cases can be charged with criminal, civil, and regulatory violations thus making it difficult to determine which violations are criminal.[8] Despite these challenges in measuring corporate crime, it is known that

> One case of corporate malfeasance can have a more serious economic impact than the entire number of street crimes in one year. An early 2000s accounting fraud by the energy company Enron, for example, has been estimated to have cost shareholders between $50–100 billion . . . The losses resulting from corporate crime are not just financial, though. The number of people who lose their lives each year as a result of occupational accidents or disease ranges from 30,000 to 76,000 . . . In 2008, the number of consumer product-related deaths in the United States stood at 35,900, compared to 16,272 people killed in "street" homicides that year . . . The 2010 Deepwater Horizon explosion killed eleven workers on site and the ensuing oil spill resulted in unknown (and unprecedented) environmental damage.[9]

The *secondary costs* of corporate crime, which may be as harmful as the primary costs, impact three areas. First, corporate crime contributes to a diminished faith in a free economy and in corporate leaders. As citizens perceive that corporate leaders are not concerned for consumers and that their decisions are motivated by greed and selfishness, they may withhold financial support for business and for economic investment in the market. Second, corporate crime contributes to the loss of confidence in political institutions, public officials, and governmental processes. Citizens want a criminal justice system that treats everyone, regardless of social status, fairly. Victims of corporate crime may lose confidence in and support for political and social institutions that fail to punish corporate offenders. Finally, corporate crime brings about an erosion of public morality when companies that flout the law set an example of misconduct for citizens to emulate.[10]

A considerable number of Fortune 500 corporations, however, have long been able to compete successfully while demonstrating a relatively high degree of social responsibility and compliance with the law. In fact, some large firms with substantial chemical releases have been found to engage in voluntary overcompliance with environmental standards. In many cases overcompliance, by which is meant that if the law requires toxic emissions reduction of 50 percent some firms voluntarily pledge to reduce emission by more than 50 percent, is intentional. "Firms often make a conscious effort to reformulate products or re-design production processes even when it is costly."[11] They belie any stereotype that all large corporations are lawbreakers or that they exhibit little concern for ethical behavior and social responsibility. Some have long-standing reputations for working closely with consumers to clarify product advertising and to improve the quality and safety of products.

Corporate goals are attained within the complex hierarchical context of expectations and social relationships. The social structure in large companies consists of those with much power—the board of directors, top executives like chairs of the board, presidents, chief executive officers, and vice-presidents; and those with less power—the middle managers, supervisors, and workers. Because aspirations and pressures within this hierarchy differ, they can be conducive to unethical or illegal conduct at several levels. In the same way, the extended relationships between the parent corporation and its subsidiaries may be crime-generating because of the immense pressure to show profits.

Corporate crime can result in both economic and physical harm. While people cringe at the increasing possibility of murder or assault, they seldom realize that the business practices of large corporations kill or injure far more persons than do individual offenders. The production and distribution of defectively manufactured products such as automobile airbags and baby cribs, kill and injure countless consumers; every year many workers are killed, maimed, and harmed by unsafe working conditions and illegal exposure to chemicals; and thousands of citizens are injured annually by corporate pollution of the air, water, and earth, as well as the illegal disposal of waste products. Investigators have found that, in some cases, chief executives have knowingly concealed the fact that certain unsafe products and hazardous environments have brought hurt, sickness, and death to many people.

Examples of corporate crime abound: abuse of the consumer can amount to reckless homicide, as in the late 1970s case of the Ford Motor Company's defectively designed subcompact car, the Pinto; crimes against public safety and health, as in the 1980 case of Proctor & Gamble's sale of tampons that caused toxic shock syndrome; abuse of workers and local communities, as in the 2006 Massey Energy Company mine explosion in West Virginia; criminal abuse of the environment, as in the 2010 Deepwater Horizon oil spill in the Gulf of Mexico; and criminal abuse in the developing world, as in Union Carbide's 1984 chemical disaster in Bhopal, India.

At the turn of the twenty-first century, the United States experienced what the US General Accounting Office referred to as a "wave" of corporate scandals that involved massive corporate financial fraud.[12]

> In 2002 and 2003 came a flood of corporate scandals involving large corporations such as Enron, Tyco, Halliburton, WorldCom, Adelphia Communications, K-Mart, Global Crossing, Merck, Qwest, Reliant Energy, ImClone, and Xerox Corporation. Most of them

involved corporations, with the aid of their accountants, inflating the worth of their assets, massive fraud, and lying to the workers, stockholders, and the public.[13]

Cases of corporate misdeeds continued into the 2010s; these included the General Motors cover-up of its faulty ignition switch, the Volkswagen emission violations, the Pfizer Celebrex false advertising scandal, the Trump University bait-and-switch scam, and the Wells-Fargo account fraud scandal.

Although Edwin H. Sutherland termed his concept "white-collar crime," what he had in mind, among other things, were the offenses committed by corporate officials. Yet, in his argument, he condemned corporations for the crime they seemed to engender. In 1948, Sutherland presented the paper, "Crime of Corporations,"[14] in which he provided materials that were to be part of the book, *White Collar Crime*, published the following year.

Sutherland obviously had some difficulty distinguishing between the behavior of corporations and the behavior of officials of corporations. It was sometime later that Gilbert Geis provided clarification and stated the problem in a precise manner:

> The major difficulty in *White Collar Crime* as criminological research lies in Sutherland's striking inability to differentiate between the corporations themselves and their executive and management personnel. Corporations are, of course, legal entities which can be and are subjected to criminal processes. There is today little restriction on the range of crimes for which a corporation may be held responsible, though it cannot, for obvious reasons, be imprisoned. For the purpose of criminological analysis, however, corporations cannot be considered persons, except by recourse to the same type of extrapolatory fiction that once brought about the punishment of inanimate objects. Sutherland attempted to resolve this obvious dilemma by maintaining, not without some acerbity, that the crimes of corporations are precisely the crimes of their executives and managers.[15]

Sutherland's pioneering work on corporate crime was a highly significant contribution to criminology, and it aroused great interest. For the criminologist, the study of corporate crime—including crimes by the corporation and crimes by corporate officials—is a pressing concern.

Definition of Behavior as Criminal

The economic and political power of the corporate world has been successful in seeing that most illegal behavior is largely punished by sanctions other than criminal. The growth of governmental regulatory agencies such as the Consumer Product Safety Commission (CPSC), the Environmental Protection Agency (EPA), and the Securities and Exchange Commission (SEC), has enabled varied sanctions to be used to deal with violations, even when the law provides criminal sanctions. Because corporate violations rarely result in criminal prosecutions, the public perceives that many such violations are of a noncriminal type, and therefore not serious in nature. This attitude tends to protect violators from the "criminal" label that invariably stigmatizes persons who are prosecuted under criminal law. In the event of a law violation, a wide range of administrative and civil penalties are available as an alternative to criminal prosecution, including warnings, injunctions, consent orders, and noncriminal monetary payments.

Even when a criminal penalty is available, it is rarely applied because of the greater amount of investigative and prosecutorial effort and time its use entails. As a result, the gravity of a corporate violation is not necessarily related to the type of penalty invoked. Consequently, the only genuine definition of corporate crime must include any corporate violations punished under either administrative, civil, or criminal law. Many see this as one way to bring corporate law violations into the same perspective as ordinary criminal offenders. Another way is to punish the corporate offenders.

> Hauling a corporate offender into court makes it explicit just where the boundary line is drawn between acceptable and unacceptable conduct in business. . . . It sends a message that the system is fair and that no one, not even powerful corporate executives, is above the law. A prosecutor . . . put it this way: "I believe that we need to send the signal that crime in the suites is just as important as crime in the streets."[16]

A national mail survey examined local prosecutor's perception of corporate crime based on community characteristics. It found that corporate prosecutions were more likely in communities with lower rates of violent street crime and stronger economies. Thus, when community members feel safe from street crime, they are more likely to demand protection from corporate crime. In more prosperous communities there are more organizational and fiscal resources available for corporate prosecutions.[17]

Today, the law defines as illegal many acts of corporations that were not illegal in the past. A series of historical developments led to many corporate activities falling into the category of illegal acts. A partial list of these developments includes (1) the advancement of technology, (2) the development of capitalist production techniques and methods, (3) rapid changes in marketing and advertising of corporate products, and (4) a growing public awareness of dangers posed to the environment by corporations. It was not until the beginning of the nineteenth century that certain business practices and activities were made illegal in the United States and in other advanced capitalist countries. Gradually such activities as the following were seen as illegal and punished in one form or another by the state: restraint of trade; false advertising; sale of fraudulent securities; theft or misuse of trademarks; manufacture of unsafe foods, drugs, and other health products; and the pollution of the environment.

During the latter part of the nineteenth century, the philosophy of *laissez-faire* and *caveat emptor* (let the buyer beware) dominated social, political, and economic thinking in the capitalist world, prohibiting the development of certain legal restrictions on business activities. New legislation grew out of industrialization, the replacement of the entrepreneur by the corporation, and the development of large-scale labor unions. In short, these new laws were largely the result of the transformation of industrial capitalism into corporate capitalism. Regulatory and administrative laws emerged that were directed chiefly at the new forms of economic enterprise.

Toward the end of the nineteenth century, an anti-monopoly movement developed in response to these new economic forces. This movement was accompanied by the belief that the problem of monopoly could be solved only through government intervention. The result was the creation of a new kind of criminal law, which not only protected private property but also assisted in maintaining a particular kind of national economy. American corporate capitalism was thus secured, rather than threatened, by the new legal restrictions on corporate activities. Antitrust law was soon enacted in the Sherman Antitrust Act of 1890. To combine in restraint of trade and to monopolize became public offenses and the federal government was empowered to proceed against serious violations of the criminal law by powerful and influential corporations. Sutherland pointed out, however, that the corporate world had it both ways: they wanted to eliminate unfair competition on the part of their corporations, but they often violated the law to their own advantage.

By 1906, Congress passed the Federal Food and Drug Act making it unlawful to manufacture or introduce any adulterated or misbranded food and drug. Offending products were to be seized, and criminal penalties provided for violations of the act. The Federal Trade Commission (FTC), established by Congress in 1914, was designed to help prevent unfair competition such as price-fixing and to deal with unethical and deceptive trade practices such as false and misleading advertising.

In the 1960s and 1970s, as citizens became more aware that corporate conduct was endangering people's civil rights, safety, and even their physical environment, they began to demand greater corporate regulation. As a result, the federal government created several new agencies. With the formation of the National Highway Traffic Safety Administration (NHTSA) in 1966, it became possible for the government to intervene in auto safety problems that resulted in thousands of needless deaths and hundreds of thousands of injuries—problems the automobile industry had previously ignored. The Occupational Safety and Health Administration (OSHA) came into being in 1970 to regulate the safety of the workplace and to protect the workforce from harmful chemicals and other substances. The EPA, also created in 1970, was designed to protect the nation's environment, including the control of air and water pollutants. After studies revealed massive injuries to consumers from their use of unsafe products, the government formed the Consumer Product Safety Commission in 1972 to ban the sale of hazardous and defective products. The purpose of the Foreign Corrupt Practices Act, passed in 1977, was to prevent widescale bribery of foreign officials by US corporations. In addition to these federal efforts, most states have created agencies of their own to regulate such harmful corporate behavior as consumer fraud and price conspiracies.

Often the corporate entities that break the law are the same ones that influence the passage of legislation favorable to the corporate structures of the country. This "circulation of elites" means that some leaders in the private field of corporate executives are recruited into top governmental regulatory positions from which they are then able to influence law and policy that advantage the corporate sector.

> Furthermore, corporate lawbreakers double as corporate lawmakers. Corporate America has saturated the legal or non-criminal world in a way that by any common standard of justice would be considered illegal and criminal, and it has obstructed legislation that would outlaw the violent activity. . . . The result is a legal system biased in favor of the corporate violator and against its victims.[18]

This relationship between corporate and political elites—what criminologists have called "state-corporate crime"—dates to the post-Civil War era and the rise of the business corporation.

> The Crédit Mobilier scandal, which came to light in 1872, is a classic historical case of the corruption that can occur at the nexus of corporate and political power. Crédit Mobilier was a construction and finance company, and a subsidiary of the Union Pacific Railroad. Both Crédit Mobilier and the Union Pacific Railroad were essentially owned by the same individuals, and when Union Pacific Railroad was awarded a multimillion-dollar federal government contract to build a transcontinental railroad to the western United States, Crédit Mobilier was given the job. It submitted inflated bills to Union Pacific Railroad, and Crédit Mobilier officials pocketed millions of dollars.
>
> All this was made possible, in part, because Oak Ames, who was not only the director of Union Pacific Railroad but also a Republican member of the US House of Representatives. Ames had secured the compliance of a number of key congressmen by selling them Crédit Mobilier stock at far below market value and allowing them to finance their investment

with expected future dividends they had not yet earned. A congressional investigation of the scandal resulted in little more than censure (official condemnation) of the participants, including Republican congressman James Garfield, who later became president, and two Republicans who served as vice president under President Ulysses Grant, Congressman Schuyler Colfax, and Senator Henry Wilson.[19]

In the major federal regulatory agencies, top executives from the corporate world are often recruited by the federal government to "do public service" as top administrators in these agencies.[20] The situation is one in which a key inner circle of technocrats and bureaucrats from the public and private sectors make official regulatory policy with regard to their own industries and corporations. The result has been not only lax enforcement but, in many cases, actual deregulation of many federal controls.

Another situation that illustrates the corporate-government nexus is when a lawmaker is appointed to a government agency to help corporations make profits. This happened in 2017 when President Trump nominated Pennsylvania Congressman Tom Marino to be Director of the Office of National Drug Control Policy. Marino withdrew his nomination following reports that he and Congresswoman Marsha Blackburn of Tennessee had repeatedly introduced a bill that protected pharmaceutical manufacturers and distributors and that weakened the Drug Enforcement Administration's ability to combat the US opioid epidemic.

There is also the relationship that Gregg Barak describes as "Wall Street looting and federal regulatory colluding," which reflects the alliance between large investment banks and the federal government. In this case, deregulation, inadequate regulation, and government "bailouts" (federal financial help provided to a corporation on the brink of bankruptcy to prevent its downfall) of lending institutions during the financial crisis of 2007–2008 resulted in the fleecing of American taxpayers.

> In an effort to prevent JP Morgan Chase, Goldman Sachs, and other megabanks from . . . ending up in either acquisition or bankruptcy, the [Obama] administration and the "high-rolling" bankers worked out a deal involving massive government bailouts. These bailout interventions for the bankers took the form of investing the taxpayers' money to pay the banks in full for their deals gone badly, for example, with AIG. . . . Contradictorily, while the economic elite from Wall Street and the political elites from Washington were in this financial crisis together, average Americans found themselves on the "other side of the street." This was most obviously the case, for example, with respect to all those homeowners "underwater" (e.g., owing more than their homes are worth) and to the failure of the government to extend credit to millions of homeowners so they could avoid foreclosures.[21]

Sociology of Criminal Behavior

In this section, we concern ourselves with the criminal careers of the executives and top-level managers who make policies and decisions for the corporation. Although corporations are indeed legal entities, individual decision-makers within these commercial enterprises make policy for them. These individuals may or may not be subjected to criminal prosecution, although the corporation itself may be. For example, the policies of Toyota, JP Morgan Chase, BP, AT&T, Exxon, Wells-Fargo, and so on—while resulting from decisions made by individuals or groups of individuals—are recognized by the legal system as policies of the corporate entity itself, and thus it is the business organization that is held responsible.

Since the first Earth Day in 1970 and the establishment of the EPA the same year, environmental pollution and concern with climate change have been taken more seriously by the American public. In addition, the character of the corporation as an offender has been understood with increased clarity. What has become obvious is that many of the nation's leading companies are committing destructive acts against the environment and against human beings. Moreover, these activities are being done systematically and repeatedly rather than randomly and occasionally. Corporate environmental crimes such as the illegal disposal of company-produced toxic waste are standard practices. For example,

> a company may simply dump the toxic waste on its own property. Alternatively, the company can truck the waste somewhere else and dump it, or more likely, hire someone else to do the same thing. Another strategy is to mix the toxic waste with other, nontoxic waste and dispose of all of it as nontoxic waste, which is much less stringently regulated and much less costly to handle.[22]

To ensure profits at a minimum of expense, such corporations willfully engage in crime. The firms themselves, as legal entities, as well as the corporate officials who make specific decisions, are increasingly being defined by the public as criminal. Once these systematic activities become normal operating procedures, they are not then the responsibility of any one individual in the corporation. Rather, they are corporate crimes, in the sense that the firm itself is the criminal. The offending individual becomes invisible, and individual accountability vanishes.

From an organizational point of view, unethical practices and law violations within a corporation can sometimes be attributed to its *internal* structure and culture rather than to such *external* factors as the unfair practices of competitors, or to a corporation's difficult financial position in the market. Moreover, in cases of unethical or illegal behavior, the complex structural relationships within large business organizations often make it difficult to disentangle delegated authority, managerial discretion, and the ultimate responsibility of top management. In one study by Marshall B. Clinard, the general theme expressed by most middle-management executives who were interviewed was that top management, particularly, the chief executive officer (CEO), sets the ethical tone.[23] These views were not due to antagonisms or to jealousy of top management; the respondents simply felt that top management dominated the overall ethical tone of their corporations. Over half of the interviewees went even further, believing top management to be directly responsible for the violation of government regulations. In fact, top management's influence took precedence, in their views, over the possibility of a pre-existing ethical (or nonethical) general corporate cultural pattern. One middle-management executive described the prime role of top management succinctly:

> Ethics comes and goes in a corporation according to who is in top management. I worked under four corporation presidents, and each differed—first was honest, next was a "wheeler-dealer," the third was somewhat better, and the last one was bad. According to their ethical views, pressures were put on middle management all the way down.[24]

In his study of pharmaceutical industry executives, John Braithwaite also found that the ethical climate of a corporation is determined by the CEO. As one executive stated:

> [The chief executive] sets the tone and the rest of management falls in line. The ethical standards of anyone other than him don't matter so much. Well, unless you have one of

those companies where an old guy at the helm has a right-hand man making all the real decisions.[25]

After he had surveyed various data, Edward Gross concluded that "most persons who will engage in crime on behalf of the organization will most likely be the officers of the organization, its top people." In elaborating this conclusion, he states:

> In sum, then, the men at the top of organizations will tend to be ambitious, shrewd, and possessed of a non-demanding moral code. Their ambition will not be merely personal, for they will have discovered that their own goals are best pursued through assisting the organization to attain its goals. While this is less true, or even untrue at the bottom of the organization, those at the top share directly in the benefits of organizational goal achievement, such as seeing their stock values go up, deferred compensation, and fringe benefits.[26]

CEOs, CFOs (chief financial officers), or boards of directors participate in key decisions not only about finances, but also about the ethical direction of a corporation in relation to workers, consumers, competitors, and the government. Neither the board of directors nor the stockholders are in charge of running a corporation, although large financial institutions and substantial family holdings may have some general influence on policy. The basis of top management control, or "managerism," lies in its strategic position and its decision-making.

Top corporate managers possess great autonomy—and, therefore, considerable power—in making decisions regarding production, investments, advertising, pricing, and marketing. The driving force of the corporate executive is the "bottom line"; often it is corporate profits, not ethical standards, that provide the ultimate test of the effectiveness of top management. The executive's rank generates identity, power, and the many perks that go with it.

Top management's character and personality often influence the internal structure of the corporation. A major distinction is between the "financially oriented" executive and the more "technical" types. Some financially oriented executives, for example, are interested primarily in securing financial prestige and quick profits for the corporation, and increased compensation for themselves. Such top executives are more likely to engage in unethical and illegal practices than are the more technical and professional types who have been trained in such specialized areas as engineering or information technology. As one middle-management executive said: "Our CEO was a technical man, an engineer, and not a financially oriented person interested in the fast buck."[27]

Aside from character and personality another factor that leads to corporate illegal behavior is executive pay and its association with corporate control. Corporate control—the discretion that executives have in determining a corporation's policies—is of two kinds: ownership control and managerial control. Ownership control over corporate policy is exercised by shareholders who make up the board of directors and have some decision-making influence in a company in which they own significant amounts of stock. Managerial control happens in corporations with widely dispersed stock ownership where managers employ various means to maximize their own welfare at the expense of the shareholders. One study looked at these two types of corporate control and their relationship to corporate crime and the compensation of top executives of the firm. The results indicate that annual salary and bonuses of top management teams and CEOs is positively associated with the incidence of corporate crime in manager-controlled firms but not in owner-controlled firms.

In studying the criminal careers of corporate executives, we are dealing with people whom the public generally see as "honorable" and who are not acting for their own private gain, but for the business organization that they represent. They work for their shareholders' investors, and for "the public." Whether looking at corporate crime as violence, theft, deception, simple greed, or any combination of the above, the public typically perceives executives and managers as fundamentally virtuous individuals who, if they transgress, are only following the orders of those higher in the corporate hierarchy. Indeed, as George B. Vold noted many years ago, there is a contradiction at work:

> There is an obvious and basic incongruity involved in the proposition that a community's leaders and more responsible elements are also its criminals. Business leaders and corporation executives by and large play important roles in civic and community affairs. They more often than not constitute an important source of imaginative leadership for community enterprises of all kinds.[28]

Corporate officials and executives are generally drawn from the middle and upper segments of US society; and even if not, they are highly regarded in the community because of their executive positions. Typically, they are graduates of prestigious educational institutions, often have served in the military, are generous contributors to charitable causes, are married with children, and are hardworking, solid citizens: persons without stigma. One study found that the offenders who commit the costliest and most damaging white-collar crimes tended to be middle-aged white men with stable employment in white-collar occupations, had college degrees, and were above average in socioeconomic status.[29]

Rationalizations, neutralizations, and self-justifications are present, for they make a distinction between what they define as simply "illegal" behavior and criminal behavior. When corporate officials violate the law, they often have the appropriate rationalizations to view their conduct. In the process, they maintain a noncriminal self-conception. For example, during a congressional hearing, an executive involved in the heavy electrical equipment antitrust case of 1961, was asked if he knew that the meetings with competitors to fix prices was illegal; he replied:

> Illegal? Yes, but not criminal. I didn't find that out until I read the indictment. . . . I assumed that criminal action meant damaging someone, and we did not do that. . . . I thought that we were more or less working on a survival basis in order to try to make enough to keep our plant and our employees.[30]

One report found that those corporate offenders whose sole offense was an antitrust violation often relied on the idea of acceptable business practice to excuse their criminality:

> Many of these defendants argue that they did not understand that what they were doing was wrong, though the probation officers often raise doubts about the true degree of their naiveté. For example, one offender was involved in a conspiracy to fix prices for reinforcing steel materials. The defendant, a college graduate with a stable marriage and three children, claimed that if "any conspiracy existed, I did not know of it or participate in it. . . . I sincerely regret this and can assure the court it will not happen again." The probation office argued on the other hand that the defendant "exercised and abused his management authority through _____'s superior market power in other areas to coordinate and police the conspiracy in this case." The defendant explained that he was taking advantage of what he thought were "ordinary business contacts."[31]

Acts by corporations or their officials on behalf of a corporation often receive considerable support from similar, even competing, individuals and businesses. In fact, the very culture of the corporate social organization may constitute group support for criminal behavior. What Andy Hochstetler and Heith Copes call "a criminogenic organizational culture" makes criminal decisions attractive to top management:

> Through interaction with other members of the organization, employees are socialized into the culture of the organization; that is, they learn the techniques, motivations, and rationalizations of criminal behavior.[32]

Law-breaking can become a normative pattern within corporations, and such norms are often shared between corporations and their executives. This creates a situation where corporate wrongdoing becomes normalized. "Normalization of deviance" happens when executives and managers become so insensitive to deviant practices that they come to define their deviant acts as normal and acceptable because they fit with and conform to the cultural norms of the organization within which they work.[33]

Not only are many businesspersons partially isolated from law-abiding definitions of business conduct, but they may also be morally disengaged. Moral disengagement,

> is an emergent phenomenon that arises out of the interactions of individuals within the collectivity with each other, where each individual not only deactivates his own moral standards but also at the same time reinforces the exonerations of other team members.
>
> [Jenny] White and colleagues studied industries whose products or production practices are damaging to human health, including the tobacco, lead, vinyl chloride, and silicosis-producing industries. Their examination of internal documents and public statements uncovered evidence of a variety of modes of moral disengagement in the research and promotional activities of each industry. Companies in these industries (and most likely all others that produce anything even remotely harmful) attempt to shape how scientific findings are interpreted. They try to socially construct scientific evidence and public debate so that their products and production practices are seen as beneficial rather than harmful to individual and social well-being. This happens in part for the obvious reason that companies need to make their products acceptable and consumers to be profitable, but also because the people who work in these companies need to feel that their behavior is justified and not morally disreputable. In other words, moral disengagement theory suggests that company leaders have to engage in a form of self-deception in order to engage in harmful practices.[34]

Businesspersons are also often shielded from criticism and find support for their activities in the media. In addition, business executives associate chiefly with other business executives, both at work and in their social lives, so the implications of corporate crime may be removed from personal scrutiny. Often the thinking is, "if we don't do this particular thing, we are at serious risk of losing a considerable share of the market," and where profit is the bottom line, there can be abundant group support to violate criminal codes and regulatory restrictions.

Corporate crime involves considerable organization among the participants. The degree of organization may range from the comparatively simple reciprocal relationships involved in a business transaction to the more complex procedures involved in the illegal activities of several large corporations acting in collusion. In this latter case, the violations may extend to many corporations and subsidiaries. The organization of the illegal activity may be quite informal, as in deceptive advertising; it may be organized very simply, as in price gouging; or it may be complex, as in the case of antitrust violations. Group support for violation was found in the savings and loan scandal of the 1980s and 1990s. Collusion with confederates was involved in the looting by top management of their own savings and loan institutions, or "thrifts." This is a type of corporate crime described by Kitty Calavita and Henry N. Pontell as "crime *by* the corporation *against* the corporation."[35]

> The most widespread techniques of looting . . . involve an array of "special deals." For example, in "nominee loan" schemes, a "straw borrower" outside the thrift obtains a loan for a third person, who is usually affiliated with the thrift from which the loan is received. Such nominee loans are a popular device for disguising violations of the regulation which limits unsecured commercial loans to "affiliated persons" to $100,000. Don Dixon of Vernon [Savings and Loan in Texas], was particularly adept at this, setting up an intricate network of at least 30 subsidiary companies for the express purpose of making illegal loans to himself.[36]
>
> Looting is not confined to inside operators of thrifts. More often than not, the scheme requires intricate partnerships with those outside the industry, usually in real estate or loan brokerage. In some cases, the outsiders themselves initiate the fraud by identifying weak thrifts as "easy targets" that are "ripe for the plucking." . . . In one infamous deal, loan broker Charles J. Bazarian Jr. engaged in fraudulent real estate transactions . . . According to charges brought against Bazarian, in one instance he borrowed more than $9.5 million from Consolidated [Savings and Loan of Irvine], putting close to $5 million of it into a partnership in which the owner of the thrift, Robert Ferrante, had a direct interest. The same year Bazarian arranged reciprocal transaction with American Diversified [Savings Bank of Costa Mesa] in which the thrift bought $15 million of "worthless" investor notes from Bazarian's brokerage firm, in exchange for Bazarian's purchase of $3.85 million in promissory notes and two pieces of real estate from the thrift.[37]

Group support sometimes takes the form of "networks of collusion" that organize and promote criminal activities, particularly among small businesses. Many business crimes such as on-the-side trading and bid-rigging conspiracies require collusion, and a network of collusion promotes crime by "providing normative support, offering protection, disseminating information, and forging connections between participants."[38]

Group support of corporate illegal behavior also happens through conspiracy, which involves several actors cooperating to carry out a crime. For example, the biggest case of corporate fraud during the early 2000s involved the energy-trading mega-corporation, Enron. The executives at Enron conspired to make the company hide massive debt and appear to be more profitable than it really was. The prestigious accounting firm, Arthur Andersen, helped Enron "cook the books" and was convicted of accounting fraud. The Enron scandal involved highly complex schemes designed to manipulate and misuse standard rules and practices of accounting. One of these schemes, which involved collusion, was called a prepay:

> While there were many variations on the theme, here's how a typical [prepay] worked: Enron would agree to deliver natural gas or oil over a period of time to an ostensibly independent offshore entity that was, in fact, set up by one of its lenders. The offshore entity would pay Enron up front for these future deliveries with money it had obtained from the lender.

The lender, in turn, agreed to deliver the same commodity to Enron; Enron would pay a fixed price for those deliveries over a period of time.

On the surface, these looked like separate transactions. But in reality, the commodity part of the deal cancelled out, leaving Enron with a promise to pay a lender a fixed return on money it had received. In other words, it looked suspiciously like a loan with interest. Nevertheless, Enron listed prepays not as debt but as trading liabilities that were supposedly offset by trading assets.[39]

Two factors influence a corporation's compliance with, or violation of, the law: (1) the corporation's own cultural or ethical climate and (2) the conduct of its top officials. Each corporation builds its own cultural history over the years: it becomes permeated with the firm's own attitudes about ethical standards and law obedience. Some critical factors in this development include the corporation's expectations of the ethical standards of top management; the emphasis on developing and maintaining a good corporate reputation; the degree of concern for employees, consumers, and the environment; the firm's customary competitive practices; and its attitudes toward continued corporate expansion and power, even at the sacrifice of social responsibility.

Just as a general pattern of respect for law obedience permeates this corporate cultural history, law-breaking can also become a pattern, regardless of the economic environment, and with or without pressures for profits. Simply put, some corporations take pride in protecting their reputations more than do others. In an interview, one Fortune 500 board chair said that ethical and law violations must be "congenial to the climate of the corporation," while another said, "Some corporations, like those in politics, tolerate corruption."[40] A middle-management executive of another corporation expressed the same view: "A corporation's history often starts from the original founders and their ethical standards prevail from the beginning; corporate reputation means a lot to some, similar to that of a Japanese corporation." Another said, "Often corporations develop a way of doing business unethically and it takes a lot at the top to change it."[41]

The other internal source of illegal corporate behavior is the role played by top management, particularly the CEO. The prior corporate cultural situation in top management is important. If the founder or subsequent influential executives have established a long history of expected ethical practices, two results can be anticipated. New top executives will be recruited to fit this pattern, or top executives will tend to go along with the established corporate practices of doing business. Corporate wrongdoing sometimes reflects the normative structure of a particular industry. That is, criminal behavior by the corporation and its executives often is the result of the diffusion of illegal practices and policies within the industry. Frequently it is not the corporate organization itself that must be examined but the corporation's place in the industry. For example, Cressey found that generally corporations in the same industry have similar rates of recidivism.[42]

A major study of corporate crime concluded that the petroleum, automobile, and pharmaceutical industries have the highest rates of illegal behavior.[43] Another study found that antitrust violators were over-represented in the petroleum, chemical, and allied products industries.[44]

That poor economic conditions do not generally cause corporate crime is shown by the fact that the oil and pharmaceutical industries characteristically have higher profits than most others, with the pharmaceutical industry having the highest.

The oil industry's long history of industry-wide violations of law includes price-fixing, illegal overcharges, theft of oil royalties, illegal political campaign contributions, and environmental pollution. Some of these violations date back to the post-Civil War era when huge monopolistic "trusts" (holding companies for a large group of corporations) were being formed. Established by

John D. Rockefeller in 1870, the Standard Oil Company was one of the late nineteenth century's largest trusts. It was the largest refinery and distributor of oil that became one of the biggest violators of antitrust laws. Rockefeller's Standard Oil monopoly ruthlessly undercut competitors by relying on price manipulations.

> By winning secret rebates from the railroads, [Rockefeller] gained a decided price advantage over competing distributors, who had to pay much higher transportation costs. . . . Whenever a small local competitor sprang up, Standard would slash its price below its own cost. The small firm would soon be facing bankruptcy, while Standard could simply make up its losses with its profits in other markets.[45]

The first legal challenge to the Standard Oil monopoly came in 1889 when the state of Ohio charged the company with antitrust violations. Indeed between 1890 and 1911, 10 states and the Oklahoma Territory filed antitrust suits against Standard Oil, none of them successful. Finally, in 1911, the US Supreme Court unanimously upheld a lower-court decision against the Standard monopoly and ordered the combination broken up into its constituent companies.

A descendant of Standard Oil, Exxon (now Exxon Mobil), was involved in one of the worse ecological disasters when, in 1989, its supertanker, the *Exxon Valdez*, ran aground off the coast of Alaska. The collision released 250,000 barrels of oil into the sea with devastating consequences for wildlife, the environment, and the region's economy. Evidence indicated that Exxon was aware that the ship's captain had a drinking problem but failed to take appropriate action. In addition, Exxon had also reduced the size of the tanker's crew, leaving them fatigued. In 1991, the Exxon Corporation pleaded guilty to a criminal charge and paid billions of dollars in criminal fines and punitive damages.

An even greater oil spill occurred in 2010. This case of environmental crime was caused by an explosion at the Deepwater Horizon oil-drilling rig located in the Gulf of Mexico only 40 miles from the Louisiana coast. The rig, which was a project of the British Petroleum (BP) corporation, killed 11 workers and injured many others when it exploded. It released nearly 5 million barrels of crude oil from its underwater well. The oil penetrated the beaches and the coastal wetlands of the Gulf and caused extensive harm to fish and wildlife. The cost of cleanup, lawsuits, and harm to the economy of the Gulf states, including the devastation of the fishing industry, exceeded $14 billion. BP and other corporate players began drilling without installing properly functioning equipment including a cement casing around the well that might have plugged the leak caused by the explosion. BP pleaded guilty to criminal charges, including 11 counts of felony manslaughter and a series of environmental crimes.

The automobile industry has long been tarnished by a general disregard for laws designed to protect consumer safety, reduce fraud, and protect the environment. There are only three American auto manufacturers in the United States: General Motors, Ford, and Chrysler (now Fiat Chrysler Automobiles). This means that the auto industry is a shared monopoly. In 2018, GM and Ford together had assets worth over $500 billion. Such huge profits allow these companies to have major social, economic, and political influence.

The auto industry has historically long resisted installing new safety devices because the added cost would cut into profits. For example, in 1929 the president of DuPont Chemicals tried to convince the president of GM to use safety glass in their cars' windshields to prevent deaths and serious injuries. The GM president felt that this addition was too costly and replied to DuPont:

> I would very much rather spend the same amount of money in improving our car in other ways because I think from the standpoint of selfish business, it would be a very

much better investment. You can say, perhaps, that I am selfish, but business is selfish. We are not a charitable institution—we are trying to make a profit for our stockholders.[46]

One of the most infamous cases of putting profits before people is that of the Ford Pinto. In the 1970s, the fastest-selling domestic subcompact, the Pinto was manufactured with a fuel system that ruptured easily in low-speed rear-end collisions. Wanting to get the car on the market as quickly as possible, Ford decided to manufacture it with the faulty gas tank despite knowing about the problem. As a result, fiery crashes involving Pintos in which the gas tank exploded occurred with some regularity. In 1978, a California jury awarded $127.8 million in punitive damages to a teenager badly burned when his Pinto burst into flames after being rear-ended by a car going 35 miles per hour. An Indiana grand jury indicted the Ford Motor Company for reckless homicide when three teen girls were burned to death after the Pinto they were in was hit from behind. The jury, however, ultimately acquitted the company. In the end, Ford had to pay millions of dollars in civil lawsuits and had to recall the Pinto.

Three other cases of manufacturing crimes involving the auto industry that have been the subject of extended public outrage and regulatory response are the following.

Case 1: Fiat Chrysler's Exploding Jeeps. The following bullet points set out a summary of key events in this case:

- November 2011: the campaign group the Center for Auto Safety (CAS) issues a report on fuel tank fires caused when Fiat Chrysler Jeeps were involved in rear impact collisions. The CAS report claims Jeeps had been involved in 185 fatal fire crashes involving 270 deaths and numerous burn injuries.
- April 2013: Fiat Chrysler Group refuses to comply with the NHTSA demand for a recall of 2.7 million vehicles.
- January 2014: Fiat Chrysler agrees to a "fix" that involves fitting a tow hitch to the back of vehicles, rather than any substantial modification to fuel tanks.
- January 2015: The CAS notes that 1 million vehicles that were supposed to have been recalled remained unfixed, and that in this period at least six people have died in rear-end collision fires.
- March 2015: Fiat Chrysler CEO Sergio Marchionne issues a further statement insisting that Fiat Chrysler Jeeps are safe.
- April 2015: *Houston Chronicle* reports that only 4 percent of Jeep Grand Cherokees and 27 percent of Jeep Liberties have been repaired in the 2 years since the recall. In this period, it also claims, 57 people have died as a result of fuel tank explosions in Jeeps. Fiat Chrysler repeats the claim that "the vehicles do not pose an unreasonable risk to safety."
- July 2015: the NHTSA (National Highway Traffic Safety Authority, the principle auto safety regulator in the US) imposes a fine of $105 million (£67.6 million) on Fiat Chrysler over recall failures. As part of the agreement, the corporation agrees to buy back 1.5 million vehicles, including the Jeeps subject to recall.[47]

Case 2: Toyota's uncontrollable acceleration. The following bullet points set out a summary of key events in this case:

- September 2007: NHTSA orders a recall of 55,000 [various Toyota and Lexus models] for problems with "all-weather" floor mats apparently catching on pedals and causing uncontrolled acceleration.

- November 2009: 3.8 million vehicles are recalled for "pedal entrapment," said to have been caused by unsecured or stacked floor mats.
- January 2010: 2.3 million vehicles are recalled for a "sticky gas pedal" problem which acknowledged a technical fault in the throttle (including 2.1 million vehicles already recalled for problems with floor mats); and an additional recall of 1.1 million vehicles for "pedal entrapment problems."
- February 2011: recall of 2.2 million vehicles for "pedal entrapment."[48]

Case 3: Volkswagen's emissions fraud. The following bullet points set out a summary of key events in this case:

- 2007: Bosch supplies software to Volkswagen in 2007 for internal testing only, warning that it was illegal to install in cars in general.
- May 2014: Researchers at the University of West Virginia find VW cars emitting up to 40 times as much nitrogen oxide than is legally permissible and alert US regulators.
- December 2014: VW recalls half a million cars in the US for "software updates" and informs the EPA it has remedied the problem.
- May 2015: The California Air Resources Board (Carb), undertakes a new series of tests, the results of which are still unsatisfactory. Carb informs Volkswagen and the US EPA.
- September 2015: VW eventually admits that 11 million vehicles worldwide are equipped with the defeat device software. The admission is limited, however, to NO_2 defeat devices in a relatively small number of diesel cars.
- November 2015: VW admits that defeat devices were also fitted to petrol engines and masked cheated CO_2 emissions; and that defeat device software was installed in a much larger range of VW-owned brands than it previously admitted, including Porsche, Audi, SEAT, and Skoda.[49]

As bad as the oil and auto industries have been in violating corporate law, the pharmaceutical industry has been even worse. The pharmaceutical industry has frequently been involved in the production and distribution of unsafe drugs and medical equipment, deceptive research, price gouging, promoting "off-label" uses of drugs, false advertising, paying physicians to prescribe their drugs, Medicaid drug fraud, and much more. Pharmaceutical corporations account for a wide variety of corporate crimes. Marshall B. Clinard provided a partial listing of legal violations committed by drug companies during the late 1990s and 2000s:

> In 2003 seven states including New York, California, and Texas brought suits against GlaxoSmithKline and Pharmacia, two large pharmaceuticals who used unethical means to let consumer drug plans select the company's drugs over competing drugs. . . . Ortho Pharmaceutical, a subsidiary of the large corporation Johnson & Johnson, was fined $8 million in 1995 for obstructing justice by persuading employees to destroy documents relating to a federal investigation of the company's Retin-A public relations campaign. . . . In 1999, F. HoffmanLaRoche Ltd, a giant Swiss pharmaceutical, operating also in the United States, was given a criminal fine of $500 million for antitrust violations involving the conspiracy of various pharmaceuticals in several countries to fix vitamin prices. In 2003 Schering-Plough was fined by the FDA for failing to manufacture its products safely. . . . Pfizer, the world's largest pharmaceutical company, in 1999 received a criminal fine of $420 million for antitrust violations involving a conspiracy to set illegal prices, market shares, and the allocation of certain areas for the sale of drugs. . . . In 2004 Bristol-Myers Squib, one of the largest

pharmaceuticals, agreed to pay $150 million to settle the SEC accusation that the company inflated its sales and earnings in a series of accounting frauds, one of the largest penalties ever imposed by a federal agency in an accounting case. . . . In 2004 ScheringPlough who, with sales of $8.3 billion, is one of the largest drug makers, agreed to pay $350 million in fines and plead guilty to criminal charges that it cheated the federal Medicaid program.[50]

The unethical practice of corporate "dumping"—exporting unsafe products that have either been banned or not approved for sale in the US—has also been common with pharmaceutical companies. Many of these products are sold in developing nations with lax or nonexistent safety regulations. For example, after the Dalkon Shield intrauterine device killed several American women and the FDA had forced its withdrawal from the US market, the manufacturer, the A. H. Robbins Company, then sold it overseas. Another type of dumping involves shipping to developing countries medications whose shelf life has expired.

Corporate crime is not only engaged in by industrial corporations—like the oil, auto, and pharmaceutical companies—but also by financial organizations, such as investment banks, brokerage houses, insurance companies, and large accounting firms. Corporate crime by such financial institutions is an outcome of what has been described as a "casino economy" which involves some element of risk, and of a "Ponzi culture" and "crony capitalism," which result from the corporate-government nexus.

The largest financial crisis to adversely affect the global economy since the Great Depression of the 1930s began in the US in 2006 when the real estate market collapsed—it then climaxed in late 2008.[51] The financial meltdown obliterated trillions of dollars of value; billions were lost through the subprime mortgage market, millions of homeowners had their homes foreclosed, and major investment banks like Lehman Brothers declared bankruptcy. The crimes that triggered a global recession involved a variety of fraudulent schemes that arose out of the real estate, mortgage, and investment banking industries. The housing market collapse resulted largely from the mortgage industry's predatory practices of making available to homebuyers "adjustable-rate loans" (that start out with a low-interest rate and through time increase to a much higher rate) and "subprime mortgage loans" (made to borrowers who could not afford to repay the loan).

During this period several prestigious Wall Street corporations, such as Goldman Sachs, were involved in *finance crime*, which David O. Friedrich's describes as "large-scale illegality that occurs in the world of finance and financial institutions."[52] For example, Goldman Sachs fraudulently repackaged financial instruments that the bank knew would decline greatly in future value and sold them to investors thus leading to huge losses when the housing market collapsed. In the end,

> [t]ens of millions of investors, taxpayers, homeowners, and consumers suffered during this economic crisis period, at least in part as victims of misrepresentations and manipulations in the world of high finance—victims, in other words, of white collar crime.[53]

Social Reaction to Criminal Behavior

In the past, the "American ethic" has consisted of a firm belief that technology is the surest way to progress, that production and consumption can achieve unlimited proportions and that the natural environment can be exploited indiscriminately by humans. The overreliance on technology, production for its own sake, and needless consumption has caused Americans to commit crimes against the environment. Many of today's crimes—corporate crimes in particular—are related to this ethic. Indeed, a great deal of corporate crime corresponds closely to what are commonly and legally accepted as legitimate behavior patterns. Much environmental destruction is supported by the Judeo-Christian religious tradition. That tradition, enhanced by Western science, has been one of "humans against nature." In the Bible, we read that humans are to "have dominion over the fish of the sea and over the birds of the air and over every living thing that moves upon the earth." From this has followed practices that range from pollution of the air and waters, to indiscriminate logging, to fracking for oil and gas, to strip-mining.

This correspondence between criminal behavior and legitimate patterns of the pursuit of financial profit is by no means limited to corporate crimes against the environment. Basic to price-fixing is an attempt by large corporations to attain a secure economic market situation. Attaining a secure economic market situation is one thing, doing so through law-violating practices and regulation evasion is quite another. It is frequently passed off as simply expedient, rational action that is necessary to attain the goal of production for profit, not production for need satisfaction. Practices such as price-fixing and insider trading are too readily accepted as models of free-market competition, whereas they are the opposite of a "free" market. Crime, from the standpoint of the corporation, may be a secondary consideration when the higher stakes involve secure economic arrangements and an ever-expanding market.

The public does not always view some of the practices that evade, skirt, or break the law as illegal behavior, and may accept them as good business practices. Such is the close resemblance between legitimate and criminal advertising. Fraudulent and deceptive advertising has been around for a long time, but only in recent decades have consumer activist groups begun to pressure for laws on truth in advertising, particularly in the drug, beauty, and health food industries. Terms such as "clinically or scientifically proven," "immunity boosting properties," "kills harmful germs," "wrinkle-free," and "anti-aging," often fraudulently used in marketing food, medications, and cosmetics, have come under increasing fire. Consequently, new and stringent labeling rules were put into effect by the Food and Drug Administration. Among other violations uncovered by consumer advocacy groups are distortions in a product's printed label of the claims for usefulness beyond what has been approved, and citations of studies (commissioned by the corporation) allegedly proving the safety or usefulness of the product.

Multinational companies are so huge and the violations so diffused and complex that it is often difficult for the public to react to crime committed by a corporation to the same degree as crime committed by an individual. As one social commentator put it:

> [I]f a person working as a part-time mechanic in his backyard were to knowingly and willfully repair or build a car for somebody that killed them, he would go to prison for manslaughter or even murder. But if a corporation knowingly and willfully were to repair or build a car that killed a human, it now has a legal exemption. It would face only civil penalties and fines under the [National Traffic and Motor Vehicle Safety] act, and none of its human decision-makers would ever be held responsible.[54]

Yet the public is not completely indifferent to corporate crimes, for generally it condemns many of them. One reason for the lack of a strong negative reaction is that consumers often do not know that they have been victimized, as, for example, when a company illegally raises the price of its product. A price conspiracy between airlines to add a fuel surcharge to airfare may produce a $10 increase in the price of a plane ticket that most passengers would not notice or would attribute to inflation, not crime, while the total cost to passengers could well be in the billions of dollars. Similarly, the relative absence of past public awareness of and reaction to consumer fraud and environmental pollution was primarily the result of the public's lack of information about these issues. In fact, public attitudes toward environmental wrongs as crimes have fluctuated.

> The late 1960s evidenced an awakening of public concern about the environment. Pollution and pesticide control became causes for the Sierra Club and other traditional advocates of conservation. In addition, as people became more affluent, their interests shifted from questions of basic survival to quality-of-life issues such as the environment. The first Earth Day in 1970, celebrated by 20 million people, elevated the environment to a top spot on the public agenda. From 1965 to 1970 public support for governmental action against pollution more than doubled to 53 percent. . . .
>
> Public interest in environmental problems declined during the 1970s: Support for more spending on pollution control dropped by more than half, from 78 percent to 32 percent. The public had come to believe that new laws, such as the National Environmental Policy Act of 1969, and the new EPA, established in 1970, were doing the job. . . .
>
> During the 1980s, public support for environmental protection grew, partly in reaction to President Reagan's downsizing of federal efforts and partly in reaction to the dire news of environmental disasters. . . .
>
> In the early 1980s, 67 percent of the public supported existing environmental law even at the cost of some economic growth. Almost half the public—more than three times the level a decade earlier—favored greater regulation of the environment. . . .
>
> The 1990s ushered in an even tougher perception of environmental protection. More than 70 percent of the American public in 1990 favored the use of jail terms when firms are guilty of purposely violating pollution laws. The following year, 84 percent of Americans believed that damaging the environment is a serious crime, and 75 percent favored holding corporate officials personally responsible for environmental offenses by their firms.[55]

In 2018, public sentiment about global warming and climate change indicated a sharp partisan divide. While 59 percent of Americans rated the quality of the environment in the US negatively, 69 percent of Republicans and only 4 percent Democrats said that global warming was exaggerated. Much of the political polarization on global warming and climate change is based on respondents' attitude toward the fossil fuel industries—coal, oil, and gas. While 89 percent of Democrats believed that global warming was caused by human activities, such as those of industry and energy supply, only 35 percent of Republicans believed that was the case.[56]

No longer are government agencies easily able to evade their legal enforcement responsibilities and their accountability to the American public. Dangerous products, false advertising, and large corporations' practices of polluting the environment are increasingly coming under public scrutiny.

Public opinion surveys have revealed that the public considers many corporate offenses equal to or even more serious than many ordinary offenses such as burglary and robbery.[57] A national probability sample conducted in 2002, at the height of the corporate crime wave, found that over 77 percent of Americans strongly support stricter penalties, including longer prison terms and higher fines for corporate executives who conceal their company's true financial condition. The analysis also indicated that African Americans were significantly more likely than whites to want stricter government regulation of the stock market and longer prison sentences and higher fines for corporate criminals.

Taken together, these findings indicate that, although Americans do not want the government to overly regulate the free market, they do support efforts to deter corporate wrongdoing through punitive enforcement of laws banning fraudulent schemes.[58]

Francis T. Cullen and his associates point out that:

> A recent round of studies reinforce the conclusion that the public has little tolerance for white-collar crime and is willing to bring it within the reach of the criminal law. To be sure, street crimes, especially violent transgressions, trigger punitive responses. Even so, clear evidence exists that the public continues to perceive many white-collar crimes to be as serious as street offenses, wants to devote more resources to the control of lawlessness in the upperworld, and wishes to get tough with company officials who break the law. For example, one poll revealed that compared to street crime, "nearly two-thirds of the sample (60.9%) felt that the federal government should devote equal or more resources to enforcing and preventing white-collar crime." In another national survey, the respondents rated bank embezzlement as more serious than a handbag robbery and rated knowingly shipping diseased meat that caused a serious illness as more serious than committing a robbery at gunpoint that caused serious injury. And still another national poll found that when asked, "Do you support or oppose stricter penalties, including longer prison terms and high fines, for corporate executives who conceal their company's true financial condition?," 94% responded either "support strongly" (77.7%) or "somewhat support" (16.3%).[59]

Studies reveal, however, that relatively few violations of the Fortune 500 corporations and subsequent enforcement actions have received much general publicity in the media. Rarely does the public have an opportunity to view a television news show about transgressions of large corporations and seldom do corporate crimes make the evening news. This may be because many of these huge corporations own and control the media.

While violent corporate wrongdoing has long attracted media attention, it has not usually been defined as criminal. For example, one study examined newspaper coverage of a 1991 fire at a chicken processing plant in North Carolina owned by Imperial Food Products, Inc. The fire resulted in the deaths of 25 workers with over 50 others being severely injured. The firm's owner had previously ordered that all safety exits be locked, the building did not have a plantwide sprinkler system, and the plant was in violation of several building codes and state laws. The firm owner and the plant manager were indicted on 25 counts each of involuntary manslaughter. In their analysis of 10 of the nation's most influential newspapers, the researchers found that, concerning the Imperial Food Products case,

> the newspapers showed little consciousness that corporate violence might be seen as a crime. The reports did not initially define the deaths as homicides, nor did they raise the possibility that the corporation or individual executives might be eligible for prosecution. In essence, the media was not proactive, but reactive: It was not until the government announced the manslaughter indictments and, in particular, the plea bargain that the criminality of the violence was reported.[60]

Another study examined news coverage of the public inquiry into the 1991 Westray mine explosion in Nova Scotia that killed 26 miners.[61] The researchers found that there were important differences in the news representation of the public inquiry as compared to the news coverage of the immediate aftermath of the disaster. In the early phase of the news coverage the press assigned blame of the explosion to physical factors like unseen dangers in the dark mine, inanimate chemical reactions, and a hazardous natural environment. By the time of the public inquiry, the press produced stories that were more suspicious of the corporation's public relations and rhetoric about who was to blame. Later the press placed the corporation in "an organization context of immorality." At no point, however, did the press designate the illegal actions leading up to the mine explosion and deaths as a crime.

Even convicted corporate offenders are often easily forgiven for their crimes. Consider the case of Massey Energy CEO Don Blankenship who in 2016 was found guilty and sentenced to a year in prison for his involvement in one of the deadliest mine explosions in US history that killed 29 of his miners—the Upper Big Branch explosion in West Virginia. Two years later Blankenship entered the Republican primary in the US Senate election in West Virginia. Though Blankenship ultimately lost the primary race, he nonetheless had broad statewide popularity because of his support for the coal industry.

Typically, newspapers like the *Wall Street Journal*, *Financial Times*, and magazines like *Business Week* and *The Economist* along with some business-themed news television networks like CNBC and websites like CNNMoney.com, regularly report illegal corporate behavior, primarily because they are financial news sources; such news is of special interest and may have significant financial repercussions. Injurious and harmful corporate actions often are not presented to the public as criminal, either by government officials or by the media, because "crime is viewed in the media as a threat to the American way of life, and the right of the state to intervene in controlling crime is presented as the only legitimate reality."[62] The mass media provide the source for determining what is and *is not* criminal. As Quinney has noted,

> A conception of crime is presented in the mass media. That conception, diffused throughout society, becomes the basis for the public's view of reality. Not only is a symbolic reality created within the society, but personal actions take their reference from that environment. Indeed, the construction of a conceptual reality is also the creation of a social reality of actions and events.[63]

Individual civil lawsuits and class action lawsuits against corporations and corporation personnel involved in malfeasance have increased since the 1970s. One of the most famous class action lawsuits brought against a major company, the W. R. Grace Corporation, involved the Woburn toxic waste case. In 1982, eight families from Woburn, Massachusetts, filed a civil lawsuit against the corporation for dumping toxic waste products in the town's supply of drinking water that caused an abnormally large number of childhood leukemia cases in the community. Grace agreed to an $8 million settlement with the plaintiffs.[64] What tends to happen in most cases, however, is that individual plaintiffs must wait years to receive relatively modest settlements, corporations file for bankruptcy to limit their ultimate financial liability, and corporations see civil lawsuits as less costly than complying with the law. The fact is that

> it is difficult to state a general principle concerning the relative effectiveness of civil suits as a deterrent to corporate crime, or to ascertain whether they result in more or less substantial punishment for offending corporations.[65]

John Braithwaite, in particular, has advocated for what he sees as a more effective deterrent to corporate misconduct: *government enforced self-regulation*, or self-policing, on the part of corporations. This occurs when a company maintains a rigorous compliance program by reporting its administrative, civil, and criminal violations to government authorities. It is a cooperative form of crime control in contrast to traditional regulatory efforts such as inspections and enforcement actions. One proposed model works as follows:

> Under enforced self-regulation, the government would compel each company to write a set of rules tailored to the unique set of contingencies facing that firm. A regulatory agency would either approve these rules or send them back for revision if they were insufficiently stringent. At this stage in the process, citizens' groups and other interested parties would be encouraged to comment on the proposed rules. Rather than having governmental inspectors enforce the rules, most enforcement duties and costs would be internalized by the company, which would be required to establish its own independent inspectorial group. The primary function of governmental inspectors would be to ensure the independence of this internal compliance group and to audit its efficiency and toughness. Such audits would pay particular attention to the number of violators who had been disciplined by each company.[66]

There are several reasons why corporations would want to comply with ethical codes and statutes: (1) they believe it is ethically right to obey the law, (2) they are concerned about their reputations, and (3) they would rather self-regulate than deal with government regulation.[67]

A deterrent strategy that has been proposed by Braithwaite is *informal social control*, defined as "behavioral restraint by means other than those formally directed by a court or administrative agency."[68] This includes such informal sanction threats as adverse publicity and stigma aimed at the crimes of powerful corporations.

One reaction to corporate crime similar to informal social control is the formal sanction of *shaming*, intended to deter future criminal behavior by managers, accountants, board members, administrators, and supervisors.

> Shaming sanctions administered by judges, courts, and legislatures for white-collar offenders serve as a process of expressing disapproval, with the intention of provoking remorse in the person being shamed.[69]

These sanctions can take the form of requiring corporate offenders to publicly apologize for their illegal acts, engage in community service, and notify all future employers of their past criminal record.

Some scholars have advocated peacemaking criminology as an alternative to dealing with corporate crime.[70] This would involve understanding that corporations, like individuals, are also a part of the "higher immorality" that is structured in the larger society. One scholar, rather than looking at how corporations engage in violence and harm, sees them as having a role in contributing to political and diplomatic peace processes. *Corporate peacemaking* concerns interventions that transnational corporations—particularly in the oil and mining industries—can take in resolving intrastate conflicts, whether at the local or national levels.[71]

Returning to the issue of crime and its social responses, Richard Quinney has noted that,

> Punishment is not the way of peace. Responses to crime that are fueled by hate, rather than generated by love, are necessarily punitive. Such responses are a form of violence that can

only beget further violence. Much of what is called "criminal justice" is a violent reaction to, or anticipation of, crime. The criminal justice system, with all of its procedures, is a form of *negative peace*, its purpose being to deter or process acts of crime through the threat and application of force. *Positive peace*, on the other hand, is something other than the deterrence or punishment of crime. Positive peace is more than merely the absence of crime and violence . . . Positive peace is the attention given to all those things, most of them structured in the society, that cause crime, that happen before crime occurs.[72]

In an empirical study, Sally S. Simpson compared the perceived effectiveness of the compliance (cooperation) and deterrence (criminalization) strategies of corporate crime control. She administered surveys to MBA students that contained hypothetical crime scenarios describing business managers participating in different types of corporate offending. Because the hypothetical manager violated the law in all scenarios, respondents were asked how likely it was that they would act as the manager did under a similar set of conditions. Results indicated that the most effective control strategies for respondents who viewed corporate crime as morally abhorrent were based on cooperation; those who did not view corporate crime as immoral were more likely to be inhibited by criminal penalties. Simpson concluded:

> Overall, managers tend not to adjust behaviors based on formal legal threats—even though they fear these threats and believe them to be consequential (to themselves and to their respective companies). Of greater significance and more important as far as prospective behavior is concerned are threats to significant relationships, feelings of guilt and responsibility for tarnishing the good name of their firm, and a system of internal compliance that is multifaceted and proactive.[73]

Whether or not formal legal threats are effective deterrents, corporate law-breaking rarely receives severe penalties. Marshall Clinard and Peter Yeager found that of penalties imposed on Fortune 500 corporations for law violations over a 2-year period, nearly half were simply governmental warnings or product recalls.[74] Even in serious or moderately serious cases, slightly more than 40 percent of the penalties imposed were merely warnings not to repeat the violation. The vast number of cases of corporate illegal behavior do not involve the use of the criminal penalty. Instead, they use civil injunctions, wherein the court enjoins the corporation from further law violations by a consent decree, which is a compromise settlement of the violations, or by a monetary penalty. Consent decrees usually state that the corporation "neither admits nor denies" the accusations. A corporate monetary fine—whether administrative, civil, or criminal—is relatively small if measured in term of billions in corporate assets and sales. Fines rarely equal the illegal profits; to some corporations, they are just another cost of doing business.

Because the United States has an exclusively criminal legal system for individuals and largely an administrative or civil legal system for corporations, the effectiveness of the criminal justice system is undermined in dealing with corporate violators. A criminal prosecution labels and stigmatizes a corporation, making it far more effective than an administrative or civil action. Obviously, the courts cannot imprison a criminally convicted corporation; the best they can do is levy a fine.

Typically, criminal actions are not brought against corporations even when the use of the product they manufacture causes severe physical injury or death. Instead, civil or administrative actions predominate. Consider, for example, the case of the Johns-Manville Corporation. Throughout the twentieth century, the Johns-Manville Corporation was a major producer of products containing asbestos, a fibrous material used primarily as a fire retardant. Since at least the 1930s, the company had full knowledge that those products caused its workers to be afflicted with asbestosis, a debilitating and usually fatal lung disease resulting from exposure to asbestos. In 1933, Johns-Manville negotiated settlements of asbestos cases in exchange for employees with asbestosis agreeing to drop all litigation against the company. Two years later, in 1935, Johns-Manville distorted the results of an industry-sponsored study on the health effects of asbestos. In 1949, the medical director of Johns-Manville advised that workers who had contracted asbestosis but who had not yet shown symptoms, should not be told of their illness. Indeed, it wasn't until 1964 that Johns-Manville warned workers of the dangers of asbestos exposure. By that time, it was too late to arrest the asbestos-related diseases—lung cancer, mesothelioma, and asbestosis—of an entire generation of workers. In 1972, Johns-Manville refused to install a dust-control system to protect its workers. The company's executives had calculated that, given the system's installation and operating costs, it was more economical to pay the annual costs in worker's compensation for employees disabled or killed by asbestos dust. In 1982, Manville declared bankruptcy to protect its assets from tort litigation. The US government called for the company to set up a trust fund to compensate victims. Neither the corporation nor any of its officers have been criminally indicted.[75]

Because a corporation cannot be imprisoned (although it can be fined or placed on probation), the only alternative is to criminally prosecute high-ranking officials. Top management can lead the firm into illegal activities, or it can create a corporate climate favorable to law violators. While company executives may be responsible for law violations within their company, the law rarely holds them personally accountable for the actions they direct. In their survey, Clinard and Yeager revealed that chief executives were convicted of failure to carry out their legal responsibility in only 1.5 percent of the total actions.[76]

Corporate executives fear imprisonment far more than they fear a criminal conviction in which a fine is imposed. If convicted, executives rarely receive prison terms, and if they do the sentences are generally below the maximum provided by the law. Typically, they are given probation, fined, or assigned some type of community service.

In discussing criminal fraud for securities violations engaged in by the leading Wall Street investment banks, like Morgan Stanley and Goldman Sachs, Gregg Barak states:

> Today's financial elite at the pinnacles of economic and political power, . . . have all consistently gotten away with much more in the way of rewards than punishments for their illegal behaviors. When punishment comes, if it does at all, it comes with "conciliating" and "compensatory" fines typically representing a fraction of the actual loot absconded with. These punishments never come with imprisonment. In sum, these types of financial frauds have never been treated as the material crimes that they are. Instead, these crimes have been treated as pardonable offenses designed primarily to re-establish social harmony in the financial markets.[77]

Since the impact of the law tends to be insignificant, corporations have a far greater fear of adverse publicity that tarnishes their corporate images and reputations. Media publicity can significantly affect corporations that have found themselves in legal trouble. In case studies of corporations that had undergone serious and highly publicized ethical or legal difficulties, media publicity related to wrongdoing tended to flow over into other unrelated issues, such as reducing corporate earnings and decreasing executive morale.[78] Because corporate illegalities receive such limited press coverage, the compulsory use of publicity, in which a corporation buys media coverage to advertise its own guilt, becomes a necessary sanction in many corporate crime cases. If the courts force corporate defendants to publish certain information about their offenses and the measures being taken to correct them, public awareness of the offense is even better assured.

John Braithwaite advocates for negative publicity—naming and shaming—with respect to corporate violations. A press conference for public corporate confession follows a restorative justice conference where the following occurs:

> There is typically a two-step process with corporate naming and shaming. The corporation is named, then internal compliance systems go to work to define personal responsibility for putting things right. . . . The plant or the mine with a poor accident record is displayed on a graph at a meeting of managers. The person in charge is asked to indicate what he or she is going to do to get his or her safety performance up to the level of other plants. Other managers tend to be nurturant, offering help to the shamed manager: "There but for the grace of God go I," they think. So . . ., the internal shaming by respected peers tends to be reintegrative. This is an important point. There are structural reasons why even external shaming of the corporation which is stigmatizing is likely to be transformed internally into reintegrative shaming within the community of corporate peers. The corporate veil is a device whose very purpose is to protect the wealth and the dignity of the powerful men it shrouds.[79]

Regardless of size, all corporations operate under a government charter that subjects them to different measures of control. Corporations obtain these national and international business charters through individual states, which benefit from the substantial revenues brought in by incorporation fees and taxes. But state governments lack the incentives and resources to examine critically the vast scope of a large chartered corporation's operations throughout the United States and around the world. Perhaps a better system would be a national corporate charter that would make the enforcement agent— namely, the federal government—a better match for the large corporations under its control. Specific penalties for corporate law violations could include obligatory management reorganization, the suspension of top executives, or even a revocation of charter. Innovative sanctions, along with greater use of criminal sanctions when appropriate, could go a long way toward controlling corporate criminality.

Derelictions by corporations and their top executives set examples that erode the moral basis of the law. When corporations disregard the rules by which the free enterprise system is supposed to operate—particularly the basic tenets of free and open competition, they endanger the system itself. The economic drive for profit, power, and productivity is not in itself criminal; it is likely to become so only when these objectives dominate all other considerations. Price-fixing offenses victimize consumers as well as law-abiding corporations. Income tax violations deprive the government and all those who depend on it for needed revenue. The criminal law alone will not assure adequate corporate compliance if those corporations that are controlled exercise political influence over regulatory agencies and courts. What is needed is increased oversight over the corporations by the public. This highlights the importance of organized and well-financed consumer groups, the grassroots opposition to corporate crime.

Notes

1 *Fortune 500, 2018.* http://fortune.com/fortune500/list/

2 Stuart Kirsch, *Mining Capitalism: The Relationship between Corporations and Their Critics* (Oakland, CA: University of California Press, 2014), 1.

3 Marshall B. Clinard, "Corporate Crime Yesterday and Today—A Comparison," in *Corporate Crime* by Marshall B. Clinard and Peter C. Yeager (Piscataway, NJ: Transaction Publishers, 2006), x.

4 Ibid., xiii.

5 Marshall B. Clinard and Peter C. Yeager, *Corporate Crime* (New York, NY: Free Press, 1980).

6 Marshall B. Clinard, *Corporate Ethics and Crime* (Beverley Hills, CA: Sage, 1983).

7 James William Coleman, *The Criminal Elite: Understanding White-Collar Crime*, 6th edition (New York, NY: Worth Publishers, 2005), 8.

8 Michael L. Benson and Sally S. Simpson, *White-Collar Crime: An Opportunity Perspective*, 3rd edition (New York, NY: Routledge, 2018), 17–18.

9 Melissa Rorie, "Corporate Malfeasance as a Social Problem," in *The Cambridge Handbook of Social Problems* ed. by A. Javier Treviño (New York, NY: Cambridge University Press, 2018), 215–235, 215–216.

10 Elizabeth Moore and Michael Mills, "The Neglected Victims and Unexamined Costs of White-Collar Crime," *Crime & Delinquency* 36, no. 3 (1990): 408–418.

11 Seema Arora and Timothy N. Cason, "An Experiment in Voluntary Environmental Regulation: Participation in EPA's 33/50 Program," *Journal of Environmental Economics and Management* 28, no. 3 (1995): 271–286, 272.

12 United States Government Accountability Office, *Court-Ordered Restitution Amounts Far Exceed Likely Collections for the Crime Victims in Selected Financial Fraud Cases*, 2005. www.gao.gov/assets/250/245227.pdf

13 David R. Simon, *Elite Deviance*, 11th edition (New York, NY: Routledge, 2018), 7.

14 Edwin H. Sutherland, "Crime of Corporations," in *The Sutherland Papers* ed. by Albert K. Cohen, Alfred R. Lindesmith, and Karl F. Schuessler (Bloomington: Indiana University Press, 1956), 78–96.

15 Gilbert Geis, "Toward a Delineation of White-Collar Offenses," *Sociological Inquiry* 32, no. 2 (1962):160–171, 162.

16 Francis T. Cullen, Gray Cavender, William J. Maakestad, and Michael L. Benson, *Corporate Crime Under Attack: The Fight to Criminalize Business Violence*, 2nd edition (New York, NY: Routledge, 2015), 348.

17 Michael L. Benson and Francis T. Cullen, *Combating Corporate Crime: Local Prosecutors at Work* (Boston, MA: Northeastern University Press, 1998).

18 Russell Mokhiber, *Corporate Crime and Violence: Big Business Power and the Abuse of the Public Trust* (San Francisco, CA: Sierra Club, 1988), 5.

19 Ronald J. Berger, *White-Collar Crime: The Abuse of Corporate and Government Power* (Boulder, CO: Lynne Rienner, 2011), 15.

20 Peter C. Yeager, *The Limits of the Law: The Public Regulation of Private Pollution* (New York, NY: Cambridge University Press, 1991).

21 Gregg Barak, *Theft of a Nation: Wall Street Looting and Federal Regulatory Colluding* (Boulder, CO: Rowman and Littlefield, 2012), 59–60.

22 Benson and Simpson, *White-Collar Crime*, 133–134.

23 Clinard, *Corporate Ethics and Crime*.

24 Ibid., 138.

25 John Braithwaite, *Corporate Crime in the Pharmaceutical Industry* (London: Routledge and Kegan Paul, 1984), 351.

26 Edward Gross, "Organizational Crime: A Theoretical Perspective," in *Studies in Symbolic Interaction*, ed. by Norman Denzin (Greenwood, CT: JAI Press, 1978), 55–85, 71.

27 Clinard, *Corporate Ethics and Crime*, 136.

28 George B. Vold, *Theoretical Criminology* (New York, NY: Oxford University Press, 1958), 253.

29 David Weisburd, Stanton Wheeler, Elin Waring, and Nancy Bode, *Crimes of the Middle Classes: White-Collar Offenders in the Federal Courts* (New Haven, CT: Yale University Press, 1991).

30 Gilbert Geis, "The Heavy Electrical Equipment Antitrust Cases: Price-Fixing Techniques and Rationalizations," in *Corporate and Governmental Deviance: Problems of Organizational Behavior in Contemporary Society* 6th edition, ed. by M. David Ermann and Richard J. Lundman (New York: Oxford University Press, 2002): 111–130, 119.

31 David Weisburd, Elin Waring, with Ellen F. Chayet, *White-Collar Crime and Criminal Careers* (New York, NY: Cambridge University Press, 2001), 66.

32 Andy Hochstetler and Heith Copes, "Organizational Culture and Organizational Crime," in *Crimes of Privilege: Readings in White-Collar Crime*, ed. by Neal Shover and John Paul Wright (New York, NY: Oxford University Press, 2001), 210–221, 214.

33 Diane Vaughn, "The Normalization of Deviance: Signals of Danger, Situated Action, and Risk," in *How Professionals Make Decisions*, ed. by Henry Montgomery, Raanan Lipshitz, and Berndt Brehmer (Mahwah, NJ: Lawrence Erlbaum, 2005).

34 Benson and Simpson, *White-Collar Crime*, 166.

35 Kitty Clavita and Henry N. Pontell, "'Heads I Win, Tails You Lose': Deregulation, Crime, and Crisis in the Savings and Loan Industry," in *Crimes of Privilege: Readings in White-Collar Crime*, ed. by Neal Shover and John Paul Wright (New York, NY: Oxford University Press, 2001), 99–127, 110.

36 Ibid., 111.

37 Ibid., 112–113.

38 Hugh D. Barlow, "From Fiddle Factors to Networks of Collusion: Charting the Waters of Small Business Crime," in *Crimes of Privilege: Readings in White-Collar Crime*, ed. by Neal Shover and John Paul Wright (New York, NY: Oxford University Press, 2001), 127–136, 131.

39 Bethany McLean and Peter Elkind, *The Smartest Guys in the Room: The Amazing Rise and Scandalous Fall of Enron* (New York, NY: Portfolio, 2003), 159.

40 Clinard and Yeager, *Corporate Crime*, 60.

41 Ibid., 66.

42 Donald R. Cressey, "Restraint of Trade, Recidivism, and Delinquent Neighborhoods," in *Delinquency, Crime, and Society*, ed. by James F. Short, Jr. (Chicago, IL: University of Chicago Press, 1976), 209–234.

43 Clinard and Yeager, *Corporate Crime*, 119–123.

44 Katherine M. Jamieson, *The Organization of Corporate Crime: Dynamics of Antitrust Violation* (Thousand Oaks, CA: Sage, 1994).

45 Coleman, *The Criminal Elite*, 53.

46 Quoted in Morton Mintz and Jerry S. Cohen, *America, Inc.: Who Owns and Operates the United States* (New York, NY: Dial Press, 1971), 260.

47 David Whyte, "It's Common Sense, Stupid! Corporate Crime and Techniques of Neutralization in the Automobile Industry," *Crime, Law, & Social Change* 66, no. 2 (2016): 165–81, 170.

48 Ibid., 171.

49 Ibid., 172–173.

50 Clinard, "Corporate Crime Yesterday and Today—A Comparison," xxii–xxv.

51 For an excellent criminological analysis of the crisis see, Susan Will, Stephen Handelman, and David C. Brotherton, eds., *How They Got Away with It: White Collar Criminals and the Financial Meltdown* (New York, NY: Columbia University Press, 2013).

52 David O. Friedrichs, *Trusted Criminals: White Collar Crime in Contemporary Society*, 4th edition (Belmont, CA: Wadsworth, 2010), 168.

53 Ibid., 169.

54 Thom Hartmann, *Unequal Protection: How Corporations Became "People"—And How You Can Fight Back*, 2nd edition (San Francisco: Berrett-Koehler, 2010), 221.

55 Yingyi Situ-Liu and David Emmons, *Environmental Crime: The Criminal Justice System's Role in Protecting the Environment* (Thousand Oaks, CA: Sage, 2000), 10–11.

56 Megan Brenan and Lydia Saad, "Global Warming Concern Steady Despite Some Partisan Shifts," March 28, 2018 Gallup Poll. https://news.gallup.com/poll/231530/global-warming-concern-steady-despite-partisan-shifts.aspx?g_source=link_newsv9&g_campaign=item_231386&g_medium=copy

57 Marvin Wolfgang, "Crime and Punishment," *New York Times*, March 2, 1980, E21; Francis T. Cullen, Bruce G. Link and Craig Polanzi, "The Seriousness of Crime Revisited: Have Attitudes Toward White-Collar Crime Changed?" *Criminology* 20, no. 1 (1982): 83–101.

58 James D. Unnever, Michael L. Benson, and Francis T. Cullen, "Public Support for Getting Tough on Corporate Crime: Racial and Political Divides," *Journal of Research in Crime and Delinquency* 45, no. 2 (2008): 163–190, 179.

59 Francis T. Cullen, Jennifer L. Hartman, and Cheryl Lero Jonson, "Bad Guys: Why the Public Supports Punishing White-Collar Offenders," *Crime, Law, and Social Change* 51, no. 1 (2009): 31–44, 39.

60 John P. Wright, Francis T. Cullen and Michael B. Blankenship, "The Social Construction of Corporate Violence: Media Coverage of the Imperial Food Products Fire," *Crime & Delinquency* 41, no. 1 (1995): 20–36, 32.

61 John L. Mcmullan and Melissa Mcclung, "The Media, the Politics of Truth, and the Coverage of Corporate Violence: The Westray Disaster and the Public Inquiry," *Critical Criminology* 14, no. 1 (2006): 67–86.

62 Richard Quinney, *Critique of Legal Order* (Boston, MA: Little, Brown, 1974), 156.

63 Richard Quinney, *The Social Reality of Crime* (Boston, MA: Little, Brown, 1970), 285.

64 A. Javier Treviño, "Truth and Environmental Justice in the Woburn Toxic Waste Case," *Contemporary Justice Review* 3, no. 3 (2000): 337–345.

65 Friedrichs, *Trusted Criminals*, 354.

66 John Braithwaite, "Enforced Self-Regulation: A New Strategy for Corporate Crime Control," *Michigan Law Review* 80, no. 7 (1982): 1466–1507, 1470–1471.

67 John Braithwaite and Brent Fisse, "Self-Regulation and the Control of Corporate Crime," in *Private Policing*, ed. by Clifford D. Shearing and Philip C. Stenning (Newbury Park, CA: Sage, 1987), 221–246.

68 John Braithwaite and Brent Fisse, "Asbestos and Health: A Case of Informal Social Control," *Australian & New Zealand Journal of Criminology* 16, no. 2 (1983): 67–80, 1.

69 John M. Ivancevich, Robert Konopaske, and Jacqueline A. Gilbert, "Formally Shaming White-Collar Criminals," *Business Horizons* 51, no. 5 (2008): 401–410, 403.

70 John F. Wozniak, "C. Wright Mills and Higher Immorality: Implications for Corporate Crime, Ethics, and Peacemaking Criminology," *Crime, Law and Social Change* 51, no.1 (2009): 189–203.

71 Natalie Ralph, *Peacemaking and the Extractive Industries: Towards a Framework for Corporate Peace* (London: Routledge, 2015).

72 Richard Quinney, "Socialist Humanism and the Problem of Crime: Thinking about Erich Fromm in the Development of Critical/Peacemaking Criminology," in *Erich Fromm and Critical Criminology: Beyond the Punitive Society*, ed. by Kevin Anderson and Richard Quinney (Urbana, IL: University of Illinois Press, 2000), 21–30, 27.

73 Sally S. Simpson, *Corporate Crime, Law, and Social Control* (New York: Cambridge University Press, 2002), 151.

74 Clinard and Yeager, *Corporate Crime*.

75 Paul Brodeur, *Outrageous Misconduct: The Asbestos Industry on Trial* (New York, NY: Pantheon, 1985); Craig Calhoun and Henryk Hiller, "Coping with Insidious Injuries: The Case of Johns-Manville Corporation and Asbestos Exposure," *Social Problems* 35, no. 2 (1988): 162–181.

76 Clinard and Yeager, *Corporate Crime*.

77 Barak, *Theft of a Nation*, 110.

78 Brent Fisse and John Braithwaite, *The Impact of Publicity on Corporate Offenders* (New York, NY: State University of New York Press, 1983).

79 John Braithwaite and Peter Drahos, "Zero Tolerance, Naming and Shaming: Is There a Case for It with Crimes of the Powerful?" *Australian & New Zealand Journal of Criminology* 35, no. 3 (2002): 269–88, 274.

7

ORGANIZED CRIME

Although most people have heard about organized crime, few understand its workings, structures, personnel, or networks. Nor do they generally comprehend its extent or the threat it poses to a society's economic and national security. It is variously perceived as sinister, secretive, terrifying, romantic, fascinating, and even necessary. Over the years it has provided the subject matter for popular culture. Not only in the United States and other industrialized countries but in developing countries as well, organized crime is mythologized as an exotic, simultaneously attractive, and repellant phenomenon. It is found around the globe, from China to the United States, Italy, Serbia, Mexico, Nigeria, Japan, Russia, and more.

Organized crime has been referred to as a business enterprise organized for the rational purpose of generating economic gain through illegal activities.[1] Another definition is that,

> [o]rganized crime is a continuing criminal enterprise that rationally works to profit from illicit activities that are often in great public demand. Its continuing existence is maintained through the use of force, threats, monopoly control, and/or the corruption of public officials.[2]

Just as in legitimate corporate organizations, organized crime provides (albeit illegally) needed—or at least desired—goods and services including gambling, loansharking, narcotics, money laundering, commercial sex, and other forms of vice.

Until the mid-1980s organized crime was chiefly identified with Italian American organized crime—also referred to as "traditional" organized crime, the Mafia, or La Cosa Nostra ("Our Thing"). In 1986, President Reagan's Commission on Organized Crime broadened this view and described organized crime as involving 11 different groups: (1) La Cosa Nostra, (2) outlaw motorcycle gangs, (3) prison gangs, (4) Chinese triads and tongs, (5) Vietnamese gangs, (6) Japanese Yakuza, (7) Cuban organized crime, (8) cocaine rings, (9) Irish organized crime, (10) Russian organized crime, and (11) Canadian organized crime.[3] Another group that may be included are street gangs. Indeed, one study found that the Gangster Disciples in Chicago exhibited many characteristics of organized crime—regarding structure and organization, criminal activities, and relationships with other criminal groups.[4] Though the Gangster Disciples' main source of income comes from the street-level distribution of powdered and crack cocaine, marijuana, and heroin, they are also involved in assaults, drive-by shootings, homicides, identification fraud, robbery, burglary, and extortion. Likewise, the California-based

Mara Salvatrucha (MS-13) street gang is involved in a variety of criminal activities including smuggling illicit drugs (primarily powder cocaine and marijuana, into the United States), human smuggling, assault, drive-by shootings, homicide, identity theft, prostitution operations, robbery, and weapons trafficking.

Like the MS-13, the Japanese Yakuza, and the Russian Vory, many organized crime groups are transnational in that they operate across national boundaries. The Federal Bureau of Investigation refers to transnational organized crime (TOC) groups as,

> those self-perpetuating associations of individuals who operate transnationally for the purpose of obtaining power, influence, and monetary and/or commercial gains, wholly or in part by illegal means, while protecting their activities through a pattern of corruption and/or violence, or while protecting their illegal activities through a transnational organizational structure and the exploitation of transnational commerce or communication mechanisms.[5]

Definition of Behavior as Criminal

Organized crime is one of the major forms of crime in US society, although numerically it does not involve a large proportion of criminal offenders. Large-scale organized crime did not exist in the United States prior to the twentieth century. During the frontier period in American history, a number of bank and train robberies were carried out by roving criminal groups such as Butch Cassidy's Wild Bunch, the Dalton Gang, and the James–Younger Gang. In cities like Philadelphia and Chicago, various adult criminal groups gained control of illegal activities in their localities, such as gambling, prostitution, distribution of beer and liquor, and various rackets.

The gangs of New York, which terrorized the city through much of the nineteenth and early twentieth centuries, included the Dead Rabbits, the Five Points Gang, and the Eastman Gang. Among their numerous crimes were armed robbery, theft, illegal gambling, extortion, racketeering, and prostitution. Many of these gang members—gangsters—included colorful characters with names like Edward "Monk" Eastman, Max "Kid Twist" Zweifach, and Louis "Louie the Lump" Pioggi. During the 1910s, the gangs flourished in Manhattan's East Side when labor unions hired gangsters to batter and kill strike breakers, intimidate workers, and raid union meetings. Gang chieftain, Benjamin "Dopey Benny" Fein, whose annual income was about $20,000, used his gang as labor sluggers:

> My first job was to go to a shop and beat up some workmen there. The man that employed me gave me ten dollars for every man that I had to use and one hundred dollars for myself. I picked out about fifteen men, and later met the man that employed me and told him that I couldn't do the job for the money that he wanted to pay—that it took more men than I had calculated on, and that I wouldn't touch it unless I was paid more money.
>
> Finally, he agreed to pay me six hundred dollars for the job. I got my men together, divided them up into squads and saw that they were armed with pieces of gas pipe and with clubs, but this time not with pistols, and when the workmen came from work the men I had got set on them and beat them up. . . . After the job was over I saw the man I had made the agreement with and asked him how he liked the way the job was done. He said it was fine and paid me the six hundred dollars in cash.[6]

These gangs prospered because they provided desired, although illegal, goods and services for the public and because of their connections with local politics. In a general way, their activities resembled those of later-day organized crime.

After the turn of the twentieth century, organized crime expanded into a wider range of offenses and extended over a larger geographical area. The event that brought about the greatest change in organized crime was prohibition, which forbade by law the sale and distribution of alcoholic beverages. When the Eighteenth Amendment to the US Constitution and the Volstead Act came into effect in 1920, organized crime was able to provide the illegal alcohol products demanded by millions of consuming Americans. Conflict between organized gangs and widespread use of violence were inevitable as rival groups competed in the liquor trade. In Chicago, the largest and strongest criminal organizations, like the South Side Gang led by Al Capone and the North Side Gang led by Dion O'Banion, dominated the scene.

At the height of prohibition in 1927, Frederic M. Thrasher published his classic book, *The Gang*, a sociological analysis of over 1,000 gangs in Chicago. One type of criminal gang identified by Thrasher was the "syndicate," which operates with business-like organization and efficiency due to its resources of money, political influence, and intelligence. The *criminal syndicate*, whose major interest is illicit liquor, gambling, and vice,

> represents a multiplication of units under a more or less centralized control either inside or outside legitimate institutions. The units may be vice resorts, gambling houses, breweries, and so on, or a variety of types of gangs or rings; diverse units may be syndicated in various combinations or those carrying the same type of illegal activity may form a single organization such as a vice or gambling syndicate. This multiplication of units is brought about by the necessity of covering a larger territory or carrying on an increased amount of business, which may be local, regional, or national in scope. The syndicate must be run on business principles to be successful. It usually has political linkages which afford protection.[7]

The larger vice, gambling, and liquor syndicates operated extensively in the Chicago suburbs and among the roadhouses located in the edge of the city and in satellite towns. These roadhouses represented "an escape from society and became important factors in maintaining the power and activities of the gang."[8] One of them, Eddie's Wonder Bar outside of Madison, Wisconsin, was owned by Chicago bootlegger, Roger "The Terrible" Touhy. A gangster hangout, the Wonder Bar had a secret tunnel that was used to smuggle liquor and help the gangsters escape from law enforcement.

A couple of years after Thrasher published *The Gang*, sociologist John Landesco completed his landmark study, *Organized Crime in Chicago*. As Landesco stated,

> with the coming of prohibition, the personnel of organized vice took the lead in the systematic organization of this new and profitable field of exploitation. All the experience gained by years of struggle against reformers and concealed agreements with politicians was brought into service in organizing the production and distribution of beer and whiskey.[9]

The so-called beer wars between competing rival factions typically concerned violation of territorial rights and produced high casualties. Indeed, between 1922 and 1926,

> the years for the control of the booze and beer business in Cook County [Illinois], 215 gangsters murdered each other. The police during these same four years, in literally running battle, killed 160 beer feudists and gangsters. Within the city limits of Chicago 42 men were slain in the booze war during the 10 months subsequent to January 1, 1926. Within Cook

County, for the same period, the total reached 64. Neither of the latter figures includes 60 other deaths which were the result of frays with policemen.[10]

Following this tumultuous period, national gangster syndicates held sway over huge criminal enterprises, ranging from corruption of city and state officials and administrations, through labor unions and industry. Underworld figures like Al Capone, "Dutch" Schultz, Charles "Lucky" Luciano, and Benjamin "Bugsy" Siegel captivated the national imagination.

Organized crime is now represented by crime syndicates and interlocking criminal networks. It has expanded to the point where leaders coordinate illegal activities on a regional, national, and international level. This era is also represented by the extension of organized crime into an increasing number of legitimate businesses and occupational activities. The characteristic features of modern organized crime can be summarized as follows:

1. Hierarchical structure involving a system of specifically defined relationships with mutual obligations and privileges.
2. Monopolistic control or establishment of spheres of influence among different organizations and over geographic areas.
3. Dependence upon the potential use of force and violence to maintain internal discipline and restrain competition.
4. Maintenance of permanent immunity from interference from law enforcement and other agencies of government.
5 Large financial gains secured through specialization in one or more combinations of enterprises.

Organized crime can be generally distinguished from other criminal behavior by the elements of illicit services and activities, violence, and immunity. According to James O. Finckenauer,

> criminal organizations exist largely to profit from providing illicit goods and services in public demand or providing legal goods and services in an illicit manner. . . . What is essential to the definition of organized crime is the ability to use, and the reputation for use of violence or the threat of violence to facilitate criminal activities, and in certain instances to gain or maintain monopoly control of particular criminal markets. Also essential is that organized crime employs corruption of public officials to assure immunity for its operations, and/or to protect its criminal enterprises from competition.[11]

Organized crime consists of several different types of individual crimes. According to Marshall B. Clinard and Robert F. Meier, seven areas of illicit enterprise predominate in the activities of organized crime: illegal gambling, racketeering, illegal drugs, usury or loan sharking, illicit sex, sale of stolen or hijacked goods, and control of legitimate business.[12] To this may be added trafficking in persons, weapons, and counterfeit products. However, the following general classification can be used to include most forms of organized crime: (1) control of illegal activities, (2) control of legitimate business, and (3) racketeering.

Control of Illegal Activities

Much organized crime traditionally has been found in areas of illicit behavior, such as gambling, loan sharking, prostitution, and narcotics. Organized crime syndicates control much of the illegal gambling in the United States, and they are the principal loan sharks and importers and wholesalers of controlled substances. In these vice activities, public sentiment is divided over their actual immorality; thus, there is limited opposition from the public when the syndicates control them. Furthermore, organized crime provides a service for sections of the public when it assures access to these enterprises. In this section, we look at organized crime involvement in gambling, drug trafficking, and human trafficking.

Gambling, particularly in the Las Vegas casino industry, was the largest source of revenue for organized crime in the US until the 1970s. Much of the organized crime revenue from gambling in Las Vegas and Atlantic City came through "skimming"—stealing cash winnings from a casino's cash boxes, cashier's cages, slot machines, and sports books before they are counted. Since then, organized crime groups have seen diminished revenues with the advent of state regulation and state lotteries. Betting on off-track horse- and dog- racing also has declined in popularity with organized crime because of state-licensed betting. Also affecting organized crime is the fact that numbers games, large dice games, and casinos have been legalized in many states.

Gambling operations are highly complex and sophisticated, utilizing the latest technologies, including the internet. Betting syndicates employ bookmakers, runners, and phone answering services in large-scale national networks. Illegal sports betting is extensive and involves all the major spectator sports in the entertainment industry, from football and baseball to hockey and boxing. In 2017, $4.7 billion was bet on the Super Bowl; 97 percent of that—or $4.5 billion— was wagered illegally.[13]

Organized crime has long been involved in "game fixing"—in pre-determining the result of a sporting event to obtain gambling payoffs. The most famous case of game fixing was the "Black Sox Scandal." In this case, eight members of the Chicago White Sox were accused of intentionally losing the 1919 World Series against the Cincinnati Reds in exchange for money from a gambling syndicate led by New York mob leader Arnold Rothstein. Another case was the 1978–1979 Boston College basketball point shaving scandal in which members of organized crime manipulated the outcomes of several games. One of the underworld figures involved was Henry Hill, a Lucchese crime family associate from New York, who bribed the players and set up a network of bookmakers. As Hill explained:

> The [BC] players loved it, because they were not dumping games. They could keep their honor. All they had to do was make sure that they didn't win by more than the point spread. For instance, if the bookies or the Vegas oddsmakers said the line was Boston by ten, our players had to muff enough shots to make sure that they won by less than the bookies' ten points. That way they'd win their games and we'd win the bets.[14]

Online gambling is unregulated. Internet gaming—or iGaming—allows gamblers to play virtual casino and poker games using their mobile devices or home computers via accounts they have established with iGaming sites operating illegally from offshore.

Gambling devices ranging from cards to slot machines and roulette wheels, all "fixed" to favor the syndicate or the house taking the bets, exist alongside legal casinos and gambling houses in many states. Even neighborhood lotteries still thrive despite state-run lotteries. The practice of "running numbers" brings in sizable sums of revenue to organized crime groups. The numbers games are more popular with poor and modest-income residents because they require less money than other forms of gambling. Numbers games involve placing a bet on a sequence of numbers. A complicated organization is required to secure the bets, record them, and pay off the winners. Numbers runners (who record the bets and collect the money from betters) are usually small-time criminals who are part of the larger syndicate. Generally, they receive up to half of the winnings.

Even though gambling for cash is illegal in Japan, Yakuza groups participate in three forms of gambling: (1) organizing various types of card, dice, and roulette games, (2) illegal bookmaking, and (3) involvement in the *pachinko* (a type of vertical pinball machine) industry, which accounts for about 4 percent of Japan's GNP. Because pachinko prizes won from games cannot be exchanged directly for money in the pachinko parlor, Yakuza gang members purchase the prizes at a fraction of their retail value. According to the Tokyo metropolitan police, this prize-exchange business developed by the Yakuza has yielded Tokyo Yakuza groups billions of yen per year.[15]

Because illegal drugs like heroin, cocaine, amphetamines, and marijuana are in great demand, trafficking in them is the largest source of income for organized crime today. Drug trafficking is a global business of enormous profits to those organizations involved in it, including the drug networks, the Mafia, and outlaw motorcycle gangs. Narcotic and drug sales are organized like a legitimate production-import-retail business involving manufacturing, importing (smuggling), and distributing.

After the Columbia drug cartels broke up in the mid-1990s, several specialized, independent working groups—"offices"—became involved in drug smuggling. Thus, if an office was infiltrated, the others were protected. As one high-level drug smuggler explains:

> They [Columbians] got connections all over the United States, people who do the smuggling, people who do the selling, people who launder money, people who take care of the money. You know, they buy and sell what they call offices. A guy got five offices. One office takes care of this. The other office takes care of different things. They tried not to put the money with the drugs. That way—before, they used to do. Now they don't. They got lots of, you know—smarter. The guy who picked up the money don't have nothing to do with the guy who's bringing it in. That way, if you get caught, you cannot tell on the guy with the money, and the guy with the money cannot tell on the guy with the drugs. All the offices go to one place, Columbia. Say, I got my office. You the head of that office. You know me, but the people working with you don't know that I am the boss. That way they cannot get to me.[16]

During the 1980s, smaller organized crime groups in the US were heavily involved in the local drug trade. Though he frequently denied any such participation, it was well-known that James "Whitey" Bulger, the head of Boston's Winter Hill Gang, was peddling drugs in his own neighborhood of South Boston.

> Bulger had an iron grip on drugs moving through South Boston and beyond. He made dealers pay "rent" on every gram of "Santa Claus," a Southie code name for cocaine. He extorted a share of everything from nickel bags to kilos, loose joints to burlap bales of marijuana. Just across from the liquor mart certain apartments in the Old Colony project, a project near where Bulger had grown up in Old Harbor, had visitors tapping at the door at all hours of the day and night. Young men, even some mothers, were selling drugs out of the homesteads—angel dust, mescaline, valium, speed, coke, and heroin— and nothing moved without Whitey's okay. (Paul "Polecat" Moore, one of Bulger's underlings in the drug business, kept a place in Old Colony.) Bulger might often refer to drugs as "fuckin' shit," but his disgust didn't stop him from making big money off the drug trade, which smoked hotter in the two projects at the rotary than it did at the more

middle-class streets of City Point. It got to where "P-dope," a heroin mixture, cost only four dollars a hit—cheaper than a six-pack.[17]

Drug-trafficking networks differ in size and complexity. However, several studies suggest that rather than large criminal syndicates with a hierarchical or corporate structure,

> higher level drug markets are composed primarily of criminal syndicates that are relatively small in size; encompass a wide variety of cultural backgrounds; and are independent, autonomous, decentralized, informal, coalitional, and situational. Illicit entrepreneurs appear to operate in loose associations of people which form, split, and come together again as opportunity arises.[18]

Though the three largest Yakuza syndicates in Japan publicly deride the drug industry, the majority of Yakuza income, about 35 percent, is derived from the trade in amphetamines. However, most of the Yakuza groups involved in the importation of amphetamines into the Japanese market are relatively small.

> Typical of these is the "M-gumi" a subgroup of the Fukuoka-based Dōjin-kai consisting of about twenty members. This group imported several hundreds of kilograms per year, meeting with Taiwanese exporters on the open sea, where amphetamines would be exchanged for ¥1,000/g. This would be distributed via parcel-delivery companies to Dōjin-kai subgroups in Hokkaidō and Kyōsei-kai subgroups of Hiroshima. At a wholesale price of ¥4,500/g, M-gumi had annual sales of ¥600 million.[19]

Syndicates that are small and tight-knit (sometimes referred to as crews or cells) have the advantages of recruiting members that are trusted and known, of closely monitoring employees, and of making it difficult to be infiltrated by law enforcement.

The Mexican drug markets, primarily involving shipments to the US, have had extraordinary levels of violence. For example, Mexico recorded over 29,000 homicides in 2017, most of them related to violence involving drug cartels like Los Zetas, the Sinaloa Cartel, and the Knights Templar. One study notes that drug-related homicides in Mexico stem from three sources: (1) successional and disciplinary issues within a drug-trafficking organization, (2) territorial or transactional issues between drug-trafficking organizations, and (3) issues arising between drug dealers and government officials.[20] Another report maintains that organized crime killings related to drug-trafficking operations in Mexico are the result of "competition"—rival cartels battling for turf to control competitive markets—and "enforcement"—government efforts to reduce drug-trafficking operations.[21] These two interacting mechanisms brought the country into a vicious cycle of violence in which battles for turf increase the incentives of law enforcement, which further increase battles for turf.

Violence also marks outlaw motorcycle gangs (OMGs), like the Hells Angels, in their extensive drug network. As one undercover law enforcement agent that infiltrated the Mongols reported:

> Sometimes the violence is the result of sheer machismo. But it also stems from a battle for control of a massive international drug economy. Figures within the OMG drug underworld are difficult to quantify accurately, but a recent Canadian prosecution against the Hells Angels gives a sense of the scope. In March 2001, local and federal law enforcement in Canada brought down a major case called Operation Springtime, during which

they seized more than $5.6 million in cash from one apartment safe in Quebec, money described as one day's drug sales. In Quebec alone the Hells Angels controlled an estimated billion-dollar-a-year distribution network, moving hundreds of kilograms of cocaine and hashish each month, with importation tentacles reaching as far as Pakistan, South Africa, the Netherlands, Switzerland, Belgium, and Jamaica. And this was just one law enforcement operation, focusing on one group of Hells Angels within one province of Canada. The Angles now have chapters in some twenty-seven countries, and they are second to the Bandidos in overall membership.[22]

Human trafficking, whose victims are primarily women and children, usually takes the form of sexual exploitation and sometimes of forced labor in manufacturing, construction, and agriculture. Although some human trafficking involves abduction, much of it has to do with the recruitment of vulnerable and desperate people through fraud, force, threat, and deception. For example, for a fee, organized crime groups may offer to help victims migrate illegally from their country (smuggling) by providing transportation and counterfeit documents. Once at the destination, the victims are exploited, usually forced into sex work or other forms of labor, and in some cases, to harvest or sell their organs.

Transnational organized crime groups are responsible for much of human trafficking, which usually involves movement across international borders and sometimes across continents. For example, Swedish police believe that the leading player behind much of human trafficking in Sweden holds a high position in the Russian-Estonian Mafia.[23] One study of human trafficking throughout South-Eastern Europe found that much of it involves criminal networks that have a well-defined organizational structure, employ a managerial approach, and respond to shifting market demands.[24] Another study[25] revealed six types of business models implemented by transnational organized crime groups that engage in the trafficking of women:

1. *The natural resource model* is typical of post-Soviet organized crime groups. These groups sell women as if they were a readily available natural resource such as timber or furs.
2. *The trade and development model* is employed by Chinese and Thai trafficking organizations. These operations control the smuggling at all stages—from recruitment through debt bondage and eventually to an assignment in a brothel in order to generate long-term profits.
3. *The supermarket model* is common among Mexican criminal organizations. It involves moving large numbers of people across the US border at low cost. It is based on large-scale supply and existing demand.
4. *The violent entrepreneur model* is characteristic of Balkan crime groups. It involves large numbers of women from the Balkans and those sold off to Balkan middlemen by crime groups from the former Soviet Union and Eastern Europe. They rely on violence in all stages of operation.
5. *The traditional slavery model* is typical of Nigerian and West African traffickers. They use female recruiters who make contracts with girls and women. By manipulating voodoo traditions, they force compliance through psychological and physical pressure.
6. *The rational actor model*, common in the Netherlands, relies on legalized prostitution and brothels to lure trafficked women.

These organized crime groups are increasingly professionalized in that they frequently reinvest their profits in criminal enterprises and legitimate business and handle trafficked victims as commodities. In addition, organized crime groups use corruption by hiring legal and business experts as intermediaries, or brokers, or by planting associates in relevant political and administrative positions.

It is sometimes difficult to find clear dividing lines between trafficking victims and trafficking perpetrators. One study disclosed that some Nigerian women who had been formally trafficked to work in the prostitution industry in Italy became partners in crime—achieving the key position of madam—with their persecutors.[26] In some cases, the trafficked woman makes a conscious choice to become one of many workers (entrepreneurs, pimps, madams, intermediaries, facilitators, etc.) involved in the sex trafficking business. In other cases, the woman has no other alternatives:

> Trafficked women are often consumed physically and psychologically. These women do not recognize any moral value and are unable to conduct a normal life. In these cases, women usually become pimps. It is very easy for women to fall into the trap and accept to become a partner in crime because it is basically the only chance to have a comfortable life. The bond with their madams is based on the expectation of a better future life. Thus, the transition from victim to persecutor is easy to make.[27]

Control of Legitimate Business

In addition to the control of illegal activities, organized crime has infiltrated legitimate businesses. This has been accomplished by employing violence and corruption and by investing large financial resources. Organized crime has used legitimate businesses as a source of valid profit and as a front for disguising criminal activities. For example, the "Pizza Connection" Mafia drug-smuggling operation of the 1970s and 1980s that imported $1.6 billion of heroin into the US used a chain of neighborhood Italian American pizzerias as fronts for their drug sales and connections. Using a legitimate business as a front also allows heads of La Cosa Nostra (LCN) a way of showing some participation in lawful employment:

> Before he was convicted, John Gotti, boss of the powerful Gambino crime family of La Cosa Nostra, filed income tax returns listing his occupation as a "plumbing supply person." Similarly, the late Joseph Colombo, head of the Profaci/Columbo LCN crime family, claimed to be a real estate salesman, Paul Castellano identified himself as a wholesale meat distributor, and Joseph Bonanno insisted that he was only a dairy product manufacturer. Carlo Gambino represented his occupation as a head of a labor consultant firm, and Anthony Corallo claimed to be a building contractor.[28]

Since the mid-twentieth century, organized crime has used legitimate business as a major source of income. In 1951, The *Kefauver Committee Report on Organized Crime* found that organized crime had infiltrated approximately 50 areas of legitimate business, including advertising, the entertainment industry, the automobile industry, banking, insurance, the liquor industry, loan businesses, the oil industry, radio and TV stations, real estate, and scrap surplus sales.[29] In 1990, a US Department of Justice study identified 49 legal business activities associated with organized crime.[30] These ranged from commercial construction and escort services to auto parts and waste disposal. Offenses related to legitimate business infiltration included bribery, embezzlement, extortion, forgery, kickbacks, tax violations, and union corruption.

Organized crime has a vested monopoly in some legitimate enterprises, such as video slot machines and electronic games. They are owners of a wide variety of enterprises, such as real estate, gambling casinos, restaurants and bars, hotels, automobile agencies, trash collection routes, laundering services, and other services. In 1970, the United States Chamber of Commerce "Deskbook on Organized Crime" stated that La Cosa Nostra controlled one of the nation's largest hotel chains and a bank with assets of more than $70 million. Organized crime often invests the profits it derives from criminal activities in legitimate businesses, and these funds establish a legal source of profits for income taxes and help to avoid prosecution. The business organizational arrangement involves consultants, accountants, and attorneys who work full-time for the organization. The control of business concerns is secured through (1) investing concealed profits acquired from gambling, drugs, and other illegal activities, (2) accepting business interests in payment of the owner's gambling debts, (3) foreclosing on usurious loans, and (4) using various forms of extortion. Somewhat related to the control of legitimate business is the infiltration of organized crime into politics. Political graft and corruption are usually mentioned as forms of organized crime. Few groups of organized criminals, however, become involved in politics for the sole purpose of economic gain. Such infiltration is usually for protection from legal interference in other criminal activities. The liaison with public officials is a method of achieving immunity from the law and should be so considered rather than regarded as a separate type of organized crime.

Criminologists have found a negative association between organized crime and a country's democracy, between organized crime and a country's long-term economic success. Organized crime not only subverts democracy; it also depends on it:

> The relationship between organized crime and the State can seem paradoxical: on the one hand, the control which the organization exerts in a given territory is intrinsically totalitarian, whereas on the other, for it to gain such control in the first place, it needs to rely on the existence of a democratic environment. Indeed, it is by exploiting the very freedoms which democratic systems offer that organized crime is able to thrive and speed-up its profit-making processes.[31]

One comparative study of 59 countries found that state and economic failure encourage organized criminal activity.[32] A state's inability to provide personal safety and collective security embolden criminal groups to infiltrate governmental agencies and fulfill those political functions. Moreover, a country that relies on an underground economy stimulates the growth of criminal syndicates as producers and suppliers of demanded goods and services. Under these political and economic conditions, the extortion practiced by a criminal organization "creates jobs for the lower cadres, offers a lucrative source of cash to the organization and, crucially, allows for the exercise of economic and political influence over a given territory."[33]

Another study indicated that some types of organized crime do bring significant revenues into a country.[34] For example, countries like Mexico, Tajikistan, and Afghanistan that dominate the production and/or trafficking of illicit drugs may, to some extent, benefit economically from their activities on these markets. However, tolerating Mafia-type organizations in the hope of beneficial effects on a country's economy frequently leads to large-scale corruption of public officials, including law enforcement and judicial officers. According to the study,

> the most important negative effect of organized crime, offsetting all possible benefits, is its pernicious impact on governance. Organized crime tends to erode the integrity of those holding a public office, including those responsible for upholding the rule of law. Where organized crime groups are powerful, legislation, policy-making, and legal rulings no longer serve the general interest but the interests of the few.[35]

The Yakuza have played a prominent role in Japan's political history. Its involvement in that country's political system is endemic, systemic, and traditional. There are approximately 22 major

Yakuza syndicates consisting of about 79,000 members. The largest Yakuza group, the Kobe-based Yamaguchi-gumi, has 39,000 members and the Tokyo-based Inagawa-kai has 10,000 members.

From the 1860s to the 1960s, Yakuza members were violence specialists in the political sphere. Their services were employed by activists, protesters, politicians, and statesmen. During that time, Yakuza use of physical force—fistfights and brawls, vandalism, threats, and intimidation—became accepted routine practice in Japanese political life.[36]

The Yakuza are politically powerful and extend their influence to the highest levels of the Japanese government. In contrast to the American mob, the Yakuza are highly politicized. Their modern history is intertwined with that of Japan's extreme right wing, a group of pro-Emperor activists who were the most virulent force behind Japan's rise to fascism and military expansion before World War II. The Yakuza constitute a violent coalition of rightists and "patriotic gangsters" that have served as a sort of paramilitary force for Japan's ruling Liberal Democratic Party, which has held continuous power in that nation's postwar politics.[37] In the early 1990s, Japan's leading politician resigned his post as parliamentary leader over mob-related scandals. He played a central role in a corruption scandal and there were links between the Liberal Democratic Party and organized crime. A short time later, a former Prime Minister who came to power with the assistance of the Yakuza was found to be at the center of an influence-peddling scandal linked to organized crime. In a case of political extortion, in 2000 the Japanese Prime Minister's home was firebombed several times by Yakuza members. In 2012, the Minister of Justice resigned due to his associations with the Yakuza.

Racketeering

The third and final type of organized crime is *racketeering*, the systematic extortion of money from persons or organizations by threats and violence. For the most part, racketeering in the United States has been concentrated in organizations engaged in the distribution of services and commodities. In the late 1920s, Landesco identified 23 racketeer-controlled trades including window cleaning, machinery moving, cleaning and dyeing, dental laboratories, and ash and rubbish hauling.[38]

Powerful organized criminal groups may extend their operations to the control of many kinds of products and services. The wholesaling of perishable products, such as fruit, vegetables, and fish, is another field of racketeering operations. Racketeering is prevalent in laundry businesses; cleaning establishments; truck, rail, and shiploading businesses; and among such workers as motion picture operators, bartenders, food service personnel, truck drivers, and retail clerks. These organizations are especially vulnerable to the operation of rackets. One of the simplest forms of this type of racketeering is the protection racket, in which persons or organizations are "protected," by payment of regular fees, for the privilege of operating without being injured, damaged, or destroyed by the organized criminals. This kind of operation may be used as a means of maintaining control over various services and commodities.

Racketeering operated successfully for many decades in controlling some groups of organized labor. The penetration of labor unions and the various trades by professional criminals dates back to the late nineteenth century. Jewish-American and Irish-American organized crime groups were the earliest labor racketeers. So too were the Chinese tongs who, at the turn of the twentieth century, dominated the laundry industry in New York City's Chinatown.[39]

> In the painful formative stages of the labor movement, it had to employ its own "muscle" drawn from the ranks of its membership to deal with Pinkerton agents and strikebreakers. In the first decade of the twentieth century, however, need arose for a more systematic and

professional approach and gangster thugs were invited into unions. They were given union cards and took active roles as pickets and union delegates. They protected fellow picketers against management goons—often employed by licensed detective agencies. The gangsters also assisted the union in keeping its members in line. It soon became clear, however, that it was easier to hire gangsters than it was to fire them. Racketeers such as Lepke Buchalter and Gurrah Shapiro came to dominate many of the industries they were invited to protect.[40]

By the 1940s, La Cosa Nostra emerged as the dominant organized crime syndicate in the US and labor racketeering was an important part of its crime families' operations. Every Cosa Nostra crime family has a documented history of labor racketeering. In some cases, two or more families exerted influence in a particular union. Moreover, practically every LCN figure in the twentieth century could be linked to racketeering.[41]

In the past, the International Brotherhood of Teamsters (IBT) was particularly vulnerable. However, other unions that have a documented history of labor racketeering are the Hotel and Restaurant Employees International Union, the Laborers' International Union of America, and the International Longshoremen's Association. During the 1970s and 1980s, the major New York City organized crime families of the Mafia controlled the construction industry and the local union of Teamsters. According to Salvatore "Sammy the Bull" Gravano, underboss of the Gambino crime family:

> In the building trades, the key to nonunion labor was Cosa Nostra control of union shop stewards, many of whom were made members or sons or relatives of members. On average, a subcontractor using union labor might expect a profit margin of 15 percent. With non-union workers, even with payoffs, the profit was 30 percent or more. If all else failed, there remained the Gambino's control of IBT Local 282, so absolute that if all of the other New York families needed Teamster assistance, they had to share the proceeds with [Gambino crime family boss] Paul Castellano.[42]

Various schemes are employed in labor racketeering. These include infiltration of certain labor unions, extortion of money from employees for union cooperation, and the cheating of union members through nonpayment of union wages or misuse of union welfare and pension funds. Workers may be forced to pay high fees and dues (payoffs) in order to find and hold jobs. Union leadership may be taken over by organized criminals. A considerable portion of the operating funds of unions may go to organized crime. Furthermore, money may be extorted or embezzled from employers. Strikes are often threatened as a means of controlling employers. The building trades are particularly vulnerable to racketeering because of the importance of purchasing materials at crucial times and the need to complete projects by a certain date.

When La Cosa Nostra first became involved in labor racketeering, there were four fundamental operations.[43]

1. Real unionization is often prevented by pretending, after the organization is paid, that the shops are really "unionized." A larger business concern, for example, may think it is cheaper to pay a certain money amount for a nonunionized union shop. Such a company may be "unionized," but the employees do not get union wages and there is no "union trouble" for the employer.
2. Employees are made members of fictitious "paper locals," which are established partly to help the employer reduce his labor costs. Cosa Nostra members may even "sell" unions to one another.

3. Employers may be threatened with strikes or violence if they do not pay bribes to Cosa Nostra members leading the controlled unions.
4. Union funds are stolen or diverted illegally from pension or welfare funds.

Many of these operations are still implemented as organized crime's infiltration into organized labor persists. In 2008, federal agents arrested over 60 Gambino-made men for crimes including labor racketeering. In 2011, law enforcement arrested nearly 120 Mafia members and associates for racketeering. In 2018, five members of the Genovese crime family were indicted for labor racketeering offenses. As legal scholar and sociologist James B. Jacobs notes,

> There is little or nothing new in labor racketeering. The same organized crime families have engaged in the same type of exploitation for much of the twentieth century. Union officers in racketeer-ridden unions often "inherit" their positions from fathers and grand-fathers. The forms of domination that appeared in the 1920s and 1930s still prevail. The cartels, bribes for sweetheart deals, extortion of employers, embezzlements from union treasuries, and frauds on pension and welfare funds all have their roots in the first half of the [twentieth] century.[44]

Sociology of Criminal Behavior

Several Dutch studies have examined specifically the criminal careers of organized crime offenders. One compared the criminal careers of those involved in organized crime with those involved in conventional crimes and found only one basic difference: that organized criminals were more likely to have prior convictions with more serious offenses.[45] Another Dutch study found that compared with conventional criminals organized criminals placed greater importance on their social relations with suppliers and clients, had access to transnational contacts, and had more contacts with co-offenders.[46] Finally, a Dutch criminologist found the following personality characteristics to be suitable for a leadership career in organized crime: extraversion, controlled impulsiveness, a sense of adventure, megalomania, and Narcissistic Personality Disorder.[47]

Another difference between conventional offenders and organized crime offenders has to do with criminal self-identification. Those involved in organized crime typically do not deny being a member of an organized crime group. This may be the case both inside and outside the world of organized crime. "In his own group," writes John Landesco, "he achieves status by being a gang-ster, with gangster attitudes, and enhances his reputation through criminal exploits."[48] Part of the self-definition of being a member of an organized crime group involves special clothing, language, tattoos, initiation rites, and so on. While this conspicuous display of group membership is true of outlaw motorcycle gangs in the wearing of "colors"—the official club patches and logos—it is more so with the Yakuza:

> Yakuza gangs occupy a place in Japanese society hard to imagine in the West. Members sport business cards and lapel pins openly identifying their underworld affiliation. Offices proudly display the gang name and insignia, much as if one found the words "Gambino Family, Manhattan Branch" emblazoned on the door of a Mafia concern.[49]

Moreover, most gangsters make no apology for their criminal careers. It is only when they come in contact with persons outside of the underworld that they find it necessary to justify their behavior. One rationalization is that everyone, including law enforcement, is involved in some criminal activity; another is that the gangster is doing it for his community. Writing in the 1920s when gangsters identified strongly with their ethnic communities, Landesco observed:

> In defense of his own criminality, when brought face to face with the righteous, the criminal becomes highly moralistic. He may deem the function of his gang that of protecting the interests of his national group or neighborhood. . . . The attitude of gangs to protect the community's safety against hostile foreign groups in the race conflict has been the basis of the status of gangsters among the law-abiding people in the neighborhood.[50]

As with any large-scale enterprise, organized crime requires a structure of positions with an accompanying hierarchy of command. It has been noted that the hierarchical structure of organized crime represents a feudal system. At the top of the clan-like pyramid are powerful leaders, the "lords," who make the important decisions and run the organization. These leaders maintain a master–serf relationship over other persons in the feudal structure. A middle echelon of gangsters, lieutenants, and cronies carry out the demands of the leaders. At the bottom of the structure are persons marginally associated with organized crime—drug dealers, prostitutes, bookies, runners— who deal directly with the public. The structure is held together by a chain of command, personal loyalties, a code of conduct, alliances with rival groups, and hostility toward law enforcement. The hierarchical structure of organized crime makes generalization about the careers of its members difficult. Some have specialized training and are directly recruited from law enforcement and even the military, while others, as young men, are given university training with the understanding that they will join the syndicate. According to Donald R. Cressey, writing about the structure and operations of La Cosa Nostra during the late 1960s:

> Cosa Nostra members occupying the higher echelons of organized crime are orienting their sons to the value of education, if only as a part of the general move toward respectability. . . . [T]hey are sending their sons to college to learn business skills, on the assumption that these sons will soon be eligible for "family" membership.[51]

In contrast to the multilevel, bureaucratic, hierarchical model of organized crime are informal models believed to be more accurate structural representations of La Cosa Nostra. Joseph L. Albini, for example, noted that the Mafia is structured by a loose system of *patron–client relationships*.[52] The "patron" holds power and influence that he can use to help or protect a "client" who reciprocates by showing loyalty and performs any service demanded in the future by the patron. In this way, patronage chains are constructed, with one man's client being another's patron. Likewise, Francis A.J. Ianni in his ethnographic study of the "Lupollo" crime family members, all of whom were related by blood or marriage, found not a formal hierarchy but an *extended kinship* network.[53] This network was rooted in notions of kinship and family based on traditional relationships of Southern Italian culture.

Many organized criminals have careers similar to the conventional offender, in which there is an association with young gang members and a long series of delinquencies and crimes. Instead of ending their careers in their early 20s, however, they continue their criminal activities in association with organized criminals. Some who grow up in certain run-down urban areas tend to emulate the older members of organized crime and aspire to a career in organized crime.

Delinquents are selected by organized criminals not on the basis of the technical knowledge they display but based on attitudes such as being loyal, willing, and trustworthy. In neighborhoods where organized crime is important, a boy might drive his uncle's car to pick up gambling receipts, or he might be given other roles to prepare for an organized criminal career. Often it is the youth gang that produces the adult gangster who uses strong-arm methods and is employed for this purpose by organized criminal groups. Gangsters and drug lords usually come from the slums of large cities or, in the case of developing countries, from poor rural areas. They generally have a conception of themselves as "tough" or "bad." Those who are successful in organized crime sometimes later become its leaders.

Sometimes, however, offenders are not minors but 30 or more years of age when they first become involved in organized crime. Such "late starters" may be recruited into organized crime through family ties, work contacts, leisure activities, or because they are heavily in debt:

> *J* (30 years) comes into contact with *A* when he runs into financial problems. *A* can readily lend him money and is not worried if the money cannot be repaid quickly. *A* now has a hold on *J*, because *J* owes him a lot of money. *A* forces him to rent premises and set them up as an XTC laboratory. The index case can be regarded as the start of a criminal career in organized crime: after the index case, *J* comes into contact with the criminal justice authorities at the ages of 36 and 38 years owing to offenses under the Opium Act.
>
> *C* (49 years) was first a car mechanic and later a process operator. After far-reaching changes in his personal life, he starts gambling and gets into financial difficulties. Through his daughter and her boyfriend he hears that a member of his "son-in-law's" family deals in the "gray market" of currency trading. *C* asks this person (*A*) if he can come and work for him as an exchange agent. Initially *A* is not very keen, but eventually agrees.[54]

It is also the case that people without any appreciable criminal record transition into organized crime in response to opportunities that arise in their legitimate business. They effectively make a career switch:

> Through a shooting club, marine engineer *A* comes into contact with *B*, a toolmaker he knows from his school days. This contact is further intensified through club life and their common interest in shooting and weapons. At a certain moment, *A* and *B* decide to turn their hobby into a job and set up a business specializing in modifying and repairing weapons—a specialty of *B*. The business does not do particularly well. When the opportunity emerges to take over a well-known weapons dealership, they seize their chance. *A* contributes the cash and *B* the machines and know-how. *A* is responsible for finance and administration, and *B* for the engineering.
>
> Through the shooting club and weapons trade fairs, *B* goes on to establish contacts with a Belgian weapons dealer. From their common interest, hobby, and occupation a friendship develops. Initially, these contacts lead to a long-term commercial relationship, in which illegal weapons are also occasionally traded.
>
> At a certain moment, this Belgian asks *B* to cooperate in a scam that a number of Belgian weapons dealers have been carrying out for some time. The Belgians put weapons on the black market on a large scale by exporting them—on paper—and then trading them illegally. It is advantageous to them to export the weapons through a business outside Belgium.
>
> The Dutch parties *A* and *B* take up the proposal and therefore become drawn into the illegal arms trade. In exchange they receive an agent's fee and may buy weapons from the Belgians at a reduced rate.[55]

Organized crime may thus provide a person with the opportunity to pursue crime as a livelihood. Selection of a career in organized crime, rather than one of the other criminal careers, is apparently dependent upon the existing social conditions, or subcultures, of the area in which the person lives. Once a part of the hierarchy of organized crime little is known of the specific mobility of the criminal from one position to another. The career histories of organized criminal offenders are not usually available because of the secrecy and nature of their work. Nevertheless, there are indications that as organized crime has moved from the bootlegging and prostitution rackets of the 1920s and 1930s into gambling, usury, drug trafficking, trafficking in women, and the control of legitimate businesses, there is more need for expertise in management operations and less need for security and secrecy, because the new operations are more open and more closely resemble legitimate corporate activity. Organized crime syndicates, therefore, are more flexible and creative and, rather than only punishing wrongdoers, they reward those in the organization who display the ability to make profits. This is the pattern of legitimate business enterprises. This skill acquired by criminal organizations is difficult to defeat.

Except for some movement up the scale in the organization, there are indications that mobility varies with the type of position in the hierarchy; for example, making money or enforcing discipline.

Progression into organized crime usually represents for the offender an increasing isolation from conventional society. While there are undoubtedly variations according to the location of the person within the hierarchy of organized crime, most organized criminals are committed to the world of crime. Their sole engagement with the larger society is concentrated on the goal of financial success, and they use illegal means to achieve it. Although they are sometimes interested in the welfare of the local community from which they come, organized crime offenders tend to have little or no interest in the well-being of the larger society (which explains their disregard for the negative effects of distributing narcotics or corrupting public officials). Several social conditions and forces in US society are conducive to the separation of the organized criminal from the larger society. In coming up through the ranks of street gangs, organized criminal offenders have been nominally separated from the dominant culture.

The leaders of organized crime are involved in activities that are in continuous conflict with the law, though in many cases they bribe corrupt law enforcement and political officials to work for them. Normally, however, a philosophy of justification allows the leaders to carry out their illegal activities. They hold the government in contempt, as well as its officials and the general public. The leaders of organized crime do, however, often choose to live segmented lives, donning the role of respectability in their community and even engaging in aid and charitable behavior. Yakuza bosses, for example, provided disaster relief (sometimes more quickly and efficiently than the Japanese government) to the victims of the Great Hanshin Earthquake in 1995 and again following the Great Tohoku Earthquake and Tsunami in 2011. Mexican cartel drug lords have also provided services to their communities including emergency food aid, housing, medication; operation of drug rehabilitation clinics; building and repairing churches, homes, roads, schools; and one-time payments/improvements enabling provision of water and electricity.[56] Nevertheless, the commitment of organized criminals remains with the world of crime, where in detachment from the values of the larger society they receive their prestige, power, individuality, and independence.

> While the Italian mafia purposely disassociated itself from mainstream society by nurturing its own subculture, their self-ostracism pales in comparison to that undertaken by outlaw motorcycle gangs, whose antisocial dress and behavior was a conscious expression of their contempt for civil society and their view that those in mainstream society are saps and suckers. This is best reflected in a comment made Jean-Guy Bourgoin, a member of the Rockers, a motorcycle club associated with the Hells Angels in Quebec. When asked what

he thought of regular "citizens," he replied, "I look at people who get up at 7, stuck in traffic for 10 bucks an hour, then come back at night. . . . They're the fools, we're the ones who are sensible."[57]

The very nature of the activities of organized crime requires that persons involved in most levels regularly associate with other criminals and receive intensive group support for their criminal activities. Since many persons in organized crime associate with a particular group of criminals (sometimes having a common ethnicity), support and prescription of behavior come not only from their criminal associates but from their communities and customers as well. For example, in the case of Alberto Anselmi and Giovanni Scalise, vicious mob executioners who worked for Al Capone in Chicago,

> almost the entire Italian group in the city was consolidated in support of these men who were bootleggers and who were accused of killing policemen, on the basis of the inflammatory and prejudicial remarks made against them by the prosecution.
>
> Even the bootlegger and the beer runner are defended by his fellow gangsters and by the sporting world, in addition, as men who are performing a valuable function in society. They may even be extolled with admiration for their bravery in risking their lives in service for their customers.[58]

Organized crime groups are organized for the sole purpose of gaining monopolistic control over a sphere (or spheres) of activity. During prohibition in the United States, for example, specific organized criminal groups competed to control the manufacture and distribution of liquor. Organized criminal groups now attempt to gain monopolistic control of drug trafficking, gambling, and various other rackets that often lead to violence and death.

Monopolistic control of a criminal activity by criminal groups often entails an interlocking domination over other illegal activities. Such interlocking interests are found in organized crime patterns similar to those in corporate business. In connection with their illicit enterprises, most organized crime groups eventually need to launder money (an endeavor requiring an elaborate structure of group support). Money laundering is the process of converting illegally earned assets to one or more alternate forms to conceal their illegalities and true ownership. Furthermore, in achieving monopolies, organized crime is not restricted by traditional political and geographical boundaries. For example, money laundering strategies involving foreign exchange activities are often required. In any event, organized crime groups generally depend on three types of group support:

> Organized crime's criminal group and protectors rely on skilled individuals, or *specialist support*, to assist in the attainment of group goals. These individuals do not share a continuing commitment to the group's goals. They are nonetheless considered part of organized crime. Specialist support includes individuals and groups who provide specialized contract services which facilitate organized crime activity, such as pilots, chemists, arsonists, and hijackers.
>
> In addition to specialists, organized crime relies on outside individuals, members of the general public, for financial and other support. *User support* includes those individuals who purchase organized crime's illegal goods and services, such as drug users and patrons of bookmakers.
>
> *Social support* includes individuals and organizations that grant power and an air of legitimacy to organized crime generally and to certain criminal groups and their members specifically. Social support includes public officials who solicit the support of organized

crime figures; business leaders who do business with organized crime; social and community leaders who invite organized crime figures to social gatherings; and those who portray the criminal group or organized crime in a favorable or glamorous light.[59]

Organizational Structure

From an organizational standpoint, all of organized crime operates on a syndicated basis. That is, skilled persons with considerable capital resources are organized to establish and maintain a large-scale, business enterprise devoted to the coordination and control of products or services. The nature of the coordination and control may be illegal, and/or the products and services may be illegal. Given the syndicated pattern of organized crime, there are questions regarding the pervasiveness and geographical extensiveness of the organization of illegal activity. For example, is it the case that in the United States there is a great number of criminal groups organized on a syndicated basis? Are some groups interlocked according to a plan? There are several different views on these questions.

The 1963 testimony of Joseph Valachi, former member of the Genovese crime family turned informer, before the McClellan congressional committee on organized crime provided clues to the syndicated nature of La Cosa Nostra in the United States.[60] He named Cosa Nostra as a group of "families" engaged in illegal economic gain. At the top of the family system was a commission that served as a court to settle disputes and inflict sanctions. Cosa Nostra presumably provided for the autonomous functioning of several organized criminal groups.

Perhaps the most complete description of La Cosa Nostra in the US was detailed in 1967 by the President's Commission on Law Enforcement and Administration of Justice. According to that report, the core of organized crime consisted of 24 groups that operated as criminal cartels in large cities across the country. At least in the case of the New York-based Five Families—Bonanno, Colombo, Gambino, Genovese, and Luchese—each is headed by a *boss*, who maintains order and maximizes profits. Beneath each boss is an *underboss*, who collects information for the boss, relays messages to him, and passes instructions down the line to underlings. On the same level as the underboss is the *consigliere*, who is a counselor or advisor to the boss. Below the level of the underboss are the *capos*, some of whom serve as buffers between upper-level and lower-level personnel, while others serve as chiefs of operating units. The lowest-level members are the *soldiers*, who report to the capos. Outside the structure of the family is a large number of *associates* who do most of the routine work in the various criminal enterprises. Finally, the 24 families are reputedly ruled by a *commission*. This body is a combination of legislature, supreme court, board of directors, and arbitration board, but functions primarily as a judicial body mediating disputes. The commission is composed of the bosses of the most powerful families and varies from 9 to 12 men.

The Yakuza's structure and organization is nearly identical to that of Cosa Nostra.[61] The basic organizational unit of the Yakuza syndicates is the *ikka*, or (fictive) families. Each *ikka* consists of a bureaucratic hierarchy with specific ranks and specialized roles. At the top level is the *kumi-chō* (family head) who has ultimate responsibility for the *ikka*'s business activities. He is advised by the *kōmon* (counselor) and by the *waka-gashira* (underboss). These are followed by the *kanbu* who may form their own internal groups that tend to be small, intimate, and cohesive. Below them are the *kumi-in*, or associates, who are employed in businesses owned by the *kanbu* and who perform the most menial tasks. Aside from this bureaucratic hierarchy, within each *ikka* are social bonds based on family relationships that connect members to each other and maintain group cohesion. These are the father–son (*oyanbun–kobun*) and brother–brother (*kyōdaibun*) relationships.

New York's Five Families

In New York City, five major Italian-American Mafia families dominate organized crime activities:

■ Bonnano crime family   ■ Columbo crime family   ■ Gambino crime family
■ Genovese crime family   ■ Luchese crime family

While the Mafia–also known as La Cosa Nostra--may no longer possess the robust national presence and influence it once had, it remains a significant threat in the extended New York metropolitan area, New England, Philadelphia, Chicago, and Detroit.

The Mafia Org Chart

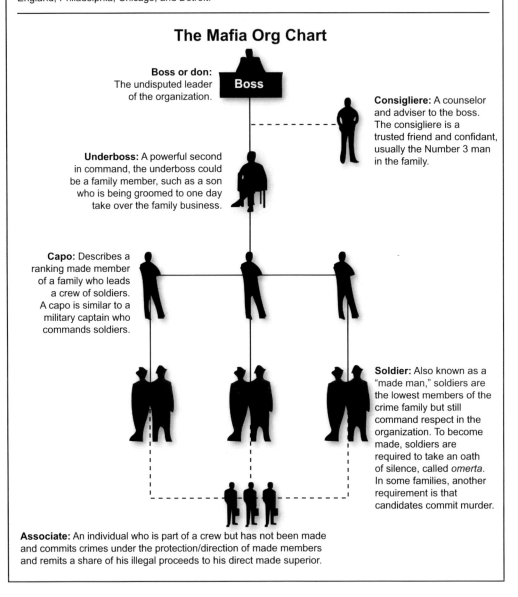

Boss or don: The undisputed leader of the organization.

Consigliere: A counselor and adviser to the boss. The consigliere is a trusted friend and confidant, usually the Number 3 man in the family.

Underboss: A powerful second in command, the underboss could be a family member, such as a son who is being groomed to one day take over the family business.

Capo: Describes a ranking made member of a family who leads a crew of soldiers. A capo is similar to a military captain who commands soldiers.

Soldier: Also known as a "made man," soldiers are the lowest members of the crime family but still command respect in the organization. To become made, soldiers are required to take an oath of silence, called *omerta*. In some families, another requirement is that candidates commit murder.

Associate: An individual who is part of a crew but has not been made and commits crimes under the protection/direction of made members and remits a share of his illegal proceeds to his direct made superior.

FIGURE 7.1   Mafia organizational chart.

Source: www.fbi.gov/file-repository/mafia-family-tree.pdf/view

Although the Yakuza syndicates do not have a commission like that of La Cosa Nostra, within the greater Tokyo area there exists a loose association of Yakuza groups—the Kantō Hatsuka-kai—that serves a similar function.

Code of Conduct

To a certain extent all career criminals observe a code of behavior in that they never inform the police, federal authorities, or prosecutors on another's activities. With La Cosa Nostra the code of conduct is highly developed and extends into areas such as the maintenance of internal discipline and the power of leadership. It is very similar to the Sicilian Mafia's unwritten code of silence, known as *omerta*, and it is effectively enforced. According to Cressey it involves

> (1) *intense loyalty* to the organization and its governing elite, (2) *honesty* in relationships with members, (3) *secrecy* regarding the organization's structure and activities, and (4) *honorable behavior*, which sets members off as morally superior to those outsiders who would govern them.[62]

Loyalty, respect, honor, and absolute obedience are expected of all members. Compliance is induced by custom, material rewards, and violence (either through beatings or executions). Subordinates should not interfere with the leader's interests, they should not inform law enforcement, and if necessary, they should go to prison to protect those in power in the organization.

Francis Ianni maintains that the Mafia code of silence, *omerta*, is based on Sicilian traditions. In his research on the "Lupollo" crime family, he found three basic ground rules: (1) primary loyalty is to the family, (2) act like a man of respect, (3) keep secret all family business.[63]

Whatever the exact rules and their origin, the code of honor has largely collapsed given that even the highest-ranking members of the New York Five Families have become government informers. For example, in 1991 "Sammy the Bull" Gravano, former Gambino underboss, admitted to involvement in 19 murders and testified against Gambino crime family head John Gotti and 35 other mobsters in exchange for a reduced sentence. In 2004, Joseph Massino, boss of the Bonanno crime family and known as "The Last Don," also turned state's evidence. Convicted on charges of murder, arson, extortion, loansharking, illegal gambling, and money laundering Massino made a plea deal to avoid the death penalty and testified against the acting boss of the Bonanno crime family.

With outlaw motorcycle gangs, their club "constitution" establishes a code of conduct. Some of the bylaws of the Hells Angels California chapter include the following: (1) all patches will be the same on the back of denim or leather jacket, nothing will show on the back except the "Hells Angels" patch, (2) there will be no use of heroin in any form, (3) all Hells Angels fines will be paid within 30 days, (5) three mandatory runs, or motorcycle outings, take place on Memorial Day, July Fourth, and Labor Day, (6) no leave period will be granted to a member except for medical reasons or if the member is hospitalized or in jail.[64]

It is also the case that,

> Triads and other traditional [Chinese] crime groups rely heavily on such factors as group identity, loyalty, and familial relationship to create a sense of belonging and extract personal commitment to sustain their profit-oriented activities. Consequently, triad societies have developed different levels of organizational imperatives such as rules, rituals, oaths, a code of conduct and chains of command, which are often sophisticated and elaborate.[65]

According to James O. Finckenauer, a variety of norms and rules govern the Chinese tong-affiliated gangs. These include respecting the tong leader, beating up members of other gangs on your turf, not using drugs, following the orders of the gang officers, and not betraying the gang. Rules violators are punished through physical assault and killing.[66]

Force and Violence

Organized crime is distinguished by its dependency on the use or threat of force and violence, plus intimidation and bribery, as methods of operation to ensure large economic gains, control illegal activities, and survive in competition with other criminal groups. The "gangster," who is usually associated with organized criminal enterprises, performs the violent acts. Continued elimination of rival gang members marks the existence of gangland warfare. Due to corruption and bribery, these killings are not usually cleared by arrest.

The infamous St. Valentine's Day Massacre of 1929 stands out as the archetype of gang warfare. Al Capone and his South Side Gang had acquired control of the illegal liquor operations in Chicago during the prohibition era. Eventually, rivals attempted to "muscle in" and compete for the large profits. Capone eventually displayed superiority over his principal rival gang with summary dispatch. On St. Valentine's Day, Capone's gangsters, disguised as police officers, lined seven members of the Bugs Moran's North Side Gang against the wall of a garage and mowed them down with submachine guns. Although such a mass killing in organized crime has never been equaled in the US, hundreds of slayings have occurred over the years in the course of competition between and within organized crime groups. Mafia "hits" on Mafia figures include the assassinations of Joe Masseria (1931), Benjamin "Bugsy" Siegel (1947), Albert Anastasia (1957), Joe Gallo (1972), Carmine Galante (1979), Angelo Bruno (1980), and Paul Castellano (1985).

Violence is also used in organized crime to defend turf and expand operations. "Biker wars" between the so-called Big Four motorcycle clubs—Hells Angels, Outlaws, Bandidos, and Pagans—have long been ongoing. The Hells Angels have sought complete control over the entire OMG subculture and frequently become antagonistic with all gangs with whom they do not have direct influence.

> While the desire to expand is a constant in most [biker] clubs, it is an increasingly costly effort that requires some coordination with the club's national and regional hierarchies: Expansion in one area can create tensions that lead to an imbalance in club relationships in other areas; thus, the granting of charters that permit use of the club name and symbols is strictly controlled at the national level. Nonetheless, each chapter is relatively autonomous in its routines, and most are left to independently decide how to deal with nearby chapters of other clubs. The club hierarchy acts mainly to support these local units and often acts informally to influence their behavior in one direction or another. This can occur at officer's meetings or through direct contacts. Chapters often negotiate with one another over either the details of how revenge should be handled or to obtain resources (equipment, weapons, manpower) for use in hostilities.
>
> When a club formally declares war, however, all such internecine fraternization is expected to end; all chapters are mandated to cooperate in any effort to target the enemy club. Without such a declaration, one chapter may seek revenge but find itself limited due to objections from other chapters. These are usually attempts to keep the club's profile low so as to avoid increased police scrutiny but may also protect local arrangements that assure peace to neighboring chapters of the two clubs. New York Pagans, for example, might seek

a war with the HA [Hells Angels] while chapters in West Virginia may seek to preserve an unspoken truce with nearby Ohio HA chapters. However, as tensions rise and the number and severity of affronts to club honor and power mount, solidarity builds within the club and inter-club truces dissolve.[67]

Examples of OMG's violence against rival gangs include the Pagan attack on the Hells Angels at a Long Island bike and tattoo show in 2002; the Hells Angels attack on the Mongols in a Laughlin, Nevada casino that same year; the shootout at a restaurant in Waco, Texas, between the Bandidos and the Cossacks in 2015.

Permanent Immunity

The existence of organized crime is dependent on the maintenance of permanent immunity from interference of law enforcement agencies. Permanent immunity is achieved in several ways. First, because the leaders of organized crime stay behind the scenes of operation, they are not usually arrested and prosecuted. Criminal activity cannot be readily traced to its leaders.

Second, persons lower in the hierarchy of organized crime who are arrested are likely to be released as a result of actions by their superiors or by the criminal organization. Such release and avoidance of prosecution and punishment are assured through bribery. For various reasons, persons not directly involved in criminal activity contribute to the protection of organized criminals. Law enforcement officials, judges, businesspersons, and even politicians provide needed services for the protection of organized criminals. Criminal justice agencies with relatively low-paid public servants, especially in developing countries, are prone to corruption by organized crime. Consider the case of Mexican drug lord, Joaquin "El Chapo" Guzman, who took advantage of the country's network of bribes and corruption to succeed in two jailbreaks. With the help of bribed prisons guards, Guzman escaped from his top-security prison in 2001. After being captured a few years later, in 2015 he again escaped from another maximum-security prison through an underground tunnel.

> In a global context, numbers of arrests or convictions for involvement in organized crime are likely to reflect police performance rather than the true extent of criminal activity. In countries where organized crime is most prevalent, investigations into such crimes will be hampered by police corruption and political interference in prosecution and sentencing. Fewer investigations or prosecutions of organized crime will be initiated or successfully completed. Low rates of court cases on corruption or organized crime in a country may point to high rather than low prevalence of such types of crime. High numbers of arrests or convictions for corruption may indicate a comparatively low prevalence of such crimes due to better policing. Police-based information on levels of organized crime will often be misleading. In the field of complex crimes, statistics of police-recorded or court-recorded crimes are a source of disinformation. The case of measuring levels of crime independently of the police is even stronger regarding organized crime and corruption than regarding common crime.[68]

A third way in which organized crime may acquire immunity is by gaining political clout through contributions to political organizations and parties. Elected officials may owe their election to organized criminals. Furthermore, regular "payoffs" to officials provide protection for organized crime. Thus, on a permanent basis, organized crime may be immune to law enforcement through political graft and corruption. According to William J. Chambliss organized crime groups are connected to business and political interests:

> Organized crime may not be something that exists outside law and government but may be instead a creation of them—a hidden but nonetheless integral part of the governmental and economic structures of the society. The people most likely to be exposed to public inquiries may be outside the government but the network of which they are a part may be organized around, run by, and created in the interest of the economic, political, and legal elites who on the surface represent the noncriminal interests of "everyone."[69]

Fourth, because organized crime provides the public with illegal and desired goods and services such as prostitution, human smuggling, and drugs, a certain amount of immunity from arrest and prosecution results from public toleration of organized crime. This toleration contributes to organized crime figures' broad public appeal. Consider that in 1920 the funeral of Chicago's James "Big Jim" Colosimo was attended by thousands of mourners. Colosimo's honorary and active pallbearers, a cortege,

> included three judges, nine aldermen, an assistant state's attorney, two congressmen, a state senator, three doctors, leading artists of the Chicago Opera Company, and current and former gamblers, divekeepers, and other criminal entrepreneurs.[70]

Finally, through the infiltration of legitimate business, organized crime is able to evade the law. Organized crime often operates behind the facade of legitimate business, obscuring its operation and making its detection difficult. Also, in the case of racketeering, organized crime escapes the law because intimidated businesspersons must contend with reprisal if a report is made. As Robert J. Kelly has noted:

> To control a business criminals do not need to actually take it over; all that is required is to control key officers and the company's assets will be at their disposal. By placing funds in a firm or helping to generate business by whatever means, criminals can significantly influence an entire business sector.[71]

In addition, organized crime and legitimate business may assist one another, as in the regulation of prices of given commodities and services or through the enforcement of labor contracts. Such mutual assistance, accompanied by public espousal of the profit motive under almost any arrangement, provides considerable assurance of immunity for organized crime.

While many citizens strongly condemn the violence and intimidation of organized crime, they are often in favor of the economic enterprise that makes it possible and the services that it provides. As already indicated, several characteristics of US society and culture give support to organized crime. In fact, it may be argued that organized crime is a result of the particular structure of American society. To begin with, the motives for organized crime are largely the same as those valued so highly in the free-market system. In fact, even in the transition to a free-market system, as happened after the collapse of the Soviet Union in the 1990s, Mafia groups in Russia emerged to enforce contracts and provide businesses with "protection" against competitors or business rivals. As one Russian investigator explains:

> These groups are not simply involved in ordinary crimes, such as stealing and killing, but also they extort money in a certain district for "protection" of places of public catering, commercial

kiosks, co-operatives, consumer service enterprises, prostitutes. Often the leaders, once they have accumulated sufficient money, enter legal business and become directors of commercial enterprises and banks. They also bribe politicians and law-enforcement agents.[72]

A great deal of organized crime in the United States is tolerated by the public because of its close relation to legitimate business. In fact, it is often referred to as the flip side of legitimate business. As George B. Vold concluded:

> One basic fact stands out, . . . namely, that organized crime must be thought of as a natural growth, or as a developmental adjunct to our general system of private profit economy. Business, industry, and finance all are competitive enterprises within the area of legal operations. But there is also an area of genuine economic demand for things and services not permitted under our legal and social codes. Organized crime is the system of business functioning in the area. It, too, is competitive, and hence must organize for its self-protection and for control of the market.[73]

Drug cartels engage in smuggling and distributing drugs, thus providing these commodities to the public. Consider that while Morocco is the world's largest producer and exporter of cannabis, Columbia is the world's largest producer of cocoa derivatives, and Afghanistan is the world's largest producer of opium, it is the United States that is one of the world's largest *consumers* of marijuana, cocaine, and heroin. Organized crime simply supplies a steady flow of a needed commodity, much as legitimate business deals in supplying the public with legal commodities. Without the demand, Los Zetas, the Pagans, and the Yakuza could not operate in the illegal drug trade.

Gambling, as a major area of operation for organized crime, is a deeply ingrained aspect of capitalist culture. In Western Canada, for example,

> video gaming and lottery machines are the newest, and possibly the largest, illicit source of gambling income available to organized crime groups. The machines can earn up to $2,000 per machine, per week, making this an extremely lucrative business. The cost of the machines ranges between $2,500 and $5,000 and is quickly paid off. Organized crime groups including the Hells Angels, Asian-based organized crime, traditional organized crime, and East European-based groups are all involved in the illegal operation of these machines.[74]

Gambling is a natural consequence of a culture that encourages success, skill, competition, and diversion.[75] The element of chance and the tendency to speculate in certain risks not only are found in illegal gambling but are a major part of investment and finance in the legitimate business world. After all, the stock market and venture capital firms do little more than investment in risks based more on speculation than on empirical data. It is little wonder that a large-scale business (legal and illegal) has developed to satisfy the demand for gambling. Moreover, living on credit with interest has become an indispensable, if precarious, feature of modern life and the US economy.

In an early writing on organized crime, Alfred R. Lindesmith stressed the social context of organized crime by noting that it is an integral part of our total culture.[76] He observed that such factors as the profit motive, indifference to public affairs, general disregard for law, laissez-faire economics, and questionable political practices have produced a fertile place for organized crime in our large cities. Similarly, sociologist Daniel Bell indicated that the development of organized crime, and gambling in particular, was due to, the jungle quality of the American business community, particularly at the turn of the [twentieth] century, reflected in the mode of "business" practiced by the coarse gangster elements, most of them from new immigrant families, who were just "getting ahead" just as Horatio Alger had urged.[77]

According to Bell, organized crime was related to immigration (ethnic) patterns and the US economy. Ianni explains this pattern as follows:

> By the 1920s and the period of Prohibition and speculation in the money markets and real estate, the Irish were succeeded in organized crime by the Jews, and Arnold Rothstein, Lepke Buchalter, and Gurrah Shapiro dominated gambling and labor racketeering for over a decade. The Jews quickly moved into the world of business and the professions as more legitimate avenues to economic and social mobility. The Italians came next.[78]

One study that contradicts the ethnic succession thesis—that organized crime was one of the "queer ladders of social mobility in American life" for racial and ethnic groups—concerned black and white involvement in illegal numbers gambling in the latter twentieth century.[79] The researchers found that African Americans who had historically been key players in numbers gambling in "East City" had not succeeded the older Italian American crime groups. The report demonstrated that Italian American organized crime had considerable advantages in illegal gambling—in the form of a combination of cultural, social, and financial capital resources—that African Americans did not.

Organized crime involvement in drug trafficking, illegal gambling, prostitution, and other vices continues without a great deal of public action against it because of a hypocrisy in which citizens try to prohibit illegal practices in which they often indulge. In this clash of values and interests, organized crime provides the illegal services that the public desires.

Social Reaction to Criminal Behavior

Although societal reaction against organized crime is strong, the public feels ambivalent about it. While more effective laws and better law enforcement may assist in the control of organized crime, the structured paradox of public indignation at illegal behavior on the one hand, and toleration and approval of such illegal behavior on the other, provides US society with its most serious handicap in the control and prevention of organized crime. Many people are complicit "victims" who have no incentive to report operations involving illicit drugs, gambling, or sex trafficking for fear of losing their availability. Targeted efforts in combating organized crime have been applied vigorously since the 1980s with some success at crippling the influence of criminal organizations, especially the Mafia. These efforts involve the use of three controversial methods: (1) confidential informants, (2) covert investigations, and (3) specialized laws.

Confidential informants provide police and prosecutors with incriminating information against criminals and criminal organizations. They usually do so in exchange for dropped or reduced charges for past crimes. However, the efficacy of using confidential informants (CIs) in law enforcement efforts at controlling organized crime is difficult to assess.

> Due to the secrecy and lack of public records, it is impossible to say precisely how many cases the FBI has been able to solve on the basis of its use of CIs. In general, the government has long maintained that certain kinds of cases would be impossible to investigate or prosecute without informants. Moreover, anecdotal evidence indicates that informants

are an important and fruitful tool. Mafia assassin Jimmy Fratianno, who spent the 1980s in witness protection, helped convict numerous mob members. The FBI has disclosed additional informant-driven successes: a three-year grand jury investigation of organized crime that led to six convictions and a $500,000 forfeiture; the investigation of three violent gangs in a northeastern city that led to thirty-five cases involving fifty-four gang members; and a two-year undercover operation that led to the indictment of four Houston City Council members.

For the same reasons of secrecy and lack of documentation, it is likewise impossible to say just how often high-level confidential informants run amok, leading to new crimes, corruption, or failed cases. But individual incidents reveal the sorts of problems that the government has contended with over the years. For example, Salvatore "Sammy the Bull" Gravano was one of the FBI's most infamous, successful, and problematic informants. A mafia hitman who confessed to nineteen murders, his 1992 testimony helped the FBI obtain nearly forty convictions, most notably that of John Gotti. The government then released Gravano and relocated him to Arizona in the witness protection program. There, he rejoined organized crime and in 2001, pled guilty to running a multi-million-dollar Ecstasy ring. In 2003, he was charged with ordering the killing of Detective Peter Calabro, but charges were dismissed when the government's sole witness died.[80]

When informants testify against organized crime, they sometimes enter the Federal Witness Protection Program, also known as the Witness Security Program or WITSEC, to avoid retribution from their co-conspirators. Administered by the US Marshals Service, WITSEC protects informants and their dependents by relocating them with new identities, jobs, and homes. These protections are often given to informants who have themselves committed serious crimes. Gerald Schur founded WITSEC in the mid-1960s:

> He was the program's creator and for thirty-four years the driving force behind it. No witnesses got protection in WITSEC without his personal attention. He wrote nearly all of the program's rules, shaped it based on his own personal philosophical views, and guided it with a steady but iron hand. During his tenure, WITSEC protected 6,416 witnesses and 14,468 of their dependents, including wives, children, and lovers. None of the witnesses who followed his rules was murdered. He was involved with *every* major Mafia witness in recent history, starting with Joseph Valachi, considered the first to tell the mob's secrets. The other gangsters form a who's who of organized crime: Joseph "the Animal" Barboza, Vincent "Fat Vinnie" Teresa, Aladena "Jimmy the Weasel" Fratianno, Joseph "Joe Dogs" Iannuzzi, and Henry Hill of the best-selling book *Wiseguy* and the popular movie *Goodfellas*. Name a mafioso who turned against the mob, and in one way or another Shur dealt with him.[81]

Covert investigations, which include the use of electronic surveillance, are perhaps the most controversial strategies for controlling organized crime. Popular accounts of undercover operations against organized crime include that carried out by William Queen, a federal agent who from 1998 through 2000 infiltrated the Mongols biker gang. Queen's testimony resulted in dozens of convictions of Mongol members, for dealing drugs, extortion, stealing motorcycles, and illegal gun sales. FBI agent Joseph D. Pistone (aka Donnie Brasco) infiltrated the Bonnano crime family during the late 1970s and early 1980s and obtained information that led to the conviction of many Mafia figures. According to Pistone:

In New York City alone, home of the main Mafia families, there were at times five or six Mafia trials going on at once. Trials coming out of our investigations got famous, such as "The Pizza Connection," the biggest heroin-smuggling case, and "The Mafia Commission," the trial of the entire ruling body of the Mafia. Because I had been living within the Mafia for so long, I had information relevant to them all, and I testified at all of them. I would be testifying at more than a dozen trials in a half dozen cities over a span of 5 years.

Ultimately, we would get more than a hundred federal convictions. By 1987, the combination of undercover agents, street agents, cops, US Attorneys, and informants had blasted the heart out of La Cosa Nostra. The Mafia would be changed forever. The boss of every single Mafia family would be indicted and/or in prison and/or dead before the trials were over. We got almost every Mafia solider we went after.[82]

During the 1980s, law enforcement engaged in an extensive web of electronic eavesdropping, the use of telephone wiretaps and microphones ("bugs"), to intercept and record conversations between Mafia members.

Extremely productive bugs were placed in the homes, social clubs, and cars of many of Cosa Nostra's top leaders. These bugs allowed the [federal] agents to listen to and record details of labor racketeering, loan sharking, cartel enforcement, crime family politics, and diverse criminal schemes. In subsequent trials the mobsters could be inculpated by their own words.[83]

There are pros and cons to employing US law enforcement undercover techniques—infiltration and surveillance—in the transnational policing of organized crime. While Americans may have few problems with covert policing, "Europeans associate undercover agents with a long history of internal spying by state security services, who used 'agent provocateurs' to infiltrate and radicalize dissident political movements, occasionally inciting acts of violence to discredit these movements."[84] The tradeoffs of undercover policing are:

(1) deception as against coercion; (2) crime detection as against prevention; (3) electronic surveillance (intruding on privacy) as against infiltration (intruding on autonomy); (4) undercover agents as against civilian informants; (5) intelligence (and national security) as against evidence (and criminal enforcement); (6) protecting society from the excessive diffusion of undercover police work (by quarantining covert methods in specialized units) as against protecting society from the specialized units (and the potentially corrupting effect of their insulation from regular police work); (7) embracing undercover policing as an effective technique as against preserving a sense of its ethical ambiguity; (8) accommodating the selection of law enforcement goals, the definition of offenses, and the rules of procedure and evidence to undercover techniques, as against preserving independent criteria for assessing whether covert tactics work.[85]

Specialized laws have also played a major role in curbing organized crime. The most powerful of these is the Racketeer Influence and Corrupt Organization Act, or RICO, that was enacted in 1970 by the US Congress. Unlike traditional criminal statutes that limit law enforcement to investigate a single crime committed by an individual offender at a specific time and place, RICO allows for the investigation and prosecution of long-standing unlawful conduct— relating to violence, the provision of illegal services (drugs, gambling, prostitution, etc.), corruption in unions and governmental affairs, and commercial fraud—committed by illicit enterprises.[86] It specifically targets people participating in an organizations' affairs through a *pattern of racketeering activity*. Because it makes it possible to bring to trial an entire group or "enterprise" associated with criminal activity, RICO has been one of the most effective weapons in fighting organized crime, particularly the Mafia, but also, for example, the Hells Angels and the now-defunct Irish-American street gang, the Westies.

Much has been written about the effectiveness of using confidential informants, covert investigations, and specialized laws in fighting organized crime. The effectiveness of *crime prevention* by law enforcement, governments, and international agencies has also been the subject of much consideration. For example, one Canadian study examined indicators of crime, as experienced at the community level, in measuring law enforcement's effectiveness in combating organized crime.[87] Advocating for a standard for success based on outcomes, the researchers recommend looking at reductions in drug crime and drug-related crime, changes in average drug seizures, improved public health, and improved public perception and confidence. They proposed three measurement approaches for improving accountability for the policing of organized crime: (1) operationalize, and standardize nationally, multidisciplinary outcome measures for the policing of organized crime, (2) measure and evaluate policing performance according to robust external methodological standards, and (3) continue to build and refine process evaluation and threat assessment methodologies.

A European study explored the possibilities of developing more effective crime prevention strategies in regard to transnational organized crime.[88] This is an area in which *enforcement*— i.e., the arresting of offenders and the interdicting of contraband—rather than *prevention* has dominated the thinking of customs agencies, banks, and the police. One reason for disregarding prevention is that the supply of persons, goods, and services provided by organized crime is not seen as preventable in the same way as conventional crimes like burglary, car theft, and credit card fraud. The study's investigators assert that data on financial crime, which can point to money laundering, can be used as an indicator in demonstrating the effectiveness of crime prevention interventions such as financial confiscation of the proceeds of crime.

Beginning in the early twenty-first century, a few economically powerful UN-member countries set up and financed transnational groups to implement proactive international policy on illicit drug trafficking.[89] However, as more countries became involved in the UN Commission on Narcotic Drugs, drug policy became increasingly reactive. As a consequence, new "informal" groups—the Financial Action Task Force, the Dublin Group, the Egmont Group, and the Paris Pact—were created to go beyond the traditional focus on trafficking and instead control precursor chemicals and money laundering. Precursors are those chemicals necessary for the processing of raw materials into illicit drugs (such as acetic anhydride and hydrochloric acid for heroin processing) or those chemicals which form the basis for the laboratory creation of illicit drugs (such as pseudepedrine and ephedrine for amphetamine, methamphetamine, and Ecstasy). These new groups are also involved in preventing money laundering, particularly as organized crime increasingly turns to electronic transfer operations to remit illicit proceeds.

Regardless of the form it takes—national syndicate, drug cartel, street gang, or transnational network—organized crime is an illegal business enterprise. It has also, however, expanded into legitimate businesses and occupations. "The character of the political economy," Richard Quinney has written, "does not stop organized crime from continuing expansion." Indeed,

> Organized crime, like legitimate business, works for maximum returns with minimum expenditure by efficient organization and skilled management. The difference is that legitimate

business operates within the law most of the time. Organized crime seems more significantly affected by economic facts of supply and demand, and the fads in consumer habits, than by legislation and sporadic attempts at formal control.[90]

Organized crime is an integral part of the global political economy. An elaborate corporate and financial structure of multinational corporations, banking institutions, and brokerage firms is tied to organized crime. Moreover, organized crime and the business world are intimately related to a country's political organization. There exists a symbiotic alliance, an institutional arrangement, between corporate crime, organized crime, and political crime.

Notes

1 Thorsten Sellin, "Organized Crime: A Business Enterprise," *The Annals of the American Academy of Political and Social Science* 347 (1963): 12–19.

2 Jay S. Albanese, *Organized Crime in Our Times*, 6th edition (Boston, MA: Anderson Publishing, 2011), 4.

3 President's Commission on Organized Crime, *The Impact: Organized Crime Today* (Washington, DC: US Government Printing Office, 1986).

4 Scott H. Decker, Tim Bynum, and Deborah Weisel, "A Tale of Two Cities: Gangs as Organized Crime Groups," *Justice Quarterly* 15, no. 3 (1998): 395–425. On why streets gangs like the MS-13 may appropriately be called organized crime groups, see Joseph Wheatley, "The Flexibility of RICO and its Use on Street Gangs Engaging in Organized Crime in the United States," *Policing: A Journal of Policy and Practice* 2, no.1 (2008): 82–91.

5 Federal Bureau of Investigation, *Transnational Organized Crime 2018*. www.fbi.gov/investigate/organized-crime

6 Herbert Asbury, *The Gangs of New York: An Informal History of the Underworld* (New York, NY: Thunder's Mouth Press, [1927] 1998), 340.

7 Frederic M. Thrasher, *The Gang: A Study of 1,313 Gangs in Chicago* (Chicago, IL: University of Chicago Press, 1927), 439.

8 Ibid., 25.

9 John Landesco, *Organized Crime in Chicago* (Chicago, IL: University of Chicago Press, 1929), 43.

10 Ibid., 97–98.

11 James O. Finckenauer, "Problems of Definition: What is Organized Crime?" *Trends in Organized Crime* 8, no. 3 (2005): 63–83, 81.

12 Marshall B. Clinard and Robert F. Meier, *Sociology of Deviant Behavior*, 15th edition (Boston, MA: Cengage, 2016), 170.

13 American Gaming Association, *State of the States: The AGA Survey of the Casino Industry*, 2017. www.americangaming.org/sites/default/files/research_files/2017%20State%20of%20the%20States.pdf

14 Nicholas Pileggi, *Wiseguy* (New York: Simon and Schuster, 1985), 174.

15 Peter B. E. Hill, *The Japanese Mafia: Yakuza, Law, and the State* (New York, NY: Oxford University Press, 2003).

16 Scott H. Decker and Margaret Townsend Chapman, *Drug Smugglers on Drug Smuggling: Lessons from the Inside* (Philadelphia, PA: Temple University Press, 2008), 43.

17 Dick Lehr and Gerard O'Neill, *Black Mass: Whitey Bulger, the FBI, and a Devil's Deal* (New York: Public Affairs, 2012), 181.

18 Frederick Desroches, "Research on Upper Level Drug Trafficking: A Review," *Journal of Drug Issues* 37, no. 4 (2007): 827–844, 832.

19 Hill, *The Japanese Mafia*, 103.

20 Peter Reuter, "Systemic Violence in Drug Markets," *Crime, Law, and Social Change* 52, no. 3 (2009): 275–284.

21 Viridiana Rios, "Why Did Mexico Become so Violent? A Self-Reinforcing Violent Equilibrium Caused by Competition and Enforcement," *Trends in Organized Crime* 16, no. 2 (2013):138–155.

22 William Queen, *Under and Alone: The True Story of the Undercover Agent Who Infiltrated America's Most Violent Outlaw Motorcycle Gang* (New York, NY: Ballantine Books, 2007), 23.

23 A Johanna Hagstedt, Lars Korsell, and Alfred Skagerö, "In the Land of Prohibition? Clients and Trafficked Women in Sweden," in *Prostitution and Human Trafficking: Focus on Clients*, ed. by Andrea Di Nicola, Andrea Cauduro, Marco Lombardi, and Paolo Ruspini (New York, NY: Springer, 2009), 186.

24 Rebecca Surtees, "Traffickers and Trafficking in Southern and Eastern Europe: Considering the Other Side of Human Trafficking," *European Journal of Criminology* 5, no. 1 (2008): 39–68.

25 Louise Shelley, "Trafficking in Women: The Business Model Approach," *The Brown Journal of World Affairs* 10, no. 1 (2003): 119–131.

26 Eva Lo Iacono, "Victims, Sex Workers, and Perpetrators: Gray Areas in the Trafficking of Nigerian Women," *Trends in Organized Crime* 17, nos. 1–2 (2014): 110–128.

27 Ibid., 123.

28 Robert J. Kelly, *The Upperworld and the Underworld: Case Studies of Racketeering and Business Infiltrations in the United States* (New York, NY: Kluwer/Plenum, 1999), 22.

29 Special Committee to Investigate Organized Crime in Interstate Commerce, *The Kefauver Committee Report on Organized Crime* (New York, NY: Didier Publishers, 1951), 152.

30 Herbert Edelhertz and Thomas D. Overcast, *The Business of Organized Crime: An Assessment of Organized Crime Business-Type Activities and Their Implications for Law Enforcement* (Loomis, CA: Palmer Press, 1993).

31 Felia Allum and Renate Siebert, eds., *Organised Crime and the Challenge to Democracy* (Abington: Routledge, 2003), 5.

32 Hung-En Sung, "State Failure, Economic Failure, and Predatory Organized Crime: A Comparative Analysis," *Journal of Research in Crime and Delinquency* 41, no. 2 (2004): 111–129.

33 Ibid., 115.

34 Jan Van Dijk, "Mafia Markers: Assessing Organized Crime and its Impact Upon Societies," *Trends in Organized Crime* 10, no. 4 (2007): 39–56.

35 Ibid., 34.

36 Eiko Maruko Siniawer, *Ruffians, Yakuza, Nationalists: The Violent Politics of Modern Japan, 1860–1960* (Ithaca, NY: Cornell University Press, 2008).

37 David E. Kaplan and Alec Dubro, *Yakuza: Japan's Criminal Underworld* (Berkeley, CA: University of California Press, 2012).

38 Landesco, *Organized Crime in Chicago*, 149–150.

39 Jeffrey Scott McIllwain, *Organizing Crime in Chinatown: Race and Racketeering in New York City, 1890–1910* (Jefferson, NC: McFarland, 2004), 130–135.

40 Kelly, *The Upperworld and the Underworld*, 50.

41 James B. Jacobs, *Mobsters, Unions, and Feds: The Mafia and the American Labor Movement* (New York, NY: New York University Press, 2006).

42 Peter Maas, *Underboss: Sammy the Bull Gravano's Story of Life in the Mafia* (New York, NY: HarperCollins, 1999), 116–117.

43 Donald R. Cressey, *Theft of the Nation: The Structure and Operations of Organized Crime in America* (New York, NY: Harper & Row, 1969), 95–98.

44 Jacobs, *Mobsters, Unions, and Feds*, 256.

45 M. Vere van Koppen, "Comparing Criminal Careers of Organized Crime Offenders and General Offenders," *European Journal of Criminology* 7, no. 5 (2010): 356–374.

46 Edward R. Kleemans and Christianne J. de Poot, "Criminal Careers in Organized Crime and Social Opportunity Structure," *European Journal of Criminology* 5, no. 1 (2008): 69–98.

47 Frank Bovenkerk, "Wanted: Mafia Boss: Essay on the Personology of Organized Crime," *Crime, Law, and Social Change* 33, no. 3 (2000): 225–242.

48 Landesco, *Organized Crime in Chicago*, 207.

49 As quoted in Frank E. Hagan, *Introduction to Criminology: Theories, Methods, and Criminal Behavior*, 9th edition (Los Angeles, CA: Sage, 2017), 351.

50 Landesco, *Organized Crime in Chicago*, 214.

51 Cressey, *Theft of the Nation*, 241–242.

52 Joseph L. Alibini, *The American Mafia: Genesis of a Legend* (New York, NY: Appleton-Century-Crofts, 1971).

53 Francis A.J. Ianni with Elizabeth Reuss-Ianni, *A Family Business: Kinship and Social Control in Organized Crime* (New York, NY: Russell Sage Foundation, 1972).

54 Kleemans and de Poot, "Criminal Careers in Organized Crime and Social Opportunity Structure," 81.

55 Ibid., 84.

56 Shawn T. Flanigan, "Motivations and Implications of Community Service Provision by La Familia Michoacána/Knights Templar and other Mexican Drug Cartels," *Journal of Strategic Security* 7, no. 3 (2014): 63–83.

57 Stephen Schneider, *Iced: The Story of Organized Crime in Canada* (Mississauga, Ontario: Wiley, 2009), 380.

58 Landesco, *Organized Crime in Chicago*, 214.

59 President's Commission on Organized Crime, *The Impact*, 31–32.

60 Peter Maas, *The Valachi Papers* (New York, NY: Putnam, 1968).

61 Hill, *The Japanese Mafia*, 65–72.

62 Cressey, *Theft of the Nation*, 171.

63 Ianni with Reuss-Ianni, *A Family Business*, 155–165.

64 Howard Abadinsky, *Organized Crime*, 11th edition (Boston, MA: Cengage, 2017), 173.

65 Sheldon Zhang and Ko-lin Chin, "The Declining Significance of Triad Societies in Transnational Illegal Activities: A Structural Deficiency Perspective," *British Journal of Criminology* 43, no. 3 (2003): 469–488, 483.

66 James O. Finckenauer, "Chinese Transnational Organized Crime: The Fuk Ching." (Washington DC: National Institute of Justice, 2006), 1–5. www.ncjrs.gov/App/Publications/abstract.aspx?ID=240164

67 James F. Quinn and Craig J. Forsyth, "The Tools, Tactics, and Mentality of Outlaw Biker Wars," *American Journal of Criminal Justice* 36, no. 3 (2011): 216–230, 219.

68 Van Dijk, "Mafia Markers," 40.

69 William J. Chambliss, *On the Take: From Petty Crooks to Presidents*, 2nd edition (Bloomington, IN: Indiana University Press, 1988), 6.

70 Jeffrey Scott McIllwain, "Organized Crime: A Social Network Approach," *Crime, Law, and Social Change* 32, no. 4 (1999): 301–323, 301.

71 Kelly, *The Upperworld and the Underworld*, 197.

72 Federico Varese, *The Russian Mafia: Private Protection in a New Market Economy* (New York, NY: Oxford University Press, 2001), 172.

73 George B. Vold, *Theoretical Criminology* (New York, NY: Oxford University Press, 1958), 240.

74 Criminal Intelligence Service Canada, *Annual Report on Organized Crime in Canada, 2000* (Ottawa, Ontario: 2000), 33.

75 Herbert A. Bloch, "The Sociology of Gambling," *American Journal of Sociology* 57, no. 3 (1951): 215–221.

76 Alfred R. Lindesmith, "Organized Crime," *Annals of the American Academy of Political and Social Science* 217, no. 1 (1941): 119–127.

77 Daniel Bell, "Crime as an American Way of Life," *Antioch Review* 13, no. 2 (1953): 131–154, 355.

78 Francis A.J. Iannni, *The Black Mafia: Ethnic Succession in Organized Crime* (New York, NY: Simon and Schuster, 1974), 13–14.

79 Darrell Steffensmeier and Jeffery T. Ulmer, "Black and White Control of Numbers Gambling: A Cultural Assets–Social Capital View," *American Sociological Review* 71, no. 1 (2006): 123–156.

80 Alexandra Natapoff, *Snitching: Criminal Informants and the Erosion of American Justice* (New York, NY: New York University Press, 2009), 142–143.

81 Pete Earley and Gerald Shur, *WITSEC: Inside the Federal Witness Protection Program* (New York, NY: Bantam Books, 2002), 5.

82 Joseph D. Pistone, *Donnie Brasco: My Undercover Life in the Mafia* (New York, NY: Signet, 1989), 12–13.

83 James B. Jacobs, Coleen Friel, and Robert Raddick, *Gotham Unbound: How New York City Was Liberated From the Grip of Organized Crime* (New York, NY: New York University Press, 1999), 133.

84 Jacqueline E. Ross, "Tradeoffs in Undercover Investigations: A Comparative Perspective," *University of Chicago Law Review* 69, no. 3 (2002): 1501–1541, 1504.

85 Ibid., 1502–1503.

86 G. Robert Blakey, "RICO: The Genesis of an Idea," *Trends in Organized Crime* 9, no. 8 (2006): 8–34.

87 Allan Castle, "Measuring the Impact of Law Enforcement on Organized Crime," *Trends in Organized Crime* 11, no. 2 (2008): 135–156.

88 Michael Levi and Mike Maguire, "Reducing and Preventing Organised Crime: An Evidence-Based Critique," *Crime, Law, and Social Change* 41, no. 5 (2004): 397–469.

89 Cindy Fazey, "International Policy on Illicit Drug Trafficking: The Formal and Informal Mechanisms," *Journal of Drug Issues* 37, no. 4 (2007): 755–780.

90 Richard Quinney, *Criminology*, 2nd edition (Boston, MA: Little, Brown, 1979), 204.

8
POLITICAL CRIME

As early as 1895, the French appellate court judge, Louis Proal, in his book *Political Crime* stated:

> The art of governing . . . has been disfigured by a great number of false maxims ["The end
> justifies the means," "The safety of the people is the supreme law"], which have made
> it the art of lying and deceiving, the art of proscribing and despoiling, under a cloak of
> legality. . . . Ordinary evil-doers who are judged by the courts are only guilty of killing or
> robbing some few individuals; the number of their victims is restricted. Political malefactors,
> on the contrary, count their victims by the thousand; they corrupt and ruin entire nations.[1]

However, it wasn't until almost a century later that these crimes *by* government, which include
human rights violations, illegal domestic surveillance, and election fraud, began to receive much
attention from criminologists.

On the other hand, crimes *against* the state—treason, sabotage, political assassinations, and
domestic terrorism—had continuously been grist for criminology's mill since at least 1892 when
Cesare Lombroso and Rodolfo Laschi published *Political Crime and Revolutions*. Here they defined
political violence as "any violent harm caused to laws established by the majority to preserve the
political, economic, or social system that it desires."[2]

In this chapter, we look at crimes against the government and crimes by the government along
the lines of our typology: definition of behavior as criminal, sociology of criminal behavior, and social
reaction to criminal behavior. Each of these types—crimes by and crimes against government—
involves different offenses, different career patterns, and different social and legal reactions.

Crime against the state is recognized in illegal attempts to oppose the government or to express
beliefs about or alter in some way (violent or nonviolent) the existing sociopolitical structure.
Since nation-states must strive to maintain power distribution within their borders, these crimes
are taken seriously and are punished accordingly. These crimes—whether in violation of laws
created for the suppression of such behavior or for other purposes (such as promulgating what
is considered an "anti-government," racist, or religious ideology, which is sometimes fueled by
conspiracy theories)—are regarded by political authorities as a threat to national security and social
order. Political crimes against the state include a wide range of classic crimes: treason, sedition,
assassination, tax evasion, rioting or inciting to riot, civil rights violations, protest violations, and

violations of law in the course of advancing "extremist" ideas and actions. Failure to conform to certain laws because of religious convictions also can be a crime against the state. An extreme example of this is seen in the refusal of the Branch Davidian religious group led by David Koresh to surrender to federal authorities on charges of firearms violations. This refusal instigated the so-called Waco siege of 1993 that lasted 51 days and that ultimately resulted in the deaths of 82 Branch Davidians and four agents of the Bureau of Alcohol, Tobacco, and Firearms (ATF).

On the other hand, crime by governments, sometimes called *state crime* or "state-organized crime," is constituted by unlawful action against citizens. An historical example is the *cause célèbre* called the Dreyfus affair, which began in 1894, when the French army and government falsely accused of treason an innocent army officer, Alfred Dreyfus, for reasons of state. This led the French sociologist, Émile Durkheim, a defender of Dreyfus, to argue that when a person's civil rights are placed above the state, there can be "no reason of State which can excuse an outrage against the person."[3]

State crime consists of the criminal violations by governments themselves, or more particularly, by the agents of the government, whether police officers, prosecutors, or presidents. State crime can be further divided into:

1. *Violations of civil liberties and rights of citizens, or failure to safeguard these liberties and rights.* For example, the Fourth Amendment to the US Constitution establishes citizens' right to privacy from government surveillance by guaranteeing that they or their property cannot be searched or investigated without a proper warrant and probable cause. In 2013, US intelligence contractor, Edward Snowden disclosed that the National Security Agency (NSA) had for years engaged in the mass, warrantless spying of US citizens.
2. *Criminal acts committed in the course of enforcing the laws of the state*, as in the case of police brutality involving minority citizens who are disproportionately targeted by police. One study that examined excessive force complaints filed with police departments in cities of 100,000 or more residents found that the higher the percentage of black and Latino populations in a community, the higher the incidence of sustained excessive force complaints.[4]
3. *Violations of international laws of warfare or national sovereignty.* Examples of this abound: the 2003 United States invasion of Iraq, the 2016 US drone strikes in Pakistan's territory along the Pakistan-Afghanistan border, and the 2018 missile strikes against Syria (although this text is concerned principally with violations of United States federal and state laws, we nonetheless include some limited discussion of international violations because many consider them political crimes).
4. *Violations of federal law by high-ranking officials, such as giving false testimony to Congress or violating Congressional policy laws.* Examples include John Mitchell, US Attorney General under President Richard M. Nixon, sentenced to prison in 1977 for the multiple crimes he committed in the Watergate affair; John M. Poindexter, President Ronald Reagan's national security advisor was convicted in 1990 for lying to Congress about key details of the Iran-Contra conspiracy; Donald Trump's former campaign chairman Paul Manafort lied to the FBI and to special counsel Robert Mueller's office about a variety of matters including Manafort's contacts with a Russian spy.

In attempting to preserve a particular social and political order, governments and their officials transgress laws that exist to protect citizens from the abuses of government in a democratic society. Often it is procedural law that is violated rather than substantive law. That governments do not usually prosecute themselves when these laws are broken does not make the violations any less criminal; it simply makes the violators harder to prosecute. Political crimes—crimes *by* or *against* the government—are particularly difficult to view objectively, for they always involve moral and ideological positions.

Any discussion of political crime is bound to be complicated by what are often conflicting views of a situation. For example, during the Vietnam era (1961–1975) those who were against the war on the grounds that it was unconstitutional vigorously opposed the government's prosecution of young men who resisted being drafted into the military. For these citizens, not only was the US government breaking the law by waging the Vietnam War in the first place, but it was making an "immoral" situation worse by punishing those who resisted the draft. For others, those who opposed the war and the "draft dodgers" were the ones guilty of crimes against the government. Similarly, some consider Snowden, who revealed that the NSA and intelligence agencies in several countries were involved in secret mass surveillance programs, to be a whistleblower, while others consider him a traitor. Thus, there is a relativity to political crime: where one side sees crime by the government, the other side sees crimes against the government. Moreover, as we know from history,

> many of those originally hailed as heroes have become political offenders and many of those regarded as political criminals have been elevated to the glorified pedestal of heroes.[5]

The so-called War on Terror declared by President George W. Bush after the September 11, 2001 attacks against the United States, posed a similar dilemma. Some saw this "war" as involving crimes by the federal government including the "extraordinary rendition," torture, and prisoner abuse of terrorist suspects as well as the indefinite detentions of prisoners at Guantanamo Bay Naval Base and the warrantless surveillance of US citizens. Others saw it as leading to the arrest of hundreds of terrorists around the world, the prevention of further large-scale attacks on US soil, and the strengthening of national security.

Events are open to interpretation, either as evidence of gross government overreach or of global terrorism and terrorists who would bring the country down by attacking civilian populations. Of course, there are many other considerations of great importance in this issue, but the point is that any discussion of political crime can be a two-edged sword. The same dilemmas arise when the state interferes with constitutional rights to free speech. Before the US Supreme Court settled the issue in 1989, flag burning was thought by some to be a crime against the state while others felt that the state, by punishing flag-burning protesters, was itself in violation of the law.

A variety of crimes against the government are crimes of *omission*, such as evasion of income tax laws, violations of customs regulations, or selling liquor without a license when one is required. We do not discuss these crimes at length in this chapter since they are more fittingly dealt with as occupational crimes, corporate crimes, or actions of organized crime.

Definition of Behavior as Criminal

Crimes against Government

All freedom, including political freedom, is qualified. The history of the United States is replete with laws that have been enacted and enforced in order to contain real or perceived threats to the status quo and/or the government. Freedom of speech was severely abridged, for example, by the Sedition Act of 1798, which provided for the punishment of anyone who uttered or published statements against the government, and by the strengthening of the Espionage Act in 1917.

The 1917 laws, sweeping and vaguely worded, constituted the most brutal attack on free speech in the US since the Sedition Act 120 years earlier. It empowered the federal government to carry out wholesale censorship of all communications, whether by mail, newspaper, telephone, telegraph, or radio. Legal controls relating to security as well as economic matters have been established during war emergencies. Concern (and what often amounted to national paranoia) over native communism—the so-called Second Red Scare—occurred during post-World War II instability and unrest.

The federal statutes are filled with other anti-subversive provisions enacted during periods of national crisis. To name only a few, the Voorhis Act of 1940 restricted the registration of persons and organizations who acted as agents of foreign powers; the Smith Act of 1940 forbade the advocacy of the overthrow of the government; the Internal Security Act of 1950 (McCarran Act) required the registration of Communist and Communist-front organizations as well as strengthened other legislation on subversion; the Immigration and Nationality Act of 1952 (McCarran-Walter Act) provided for the deportation of resident aliens because of "disloyal" beliefs and associations; and the Communist Control Act of 1954 required the registration of Communist party members with the Attorney General. In addition to such legislation, loyalty and security programs have been initiated and blacklist procedures established. Moreover, the 2001 USA PATRIOT Act authorized the indefinite detention of immigrants; allowed law enforcement officers to search private premises without the owner's or the occupant's consent or knowledge; and permitted the FBI to search telephone, e-mail, and financial records without a court order. In addition, Executive Order 13769—also called the "Muslim ban"—signed by President Trump in 2017 prohibited people from predominantly Muslim countries from entering the US, purportedly as a way of controlling terrorism.

The greater a country's political freedom, the greater the effort needed to preserve and enhance it. This is the case with established democracies like the US, the UK, and France that generally allow freedom of expression and of the press. It is equally true that the less political freedom, the more difficult it is to create a just and representative government. An example of this is the Arab Spring uprisings, which began in 2010 in response to oppressive regimes throughout North Africa and the Middle East. The uprisings faded a couple of years later as Arab Spring demonstrations were met with violence from authorities, pro-government militias, counter-demonstrators, and militaries.

But the existence of political freedom does not automatically require tolerance on the part of society. There may be laws guaranteeing demonstrations and freedom of speech, but these do not ensure that other laws will not be invoked when violence and hatred are involved. For example, the Unite the Right rally that occurred in Charlottesville, Virginia, in 2017 involved white supremacists who gathered to oppose removing a statue of Robert E. Lee. Carrying Confederate battle flags, Gadsden flags, and a Nazi flag, the protesters chanted Nazi slogans, including "Jews will not replace us." One white nationalist drove his car into a crowd of counter-protesters, hitting several and killing one. Despite the fact that President Trump drew a moral equivalence between the white nationalists and the counter-protesters stating that there were "very fine people on both sides," the white nationalist who drove into the crowd was convicted of first-degree murder.

In the 1960s, demonstrators for civil rights, social justice, and other causes were arrested on such charges as disorderly conduct, breach of peace, parading without a permit, trespassing, loitering, and violation of fire ordinances. Other protesters were legally harassed for refusing to pay income taxes used for military purposes, for picketing military bases, and for failing to register for the draft. More recently, criminal law was used to arrest and prosecute ranchers who protested government rules against grazing cattle on federally-owned land. For example, in 2014, Nevada cattle rancher Cliven Bundy's refusal to pay grazing fees to the US government led to an armed confrontation between Bundy's supporters and law enforcement. These behaviors share the common element that the offenders are pursuing values out of conscience and conviction, which are different from those of the groups that formulate and administer criminal law. The result is that some persons and organizations are defined as criminal. The challenge is to determine whose interests and values are reflected in law.

Criminal laws established to control perceived and real threats to the state are patently political. They make no attempt to cover up their direct political intent. Existing governmental policy is to be honored and protected from all internal or external dangers. Even when certain procedural guarantees are recognized, such as due process, equal protection, and the right to civil disobedience, the law can be qualified at every point to maintain the status quo. This was the point that Martin Luther King, Jr. brought out in his 1963 "Letter from Birmingham Jail":

> Sometimes a law is just on its face and unjust in its application. For instance, I have been arrested on a charge of parading without a permit. Now, there is nothing wrong in having an ordinance which requires a permit for a parade. But such an ordinance becomes unjust when it is used to maintain segregation and to deny citizens the First Amendment privilege of peaceful assembly and protest.[6]

One tactic used by all governments against their citizens—usually those advocating political and social change—is the refusal to publicly and legally recognize the concept of political crime. In the case of the United States, the doctrine of legalism seems to justify this: obedience to existing law is a moral absolute. Political theorist Judith N. Shklar stated that legalism is pervasive throughout Western society. It is a moral code of conduct as well as a common ethos that extends from the individual level to the institutional level:

> To a great extent [legalism] has provided the standards of organization and the operative ideals for a vast number of social groups, from governmental institutions to private clubs. . . . Lastly, it has also served as the political ideology of those who cherish these [Western] systems of law and, above all, those who are directly involved in their maintenance—the legal profession, both bench and bar.[7]

Since opposition to the government could not be legally *and* morally recognized, political crime as a concept could not be incorporated into the law. Political offenders normally have been dealt with under "nonpolitical" laws. The political offender has been officially labeled and handled in the same way as the conventional offender. To admit the concept of political crime into domestic jurisprudence would be to recognize the limitations of liberal democracy. This doctrine is called "democratic elitism," wherein those in power, according to our present legal system, can effectively use the law to their own advantage. This point was made over a century ago by British historian L.T. Hobhouse who observed, "The function of State coercion is to override individual coercion, and, of course, coercion exercised by any association of individuals within the State."[8]

Crimes by Government

In the past, criminologists, like most people, had been reluctant to face the possibility that government can act criminally. Following the classic image of government formulated by political philosophers such as Jeremy Bentham and John Stuart Mill, Americans tended to regard the US government as being above the law. Since governments supposedly have sovereignty over the people, governments are to control the citizenry—not regulate themselves. The classic idea is that governments need not self-regulate since they are simply expressions of the will of the people. Only the *critical perspective* in criminology sees that government uses various kinds of criminal laws "as political weapons, . . . to authenticate and limit the political action of those who would appear to jeopardize the stability and survival of the existing political order."[9] However, an examination of criminology textbooks published between 1990 and 1999, found that they largely ignored the critical perspective.[10] Thus, as long as the classic tradition is followed—with government having complete sovereignty—the immunity of government from the law is tacitly accepted.

Largely as a result of nefarious events involving deceptions, cover-ups, and corruption on the part of government and politicians since the 1960s—such as the Pentagon Papers, the Watergate scandal, the My Lai massacre, the Iran-Contra scandal, and the Whitewater controversy—there is now recognition that the government must be subject to its own laws as well as to international law. No longer is government accepted as being immune from law or incapable of violating it. Government claims of "executive privilege," "national security," and "can't indict a sitting president" are no longer as readily accepted by the public as in the past. The Nuremberg war crimes trials of 1945–1946 set a precedent for all governments: "If certain acts and violations of treaties are crimes," the Chief Prosecutor at Nuremberg observed, "they are crimes whether the United States does them or whether Germany does them." Consequently, we have come to understand that the state itself is capable of crime—the social harm and suffering of vast multitudes both at home and abroad.

A critical conception of democracy makes it apparent that governments as the principal makers and enforcers of law can themselves be lawbreakers. If the law is an institution of the citizenry, then that same law can be used to protect citizens from harms committed against them by those who act in the name of the government. In the past, we have tended to accept a double standard toward crime. The major emphasis has been on crimes against the government or crimes "against society," to the virtual neglect of crimes committed by the government against the people who create it and to whom it is responsible. While individual violence (e.g., homicide) or collective violence (e.g., rioting) have been viewed as criminal, similar actions by the government (e.g., excessive force, riot control) have either not been seen as acts of violence or have been regarded as acts of "legitimate violence." However, the violence employed by law enforcement officers in quelling a civil protest can easily pass over the line into police brutality. Or the violence of the military in maintaining world hegemony and control over valued resources can become problematic with regard to lawful behavior.

Since the 1980s, criminologists and others have taken note of state crime. It was William J. Chambliss's 1988 presidential address to the American Society of Criminology that activated criminological interest in crimes of the state. The concept, however, is difficult to analyze and define, for if a state definition of crime is the only one used, then we are left with the fact that crime is what the state says it is, and governments are not inclined to prosecute themselves. However, if the definition of state-organized crime proposed by Chambliss is accepted, then crime by the government "consists of acts defined by law and committed by state officials in the pursuit of their job as representatives of the state."[11] In one of the first books on state criminality Gregg Barak distinguished between corporate crime and state crime:

> Like the study of corporate crime, the study of state crime involves examining behaviors and processes committed by agents and organizations that are both socially acceptable and politically powerful. . . . Although both corporate and state criminality can potentially undermine

the very stability of the [capitalist] system the corporate state strives for, crimes by the state pose the greater threat to the system as a whole. State criminality, in order words, creates inherent contradictions which simultaneously threaten the legitimacy of the prevailing political order yet accommodate the very same behavior in the name of common interests or national security.[12]

While Barak made a conceptual distinction between corporate crime and state crime, others saw a nexus between the two and in the 1990s began to focus on *state-corporate crime*—"a form of organizational misconduct that occurs at the interstices of corporations and governments."[13] Criminologists have traced the intellectual origins of the concept to the theorizing and research conducted by Richard Quinney.[14] One important book on state-corporate crime considered cases like the 1986 space shuttle *Challenger* explosion, the National Highway Transportation Safety Association's (NHTSA) failure to adequately respond to the Bridgestone-Firestone and Ford tire problems, and the 2001 US invasion of Iraq.[15] While state-corporate crime is an important area of study, this chapter will consider political crimes that involve only the state and state officials.

One such political crime was the Watergate scandal of the 1970s when President Richard M. Nixon and his associates committed "high crimes and misdemeanors" that resulted in the imprisonment of 25 high-ranking officials, including the Attorney General and two top presidential aids. Nixon was spared from possible criminal action by a presidential pardon. The violations of law by these men included obstruction of justice, conspiracy to obstruct justice, perjury, accepting contributions or bribes from corporations, bribing persons to prevent testimony, illegal tactics or "dirty tricks" in conducting election campaigns, and the misuse for personal purposes of the FBI, the CIA, and the IRS. In the mid-1980s, President Ronald Reagan authorized sending arms illegally to Iran in exchange for the political hostages they held. Some administration officials, including Marine Corps colonel Oliver North, were involved in two operations, one that would exchange arms for the hostages, another that would funnel the profits from the arms sale to aid the "Contras," the political guerrillas in Nicaragua. Although no hostages were ever actually returned in exchange for arms, the sending of money to the Contras had been expressly forbidden by Congress.

A problem in this area of criminal activity is that it is difficult to gather reliable data and cite empirical studies regarding crimes by the government. Still, in the case of war crimes and mass atrocities, as with all governmental crimes, acts in violation of the law may be observed and studied as criminal offenses. And there are those instances in which the legal apparatus rises above the narrower interests of particular states and governments and even political parties. The crimes of government are recorded in legal and social history.

Sociology of Criminal Behavior

Crimes Against Government

Political crime against the government is endemic and pervasive in American history, from Benedict Arnold's treason, to Julius and Ethel Rosenberg's conspiracy to commit espionage; from Henry David Thoreau's tax resisting, to Daniel Berrigan's civil disobedience activities; from former CIA officer Aldrich Ames's espionage, to former FBI agent, Robert Hanssen's espionage; from John Wilkes Booth's assassination of President Lincoln, to Timothy McVeigh's domestic terrorism. The names of political criminals leap from the pages of our history, and while they make strange bedfellows, they have in common their opposition to the existing social order.

Political offenders share some general characteristics. First, they usually do not see themselves as criminals and do not identify with a life of crime. However, when the government continues to define these persons as outlaws, they may begin to conceive of themselves as political criminals. In fact, to do so may become part of their conscientiously held beliefs and lead them to hold a moral conviction to violate what they see as unjust laws. Thoreau was briefly incarcerated for refusing to pay the poll tax used to finance slavery and the Mexican–American War, both of which he opposed. In his 1849 essay, "Resistance to Civil Government" Thoreau wrote:

> Under a government which imprisons any unjustly, the true place for a just man is also a prison. . . where the State places those who are not with her, but against her,—the only house in a slave State in which a free man can abide with honor. . . Cast your whole vote, not a strip of paper merely, but your whole influence. A minority is powerless while it conforms to the majority; it is not even a minority then; but it is irresistible when it clogs by its whole weight. If the alternative is to keep all just men in prison, or give up war and slavery, the State will not hesitate which to choose. If a thousand men were not to pay their tax bills this year, that would not be a violent and bloody measure, as it would be to pay them, and enable the State to commit violence and shed innocent blood.[16]

Second, for most political offenders the objective is not to break the law for its own sake, but to change social conditions or governmental policies which they see as oppressive, tyrannical, or unjust. Violation of the law is usually incidental and necessary to make their case or be heard. Normally law-abiding citizens, they violate the law only when doing so makes a political point or has the potential of bringing about a desired change. In these instances, crime can be a political tactic.

In analyzing political crime in late nineteenth-century Europe, Cesare Lombroso distinguished between "revolution," which he saw as bringing about progressive social change, and "revolt," which he saw as socially destructive. In fact, Lombroso

> Sees revolution and the adaptive changes it brings in society as absolutely necessary for the progress of society. He realizes that insurrection sometimes leads to results which are socially destructive and which impede progress more than they further it. These he calls "revolts." They are the work of a minority, inspired by an excessive love or hatred of change, who seek forcibly to establish systems or ideas rejected by the majority. Unlike revolutions, revolts may break out for merely temporary causes—a famine, tax, or official tyranny which suddenly disturbs the order of daily life. Lombroso admits, however, that it is often impossible to distinguish between the two, and whether one has a "good" revolution or "bad" revolt depends on the outcome of the insurrection—victory by the insurrectionaries being proof that their ideas have permeated the masses. This benevolent attitude toward political crime leads Lombroso to recommend lenient punishments such as banishment or transportation for political crimes, whereas in the case of common crimes he was an advocate of the rigorous use of the death penalty.[17]

Richard Quinney in *Class, State, and Crime* stated that, under capitalism, the political crimes of the working class,

> range from unconscious reactions to exploitation, to conscious acts of survival within the capitalist system, to politically conscious acts of rebellion. These criminal actions, moreover,

not only cover the range of meaning but actually evolve or progress from *unconscious reaction to political rebellion*. Finally, the crime may eventually reach the ultimate stage of conscious political action—*revolt*. In revolt, criminal actions are not only against the system but are also an attempt to overthrow it.[18]

Thus, many crimes against the government involve protests, uprisings, and expressions of dissent that aim to change some existing social, political, or legal structure. Those who protest may be sincerely expressing their conviction to a value. This was the case, for example, with the thousands of "Yellow Vest" demonstrators—rightists and leftists—who took to the streets in France in 2018 to protest president Emmanuel Macron's proposed fuel tax increases, the high cost of living, wealth inequality, and their belief that Macron's centrist government was out of touch with working people. In the US case of the white-identity groups of the Alt-Right, some of their more radical members who sometimes advocate violence seek to create white "ethnostates" in the US, to implement policies to encourage nonwhite people to leave the country, and to end mass immigration into the country.[19]

Insurgents may also be paid agents of a foreign government, members of a domestic or international terrorist organization, or acting on their own as a "lone wolf." An example of the latter is Ted Kaczynski, also known as the Unabomber, who was a serial mail bomber. Between 1978 and 1995, Kaczynski attempted to start a revolution by conducting a nationwide bombing campaign targeting people involved with modern technology. He killed three people and injured 24. In his "Unabomber Manifesto," Kaczynski claimed that technological society suppresses human freedom and self-esteem. He stated that, "We have no illusions about the feasibility of creating a new, ideal form of society. Our goal is only to destroy the existing form of society."[20]

Many of these crimes—treason, violent civil unrest, murder—arise out of a perceived conflict between ideological beliefs and state laws. Most such acts are prompted by a desire to improve the world or dismantle the existing political system. Political conviction is considered by some to be one of the main definitional criteria of political criminals.

Finally, citizens arrested for crimes against the state do not have personal benefit in mind. They seek to effect change in the larger social context. Their actions are usually directed toward public gain rather than private gain. The typical political offender regards his or her behavior as important for a larger, higher purpose. Martin Luther King, Jr. did not have himself arrested in order to further his own career, but rather to change racist laws and racial discrimination practices. The same may be said for some involved in the 2014 unrest in Ferguson, Missouri, who, during a protest of police brutality, discrimination against African Americans, and application of racial stereotypes, engaged in vandalism, looting, and rioting. The police response—using dogs for controlling the protesters, deploying rooftop snipers to monitor the crowds, and bringing in military-style armored vehicles—inflamed tensions between police and protesters. Despite these destructive acts, the purpose is larger than a single individual's advancement, and the arrested protester does not usually consider himself or herself to be an outlaw or a criminal. In fact, it is the government and its law and policy that is seen as criminal.

Political protest that sparks off into violence, disorder, looting, or mayhem revolves around a major "flashpoint" incident.[21] Normally law-abiding citizens who have no criminal career seem to go suddenly berserk due to forces beyond their control. They lose control over their own actions. Unless they have a history of this behavior, and most do not, they have no criminal career, nor do they see themselves as felons and radicals. This identity ambiguity is particularly true in democratic societies.

Democratic institutions make the policing of protest intrinsically morally ambiguous:

protesters are not criminals, but citizens participating in the political process; they are not motivated by willful self-interest but are expressing a grievance or altruistically pursuing the collective good; and thus any conflict between protesters and the police tends to be a battle of moral equals in which both sides are seeking the approval of bystanders.[22]

The point is that the majority of the protesters, whether of the left or the right, do not consider themselves to be criminals. Their conviction is to a higher cause and they have suddenly been caught up in a vortex of forces beyond their control, forces often caused by the actions of agents of the state itself. In any event, in contrast to conventional criminals, convictional criminals frequently want to publicize their cause:

> Dramatic publicity is therefore almost a necessity for the convictional criminal in order to make the public understand his actions. . . . His crime may serve as an example to would-be followers. As the convictional crime may even be supported by public opinion, punishment of the offender may fail to deter later convictional crimes. Moreover, punishment may serve only to interest others in the given ideal and to recruit members for other convictional violations of law.[23]

There has been only a limited attempt to describe the more specific personal and demographic characteristics of those who engage in political behavior that may eventually come to be defined as criminal. Lombroso, for one, considered political criminals to be a subgroup of "criminals by passion." He suggested that "criminals by passion can be characterized by a high degree of affectability which, under stress in unusual circumstances, develops a passion that leads to crimes with violence."[24] Furthermore, stated Lombroso, political criminals have a heightened sensitivity to stimuli, great intellect, and altruism:

> In nearly all political criminals by passion we have noticed an exaggerated sensibility, a veritable hyperesthesia, as in the ordinary criminals by passion; but a powerful intellect, a great altruism pushed them towards ends much higher than those of the latter: it is never wealth, vanity, the smile of woman . . . which impel them, but rather the great patriotic, religious, scientific ideals.[25]

A few years later, in 1916, Marxist criminologist Willem Bonger viewed political criminals as members of the economically "oppressed class." According to Bonger, "the political criminals . . . risk their most sacred interests, their liberty and their life, for the benefit of society; they injure the ruling class only to aid the oppressed classes, and consequently all humanity."[26]

We now know that at any historical period such characteristics as age, gender, ethnicity, and social class do not differentiate political offenders as a group from the general population.[27] However, concerning differences between political criminals themselves, one study found evidence distinguishing between nonviolent and violent political extremists. The results showed that lack of stable employment, having radical peers, a history of mental illness, and criminal record had significant effects on participation in political violence.[28]

Political criminals also differ more from one another according to the type of political crime or "cause" than they do from the noncriminal population. For example, in regard to social class, people in the anti-government Patriot Movement, some of whom have committed or supported illegal acts of violence, are largely of the working class,[29] while the members of radical environmentalist groups like the Earth Liberation Front, responsible for about 600 criminal acts between

1996 and 2002,[30] have been from the middle stratum of US society. Likewise, with respect to racial background, politically oriented movements, especially those based on a politics of identity, have differed greatly from one another in their ethnic composition. For example, racist hate groups like the Nation of Islam consists of black Muslims while the American Freedom Party attracts primarily white Christians. Ultimately, demographic and psychological factors play only an incidental role in the creation of the political offender. As one legal scholar has observed:

> The insurgent or armed guerrilla is likely to differ drastically in both personal history and psychological makeup from the political activist who refuses military service, and the offender who engages in lone dissent is not like the offender who joins in collective protest. In particular, rebels committed to violent and militant action may not necessarily resemble those who scrupulously adhere to peaceful action.[31]

Thus, it appears that the crucial factors in the career of the political offender are not personal and social characteristics per se, but rather the values of the offender and the value systems that the offender actively espouses.

For example, during the turbulent period of the war in Vietnam, those who resisted the war and the draft (compulsory military conscription) differed considerably from one another in personal and social characteristics. During those years, criminologist John Wildeman observed that:

> Violation of Selective Service law, then, does not seem to be a criminally defined behavior that is typical of any one particular segment of our society with the notable exception of age and sex structures. Resistance to the arbitrary domination of power on the part of those held in subjection to that power is as ubiquitous and extensive as is that power itself. As the power of the government reaches across the void deeply into the lives of all the people, holding them in subjection to its criminal war policies, so too resistance and opposition to this incredible domination is found in every segment of the social structure.[32]

Political criminals, including anarchists like Ted Kaczynski, are committed to some form of social order. The social order they have in mind, however, differs from the existing order. It is because of their commitment to something beyond themselves and conventional society that they are willing to engage in criminal behavior. Persons who occasionally engage in political crime are interested in their society, but at times find it lacking in critical ways. In short, they often want to create a better world by their actions. Consequently, they may sever their commitment to the existing social order in place of a more just and desirable (according to their values) social order that could replace it. The society to which they are committed may be a modification of the one that exists or may be an entirely new one, as in the case of authentic social revolutions. The French Revolution at the end of the eighteenth century and the Russian Revolution at the beginning of the twentieth century swept away old orders that defined the actions of the triumphant revolutionaries as criminal. In every case, whether it be a total or partial change that is sought, the existing society and its policies, social structures, and values always serve as a reference point for political offenders.

The traitor and the spy provide the classic examples of the political offender who is committed to another social order. (However, some spies, like the Americans Christopher Boyce and Andrew Daulton Lee, known as "the Falcon and the Snowman," are motivated by nothing more personal monetary reward.) The traitor is guilty of treason in giving aid to another government that is antagonistic to his or her own government or adhering to enemies of the state. The spy, however, is more often a citizen of another country and in the course of espionage obtains classified and sensitive information, often of a valuable military, diplomatic, or intellectual property nature, for a foreign power. The spy is committed to his or her own country but is not attached to the country from which he or she secures the information, the country in which the spy is regarded as a political criminal. Long periods of such an offender's career may be devoted to spying, as, for example, CIA officer Aldrich Ames who engaged in espionage for the Soviet Union and Russia for 9 years (1985–1994). An even longer spying career was that of FBI agent Robert Hanssen, who worked for Soviet and Russian intelligence services for over 20 years (1979–2001).

The nature of the self-conceptions, morality, and rationality of political offenders is obvious in the accounts they give of their actions. This is demonstrated in the beliefs of American domestic terrorist Timothy McVeigh, who in 1995 detonated a truck bomb in front of Oklahoma City's Alfred P. Murrah Federal Building that killed 168 people, 19 of whom were children in a daycare center. Motivated by anti-government sentiment, McVeigh offered a justification for the bombing:

> I chose to bomb a federal building because such an action served more purposes than other options. Foremost, the bombing was a retaliatory strike; a counter attack, for the cumulative raids (and subsequent violence and damage) that federal agents had participated in over the preceding years (including, but not limited to, Waco.) From the formation of such units as the FBI's "Hostage Rescue" and other assault teams amongst federal agencies during the '80's; culminating in the Waco incident [with the Branch Davidians], federal actions grew increasingly militaristic and violent, to the point where at Waco, our government—like the Chinese—was deploying tanks against its own citizens.
>
> Knowledge of these multiple and ever-more aggressive raids across the country constituted an identifiable pattern of conduct within and by the federal government and amongst its various agencies. . . . [F]ederal agents had become "soldiers" (using military training, tactics, techniques, equipment, language, dress, organization, and mindset) and they were escalating their behavior. The . . . bombing was also meant as a pre-emptive (or proactive) strike against these forces and their command and control centers within the federal building. When an aggressor force continually launches attacks from a particular base of operation, it is sound military strategy to take the fight to the enemy.
>
> Additionally, borrowing a page from US foreign policy, I decided to send a message to a government that was becoming increasingly hostile, by bombing a government building and the government employees within that building who represent that government. Bombing the Murrah Federal Building was morally and strategically equivalent to the US hitting a government building in Serbia, Iraq, or other nations. . . . Based on observations of the policies of my own government, I viewed this action as an acceptable option. From this perspective, what occurred in Oklahoma City was no different than what Americans rain on the heads of others all the time, and subsequently, my mindset was and is one of clinical detachment. (The bombing of the Murrah building was not personal, no more than when Air Force, Army, Navy, or Marine personnel bomb or launch cruise missiles against government installations and their personnel.)[33]

It seems clear that an understanding of political offenders calls for a conception of people that differs radically from the one that was employed by criminologists in the past. The view that the criminal is largely a product of impersonal forces beyond the individual's control has proven inadequate for the study of the political offender. Human introspection and critical thinking are obvious in the careers of all types of political offenders. Only humans are reflective beings capable of considering alternative actions and of breaking from the established social order. A purposive, voluntaristic conception of people and their behavior is thus essential to the study of human behavior in general and political crime in particular. As Richard Quinney has written:

> Protest on a large scale can be interpreted as a desire by persons to find meaning, identity, or a "reality world." Dissatisfaction with present values and norms can produce a response by entire groups of people . . . "Political extremism," some of which may be defined as criminal or may result in criminal offenses, appears to be a conscious attempt by individuals to improve particular situations. Violation of the law may be carried out as a protest against policies and conditions that are regarded by some persons as unjust. Behavior that is defined as criminal may at times be the only appropriate means for achieving desired ends.[34]

Quinney asserts that the underlying character of much criminal behavior is political in nature, rather than being merely deviant or pathological. Thus,

> The actions of the criminally defined are not so much the result of inadequate socialization and personality problems as they are conscientious actions taken against something. For many persons, behaviors that can readily be labeled as criminal may be the only appropriate means for expressing certain thoughts and feelings—and the only possibilities for bringing about social changes. The traditional channels of the political process may be inappropriate or may be insensitive for the grievances of much of the population.[35]

Crimes by Government

As with crimes against the government, crimes *by* the government and its officials are many and complex. Often it is difficult to speak of the criminal careers of individual offenders in this case, for the crimes frequently result from bureaucratic and impersonal state institutions wherein individuals become invisible. As such, the perpetrators, and even the crimes themselves, become difficult to identify with precision, much less prosecute them.

Crimes by government and government officials include illegal violations of congressional laws and policies by personnel in the executive branch, illegal concealment of information to congressional committees, election fraud, and accepting payoffs. They also encompass violations of law by state and federal authorities, such as bilking the government for personal expenses like travel, violating franking privileges, or accepting bribes. Consider, for example, that between 2009 and 2011 Illinois Governor Rod Blagojevich was impeached, convicted, and removed from office for soliciting bribes in return for appointment to President Barak Obama's vacated US Senate seat. Another example involving a brazen misuse of power occurred in 2018 when Administrator of the Environmental Protection Agency (EPA), Scott Pruitt, was forced to resign from office. Pruitt resigned amid mounting ethics scandals including, (1) frequent use of first-class commercial air travel as well as frequent chartered private jets and military flights at exorbitant costs to taxpayers, (2) spending over $40,000 to install a soundproof phone booth in his office, (3) attempting to purchase two expensive desks, one of them bulletproof, valued at over $70,000, (4) leasing a condo at a deeply discounted rate from a lobbyist whose clients were regulated by the EPA, (5) using aides to find a job for his wife, (6) giving pay raises to close aides that were considerably higher than salaries paid to those in similar positions, (7) using his security detail to run personal errands for him. As Chambliss noted long ago:

> Presidents, vice presidents, congressmen, senators, governors, and racketeers, are implicated in a ubiquitous system of payoffs and favors, backscratching, stealing, campaign contributions, and personal aggrandizement.[36]

Under the classification "crimes by government" may be added crimes by the police, who are traditionally the most obvious and visible governmental offenders. Police brutality, and other forms of misconduct, such as corruption and fraud, are chronic and endemic in the US and have been documented throughout the history of policing in America. Police brutality is the unauthorized, unwarranted, and criminal use of force and violence in taking a citizen into custody. Forms of misconduct include actions like entrapment, racial profiling, accepting payoffs to alter sworn testimony, stealing from burglarized establishments, being "on the take," planting weapons or drugs on suspects, and selling confiscated controlled substances and weapons. One criminologist has stated that police corruption,

> generally refers to officers who do something against their duty, or who do not do something, in return for some gain or promise, though it may also refer more broadly to police abuse of power.[37]

One study found that highly publicized incidents of police brutality and corruption in Los Angeles and New York City had a dramatic increase in citizens' unfavorable attitudes of the police. Police brutality toward blacks and Latinos, in particular, may result in people in those communities becoming "less cooperative toward officers and more predisposed to accept allegations of police misconduct, even when officers act properly."[38]

While police officers as a category do not have a criminal career, it nevertheless has been documented that a substantial minority has been seduced into misconduct by situations in which the job of policing places them. Jerome H. Skolnick and James J. Fyfe have found that the quasi-military structure of police agencies and the occupational subculture of policing may promote police brutality. Police also tend to use excessive force on those who fit the stereotype of dangerous people, which in many cases are residents in minority communities.[39]

Police crimes must be seen within the context of their careers as peace officers. The young police recruit, during the training period, adopts a particular outlook on the work and develops a justification for using procedures in the line of duty that are seen in the subculture of policing as being "expedient." In other words, officers learn an ideology that later affects their work. Because of the nature of police work, a rationale exists among the police for the use of harsh and frequently illegal methods. It is the fate of police work that a certain amount of criminality can easily be built into the career of the police officer. Just as any other employee placed at risk of committing crime because of the nature of the job, the police officer begins to develop a criminal career with the first illegal act, whether it be an act of excessive force or other misconduct. From that point on, resistance to temptation begins to erode, and exposure to others who are willing to break the law tends to snowball into a career in crime. The idea is that the nature of policing easily lends itself to the production of a limited number of isolated rogue individuals, a few "bad apples." However, at least in the case of racial profiling by the police, some scholars reject the "bad apples" thesis:

> The implication of the "bad apples" perspective is that all we need to do to solve the problem of racial profiling is provide police officers with more training in race relations and cultural sensitivity, or recruit a limited number of people of color. This, of course, leaves unchanged the structure of policing as well as the core ideology of police officers—their beliefs, values, and norms.[40]

Governmental crimes are also committed by those involved in government policy-making and the execution of policies; these are elected or appointed federal, state, or local officials and their subordinates, as well as those involved in military structures, from admirals and generals. Consider, for example, that three-star Army general and former national security advisor Michael Flynn lied to the FBI (a felony) about potentially promising quid pro quos to the Russian ambassador to the United States during the Trump presidential transition. Here again, the evolution of a criminal career is difficult to document.

In the last analysis, anyone who engages in criminal acts constructs rationalizations to justify their actions and to provide appropriate self-conceptions. Governmental criminals do the same thing. The police officer is just "doing what is necessary to get the job done," or doing what is "expected" of him or her. Soldiers involved in war crimes are usually able to convince themselves that they were merely carrying out orders from superiors. This was the case for example, in the massacre of approximately 400 unarmed South Vietnamese civilians by US troops in the village of My Lai during the Vietnam War. US Army Lieutenant, William Calley, Jr. was court-martialed for murdering 22 unarmed men, women, children, and infants at My Lai. His main defense was that all superior orders were legal. According to Calley:

> I was ordered to go in there and destroy the enemy. That was my job that day. That was the mission I was given. I did not sit down and think in terms of men, women, and children. They were all classified as the same, and that's the classification that we dealt with over there, just as the enemy. I felt then and I still do that I acted as I was directed, and I carried out the order that I was given, and I do not feel wrong in doing so.[41]

Further, it is often difficult to convict those involved in state-sanctioned crime. Consider, for example, the 2004 torture and physical, sexual, and psychological abuse by US military personnel of Iraqi detainees at Abu Ghraib prison in Baghdad. Many such practices were considered "standard operating procedures" by military intelligence officers. Criminologists have stated that the abuse at Abu Ghraib as not an isolated case but represented a widespread pattern that was part of a larger "culture of abuse."[42] As one scholar noted:

> As testimonies from prisoners, military personnel, and investigative reports have shown, it was not a matter of a few rogue MPs [Military Police officer's] on the night shift. In the case of Iraqi prisoners in US custody, there is significant evidence that immediate superior officers were aware that prisoners were being tortured, and that these practices were not limited to the Abu Ghraib prison. . . . And as the torture memos and other internal state documents show, responsibility for these abuses does not stop with superior officers in Iraq but goes right to the top of the Pentagon and the White House.[43]

Like Calley before him, Abu Ghraib prison guard, Charles Graner Jr., who was convicted of indecent acts, dereliction of duty, conspiracy to commit maltreatment, and assault consummated by battery, had as his main defense that he was following orders.

Crimes Against Government

The extent and nature of group support for political crimes against the state varies. Some political offenders receive less group support than others. Clearly, group support for terrorist activities tends to be high:

Although people can engage in politically violent acts alone, the process of communicating terrorism is aided by belonging to or leading a terrorist group, and the frequency of one's violent acts likely increases in a group setting and with organizational support. This interpretation is complementary with differential association theory, which would allow that terrorism, like any other crime, is learned behavior reinforced by socialization into the group.[44]

Also, the groups to which political offenders belong differ greatly in their ideologies, loyalties, and motives. In addition, the social organization of groups supporting political crime varies with the group's size, cohesiveness, formality of organization, duration, geographical distribution of members, and patterns of leadership. Finally, groups differ in the techniques and tactics used by members in the course of committing offenses. Techniques and tactics include such diverse forms as face-to-face recruitment, websites and propaganda videos, nonviolent coercion, passive resistance, inciting to riot, rallies, marches, strikes, suicide attacks, bombings, siege warfare, guerrilla warfare, and the passing of information to the enemy of the state. The activities of terrorists, dissident and outlawed political movements, and traitors illustrate this.

In some cases, there is a relatively high degree of group support for crimes against the state. Except for the isolated zealot or mentally ill person, most of these actions are not carried out alone. In the case of the lone wolf terrorist, for example, although the act of political violence is that of the individual and is prompted by an individual decision, there is usually a large reference group, organization, or network of like-minded people who radicalize, inspire, and "enable" the terrorist. One study on lone wolf terrorists in fifteen countries found that there is a

> Variable degree of commitment to and identification with extremist movements among lone wolf terrorists. Although lone wolf terrorism results from solitary action during which the direct influence, advice, or support of others is absent, such action and its justifications clearly do not take place in a vacuum. The analytical distinction between lone wolf terrorism and group-based terrorism is often somewhat problematic in practice, since group dynamics may also influence, at least to some extent, individuals who operate autonomously.[45]

Recent events of civil strife demonstrate the extent to which criminally defined political behavior receives group support. In many cases, most of the activity (ranging from protests to riots to uprisings) is of a collective nature. Moreover, group cohesiveness plays an important part in many of the crowd actions, such as the race demonstrations in 2014 in Ferguson, Missouri and in 2015 in Baltimore that were triggered by the police killings of African American men.

> The crowd culture will vary with the nature and composition of the crowd. A crowd may be homogenous in its composition, drawing on a permanent sense of its own identity derived from occupational, ethnic, or other forms of group membership. Individuals in such a crowd are more likely to feel that the crowd is an extension of their own social identity, experiencing and expressing a permanent sense of *crowd solidarity*.[46]

Similarly, the race riots of the 1960s occurred largely through shared experiences and group support. Grievances that had accumulated for years finally were raised to the level of group consciousness. Entire segments of the population became aware that the inner-city grievances of economic deprivation, racial discrimination, poor housing, and consumer exploitation could be attacked.

What the government defined as violence was for many African Americans a means of achieving just demands and basic human rights. Assessing the situation at the time, an urban historian summarized the events as follows:

> Reasons may be obscure, but results are clear. The blacks—or at any rate a substantial minority of them—refuse to tolerate racial discrimination, economic deprivation, consumer exploitation, and involuntary residential segregation any longer. Instead they intend to call attention to their grievances, to share in the benefits of affluent America, to even the score with white merchants, and ultimately to gain control over their communities. They have long tried to do so through elections, demonstrations, education, training, and other conventional channels; and they will probably continue to do so. But the riots made it quite clear that where the blacks find these channels obstructed, they will not be confined by them. Nor will they be bound by the fear of arrest, the concern for personal safety, the commitment to orderly social change, the trauma of white racism, and the other restraints on rioting in the United States. Under these circumstances it is not remarkable that a significant minority of the blacks are now prepared, even determined, to resort to violence until their grievances are redressed.[47]

In the course of political socialization (radicalization) and life experience, individuals and groups develop a conception regarding the relative legitimacy of existing political institutions and actions. A political system—the state and its policies—is regarded as legitimate when the authority of those in control is respected, and the procedures in the political process are believed to be appropriate. Groups generally regard a political system and its actions as legitimate or illegitimate based on whether the values of the system accord with their own. The acceptance of particular societal values tends to maximize the legitimacy of the existing system. Groups that do not share these values are more likely to question the legitimacy of the system and are likely to engage in oppositional political behaviors and extremist politics that may be defined as criminal. For these citizens, to do otherwise is to be alienated from contemporary life and to withdraw from the realm of the social as an agent of change. Such a withdrawn populace is controlled without a great deal of effort on the part of political leaders. Traitors, in their own eyes, are loyal to some value, social structure, or ideal that they and the network that supports them value as worthier of allegiance than the existing structure. Such citizens are conscientiously following a set of norms and values that differ from those of the individuals, institutions, and segments of society that possess the power to define what being a good and loyal citizen means.

A consideration of the July 20, 1944, plot to assassinate Adolf Hitler during World War II sheds light on the degree of group support for these actions. The assassination attempt was a *coup d'état* against the Nazi regime orchestrated by a group of German military officers who aimed to seize power in Berlin and make peace with the western Allies. Though the number of military conspirators who led the failed plot was only about eight, group support was extensive given that the Nazi secret police arrested about 7,000 members of the German resistance thought to be involved in the coup attempt; of these, nearly 5,000 were executed.

Crimes by Government

In crimes by the government, governmental offenders are often supported by their fellow workers. A major reason for this is that the illegal activity that the law-violator engages in is usually an integral part of governing and maintaining social control. For example, from time to time police officers are convicted of extorting large sums of money from drug dealers—a simple case of blackmail and extortion. However, the officer who breaks the law by using unnecessary force in making an arrest, or who shoots a citizen, may be following the norms of his or her group. In his study on corruption and organized crime, Chambliss found a crime network of cooperation and conspiracy between police, politicians, and mobsters:

> At the very least, I was convinced from my Seattle research that a symbiotic relationship between politics, law enforcement, legitimate business, and organized crime was absolutely necessary for organized crime to survive and flourish as if does in America.[48]

Police officers backed by group effort frequently give little consideration to the legality of their actions in the course of enforcing other laws. The law that exists to protect the citizen from the abuses of government authorities is often seen by the police officer as an obstacle to law enforcement. From the viewpoint of the police, the civil liberties of the citizen are often an impediment to the performance of the job. In such a context of group support, laws—usually procedural laws—may be broken by those charged with enforcement of the law. When the state attempts to silence political dissent and dissenters by interfering with freedom of assembly or speech, whether by violent or nonviolent means, it frequently breaks laws. According to Austin T. Turk, how the government reacts to the actions of political dissenters and resisters varies with how the actions are perceived:

> If an act is believed to be no more than a spontaneous idiosyncratic "deviation" by a few resentful individuals, the kind and degree of criminalization will vary fairly directly with the openness and the violence of the resistance. Calculated acts as part of a program of resistance by an organization will elicit a relatively severe response, with the choices of legal or extralegal and direct or indirect control tactics depending upon the degree of perceived threat. The perceived relative power . . . of the opposition will be an additional contingency affecting the form and degree of official response to calculated and organized resistance.[49]

The crimes committed by government officials as part of the Watergate affair represented acts of collusion taken to the extreme. Consider that the burglars who broke into and bugged the headquarters of the Democratic party were paid by President Nixon's re-election committee; that US Attorney General, John Mitchell participated in preliminary discussions about wiretapping the Democratic headquarters; that the White House attempted to halt the FBI investigation of Watergate; that the president's advisors resisted attempts by the special prosecutor, the courts, and Congress to get information on the case. This tangled web of activities would not have been possible without the knowledge and cooperation of a close network of like-minded government employees, politicians, agents, and appointed officials—a very tight group-support network of individuals sharing the same zeal, commitment, and ideology.

Social Reaction to Criminal Behavior

Crimes Against Government

The behavior associated with crimes against government in the United States is normally consistent with the democratic principle of the right of expression and the right to dissent. The right of petition and association is guaranteed in the First Amendment of the Federal Constitution, which states that Congress shall make no law abridging "the right of the people peaceably to assemble, and to petition the Government for a redress of grievances." Aside from terrorist crimes against government, most political dissent is in conformity with what is commonly regarded as legitimate behavior. It is true that one cannot hold a rally without a permit, one cannot block traffic, or physically attack striking workers in a union protest, one cannot block access to an abortion clinic, and one cannot incite others to violence and riot. But even these actions, while usually in violation of local ordinances and laws, are commonly regarded as minor violations that do not depart radically from legitimate behavior.

In fact, there are limits to freedom of expression. Although the behaviors included in political crime may correspond in principle to the democratic values of US society, the commission of the acts is restricted to what is generally regarded as politically legitimate. The boundaries and definitions of political freedom are by no means consistent within any political democracy. The degree of dissent that is regarded as legitimate varies from one time period to another. During some periods a considerable amount of dissent may be tolerated because it does not seriously threaten the stability of the government. However, during times of civil unrest and dissatisfaction with state policy, dissent may be suppressed with overwhelming police force or the use of the courts to exhaust the scant resources of dissident political or social movements. The point is that political legitimacy and the limits of governmental tolerance of dissent are concepts that are manipulated and defined by those in control of the state. When serious threats to state legitimacy are exerted by those outside the power structure, then the boundaries of political legitimacy may be severely restricted, and the dissenting behavior considered to be well outside legitimate and acceptable limits.

Abstract freedoms may flourish with ease. When protests and actions become effective, civil liberties can be withdrawn. Not only may civil liberties be abridged, but repressive laws may be used to suppress potentially effective action. It is with these realizations that many individuals and groups in US society engage periodically in actions that threaten existing social and political arrangements. Many feel that human rights are not being fulfilled or are being violated and that they have the right to create a society that promotes these basic human rights. Thus, we are aware that many actions are political, and in so being are often illegal. What is defined as criminal may actually be the fulfillment of basic human rights. Crime against government in such times expresses these rights.

Crimes by Government

The correspondence between the crimes of government and legitimate behavior patterns is simple and direct: They tend to be the same, in that those who legislate and enforce the law (thus determining what is to be regarded as legitimate) are in the position of violating the laws themselves without being criminally defined. For example, in the US, none of the various state's legal codes contain a crime labeled as crimes of state. There is no law that holds the state responsible for any crime or that holds criminally responsible those who collectively participate in crimes of mass atrocity.

> State officials are criminally responsible on an individual basis in every state, but the forms of criminal responsibility, the evidentiary requirements, and the political influences on the investigation, prosecution, and adjudication processes afford wide latitude of impunity to state actors.[50]

While there are behaviors beyond the law that stipulate the illegitimacy of certain governmental actions, as concerns the official interpretation of the law, what government does is legal. It is when the law on occasion is invoked against government authorities that the incongruity between their criminality and a higher morality is made clear.

The civil rights movement during the 1960s illustrates the conflict between criminal and legitimate behavior. Although the US Supreme Court had defined various forms of racial discrimination as criminal, communities in the South, supported by their elected or appointed officials, held that the traditional patterns of discrimination were legitimate. It was argued at the time that Southern history was characterized by governmental crime.[51] Southern political power denied political identity to the black population and violated basic constitutional rights such as the equal protection of the law. By developing this pattern of "exclusive" politics, the South created a police state rather than a political community. African Americans were forced to accept subservient social status by techniques of extralegal violence supported by police control. Government authorities, as well as community members, responded to the civil rights movement by committing various criminal offenses. African Americans who attempted to vote in primaries were assaulted and beaten, their homes bombed, and they were sometimes murdered.

As has been discussed, government agencies and their functions are legitimate and approved in a democratic process. However, such governmental functions are often marred by illegal behavior in their application. Examples include the use of violence by correctional officers against inmates. Prison inmates are to serve time, be punished and treated for their offenses, yet the prison staff members who perform these functions on the part of the state may violate criminal laws in the course of their duties. Their crimes are in close correspondence to the objectives of security and punishment. Correctional officers are expected to do what is necessary to maintain security and order in the prison. The result is sometimes governmental crime by these officers.

> When officers do beat convicts, it is often out of retaliation, because the latter have attacked officers or have instigated or participated in work strikes, riots, or escape attempts. Occasionally, correctional officers have been accused and convicted of torture. . . . Also, if staff violence occurs, then the violence is usually done discretely in ways to minimize witnesses. It often takes place when the correctional officers have power in numbers.[52]

Most incidences of crimes committed by corrections officers become known to the public following the prison riots that occur across the country periodically. One of the most brutal of these riots happened in 1980 at New Mexico State Penitentiary that resulted in 33 inmates being killed and 400 injured. One study found that the New Mexico riot was in part due to "breakdown processes"—the termination of educational, recreational, and other rehabilitative programs; overcrowding; idleness; and a generally poorly-administered prison system. One inmate described the disorganized conditions in the prison before the riot: "It was unlivable before the riot. . . . It's been too crowded, the food is bad, the goddamn guards talk to you like you're a dog. We're not dogs."[53]

Another example of the correspondence between the crimes of government and the activities the government regards as legitimate can be seen in surveillance of citizens by the government. Governmental surveillance, according to a series of supreme court rulings, is illegal in most situations. Such techniques as unreasonable search and seizure, interrogation, wiretapping, and various forms of electronic surveillance have been declared unconstitutional except in a very few cases. Nevertheless, government agents continue to engage in these forms of surveillance. This was dramatically brought to public attention when Edward Snowden revealed that in investigating suspicious activity the NSA had been vacuuming up the phone data of millions of ordinary American citizens.

According to Jeffrey Ian Ross, there are six interrelated causes of illegal domestic surveillance.[54] First, individuals or groups are targeted for illegal domestic surveillance because of certain characteristics—such as nonconforming political opinions, ethnicity, or religious identification—that identify them as threats to national security. Second, because of the difficulty that individuals and organizations labeled as subversive have in demonstrating that they are not threats. Third, because of the national political climate of the time, whether it be anti-communist, anti-fascist, anti-Muslim, or anti-immigrant. Fourth, because of the belief by governmental agents that illegal surveillance is necessary for the protection and preservation of the status quo. Fifth, because of inexperienced and overzealous government agents who take extreme measures is conducting official investigations. Sixth, because of poorly trained state officials that use illegal surveillance haphazardly.

Crimes Against Government

Political criminals frequently present a serious threat to the existing social, political, and economic order. They are dealt with according to the officially defined seriousness of the threat. The more serious the threat, the harsher the punishment. In addition, as Durkheim noted long ago, the more absolute the government regime, the more severe the penal sanctions employed.[55] Various types of absolutist governments (communist regimes, one-party states, theocracies) tend to inflict brutal criminal punishments that include execution, public stoning, torture, and mass incarceration—punishments that themselves may be considered crimes under international law.

Even in democracies, legal reactions to political crime have been particularly severe. For example, during World War II the average sentence for conscientious objectors was more stringent than for many other convicted criminals. Nearly 90 percent of the convicted conscientious objectors were sentenced to prison, with over 30 percent receiving a 4- to 5-year term. For the entire period, only a little over 4 percent of the cases were granted probation.[56]

In 1927, the state of Massachusetts executed in the electric chair Italian-born American anarchists Nicola Sacco and Bartolomeo Vanzetti for a crime that many believe they did not commit—not only because they were poor Italian immigrants but mainly because they were anarchists. Other crimes against the government, such as blocking road traffic, inciting to riot, and engaging in disruptive demonstrations, receive more lenient penalties. The degree of threat posed by the crime to the existing social order, the status quo, or the existing power structure becomes the barometer by which the punishment is calculated.

Public reaction to activity regarded as threatening to political authority has taken many forms. In the United States, a stereotyped conception of the leftist radical long predominated as a general form of reaction. Writing in the mid-twentieth century, sociologist Edwin M. Lemert stated:

> The stereotyped ideas about radicals which lurk in the consciousness of the masses of people are easily provoked in experimental free-association reactions to the term, embracing such associations as "red," "alien," "dirty," "soapbox agitation," "Godless," "free lover," "bewhiskered," "bombs," and "sabotage." Stereotypes such as these, circulated in newspapers, fiction, and artistic representations, have been highly colored by beliefs which grew up around anarchism in the nineteenth century and the IWW in the twentieth. Reports of assassinations by Russian revolutionaries and by anarchists in European countries, the assassination of President Garfield by an anarchist, along with the Haymarket riots in Chicago and

IWW violence at Homestead, Pennsylvania, and elsewhere, did much to shape the American fixed notions of the radical. Not only has this older anarchistic stereotype remained alive, but it tends to be applied indiscriminately to socialists, Communists, pacifists, and other radicals, as well as to progressive or moderate reformers.[57]

While social disturbances can be interpreted by the public as legitimate protests, criminal conceptions are more easily and readily drawn. It is simpler to regard a public disturbance or protest as a crime or rebellion rather than to search for the motives and the grievances behind the actions. The designations are frequently simplistic and derogatory. Moreover, public perceptions of racial protests tend to differ by race. For example, a 2017 poll found that while 83 percent of African Americans had a favorable view of the activist movement that protests police brutality, Black Lives Matter, only 35 percent of whites had a favorable view.[58]

Negatively labeling political criminals is a way of opposing, dehumanizing, and controlling them. According to Turk:

> Characterizations of political criminals by officials and respectables emphasize the moral and/or intellectual deficiencies of anyone challenging, or even relatively indifferent to, the structures and personages of authority. The inadequate socialization and consequent intellectual disabilities of political criminals may be asserted, while even those few who are recognized to be genuine in their moral convictions may still be depicted as tragic objects to be pitied rather than admired.[59]

Rejecting the stereotype of the hooded, dim-witted bigot, the radical right attempts to influence public perception by projecting the image of what George Hawley calls "highbrow white nationalism":

> Avoiding the violence and pageantry of the Klan and various neo-Nazi groups, the highbrow white nationalist movement, complete with quasi-scholarly journals, books, and websites, has been around for decades. This variety of white nationalism presents itself as a movement of serious scholars and social observers—including many people with impeccable academic credentials. The people associated with this variety of white nationalism tend to maintain a civil tone, avoiding the racial slurs, threatening language, and vitriol for which groups like the KKK and skinhead gangs are known.[60]

Political leaders and public officials often set the framework for societal reaction to political offenders. For example, following World War I, when some people and groups were calling for the release of radicals and pacifists from prison, then Senator Warren Harding declared:

> No true American will argue that our laws should not be enforced. I refer to laws, no matter what nature, whether they be those which deal with ordinary crimes and misdemeanors, or those which deal with acts of treason to the United States, threatening the Constitution and the fabric of social organization. I wish no one to misunderstand me, and therefore, I will say as plainly as I can that, for my part I can see no essential difference between ordinary crimes on the one hand and political crimes and political prisoners on the other hand. If there is a distinction, surely it is not a distinction which favors political crimes or political prisoners. The thief, or ordinary criminal, is surely less of a menace to those things which we hold dear than the man or woman who conspires to destroy our American institutions.[61]

While such an absolutist reaction to political criminals is common, there sometimes also occurs a temporal transformation in the public perception whereby rebels are eventually vindicated by history as respected leaders. This happened, for example, in the cases of Menachem Begin of Israel, Lech Walsea of Poland, Vaclav Havel of the Czech Republic, and Nelson Mandela of South Africa, all of whom were previously regarded as agitators or terrorists. The sentiment was most dramatically expressed by Cuban revolutionary leader Fidel Castro during his 1953 court trial when he declared: "History will absolve me." Aside from a societal redefinition of the political offender there sometimes occurs a kind of collective disavowal of criminality.

> An interesting example of societal reaction to individuals charged with complicity in war crimes is that of Kurt Waldheim, former secretary general of the United Nations and Austrian president. On the eve of the election for the presidency of Austria charges were levied (but never prosecuted) that Waldheim had, as an SS officer during World War II, transmitted orders to Axis troops to shoot Yugoslav partisans, burn their villages, send resistance supporters to concentration camps, and supervised "ethnic cleansing" operations. Despite these charges Austrians, who as a nation have never fully acknowledged their complicity in Hitler's Third Reich, elected Waldheim to the presidency.[62]

Government officials and the media shape the public's conception of the political offender. A social reality of crime is created. This is illustrated in the following comment made by a respondent who was part of a study on how terrorists are perceived by Australians working in inner-city Melbourne:

> Terrorism and terrorists, especially when I worked at [Melbourne city shopping strip], I found it very difficult. When I think about terrorists and the terrorist threats I think about *the* certain race, I think about what's happening in Iraq, I think about people of that kind of race. As soon as I see one [a Muslim] I think shit, you know. Especially if they are walking around [Melbourne city shopping strip], I think to myself it is such a big complex and there are a lot of those people around there; it really wouldn't surprise me if something happened to that place. Like every time you hear a fire drill, an alarm, or you hear something happening, for example, like . . . fire drills, the sirens, anything to do with that. You maybe think shit, something has happened and they [Muslims] are the first people you think about.
>
>   I certainly treated people differently. As soon as an Arabian, a Musso, as soon as a Muslim walked in, what I classified as a Mussi, I would genuinely try to stay away from them only because I didn't want to come into contact or have to deal with people like that. It sounds a bit racist but, just the mentality after September 11 and what you see on TV does make me have this kind of, I've given them a stereotype basically.[63]

Incarceration, deportation, and exile have been used in the US as a means of controlling radicalism. One of the most dramatic uses of deportation occurred during the First Red Scare on November 7, 1919, when federal agents, under the direction of Attorney General A. Mitchell Palmer, staged a series of nationwide dragnet raids and detained for deportation several thousand alien members of the Union of Russian Workers, the Communist Labor party, and the Communist party.

> The roundup of Russians continued through the night and into the next day. The police burst into apartments and dragged people from their beds. Sometimes they had

arrest warrants, but usually they simply arrested everyone they found. In the end, the Department of Justice had grabbed more than one thousand people in eleven cities. Approximately 75 percent of those arrested were guilty of nothing more than being in the wrong place at the wrong time, and many were quickly released. Others were not so lucky. Nearly one hundred men were locked up in Hartford, Connecticut, for almost five months. Many of them were denied access to a lawyer or even knowledge of the charges against them. Probably half were Russian workers whose only crime was that they could not speak English. When a lawyer finally succeeded in getting inside the jail, ten of the men were released with no bail.[64]

No criminal proceedings were involved as a result of the raids. Attorney General Palmer did not try to prosecute actual crimes of radicals against the United States because this would have required an indictment and a trial by jury. Rather, he relied on an administrative process for the apprehension and deportation of radical aliens and thereby circumvented normal legal procedures. Some notable people who have been deported or exiled from the US include Emma Goldman, Charlie Chaplin, and Rosaura Revueltas.

The same year as the Palmer Raids, 1919, American anarchist, Emma Goldman and 248 radical "aliens" were deported to the Soviet Union under the 1918 Alien Act, which allowed for the expulsion of any alien found to be an anarchist. Later, at the height of the Second Red Scare, film star Charlie Chaplin was accused of supporting left-wing causes by Senator Joseph McCarthy and deemed to be a security risk by the FBI. As a result, Chaplin was banished from the United States in 1952.

> After setting sail from New York City [for Europe] aboard the *Queen Elizabeth* on September 18 [1952], . . . Chaplin and his family received bad news: A spokesman for Attorney General James McGranery announced on September 19 that Chaplin's re-entry permit had been revoked and that Chaplin would have to answer INS [Immigration and Naturalization Service] questions about his political views and moral behavior before he would be allowed to reenter the country. McGranery's spokesman told the press that his office had "a pretty good case" against Chaplin. Ten days later McGranery told the press that Chaplin "is in my judgment an unsavory character," and charged him "with making statements that would indicate a leering, sneering attitude" toward the country whose hospitality enriched him.[65]

Two years later, in 1954, Mexican stage and film actress, Rosaura Revueltas, was incarcerated and then deported from the United States to Mexico during filming of the pro-labor movie, *Salt of the Earth*. Shortly after a US Congressman charged that the movie was being made "under Communist auspices," INS officers arrested Revueltas "on questionable charges of failure to have her passport stamped on entry (a government error)."[66] The Hollywood Screen Actors Guild took these actions against Revueltas as a means of halting the film's production.

More direct and immediate reactions have taken place, as in the intentional killings by police in such disturbances as the Haymarket riot of 1886 and the Pullman strike of 1894. Police intimidation and brutality have been evident in more recent times in the handling of "race riots." Some of the violence that has occurred in such disorders has been provoked by racial profiling and police aggression usually leading to the death of a young African American man.

> Racially targeted police violence inflicts an ugly wound: it undermines the legitimacy of the state and sends the message that the lives of some of its citizens are not valued. . . .

a particularly egregious incident of police violence, such as the killing of an unarmed youth, may incite riots. Most riots begin as nonviolent gatherings and pleas for justice by families, friends, and neighbors of the victims. Police repression of such gatherings encourages others to join the fray. Network ties between residents of an affected area and those who live in places with similar conditions lead to riot diffusion, particularly to areas where affected minorities comprise the majority of residents.[67]

Judicial proceedings have defined and limited a variety of crimes against the state. The courts have been used by most governments on behalf of political goals. Otto Kirchheimer, in an analysis of the court's role in the control of opposing political viewpoints and actions, noted that three types of political trials have been used to accomplish the goals of the political authority:

1. The trial involving a common crime committed for political purposes and conducted with a view to the political benefits which might ultimately accrue from successful prosecution.
2. The classic political trial: a regime's attempt to incriminate its foe's public behavior with a view to evicting him from the political scene.
3. The derivative political trial, where the weapons of defamation, perjury, and contempt are manipulated in an effort to bring disrepute upon a political foe.[68]

The United States has a rich history of political trials. While there have only been a few dramatic trials for treason, the courts have been used by the government on numerous occasions for political purposes. Jens Meierhenrich and Devin O. Pendas have conceptualized political trials as an instance,

> in which at least one government is a claimant, an object of claims, or otherwise associated with the [court] proceedings; the outcome of the proceedings crystalizes or communicates a political conflict, often but not necessarily, over the distribution of social resources of one sort or another; *or* courtroom proceedings are directed at the defeat of a political enemy, real or imagined.[69]

In political trials, often the goal of the state is not to actually secure a conviction, but rather simply to harass the dissident individual, group, or organization, drain its energies (and more importantly its finances) to the point of collapse. As long as governments regard certain persons and groups as threats to their functioning and to their existence and stability, criminal law will be used for political purposes. And as long as people have the will to oppose oppressive governments or their policies, there will be behaviors that the courts define as criminal.

Crimes by Government

In the United States today, public reaction to governmental crime depends largely on partisan motivated reasoning. Due to partisan allegiance, Republicans tend to react strongly to crime committed by Democratic politicians and Democrats tend to react strongly to crime committed by Republican politicians. It is difficult for the public to form unbiased opinions about governmental crime for two reasons. First, the information that the public gets is often refracted through a partisan lens, whether in cable news, talk radio, websites/apps, or social media. What the public gets, and often wants, is a one-sided account of what the government is doing. The second problem in reference to public opinion about governmental crime—political corruption, obstruction of justice, abuse of power—is the way in which powerful politicians manipulate the conceptions that are presented to the public. The president of the United States, for example, can use the bully pulpit to advance his ideology; attack the press as "the enemy of the people"; issue untruths, misinformation, and propose "alternative facts."

Instances of possible crimes by government, governmental agencies, or state officials are typically shrouded in deceit, cover-up, and counter-accusation for years after the fact. Questions and doubts are planted, but the truth is elusive, and allegations are rarely resolved. It is for this reason that public reaction to governmental crime is dulled and rendered impotent. Regarding ambiguity and deceit, examples are abundant. President Nixon was never tried for crimes in the Watergate affair, being protected by a presidential pardon from his successor, Gerald Ford. Oliver North, who was charged with lying under oath and destroying government documents in his participation in the Iran-Contra scandal had his conviction overturned on appeal because he had been granted immunity. President Bill Clinton was impeached by the House of Representatives for perjury and obstruction of justice, but the Senate acquitted him of those charges. One criminologist has observed:

> Politicians, police officers, and regulatory inspectors do not necessarily resemble criminals on the surface, yet it is well known that some of them engage in a variety of crimes, including political corruption. Political corruption remains a fundamental problem for advanced industrial democracies. Within the cultures of politics and policing, there remains a veil of secrecy and a distrust of outsiders encouraging corruption to take place undefeated. In some cases, the violation of laws is fundamental to the occupational cultural norms and values of politics and policing. Thus, quite often both the public and the state expect these corrupt activities to go hand in hand.[70]

When governmental crimes are detected, legal processing is typically weak, protracted, and evasive. The results are usually predictable: the charges are dropped, the defendants are cleared, or, at most, an official may be dismissed from his or her former responsibilities. It often happens that misdemeanor and felony convictions are reversed on appeal, or they are expunged, as was the case when President George H.W. Bush pardoned several high officials in connection with the Iran-Contra affair. Legal processing of crimes by the state (and the accompanying public reaction to those crimes) tends to be weak unless the truth is quickly revealed, and the case is vigorously prosecuted.

There are, however, several internal and external mechanisms that can be used to control state crime.[71] State agencies (the police, national security/intelligence agencies, the military, and educational institutions) and state actions against groups (labor, indigenous peoples, refugees, immigrants) are subject to controls that are internal to the agency. These include investigations by ombudsmen, inspector generals, and integrity officers. Internal mechanisms that control state crime may involve criminal law, interest groups, and opposition political parties. Control mechanisms external to the state include international law, international humanitarian law, international human rights law, and laws of air, sea, and space. External control of state crime may be exerted by international bodies such as the United Nations, the International Court of Justice, and the International Criminal Court. In addition, Jeffrey Ian Ross identifies alternative reactions that victims, activists, and oppositional groups can use to resist state crime. These forms of resistance include social protest, defiance, and the use of news media to publicize crimes by government.

Notes

1 Louis Proal, *Political Crime* (New York, NY: D. Appleton and Co., 1898), xiii–xiv.
2 As cited in Jonathan Daly, "Political Crime in Late Imperial Russia," *Journal of Modern History* 74, no. 1 (2002): 62–100, 68.
3 Émile Durkheim, "Durkheim's 'Individualism and the Intellectuals,'" trans. by Steven Lukes, *Political Studies* 17, no. 1 (1969), 14–30, 22.
4 Brad W. Smith and Malcolm D. Holmes, "Police Use of Excessive Force in Minority Communities: A Test of the Minority Threat, Place, and Community Accountability Hypotheses," *Social Problems* 61, no. 1 (2014): 83–104.
5 Stephen Schafer, *The Political Criminal: The Problem of Morality and Crime* (New York: Free Press, 1974), 5.
6 Martin Luther King, Jr., *A Testament of Hope: The Essential Writings and Speeches*, ed. by James M. Washington (San Francisco, CA: HarperOne, 2003), 294.
7 Judith N. Shklar, *Legalism: Law, Morals, and Political Trials* (Cambridge, MA: Harvard University Press, 1984), 1–2.
8 L.T. Hobhouse, *Liberalism* (London: Oxford University Press, 1911), 147.
9 Richard Quinney, *The Social Reality of Crime* (Boston, MA: Little, Brown, 1970), 56.
10 Richard A. Wright, "Left Out? The Coverage of Critical Perspectives in Introductory Criminology Textbooks, 1990–1999," *Critical Criminology* 2, nos. 1–2 (2000): 101–122.
11 William J. Chambliss, "State-Organized Crime," *Criminology* 27, no. 2 (1989):183–208, 184.
12 Gregg Barak, ed., *Crimes by the Capitalist State: An Introduction to State Criminality* (Albany, NY: State University of New York Press, 1991), 7.
13 Ronald C. Kramer, "The Space Shuttle Challenger Explosion: A Case Study in State-Corporate Crime," in *White Collar Crime Reconsidered*, ed. by Kip Schlegel and David Weisburd (Boston, MA: Northeastern University Press, 1992), 215.
14 Ronald C. Kramer, Raymond J. Michalowski, and David Kauzlarich, "The Origins and Development of the Concept and Theory of State-Corporate Crime," *Crime & Delinquency* 48, no. 2 (2002): 263–282.
15 Raymond J. Michalowski and Ronald C. Kramer, eds., *State-Corporate Crime: Wrongdoing at the Intersection of Business and Government* (New Brunswick, NJ: Rutgers University Press, 2006).
16 Henry David Thoreau, "Civil Disobedience," in *Walden and Other Writings of Henry David Thoreau*, ed. by Brooks Atkinson (New York, NY: The Modern Library, 1992), 679–680.
17 Barton L. Ingraham, *Political Crime in Europe: A Comparative Study of France, Germany, and England* (Berkeley, CA: University of California Press, 1979), 224.
18 Richard Quinney, *Class, State, and Crime: On the Theory and Practice of Criminal Justice* (New York: Longman, 1977), 59.
19 George Hawley, *Making Sense of the Alt-Right* (New York, NY: Columbia University Press, 2017), 15–16.
20 Christopher C. Harmon, *Terrorism Today*, 2nd edition (New York, NY: Routledge, 2008), 13.
21 David Waddington, *Public Order Policing: Theory and Practice* (Devon: Willan Publishing, 2007), 48–52.
22 P.A.J. Waddington, "Controlling Protest in Contemporary Historical and Comparative Perspective," in *Policing Protest: The Control of Mass Demonstrations in Western Democracies*, ed. by Donatella Della Porta and Herbert Reiter (Minneapolis, MN: University of Minnesota Press, 1998), 129.
23 Schafer, *The Political Criminal*, 152–153.
24 Ibid., 134.
25 Cesare Lombroso, *Crime: Its Causes and Remedies* (Boston, MA: Little, Brown, 1911), xxv.
26 Willem Adriaan Bonger, *Criminality and Economic Conditions*, trans. by Henry P. Horton (Boston: Little, Brown, 1916), 649.
27 See Edwin M. Lemert, *Social Pathology* (New York, NY: McGraw-Hill, 1951), 180–187.
28 Gary Lafree, Michael A. Jensen, Patrick A. James, and Aaron Safer-Lichtenstein, "Correlates of Violent Political Extremism in the United States," *Criminology* 56, no. 2 (2018): 233–268.
29 Carolyn Gallaher, "On the Fault Line: Race, Class, and the U.S. Patriot Movement," *Cultural Studies* 16, no. 5 (2002): 673–703.
30 Stefan H. Leader and Peter Probst, "The Earth Liberation Front and Environmental Terrorism," *Terrorism and Political Violence* 15, no. 4 (2003): 37–58.
31 Nicholas N. Kittrie, *Rebels with a Cause: The Minds and Morality of Political Offenders* (Boulder, CO: Westview, 2000), 80.
32 John Wildeman, *War Resistance and the Governmental Process* (Hofstra: Department of Sociology: Hofstra University, 1971), 27.
33 As quoted in Katheryn Russell-Brown and Angela J. Davis, *Criminal Law* (Thousand Oaks, CA: Sage, 2016), 311.

34 Richard Quinney, "A Conception of Man and Society for Criminology," *Sociological Quarterly* 6, no. 2 (1965): 119–127, 122–123.

35 Richard Quinney, *The Problem of Crime* (New York, NY: Dodd, Mead & Co., 1970), 180.

36 William J. Chambliss, *On the Take: From Petty Crooks to Presidents*, 2nd edition (Bloomington, IN: Indiana University Press, 1988), xiv.

37 Maurice Punch, "Corruption (Police)," in *Dictionary of Policing*, ed. by Tim Newburn and Peter Neyroud (Devon: Willan Publishing, 2008), 51.

38 Ronald Weitzer, "Incidents of Police Misconduct and Public Opinion," *Journal of Criminal Justice* 30, no. 5 (2002): 397–408, 406.

39 Jerome H. Skolnick and James J. Fyfe, *Above the Law: Police and the Excessive Use of Force* (New York, NY: The Free Press, 1993).

40 Carol Tator and Frances Henry, *Racial Profiling in Canada: Challenging the Myth of "A Few Bad Apples"* (Toronto: University of Toronto Press, 2006), 17.

41 As quoted in Edwin L. Battistella, *Sorry About That: The Language of Public Apology* (New York, NY: Oxford University Press, 2014), 160.

42 Alette Smeulers and Sander van Niekerk, "Abu Ghraib and the War on Terror—A Case against Donald Rumsfeld?" *Crime, Law, and Social Change* 51, nos. 3–4 (2009): 327–349.

43 Dawn L. Rothe, *State Criminality: The Crime of All Crimes* (Lanham, MD: Lexington Books, 2009), 57.

44 Jeffrey Ian Ross, *The Dynamics of Political Crime* (Thousand Oaks, CA: Sage, 2003), 72–73.

45 Ramón Spaaij, "The Enigma of Lone Wolf Terrorism: An Assessment," *Studies in Conflict & Terrorism* 33, no. 9 (2010): 854–870, 866.

46 David Waddington, Karen Jones, and Chas Critcher, *Flashpoints: Studies in Public Disorder* (London: Routledge, 1989), 162.

47 Robert M. Fogelson, "Violence and Grievances: Reflections on the 1960s Riots," *Journal of Social Issues* 26, no. 1 (1970): 141–163, 160.

48 Chambliss, *On the Take*, 154.

49 Austin T. Turk, *Political Criminality: The Defiance and Defense of Authority* (Beverly Hills, CA: Sage, 1982), 108–109.

50 M. Cherif Bassiouni, "Crimes of State and Other Forms of Collective Group Violence by Nonstate Actors," in *State Crime: Current Perspectives*, ed. by Dawn L. Rothe and Christopher W. Mullins (New Brunswick, NJ: Rutgers University Press, 2011), 1–21, 12.

51 Joseph C. Mouledoux, "Political Crime and the Negro Revolution," in *Criminal Behavior Systems: A Typology*, ed. by Marshall B. Clinard and Richard Quinney (New York, NY: Holt, Rinehart, and Winston, 1967), 217–231.

52 Jeffrey Ian Ross, *An Introduction to Political Crime* (Bristol, UK: Polity Press, 2012), 145.

53 Bert Useem, "Disorganization and the New Mexico Prison Riot of 1980," *American Sociological Review* 50, no. 5 (1985): 677–688, 681.

54 Ross, *An Introduction to Political Crime*, 102–104.

55 Émile Durkheim, "Two Laws of Penal Evolution," *Economy and Society* 2, no. 3 (1973): 285–308.

56 Lemert, *Social Pathology*, 203–204.

57 Ibid., 200.

58 Harvard-Harris, *Monthly Harvard-Harris Poll: July 2017*, p. 168. https://caps.gov.harvard.edu/files/caps/files/crosstabs-hcaps_july-wave_topline-memo_registered-voters_custom-banners.pdf

59 Turk, *Political Criminality*, 72.

60 Hawley, *Making Sense of the Alt-Right*, 26.

61 B. L. Ingraham and Kazuhiko Tokoro, "Political Crime in the United States and Japan: A Comparative Study," *Issues in Criminology* 4, no. 2 (1969): 145–170, 162–163.

62 Frank E. Hagan, *Political Crime: Ideology and Criminality* (Needham Heights, MA: Allyn and Bacon, 1997), 184.

63 Luke Howie, *Terrorism, the Worker and the City: Simulations and Security in a Time of Terror* (Surrey: Gower, 2009), 117.

64 Christopher M. Finan, *From the Palmer Raids to the Patriot Act: A History of the Fight for Free Speech in America* (Boston, MA: Beacon Press, 2007), 2.

65 Charles J. Maland, *Chaplin and American Culture: The Evolution of a Star Image* (New Haven, CT: Princeton University Press, 1991), 280.

66 James J. Lorence, *The Suppression of* Salt of the Earth: *How Hollywood, Big Labor, and Politicians Blacklisted a Movie in Cold War America* (Albuquerque, NM: University of New Mexico Press, 1999), 83.

67 Cathy Lisa Schneider, *Police Power and Race Riots: Urban Unrest in Paris and New York* (Philadelphia, PA: University of Pennsylvania Press, 2014), 25–26.
68 Otto Kirchheimer, *Political Justice: The Use of Legal Procedure for Political Ends* (Princeton, NJ: Princeton University Press, 1961), 46.
69 Jens Meierhenrich and Devin O. Pendas, eds., *Political Trials in Theory and History* (Cambridge: Cambridge University Press, 2016), 48–49.
70 Ross, *An Introduction to Political Crime*, 99.
71 Jeffrey Ian Ross, "Controlling State Crime and Alternative Reactions," in *The Routledge International Handbook of Crimes of the Powerful*, ed. by Gregg Barak (New York: Routledge, 2015), 492–502.

INDEX

Note: Page numbers in *italic* refer to figures.

public opinion: and corporate crime 130–131; and organized crime 164–168
public order crime 11, 55; and commercial gain 78; decriminalization of 85–86; definition of 55–60; international differences in 79; social reaction to 77–87; sociology of 60–77
public reactions, to crime 6–7
publicity 180; adverse 135–136
punishment: of corporate crimes 115–116, 133–134; for occupational crime 107; of political criminals 191; by sanction 115; for violent crime 32–33
pyramid schemes 96

Queen, William 165
Quinney, Richard 40, 51, 94, 100, 102, 133, 167, 177–178, 183

race: and alcohol consumption 73–74; and drug arrests 85; and drug penalties 60; and drunkenness 66; and violence 24
racism 5, 17, 172, 181, 186–187, 190; by police 184
racketeering 150–152, 162; laws against 166–167
radicalism 191–193
radicalization 187
rape 15, 18, 26; and criminality 19; and personal relationships 29; sentences for 33; victim precipitated 28; and victim-blaming 28
rational choice model 50
rationality 7–8
rationalization 98–100; by governmental criminals 185; of corporate crime 121
re-offending, by rapists 19
recidivism 86; and alcoholism 64; in corporate crime 124
Reckless, Walter C. 6
recognition 50
reconciliation, victim–offender 33–34
Regan, President Ronald 84, 172, 177
regulatory agencies 115
reintegrative shaming 108
religion: and alcohol use 65–66, 73–74; and drunkenness 57; embezzlement in organizations 101–102; and the environment 129
repeat offenders 64, 99
resistance, forms of 196
restorative justice (RJ) 33–34, 51–52, 136
retaliation 21
revolt 178
revolution 178
Revueltas, Rosaura 194
riots 15, 31–32, 186–187, 194; in prison 190
robbery 15, 18, 29; and drunkenness 65
Rockefeller, John D. 125
role-career model 6
Roof, Dylann 32
Rosenfeld, Richard 104

Ross, Edward A. 93
Ross, Jeffrey Ian 191, 196
Rothstein, Arnold 144
running numbers 144–145

Sacco, Nicola 191
Sampson, Robert J. 24
saunas 72
Schur, Edwin M. 104
Schur, Gerald 165
secrecy, in organized crime 159
Securities and Exchange Commission (SEC) 95, 115
self-concept: of addicts 68; noncriminal 97–100; of occupational criminals 97; and political crime 179–180
self-control 5
self-esteem 5
self-identity: criminal 152, 179–180; loss of 49
self-interest, and political protest 179–180
self-justification 121, 182–183
self-regulation, government-enforced 133
serial murderers, typology of 5
sex, as commodity 79
sex workers see prostitutes; prostitution
sexual assault 18
sexual conduct 56
sexually transmitted diseases/infections (STDs/STIs) 56–57, 63, 72–73, 80
shame (shaming) 99, 108, 133, 136
Sharia law 79
Shklar, Judith N. 175
shoplifting 40, 42, 50; adolescent groups in 49; occasional 45, 47; and private justice systems 52; and prostitution 63; rationalization of 48; techniques 46
silence (omerta), in organized crime 159
Simpson, Sally S. 134
Singer, Merrill 75
situated interaction, Luckenbill's stages of 28
situated transaction 27–28
skimming 144
Skolnick, Jerome H. 184
Snowden, Edward 172, 190
social class, and violence 25–26
social criminals 6
social drinking 73
social interaction, and violence 26–28
social networks, and drug use 76
social occasion 28
social reaction 6–8; to corporate crime 128–136; to crimes against government 188–189; to crimes by government 189–191; to criminal behaviors 10–11; to occasional property crime 50–52; to occupational crime 102–109; to organized crime 164–168; to political crime 188–196; to public order crime 77–97; to violent personal crime 30–34
social relationships 27

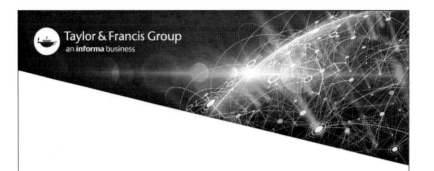

Made in United States
North Haven, CT
30 August 2022

23429601R10122